African American Childhoods

Historical Perspectives from Slavery to Civil Rights

Wilma King

AFRICAN AMERICAN CHILDHOODS
© Wilma King, 2005.

First published in 2005 by
PALGRAVE MACMILLAN™
175 Fifth Avenue, New York, N.Y. 10010 and
Houndmills, Basingstoke, Hampshire, England RG21 6XS
Companies and representatives throughout the world.

PALGRAVE MACMILLAN is the global academic imprint of the Palgrave Macmillan division of St. Martin's Press, LLC and of Palgrave Macmillan Ltd. Macmillan® is a registered trademark in the United States, United Kingdom and other countries. Palgrave is a registered trademark in the European Union and other countries.

ISBN 1–4039–6250–2
ISBN 1–4039–6251–0 (pbk.)

Library of Congress Cataloging-in-Publication Data

King, Wilma, 1942–
    African American childhoods : historical perspectives from slavery to civil rights / Wilma King.
        p. cm.
    Includes bibliographical references and index.
    ISBN 1–4039–6250–2—ISBN 1–4039–6251–0 (pbk.)
    1. African American children—History. 2. African American children—Social conditions. 3. African Americans—History. 4. African Americans—Social conditions. 5. United States—Race relations. 6. United States—Social conditions. I. Title.

E185.86K57 2005
305.23'089'96073—dc22   2005048688

A catalogue record for this book is available from the British Library.

Design by Newgen Imaging Systems (P) Ltd., Chennai, India.

First edition: November 2005

10 9 8 7 6 5 4 3 2 1

Printed in the United States of America.

In memory of George Breathett, who said,
"Write a paragraph a day," and Charlotte Fitzgerald,
who said, "Always keep something in the mail."

All you dark children in the world out there,
Remember my sweat, my pain, my despair.
Remember my years, heavy with sorrow—
And make of those years a torch for tomorrow.
Make of my past a road to the light
Out of the darkness, the ignorance, the night
—"The Negro Mother"
Langston Hughes

CONTENTS

LIST OF ILLUSTRATIONS

Part I

INTRODUCTION

At the beginning of the twenty-first century, childhood and adolescence have a more prominent place in the national discourse than at any other point in American history. Public policy debates rage over how to protect children from harmful influences in the media: on television, in popular music, in video games, and on the Internet. The intractable problems of childhood homelessness and poverty receive frequent media attention. The question of how to deal with children with psychiatric problems has come to the fore with controversies over drugs, like Ritalin, and violent incidents, like the one at Columbine High School in Colorado. Recent charges of molestation against Catholic priests have given the issue of sexual abuse of children a renewed prominence. School reform issues like testing and vouchers have become volatile topics in political campaigns.

The August 7, 1998, essay in the *Chronicle of Higher Education*, "The Meaning of Children in Culture Becomes a Focal Point for Scholars," recognized the increased interest in studying childhood among academics. But historian Steven Mintz suggested that childhood was not the sole purview of scholars when he commented:

> For more than a decade childhood has been the major battleground in the culture war. Today, virtually every public policy issue, from gun control to the Internet, focuses on children. Books dealing with children, by such writers as Mary Pipher, David Elkin, and Christina Hoff Sommers, regularly stand atop the best-seller list.

Scholars may readily examine the larger historical debates, place children in the center, and determine how the issues, be it pornography on the Internet or reductions in aid to dependents, impact the lives of children over time.[1]

Artistic and literary representations of the varied experiences of American childhood have proliferated recently. In all probability this is related to nostalgic reflections of the artists' childhoods along with the recognition of the relatively brief period, childhood, in the lives of a graying American population. The last decade has witnessed a flourishing of autobiographical "coming of age" or "growing up" narratives of people of wide-ranging regional, class, religious, and ethnic backgrounds. Included among these are Patricia Riley, ed., *Growing Up Native American* (1993); Joyce A. Ladner, *Tomorrow's Tomorrow* (1995); Rebecca Carroll, *Sugar in the Raw* (1997); Sonsyrea Tate, *Little X* (1997); Michael L. Cooper, *Indian School* (1999); Frances Esquibel Tywoniak, *Migrant Daughter: Coming of Age as a Mexican American* (2000); Dalton Conley, *Honkey* (2000); Cathy Luchetti, *Children of the West: Family*

Life on the Frontier (2001); Sandra Day O'Connor and H. Alan Day, *Lazy B: Growing Up on a Cattle Ranch in the American Southwest* (2002); and Antwone Quenton Fisher, *Finding Fish: A Memoir* (2002).

Other books provide recollections of coming of age in particular noteworthy periods of time such as slavery, World War II, segregation, or the Great Depression. Among the publications are Dorinda Makanaonalani Nicholson, *Pearl Harbor Child: A Child's View of Pearl Harbor—from Attack to Peace* (1993); Laurel Holliday, ed., *Dreaming in Color, Living in Black and White* (2000); Jordana Y. Shakoor, *Civil Rights Childhood* (1999); and Harriet Hyman Alsonso, *Growing Up Abolitionist: The Story of the Garrison Children* (2002) provide firsthand accounts of their lives during identifiable moments in American history.[2]

The proliferation in scholarship on childhood and adolescence since the 1960s is related to the emergence of social history and the complication of lives and events through color, class, gender, and age analyses. A natural outgrowth of this historical shift is an abundance of publications about women many of whom are mothers and educate or design consumer products for children's use, create entertainment for their pleasure, or lobby for their welfare. Concomitant with the growth and development of women's studies is the relatively new field, history of children, with much of its scholarship produced since 1960; the appearance of Philippe Ariès's *Centuries of Childhood* in English in 1965 being a major landmark. The past ten years have yielded an abundance of compelling work; encyclopedias of girl- and boyhood, several essay collections, and monographs. *Small Worlds: Children and Adolescents in America, 1850–1950*, edited by Elliott West and Paula Petrik (1992), *Generations of Youth*, edited by Joe Austin and Michael Willard (1998), and *Childhood in America*, edited by Paula Fass and Mary Ann Mason (2000) are few examples of the scholarship shaping this emerging field. Kathleen Thompson and Hilary MacAustin recently published two compelling visual treatments of the topic in *Children of the Depression* (2001) and *America's Children: Picturing Childhood from Early America to the Present* (2002). The judiciously selected images in these works often convey far more about their subjects than is possible with mere words.

Scholars who concern themselves with the reactions of youngsters to historical events, such as the September 11, 2001, attacks on New York City's World Trade Center and the Pentagon in Washington, DC, are likely to answer questions about a child's memory of the event, its impact upon the psyche, or how it will shape the child's future. The answers are relevant to a more nuanced understanding of historical events.

Despite the growing interest in childhood and the outpouring of new publications on the subject, a void remains in the general literature about African American children in a historical perspective. To be sure, Frederick Douglass's narratives remain in print and are omnipresent on syllabi for American and African American history courses at colleges and universities across the United States. The same is true of the slave-born Harriet Jacobs's *Incidents in the Life of a Slave Girl*, Booker T. Washington's *Up From Slavery*, and the freeborn Charlotte Forten Grimké's *Journals*. These narratives chronicle the lives of selected nineteenth-century children, while Anne Moody's popular twentieth-century narrative, *Coming of Age in Mississippi*, touted as "the classic autobiography of growing up poor and black in the rural South," appears regularly on required or suggested reading lists in history and women's study courses.

As invaluable as these sources are, they still have the limitations of being personal narratives. It is problematic to draw wide-ranging conclusions about the experiences of children in these periods from such sources.[3]

To offset any disadvantage associated with the personal narratives, other sources, such as wills, divorce decrees, church records, newspaper commentaries, diaries, letters, and autobiographies, undergird this study. Furthermore, the narratives of former slaves, collected by the Works Progress Administration (WPA), tell much about newly freed *children* as they made their transition from slavery to freedom.

African American Childhoods seeks to fill a vacuum in the study of African American children. While not a comprehensive historical examination, it is a collection of essays addressing selected resounding themes in American history, asking how major events, including the trans-Atlantic slave trade, Civil War, Great Depression, and modern Civil Rights Movement, impacted or changed the lives of black children. *African American Childhoods* challenges the "traditional" ways of historical thinking about black children. For example, a significant number of enslaved children did not live on plantations during the antebellum era. One chapter herein examines the lives of children living in professional households serving doctors, lawyers, and politicians.

Another chapter looks at free black children in the slave era, while yet another relates the life of a black teenaged girl during the Great Depression. Recovering the voices and experiences of these children reveals nuances about their legal status, class standing, and social development that counter accepted historical wisdom.

Attempting to recapture the voices from the nineteenth and early twentieth centuries is a daunting task, especially when one recognizes that black children generally had little opportunity to record events in their lives and even more rarely did such accounts come to be published. Charlotte Forten's journals are exceptional in this regard. For freeborn blacks, a handful of autobiographies exist that help to illuminate their childhoods before 1865, yet there is no great body of data about their experiences comparable to the WPA narratives collected in the 1930s that tell so much about the lives of enslaved girls and boys. Yet even these invaluable sources are problematic. Critics readily question their usefulness stating that interviewees were aged and interwove events into their accounts of childhood that occurred when they were no longer children, and that many published narratives were influenced by white amanuenses.[4]

This volume seeks to provide a counterbalance to the limitations of such sources through a careful comparison and analysis of a variety of sources. This collection of essays is subdivided into two parts. The essays in the first section examine the lives of children before emancipation while the second provides twentieth-century perspectives. The first section starts with chapter one, Africa's Progeny Cast upon American Shores, an overview of African children's experience of being introduced into English-speaking North America via the Atlantic slave trade. Chapter two, Minor Players in Bondage: Interactions between Enslaved and Slaveholding Children in the Old South, discusses relationships between black and white children, paying particular attention to Thomas Jefferson's observation of slaveholding children. He noted that they imitated the "whole commerce between master and slave" from observing their parents. A major question that the essay poses is whether Jefferson's remarks were applicable to black slaveholding children as well.

Chapter three, Within the Professional Household: Slave Children in the Antebellum South, examines the lives of selected children coming of age within the homes of medical doctors, lawyers, and politicians to determine if their lives differed significantly from those of children owned by planters. The essay employs a model containing three categories formulated by historian Eugene D. Genovese for comparing the treatment of slaves in different countries. Based on the model, an examination of (1) day-to-day conditions, (2) family integrity, and (3) chances for gaining an education, practicing religion, and securing freedom will yield data about the treatment of enslaved children in professional households. The results may be compared with that of the children in the households of planters or yeomen.[5]

The relatively large number of free black boys and girls before 1865 is the subject of chapter four, No Bondage for Me: Free Boys and Girls Within a Slave Society, which emphasizes their growing up, education, work, and participation in social reform or protest movements before slavery ended. Chapter five, "Dis was atter freedom come": Freed Girls and Boys Remember the Emancipation, answers questions about the essence of liberty for black children in a new era (1867–1900) as they reunite with family members, attend school, join the labor force, and make life meaningful after the Civil War.

The second part of this collection examines several major historical events, issues related to federal funding, and media presentations, that affected African American children. Chapter six, Black and Red Education at Hampton Institute: A Case Study of the Shawnee Indians, 1900–1925, views the social and historical construction of race at Virginia's Hampton Agricultural and Normal School and its link to federal appropriations for Indian education. Several Oklahoma-born students of African descent enjoyed federal support at the institution due to their classification as Native Americans. Following the loss of federal dollars in 1912, the institute's administrators reclassified the Shawnees as African American and housed them with other black students.

Chapter seven, What a "Life" This Is: An African American Girl Comes of Age during the Great Depression in Urban America, 1929–1939, incorporates diaries kept by a fifteen-year-old Mississippi-born girl into a discussion that reveals a personal account about coming of age during the worst economic depression in American history. The diaries offer a rare glimpse of how a black child lived during the early days of the depression. Her life contrasted sharply from the stereotypically imagined children seen in chapter eight, The Long Way from the Gold Dust Twins to the Williams Sisters: The Presentation of African American Children in Selected Nineteenth- and Twentieth-Century Print Media. This essay raises questions about the impact of negative images of black children and shows why such characterizations have largely faded from the media.

Chapter nine focuses on the looming threats of physical violence toward black children throughout the nineteenth and twentieth centuries. Such an inhospitable environment gave rise to mass action as seen in chapter ten, Emmett Till Generation, which emphasizes the place of youngsters in the Civil Rights Movement beginning with *Brown v. Board of Education* (1954) and ending with the Civil Rights Act of 1964. The bravery of black children, whether entering Little Rock's Central High School or marching in the streets of Birmingham, Alabama, was vital to the success of the modern Civil Rights Movement.

The Civil Rights Movement continues to shape the lives of African American children and youth today. A special feature in the June 7, 1999, *Newsweek* noted the rise in black employment and home ownership along with the declining rate of out-of-wedlock births. According to the article, more black males and females were attending college than ever before.

Although the observations indicate progression toward social and economic goals, they do not suggest that further inquiry into the condition of the majority of America's black children should cease. Instead, it is vital to continue efforts to answer questions about the consideration given to African American children in public policy debates related to health, the welfare system, child protective services, gun control, substance abuse, resegregation, and violent or misogynistic imagery in the media.

There are multiple areas into which the research on African American children may be directed. I am hopeful that additional scholarship about black children will become available to open the windows into their struggles and dreams.[6]

Figure 1   Cape Coast Castle, Ghana, West Africa
Source: Courtesy Warner Foreman Archives, London, England.

CHAPTER ONE

AFRICA'S PROGENY CAST UPON AMERICAN SHORES

[Charlotte] did comfort me when I was torn from my dear native land.[1]
—Sarah Margru

"Your image has been always riveted in my heart, from which neither time nor fortune have been able to remove it; so that, while the thought[s] of your sufferings have damp[en]ed my prosperity, they have mingled with adversity and increased its bitterness," wrote Olaudah Equiano, also known as Gustavus Vassa, as he reflected about the fate of his beloved sister. In 1756, one woman and two men raided Isseke, Equiano's village in present-day Nigeria, while the adults were working in a common field nearly an hour away by foot. The raiders kidnapped Olaudah, whose name means "the fortunate one," and his sister. He was eleven years of age at the time.[2] The children, descendants of a slaveholding Ibo chief, were aware of a previous battle between the Ibos and "their enemy." The warfare resulted in taking prisoners who were kept within the community or sold away. Fighting among different ethnic and language groups was not unusual in this part of West Africa, and it probably intensified with the increased European demand for slaves.[3]

This essay attempts to reconstruct the experiences of girls and boys kidnapped, sold, and transported into the Americas. Children constituted a significant portion, an estimated one-fourth to one-third, of the slaves in the trans-Atlantic slave trade. To be sure, there were shared experiences among kidnapped Africans, especially when crossing the Atlantic; but one must keep in mind that individual experiences varied greatly. Young boys and girls often walked about the decks unfettered while men were confined to the ship's hold, and women ordinarily traveled on the quarterdeck. Differences in physical condition, age, and life experience all tempered the Africans' responses to enslavement. No doubt children understood some facets of what was happening to them, but they, like the adults, had no way of knowing what the future held in store.[4]

A researcher trying to recover the voices of youthful Middle Passage survivors encounters many obstacles: most young enslaved Africans were not literate and lived under extremely harsh conditions once in the Americas. This essay does not claim that the survivors' autobiographies are representative of the whole because of the paucity of firsthand accounts and obvious male biases. Nevertheless, this recovery effort may be collaborated by official records, ship manifests, and journals kept by crew members to provide a broader picture.[5]

With few exceptions, the published narratives of young Middle Passage survivors mention other children and some facet of an idyllic childhood before the raids resulting in their enslavement in the Americas. A memoir by the former slave Florence Hall recounts playing in an open field with peers when kidnappers took her along with several playmates. Similarly, the young boy Ottobah Cugoano was playing in a field with eighteen or twenty children when he was "snatched away from [his] native country." Finally, the teenager Boyrereau Brinch told of the life-altering day when he and his young companions set out to bathe in a river that was a distance from his home. With his family's blessings and "a heart lighter than a feather," Brinch claimed, he and his peers "could anticipate no greater pleasure, and knew no care." Their mirth came to an end when they were "waylayed by thirty or forty more of the same pale race of white *Vultures*" who took eleven of the fourteen children. The kidnapping of Hall, Cugoano, Brinch, and their friends did not differ dramatically from what Equiano and his sister experienced.[6]

Several narratives indicate that some children had a working knowledge of potential dangers from "raiders." The Guinea-born Venture Smith vividly recalled the invasion of his village and kidnapping of his people. He estimated that he was only six years old thus making the year 1729. Smith suggested that the intruders were "instigated by some white nation." Whether motivated by Europeans or their own initiatives, the raiders greeted the child with "a violent blow on the head with the fore part of a gun, and at the same time a grasp around the neck." Afterward, Smith watched as the men "closely interrogated" his father before they "cut and pounded on his body with great inhumanity." "I saw him," Smith wrote, "while he was thus tortured to death." To witness such a tragedy was devastating. Smith reflected on the murder much later and admitted, "The shocking scene is to this day fresh in my memory, and I have often been overcome while thinking on it."[7]

One small boy could do nothing to save his father or people from being over powered by the large continuously moving army of slave raiders. As it entered one village after another, the army "laid siege and immediately took men, women, children, flocks, and all their valuable effects . . . then went on to the next . . ." said Smith. Although his family had been forewarned, it was too weak to withstand the assault.[8]

Knowing that raiders would and did overrun villages and take prisoners had prompted the adults of Isseke to prepare themselves against invasions and for waging war. According to Equiano, when the adults went out to work, they carried "firearms, bows and arrows, broad two-edged swords and javelins" along for protection. "All [were] taught the use of these weapons; even our women are warriors," wrote Equiano, "and march boldly out to fight along with the men."[9]

The warriors were of no help to Olaudah or his sister. As a result, the children were catapulted into an unimaginable destiny. Their grief was overpowering, and their only relief was falling asleep in each other's arms. After more than a day's journey, the raiders separated Olaudah from his sister. Their pleas to remain together fell upon deaf ears. Afterward, Equiano refused to eat and "cried and grieved continually" about the condition of his sister.[10]

Without a comparable narrative by the Equiano girl, there is no way of knowing exactly how she responded to the shock of kidnapping and detachment from her brother and other loved ones. One cannot assume that age or gender mitigated her condition. However, it is reasonable to posit that she, Olaudah's "dear partner," in all of his childish sports and the "sharer of [his] joys and sorrows," would display emotions similar to what he reported:

> I was quite oppressed and weighed down by grief after my mother and friends; and my love of liberty, ever great, was strengthened by the mortifying circumstances of not daring to eat with the freeborn children, although I was mostly their companion.

His sorrow at being separated from his immediate family and village was exacerbated by his loss of freedom and by the humiliation of his lowly new status.[11]

Perhaps, there were ameliorating factors for the young Equiano girl like those of her sibling. He encountered a few older West African women who comforted him. Included among them was one of the wives of an African chieftain who once owned him. In fact, Equiano claimed the kind woman "was something like [his] mother."[12]

At length, perhaps several months and as many owners, Equiano and his sister were reunited. "As soon as she saw me," he wrote, "she gave a loud shriek, and ran into my arms." Neither child could speak. They simply "clung to each other in mutual embraces" and wept. The trader indulged them. The "joy of being together" again made them forget what Olaudah Equiano termed as their "misfortunes."[13]

Neither Olaudah nor his sister realized how quickly their modicum of happiness would turn again to sorrow. Once traders snatched her away for the last time, Olaudah reflected about the wretchedness of his own situation and the anxiety intensified as he worried "after her fate." He feared that her sufferings would be greater than his own. Perhaps his anxiety was grounded in gender concerns thinking she was not old or strong enough to fend for herself or to protect herself from sexual exploitation. Nevertheless, he knew that he "could not be with her to alleviate them." It would have been an esteemed pleasure, Equiano wrote, to "encounter every misery for [her] and to procure [her] freedom by the sacrifice of my own."[14]

Equiano, like his sister, had no choice in the matter. She may have been subjected to what he described as "the violence of the African trader, the pestilential stench of a Guinea ship, the seasoning in the European colonies, or the lash and lust of a brutal and unrelenting overseer." What happened to the Equiano girl remains unknown, but she probably suffered a fate that did not differ greatly from that of the other girls who were kidnapped and integrated into domestic slavery in West Africa, or those sold to Europeans and transported to a life of bondage in the Americas or the Sahara.[15]

Olaudah Equiano's lengthy narrative is the proverbial window into the lives of African boys and girls who endured kidnapping, sale, and removal from Africa to the New World through the Middle Passage. The narrative first appeared in 1789 and questions about its authenticity soon followed. Questions still remain about whether the author was indeed the West African-born Olaudah Equiano as claimed or the South Carolina-born Gustavus Vassa. The veracity of the author's place of birth is important; however, specific details in the catalogue of other events in his life are remarkably accurate. The narrative by a man calling himself Olaudah Equiano or Gustavus Vassa cannot be discounted because it is not at variance with other narratives describing kidnapping, sales, and travel from Africa into the Americas.[16]

The narrative of James Albert Gronniosaw and Ottobah Cugoano are useful in this regard. As a young boy, Gronniosaw fell into the hands of slave traders and experienced what he described as a "very unhappy and discontented journey" from his village to the seacoast. The sadness and disappointment associated with being kidnapped became more poignant for Cugoano as he reached the seashore and saw many of his countrymen "chained two and two, handcuffed, and some with their hands tied behind." He empathized with their misery crying bitterly but in vain.[17]

Unlike some of the autobiographers, Augustino, a West African who was kidnapped when he was about twelve years of age, does not focus on the kidnapping or the overland trek to the seaside, but his account is of the trans-Atlantic voyage he endured.[18]

An estimated 11,863,000 Africans survived the Middle Passage but less than 1,000,000, primarily Bantu-speaking people were destined for what is now the United States. The majority of all slaves came from west-central Africa, an area of prominence early on and continued in importance until the end of the slave trade. Angola and the Zaire River basin were the sources of an estimated 40 percent of the slaves in the trans-Atlantic trade. Other regions, including Sierra Leone and Senegambia along with the Gold Coast, the Bight of Benin, and the Bight of Biafra, supplied a vast number of slaves.[19]

On occasions slave traders sought young children specifically, as was the case in 1746 when William Ellery, owner of the *Anstis*, told Captain Pollipus Hammond, "if you have good trade for the Negroes . . . purchase forty or fifty Negroes. Get most of them mere Boys and Girls, some Men, let them be Young, No very small Children." Nearly twenty years later, entrepreneurs John Watts and Gedney Clarke discussed sending a ship to Africa to procure slaves for sale in New York. "For this market," wrote Watts, the slaves "must be young the younger the better if not quite Children, those advanced in years will never do." In general, the most marketable age was between ten and twenty-four years old. According to the October 22, 1717, minutes of the South Sea Company, children sold best on the "Windward Coast," referring to a group of islands including St. Lucia and Grenada in the Caribbean Sea, where potential purchasers were poor and could not afford the price of adults.[20]

It is impossible to determine the exact number of children who survived the Middle Passage because of irregularities in reporting, especially where infants were concerned, and the lack of a standard definition of a child. Dr. James Houstoun, chief surgeon at Cape Coast Castle in 1722 noted that children under ten years of age were occasionally listed in the company books as "women." In actuality, more children than women survived the Middle Passage.[21]

The transporting of African children was significant to the extent that it is mentioned in the bill passed by the British Parliament entitled "An Act to Regulate the Carrying of Slaves (1788)" saying if the cargo constituted of more than two-fifths children measuring less than four feet four inches in height, every five such children were deemed equal to four adults. Boys and girls were smaller than adults; therefore, more children could be transported. On occasions children made up the majority of a cargo. The *Margarita* and *Maria* are illustrative. The *Margarita* sailed from Africa in 1734 with ninety-three Africans aboard. Eighty-seven percent of the slaves were sixteen years of age or younger. The average age of the children was 13.4. The *Maria* sailed in 1790 with eight crew members and eighty Africans on board. Ninety percent of the Africans were listed as children. Among them were forty-nine boys and twenty-five girls.[22]

One is left to ponder the conditions under which the children aboard the *Margarita* and the *Maria* crossed the Atlantic. Were they free to stroll about on the deck while the few black men and women aboard remained in the hold or quarter deck? Could they console each other in their hours of loneliness and weariness? Regardless of the manner in which these children traveled, nearly all of the survivors' narratives contain sorrowful lamentations about separations from their families in Africa.

Phillis Wheatley is not unusual in this regard. She was born in Gambia several years before the 1756 raid on Olaudah Equiano's village. Raiders kidnapped and sold the child to overseas traders when she was less than ten years of age. She imagined the grief her parents experienced when the thieves seized her. As a poet she wrote, "I, young in life, by seeming cruel fate was snatch d from Afric's fancy'd happy seat: What pangs excruciating must molest, What sorrows labour in my parent's breast?" Seemingly resigned to her own destiny in colonial North America, Wheatley consoled herself with religion. "On being brought from AFRICA to AMERICA," included in her *Poems on Various Subjects* (1773), proffers that "mercy" brought her from a "Pagan" land and taught her "benighted soul to understand" that redemption existed in Christ. Some critics interpret the poem as an indication of unqualified gratitude for introduction to Christianity without including a concomitant analysis of "To the Right Honourable WILLIAM, Earl of Dartmouth, His Majesty's Principal Secretary for North America, &c.", published in Wheatley's first volume of poems. After explaining her love of freedom to the Earl, Wheatley asks, "And can I then but pray [that] Others never feel tyrannic sway?" Coming to America and being exposed to Christianity were highly significant occurrences in her life, but they never eradicated the piercing memory of being snatched from Africa's "fancy'd happy seat."[23]

Wheatley, like other children, wrenched from Africa, left a familiar world of family and friends for an alien existence in distant lands. "I often reflected with extreme regret on the kind friends I had left," reported James Albert Gronniosaw. He continued, "the idea of my dear mother frequently drew tears from my eyes." The lamentations of Sarah Margru, a survivor of the 1839 mutiny aboard the *Amistad*, are similar to Gronniosaw's. She described a "low Spirit" that engulfed her whenever she thought of her birthplace. "Africa is my home I long to be there," she wrote, "My heart is there." Aside from her heart, the people she loved were in the country she admired.[24]

Imprisonment, sale, passage across the Atlantic Ocean, and enslavement in the Americas obviously changed the lives of children as well as those of their loved ones left in Africa. Both Africans and Europeans must share the responsibility for the trauma these children suffered. "We cannot take the simple attitude," asserts historian Walter Rodney, "that the whites were the villains and the blacks were the victims." The nature of their participation differed, yet it was complementary. Europeans interested in acquiring laborers for American plantations led no major invasion into West African to conquer governments and kidnap Africans. With the exception of the Portuguese penetration in Angola, Europeans did not go inland to seize slaves.[25]

Instead, Africans and Europeans engaged in a brisk business of bartering human chattel for consumable goods. This systematic procedure commenced as Africans developed a fondness for European textiles, iron, guns, and ammunition in addition to

> common red, blue, and scarlet cloth, silver and brass rings, or bracelets, chains, little bells, false crystal, ordinary and course hats; Dutch pointed knives, pewter dishes, silk sashes, with false gold and silver fringes; blue serges; French paper, steels to strike fire . . . looking-glasses in gilt and plain frames, cloves, cinnamon, scissors, needles, course thread of sundry coulors . . . Lastly, a good quantity of Coignac brandy. . . .

One scholar surmised that the "demand for this or that item shifted dramatically, often to the consternation of merchants who brought thousands of items only to find no demand for them." The vacillation in desires reflects the behavior of consumers who were responding to "changing fashions of nonessential commodities" rather than basic needs.[26]

Africans paid for their purchases with textiles, gold dust, hides, beeswax, elephant teeth, feathers, and human beings. According to the log and account book of the New England slaver, *Snow Greyhound*, several children were traded for rum and tobacco. Venture Smith claimed Robertson Mumford, a crew member on a Rhode Island slaver, carried him aboard the ship after exchanging him for "four gallons of rum and a piece of calico." James Albert Gronniosaw, also a small child when taken from Africa, declared that he was sold "for two yards of check [fabric]." Such trades were possible because of internal conflicts among Africans combined with the absence of reservations about ridding themselves of surplus slaves—spoils of war—seemingly to fill an insatiable desire for foreign goods.[27]

As demands for more black laborers increased in the sixteenth and seventeenth centuries, European traders and African leaders supplied the workers through an organized business system. Fortified castles, built with the permission of African rulers, along the seashore at Christianburg, and Cape Coast, or Goree, Whydah, and Bissau served as sites for negotiations between traders, black and white. The castles were also holding places, or "barracoons," where slaves remained until an oceangoing vessel arrived to transport them to the Americas.[28]

Once the international slave trade reached this level of sophistication, the method of filling demands changed. Europeans exploited divisions among Africans based on class and culture for their own purposes. At the same time, African leaders realized the profit-making potential in kidnapping men, women, or children by continuing to fight old enemies or starting wars with new ones. In their discussion of slave trading and warfare in West Africa, historians Michael L. Conniff and Thomas J. Davis write, "civil wars and the related breakdown of authority allowed soldier-slavers to become a serious problem. The Imbangala mercenaries pillaged many regions of Angola in the seventeenth century, unimpeded by the states weakened by war." Endemic warfare in the kingdom of Kongo, in the late seventeenth and eighteenth centuries, resulted in bandits terrorizing villages. Similar conditions existed in the kingdom of Benin during the eighteenth century. Ultimately, the disorder and warfare meant the loss of freedom for many Africans who were enslaved in Africa or the Americas.[29]

The pithy remark, "Enemies of our Country seized and sold us to the white people, for the love of drink, and from the quarrels of their chiefs," suggests that the enslaved Eboe girl, Florence Hall, had grown to understand the intricate dimensions of the international slave trade.[30]

Aside from that style of greed, some enslavements resulted from the wrongful abuse of power in the hands of priests, chiefs, or judges. John Barbot, agent-general for the English Royal Company of Africa in the 1670s said, "The kings are so absolute, that upon any slight pretense of offence committed by their subjects, they order them to be sold for slaves without regard to rank, or possession."[31]

The misuse of power figures importantly in the explanation of why a fifteen-year-old girl was among the Africans on the brig *Ruby* of Bristol. Nicknamed "Eve" because she was the first woman aboard the slaver, the teenager conveyed a sad tale, perhaps through an interpreter to the ship's doctor James Arnold, about a goat appearing mysteriously in her father's garden. One of the village's great men, whom she believed had it placed there, accused her father of theft. As restitution, the father had to give up one of his three daughters, and the headman selected Eve whom he sold to overseas traders.[32]

One is left to wonder what precipitated the subsequent enslavement of Eve's eight-year-old sister whom traders brought aboard the *Ruby* three months after Eve's arrival. It was not unusual for slavers to remain on the coast, several months or longer, while the captain continued trading until he acquired the desired number of slaves. Hence, the enslavement of the two children aboard the *Ruby* at different times. Perhaps the meeting of the two children was similar to the reunion between Olaudah Equiano and his sister. It was impossible to tell how long the two girls remained together. If both children survived the voyage, it is possible that they would disembark and be sold into the same community. If this indeed were the case, the possibility of the girls maintaining a familial relationship was plausible. Otherwise, they, like millions of other Africans without regard for age, would endure further separations from real and fictive kin.[33]

The consequences of the Atlantic slave trade on Africa demographically and economically remain topics of serious debate. Joseph Miller's study of Angola where the estimated displacements were as high as 100,000–120,000 souls per year asserts that the repercussions upon the region were significant. Similarly, Patrick Manning developed a simulation model that uses statistics to measure demographic changes in trading and exporting areas. He claims that the overseas slave trade had a devastating impact on Africa and served as a catalyst for the growth of slavery on the continent. Paul Lovejoy is clear in saying the "European slave trade across the Atlantic marked a radical break in the history of Africa" as a "major influence in transforming African society." By contrast, David Eltis asserts that the Atlantic slave trade was not sufficiently widespread to have a significant jolt upon the course of African history. The suppression of the overseas slave trade, concludes Eltis, was also of marginal influence upon the continent's historical path. Historical disagreements aside, the slave trade robbed Africa of millions of girls, boys, women, and men whose energy and creativity contributed nothing toward the improvement of their homeland.[34]

When examining the impact of the slave trade on children, it is evident that this international commerce changed the lives of children who remained in Africa and those taken to the Americas. The loss of a great number of men among people who practiced polygyny was offset by continued reproduction, consequently women carried on in their positions as caregivers with the assistance of other women, but the quality and quantity of time spent with their offspring changed. Also of importance are the demographics of those left behind and the relationship to the quality of their lives. In regions where the preponderance of the slaves exported were males between twelve and sixty years of age, a disproportionate amount of work shifted to women. Without the greater majority of able-bodied men to fell trees and clear fields for the women to cultivate, the women's work increased as they filled voids created by the loss of strong healthy men.[35]

In the absence of these men, women spent more time clearing fields and less time cultivating. This resulted in less agricultural produce for subsistence and disposal as marketable surplus commodities. In a similar vein, there were fewer men hunting, fishing, and raising livestock. Therefore, diets contained fewer sources of protein unless those left behind used alternative ways to sustain themselves.[36]

What happened to persons remaining in African villages was as important as what lay ahead for those taken away from their homelands. Upon arrival at the seacoast, children and adults were imprisoned while awaiting the final processing before sailing into the Atlantic's middle passage. Traders selected the able-bodied from those who were less-able by examining naked males and females "even to the smallest member . . . without the least distinction or modesty."[37]

Afterward, traders branded able-bodied slaves with the name or symbol of the trading company. William Bosman, chief factor of the Dutch West India Company at Elmina and author of *A New and Accurate Description of the Coast of Guinea, Divided into the Gold, the Slave, and the Ivory Coasts, etc* (1701), claimed branding seemed "very barbarous" but declared it was "followed by meer necessity." This "necessity" prevented African traders from exchanging hearty slaves in place of those deemed unfit. Bosman asserts that whites took "all possible care" not to burn the slaves "too hard, especially the women, who are more tender than the men." The pain subsided over time, but branding made an indelible imprint on the slaves' psyche and was a visible reminder of the suffering they endured.[38]

There was little attention to the comfort of Africans during their voyages. Augustino recalled that "The clothes of all the negroes going on board ship were stripped off . . . even to the last rag." Some captains provided cloth for the Africans to cover themselves and mats for them to lie upon; others did not. One former crew member wrote, "The Hollanders and other Europeans take no such care in transporting their slaves to America, but ship them poor and faint, without any mats, or other necessaries."[39]

Commonplace discussions of this facet of the slave trade, also known as the Middle Passage, including descriptions of bad food, stale water, severe crowding, and other conditions such as those offered by a crew member aboard a slaver who wrote,

> It is pitiful to see how they crowd those poor wretches, six hundred and fifty or seven hundred in a ship, the men standing in the hold ty'd to stakes, the women between decks, and those that are with child in the great cabin, and the children in the steerage, which in that hot climate occasions an intolerable stench.[40]

In addition, space allotments varied according to gender and age. Adult males had a space that was six feet long by sixteen inches wide, and two feet seven inches high. Space for women was not as long measuring five feet ten inches long by sixteen inches wide. Boys and girls received even less space. Young males were to fill no more than five feet by fourteen inches while small females had four feet six inches by twelve inches. Despite the usual space allotments, the Philadelphian, William Chancellor, a surgeon aboard the sloop *Wolf* in 1750, claimed that the vessel that sailed from New York did not have a quarterdeck or platform to accommodate very young children. Although this was true, children of three and four years of age were taken aboard the ship. Without a special space for the children, said Chancellor, "They lie on Casks & it is no wonder we loose them so fast."[41]

With or without assigned spaces, children were often unfettered and could escape the heat and stench of the hole. As a young boy, Augustino remembered that he walked on the deck and breathed fresh air, but that was only a temporary respite from the ship's inhumane living conditions and contagious diseases. "The shrieks of the women, and the groans of the dying," wrote an eyewitness, "rendered the whole a scene of horror almost inconceivable."[42]

During the trans-Atlantic crossing children saw and experienced things for which an adult would be unprepared; the voyage presented a sharp contrast to some children's lives prior to being kidnapped. Augustino remembered his voyage across the Atlantic when "five, six, ten, sometimes even a dozen died in a day" due to the "excessive heat" and "insufficient supply of water." Venture Smith reported that smallpox ravished the ship as he crossed the Atlantic in the 1730s. When the vessel reached Barbados, only 200 of his estimated 260 shipmates were still alive.[43]

Smith said nothing about the victims' age or gender and did not comment about his reaction to the illnesses and deaths surrounding him. By contrast, Dr. Chancellor made specific notations about the morbidity and mortality rates among children aboard the *Wolf*, who died of flux, worms, measles, and dropsy. On May 29, 1750, the doctor noted that forty-three young slaves were sick with measles. A five-year-old girl among them died that day. The prognosis for the remainder was not good and caused him to write, "[I] imagine that more will tip off." On May 30, 1750, he went among the slaves at morning, noon, and afternoon. With each visit he discovered another child dead. The stressful situation caused the doctor to write, "It is impossible for you [readers] to conceive or me to describe the Torture I sustain at the loss of these Slaves." If the doctor were so affected, what did the children among the sick and dying experience? Moreover, what did the children think as they saw the adults sending the youthful victims overboard to a "watry grave?"[44]

In addition to enduring an existence permeated by death, young survivors often coped with rampant sexual exploitation that was not confined to the ships but sometimes began as females waited in barracoons until loaded on the ships. Boyrereau Brinch wrote about "common sailors" ravishing "women in the presence of all the assembly." He also claimed that mothers and fathers sometimes witnessed their "daughter's being *dispoiled*." James Pope-Hennessy, author of *Sins of the Fathers: A Study of the Atlantic Slave Traders, 1441–1807*, had tales of his own to tell about the sexual exploitation of African women. "Disagreeable, indeed repellent, as this subject may seem," he wrote, "it is one of the greatest pertinence to the history of the coloured populations of the West Indies, the Southern States of America and the other trans-Atlantic slave plantations."[45]

Ottobah Cugoano remarked about the occurrence saying, "It was common for the dirty filthy sailors to take the African women and lie upon their bodies." The veteran slaver John Newton concurred and admitted that on some ships "the licence . . . was almost unlimited." It was not a universal practice, but it was "too commonly, and, I am afraid, too generally prevalent," Newton wrote. When it came to his attention on board his own ship, Captain Newton fussed. On Wednesday, January 31, 1753, a crew member, William Cooney, seduced "number 83," an African woman, "down into the room and lay with her brutelike in view of the whole quarter deck." This raised Newton's ire.[46]

Newton placed Cooney in irons. His action served notice to the crew that such behavior would not be tolerated. It also sent a message to females, without regard for age, that as captain he would take some measures to prevent further abuse. Other slavers may have had more ambivalent attitudes about this behavior. When commenting about sexual exploitation, one captain of a slaver suggested that it would not "fail to have conditioned their [the slaves] attitude, and consequently that of their descendants, to the white men who claimed to own them."[47]

No doubt the traumatic conditions associated with enslavement kindled a strong desire for reunification with families and manifested itself in defiant behavior from the outset. Several of the narratives, including one by Cugoano, affirm that the children attempted to evade kidnappers, but he wrote, "pistols and cutlasses were introduced, threatening, that if we offered to stir, we should all lie dead on the spot." The resistance by children in Cugoano's company did not differ drastically from Florence Hall and her peers. Of their response, Hall wrote, "cries and screams were raised, but raised unheard, if heard, unattended."[48]

Resistance to enslavement and all of its manifestations was a continuous theme whether Africans, young and old, were fighting their captors—black and white in their villages, while marching from the interior to the shore, or on board ships in the Atlantic. Refusing to eat and attempting to commit suicide by jumping overboard were the most commonly reported forms of active resistance. Based on his experience as a child in the Middle Passage, Augustino remembered that youngsters were also among those who chose death over what they considered a worse fate. He recalled: "The young ones had the right of coming on deck, but several of those jumped overboard, for fear they were being fattened to be eaten."[49]

Crews countered resistance by forcing recalcitrant males and females to eat. Since the Africans appeared to be more affected by pain than death, the crew dissuaded them from jumping overboard and drowning themselves by using netting or rigs. Other acts of defiance included rebellions and mutinies. In his "Shipboard Revolts, African Authority, and the Slave Trade," an essay based on data collected about trans-Atlantic slaving vessels between 1650 and 1860, David Richardson, estimates that mutinies occurred on as many as 10 percent of the voyages with up to 10 percent of lives lost in the uprisings.[50]

Given the relatively large percentage of children in the Middle Passage, it is unlikely that many girls and boys failed to witness such bloody tumults.

To witness a mutiny was one thing, but to participate in one was a different matter. A 1734 warning issued to Samuel Rhodes, captain of the Massachusetts slaver *Affrica*, by its owner Samuel Waldo attests to the possibilities of trouble from youthful passengers. "For your own safety as well as mine," said Waldo, "You'll have the needful Guard over your Slaves, and putt not too much confidence in the Women nor Children lest they happen to be Instrumental to your being surprised which might be fatall." Such advice was worth heeding. Apparently the *Henrietta Marie's* owner was of a similar mind. More than eighty pairs of shackles of the appropriate size for small hands were onboard the *Henrietta Marie*.[51]

John Newton, who after nine years as a slaver became a minister and abolitionist noted, "It is not to be expected that [Africans] will tamely resolve themselves to their situation." Based upon his experience, Newton added, "It is always taken for granted, that they [Africans] will attempt to gain their liberty if possible." Consequently, crews stood ready with both lethal weapons and whips to put down resistance from the rebels on board. In 1721, William Snelgrave, captain aboard the London based *Henry*, observed that the crew on the ship secured the human cargo "very well in Irons, and watch[ed] them narrowly," yet they revolted. When asked "what had induced them to mutiny," the Africans explained that they had been carried away from their homes and were "resolved to regain their Liberty if possible."[52]

In Ottobah Cugoano's account of the kidnap and passage across the Atlantic, he refers to a plot among the boys and women. With more liberty than men, the women and boys planned to "burn and blow up the ship, and to perish all together in the flames." "Death," wrote Cugoano, "was more preferable than life." The rebels were not successful because "one of their own country-women, who slept with some of the head men of the ship" betrayed them.[53]

Although it is not known how many children witnessed the mutiny aboard the *Robert* of Bristol in 1721, their presence is of special interest. According to Captain Harding, Tomba, an enslaved African, "combined with three or four of the stoutest of his Country-men to kill the Ship's Company." That they were outnumbered did not dissuade the insurrectionists. The press of freedom was worth the risk. And, their quest was nearly successful due to "a Woman-Slave, who being more at large, was to watch the proper Opportunity." The moment came when they "had a Shore to fly to" and she noticed that only five whites, all asleep, were on the deck. She passed that information to Tomba along with "all the Weapons that she could find," one hammer. He and his followers, including the woman, seized and killed three sailors.[54]

The crew put down the insurrection quickly and sentenced both the "Abattoirs" and "Actors" to "cruel Deaths." Before executing them, the crew forced several rebels to "eat the Heart and Liver of one of [the whites] killed." The woman's cruel fate included being "hoisted up by the Thumbs, whipp'd, and slashed with Knives before the other Slaves till she died." Such a punishment in the presence of shipmates, young or old, served as a vivid reminder of what lay ahead if any of them followed her lead.[55]

Any lessons to be learned applied only to the Africans, young and old, aboard the *Robert*. Other Africans embarking on voyages across the Atlantic would know nothing of the woman's participation in the mutiny or about her execution. Besides, the loss of liberty and facing an unknown future did not dissuade would-be-mutineers.

Certainly, this was true of the Africans aboard the *Thames*, December 15, 1776, who attempted to take over the ship. When they failed, thirty-two Africans, considered the "best Slaves" jumped overboard. Among that number were some boys.[56]

Perhaps the most widely publicized and far-reaching mutiny occurred July 1, 1839, when Africans aboard the 120 ton Spanish slaver *Amistad* killed the captain and several crew members before commandeering the ship during a rainstorm when many Africans were on the deck. Joseph Cinqué, the "master spirit" of the insurrection, intended to return to Africa. Without navigational skills, he depended upon the maritime knowledge of crew members José Ruiz and Pedro Montes. Instead of sailing for Africa, the two men maneuvered along the North American coast for nearly two months and finally attracted the attention of the *USS Washington*, a revenue cutter near Long Island, which directed them ashore.[57]

Among the thirty-six *Amistad* captives who survived the mutiny and imprisonment were four children ranging from seven to twelve years of age. They had come from different villages in the Congo and did not know each other previously. The mutiny must have been a frightful episode for the children. Sarah Margru, remembered one of the other girls, Charlotte, who showed great maturity despite her youth. She, Charlotte, "did comfort me when I was torn from my dear native land," wrote Margru. Moreover, it was Charlotte, Margru added, who "used to tell us that one day we shall all see our native land."[58]

Charlotte's prediction became a reality for her shipmates, but few other Middle Passage survivors ever saw their native land again. The majority of the Africans stepped ashore and into perpetual servitude when owners of mines, plantations, shops, and businesses bid for their labor at private and public sales.[59]

Enslavement in the Americas was not a monolithic occurrence. As a result, the girls and boys experienced ownership at the hands of brutal and benign owners across regions. Observations made by the freeborn, New Yorker Solomon Northup who had fallen prey as an adult to traders and enslaved for twelve years noted:

> There may be humane masters, as there certainly are inhumane ones—there may be slaves well-clothed, well-fed, and happy, as there surely are those half-clad, half-starved and miserable; nevertheless, the institution that tolerates such wrong and inhumanity . . . is a cruel, unjust, and barbarous one.[60]

The paucity of written narratives by persons, especially females, enslaved as children make it virtually impossible to evaluate the impact of slavery upon their lives. Florence Hall's memoir is a rarity in this regard. Despite its brevity, Hall's well-chosen words convey the meaning of slavery for her. For example, she described being stripped of her beads and shells. Additionally, she wrote:

> My Eboe name was Akeiso—the loss of which soon put an end to all recollections of my people—another name—a strange language & new master confused my mind, and while ignorance of each, made my labour more troublesome, yet the dread of punishment compelled me to work.

Hall, like millions of other Africans, had been divested of her "trinkets," name, and language when thrown into a new world of work. When remembering the disembarkation, Hall lamented further about the great losses she and other Africans endured. "We," she wrote, were "consigned to foreigners and Slavery." Even more poignant, she added, "We [had] left our Country and our freedom."[61]

Enslaved children who had never known freedom in the Americas were incapable of making a comparable analogy as did Northup, who was enslaved as an adult with two dependant children, yet they would agree that their loss of liberty whether in Africa or the Americas was cruel, unjust, and barbarous. The testimony and action of many enslaved boys and girls who came of age in the New World suggest that many of them adapted to bondage and found some solace in their families, leisure activities, and religion. But, they were never content with the idea of perpetual servitude for themselves or their offspring.

Figure 2 Magby Peterson and his nanny, 1868

Source: Florida Department of Archives and History, Tallahassee, Florida.

CHAPTER TWO

MINOR PLAYERS IN BONDAGE: INTERACTIONS BETWEEN ENSLAVED AND SLAVEHOLDING CHILDREN IN THE OLD SOUTH

I alwas' played wid de white chilluns til I wuz big enough to be put to wuk an' den onto de field.

—Manus Brown[1]

As a way of entertaining two young visitors in 1848, Launcelot Minor Blackford, son of white slaveowners in Virginia, built a small cart in which they could ride. Afterward, the eleven-year-old diarist "got all the little children who could well do it and hitched them to the carriage [and] made them run around the yard with Alice or Richard on it." Blackford added, "They seemed to enjoy it very much." As written, the identity of all the little children who could pull the carriage remains unknown. Were his miniature beasts of burden black or white? What were their ages? Did Blackford harness boys as well as girls? Were the little children who pulled the cart active agents or helpless victims in Blackford's entertainment? Answers to these questions are as important as knowing the identity of the children whom Blackford said "seemed to enjoy [the ride] very much." Was he referring to Alice and Richard who rode in the carriage or to the little children who towed it?[2]

The intent herein is to examine interactions between children, free and unfree, in the Old South to determine the extent to which Thomas Jefferson was correct when he argued that children imitated the "whole commerce between master and slave" from observing their parents' actions with bound servants. Afterward, slaveholding children, according to Jefferson, put on the same airs when interacting with enslaved persons. Conventional wisdom suggests that Jefferson was referring to white children, but it is reasonable to ask if his analogy was also applicable to black slaveholding children. Ordinarily, one thinks of slave–slaveholder relationships in terms of black and white, but blacks also owned other blacks. The relatively small number of black slaveholders and the general paucity of readily available manuscripts attributed to them tends to preclude serious general studies of relationships between black slaveholders and the black folk they claimed.[3]

Despite differences in the size of the black slaveholding population and the number of slaves they possessed when compared to whites, this facet of American history warrants study to answer questions such as, "Were there differences in the way black and white slaveholding children interacted with enslaved children within the confines of their households (dwellings and surrounding property)?" "How important are age, color, and gender differences in defining relationships between slaveholding and enslaved children?" Answers to these questions are most readily available through an examination of relations between enslaved and slaveholding children as they played together, learned their letters, and performed chores.[4]

Relationships between enslaved and slaveholding children did not follow uniform patterns. Much depended upon slaveholders' reason for owning slaves as well as the owners' color, size of household, and attitude toward their children associating with enslaved girls and boys.

The exploitation of labor for profit-oriented motives appears to have been primary reasons for owning human beings. However, historian Carter G. Woodson argued that black slaveholders had different motives. Based upon his study of the 1830 census, the historian declared that benevolence and interests in the personal freedom of relatives and friends were important incentives for blacks owning slaves. Several states enacted legislation that demanded a freed person's egress from the state within a specified time or risk reenslavement. Some states prohibited ingress by free blacks, while others denied manumissions altogether. Additionally, the costs of manumissions and capitation taxes were often prohibitive. As a result, blacks owning relatives and friends held their kin and acquaintances to avoid egress or other obstacles associated with manumission.[5]

While there may have been some cases where Woodson's thesis was valid, recent scholarship challenges this notion as a primary motivation in all cases, and argues that African Americans also owned slaves solely for pecuniary reasons. Woodson's work denies the relationship between color and class among African Americans, especially in the nineteenth-century South where emancipations were often linked to special circumstances rather than mass liberations, as in the North during the Revolutionary War era. It was not unusual for southern whites to free biracial offspring and bestow property, *real and personal,* upon them. Furthermore, mixed race children often intermarried persons of like backgrounds to maintain and solidify their assets. Consequently, the mulatto ownership of dark-skinned persons was not entirely unusual.[6]

Wills often leave little doubt about the nature of interpersonal relationships between slaveholders of color and the persons they owned. The last wishes of Betsy Sompayrac, a free woman of color in Natchitoches, Louisiana, reflect an economic interest in slaves as chattel but also reveal a level of complexity in these relationships that precludes generalizations. Sompayrac, a small slaveholder and mother of four children, dictated her final wishes to the parish judge on January 15, 1845. Concerned about the financial impact her death would have upon the welfare of her three minor children, Sompayrac sought to guarantee a degree of financial security by parceling out personal property, a woman and her four children, among her offspring. Sompayrac's son, Daniel, fell heir to the "boy Alexander." Another "boy," James, along with the "boy" Solomon, became the property of Sompayrac's son, Stephen. The "little negro girl named Elizabeth" and the woman, Jane, were set aside for Sarah Ann Sompayrac. The *bequests* were not as simple as it appears on the surface.[7]

Intricate stipulations of the will prevented Sarah and Stephen Sompayrac from benefitting from their inheritances permanently. Five-year-old Solomon was Stephen's property only until he reached thirty years of age in consideration of his status as Sompayrac's godson. Accepting oversight as a guardian, if necessary, meant committing oneself to a child's emotional, physical, and religious well-being, as if he or she were one's own offspring. Sompayrac cared for Solomon, but her sentiments were not as strong as for her own children. Consequently, she did not free him outright.[8]

Even more arresting than Solomon's treatment were the conditions affecting the woman Jane. She would become Sarah's property only after the liquidation of Sompayrac's debts. Rather than requesting the sale of her real property, Sompayrac asked the executors to rent her home and to hire Jane out with the proceeds earmarked for creditors. After paying the debts, Sarah could take possession of Jane but not of her progeny. Sompayrac requested that if Jane had any additional children, they would belong to her older son Benjamin, who was absent when she dictated the will, if he ever returned to Natchitoches.[9]

The Sompayrac raises more questions than it answers about relationships between young black slaveholders and the children they owned. What services would the slave boys, Alexander, James, and Solomon, perform for their owners, Daniel and Stephen? Would the enslaved boys, ranging in age from four months to eight years old, show deference to their young "masters" or would they treat each other as equals because they were of the same color? Did Sompayrac's daughter Sarah view the "little girl Elizabeth" as a playmate and Jane, aged thirty-five, as a surrogate mother? Would gender distinctions determine if Sompayrac's sons were more likely to manage their slaves with less difficulty than Sarah? What were the conditions under which each child learned the role that he or she was to play in a "master-slave" or "mistress-maid" situation? What influence did their parents have in the matter?[10]

After an especially trying day in December 1844, Anna Matilda Page King, wife of a white Saint Simon's Island, Georgia, planter who owned more than one hundred slaves, wrote to him saying she would not object to ridding themselves of the slaves and leaving the "wretched" country. "I am more and more convinced," she admitted that "it is no place to rear a family of children." It was not unusual for Anna King, mother of ten children, to worry about their educational opportunities, character development, moral courage, and principles. She believed, "none but a parent (who tries to do their [sic] duty) can know how great a trial it is to raise a family of children in the right way." In her opinion, "To bring up boys on a plantation [with slaves made] them *trianical* [sic] as well as lazy." She added, "and girls too." King did not elaborate, but it is well-known that whites, young and old, were in positions of racial hegemony to demand and receive both deference and services from blacks, young and old.[11]

Anna Matilda King was not alone in her concerns about her children developing imperious behavior. The British-born Frances Kemble's well-known comments about the slaves, young and old, who surrounded her daughter and eagerly obeyed her "little gestures of command" are informative. Her child said something about a swing, according to Kemble, and in less than five minutes, headman Frank had one erected for her, and a dozen black boys and girls were ready to swing little "missis." Kemble shuddered at the thought of her child learning to rule her black peers despotically before comprehending the first lesson of self-government. Kemble suggested that she could avoid this foreboding future by removing herself and the child from the plantation South, which she described as "misery and ruin."[12]

The majority of slaveowners, like Anna Matilda King, did not extricate themselves or their children from slaveholding surroundings. Instead, many taught their children to behave charitably, in word and deed, toward enslaved persons of all ages. For example, as a young girl, Minerva Cain Caldwell received words of wisdom about the subject from a relative. The advice warned against offending relatives, friends, and servants who provide for their "comfort and gratification." The 1833 letter urged treatment "with much feeling" and "as little trouble as possible." The pithy reminder, "You will have to answer at the bar of God, for your conduct towards them," followed.[13]

By the 1830s, the idea of paternalism as a reciprocal obligation between slaveholders and slaves sharing mutual benefits was sufficiently widespread to the extent that an antebellum agricultural journal posited that slaveholding children should "be taught that it is their duty to regard [enslaved persons] with benevolence, to administer to their wants, and to protect them from injury" without "terms of familiarity." Although this advice appears praiseworthy, it is charged with the makings of unequal associations and the assumption that slaves needed white hands, even young small ones, to care for and protect them. Advice of this kind would appear unnecessary for persons owning relatives and friends for benevolent reasons.[14]

Ordinarily, such discussions, ownership of relatives and friends, focus more on blacks owing other blacks as suggested by Woodson rather than the charitable acts by whites who owned relatives. Certainly, exceptions existed. For example, a British officer in the United States between 1806 and 1809 deputed to investigate American claims against the Crown noted one such exception:

> Col H's servants (slaves) are mostly his own children. His coachman is his own son. He has adopted a little girl [,] daughter of a female slave who was also his daughter tho now dead. This adopted daughter being white tho born a slave & of a yellow mother he and Mrs H treat her with as much care & attention or more than if she was their legitimate child. She sleeps in the (same) bed with them calls them father & mother while her uncles, aunts etc are serving the table.

The intricacies of slaveownership in the colonel's household calls attention to the complexities of slavery and its impact on all persons involved. It gave pause to the officer who ended the journal entry by writing, "So much for Virginia manners." [15]

The officer did not provide the child's age or that of her uncles and aunts who served the table; yet, he is clear in saying that the colonel's adopted granddaughter was "quite a spoiled child." Indeed, she enjoyed privileges that were denied to other enslaved persons in the household. Under the circumstances, it is reasonable to ponder whether the young girl imitated her grandparents in exercising power over the slaves or interacted with them on terms of equality.[16]

No doubt some slaveholding parents disapproved, unequivocally, of associations between their children and enslaved boys and girls because of their notions about the superiority of slaveholders and inferiority of slaves along with wishes to maintain socially constructed distinctions based upon color and status. Added to these objections were the circumstances involving children who shared common paternity but not the same color and status. White women, particularly those who suspected their husbands of infidelity or had confirmed it, often objected to the presence of enslaved mulatto children and treated them poorly.[17]

Other white parents objected to interplay between their children and enslaved boys and girls whom they believed were "corrupting influences" upon their own offspring. For example, Mary Chaplin, wife of a South Carolina cotton planter, complained that "the little Negroes are ruining the children" by teaching them "badness," which included "bad manners, crossing swollen creeks, eating green fruit." These transgressions are the kinds of things to which children resort when they have time on their hands and are not under the careful supervision of adults. Perhaps the white and black children in the Chaplin household shared equally in the "badness." If this is the case, the white children were also in a position to skew accounts of events against the black ones to avoid chastisement at the hands of a mother who found it difficult to believe her offspring acted badly on their own.[18]

The freedman William Johnson, a prosperous Natchez, Mississippi, barber and slaveowner, objected to interactions between free and enslaved blacks. Diaries kept by Johnson between 1835 and 1851 reveal his views about associations between the free black apprentices he hired and their enslaved acquaintances. "Fraternization with slaves," Johnson's biographers write, "was out of the question—or so he thought." The slave-born Johnson, a barber, grumbled about the apprentices' interests in attending "darkey parties," entertainments for slaves arranged by slaveowners. Although Johnson groused about the behavior of his apprentices, and not his own children, it is reasonable to think that the barber would have also objected to his children attending the "Darkey Ball."[19]

Sylvester Sostan Wickliffe, a freeborn Louisianan told a Works Progress Administration (WPA) interviewer that his uncle, Romaine Vidrine, owned " 'bout thirty-eight" slaves and observed distinctions in his position as a slaveowner. According to Wickliffe,

Dey was a big dif'ence make [*sic*] 'tween slave niggers and owner niggers. Dey so much dif'ence as 'tween white folks and cullud folks. My uncle wouldn't 'low slave niggers to eat at de same table with him or with any of us free-born niggers . . . He ain't never 'low none de slaves be familiar with him.

Wickliffe did not explain Vidrine's rationale but understood that his uncle behaved much like white slaveholders.[20]

Free blacks in the small towns and rural areas of the South sometimes refrained from open association with slaves, especially those outside their kinship circle. Free persons tried to perpetuate an image of social divisions between slaves and themselves to protect their own liberty. Many whites abhorred the idea of free blacks among them thinking that freepersons inspired their contemporaries in bondage to desire freedom and act upon their ambitions for liberation. To insulate themselves from such charges, some free black southerners objected to associations with enslaved persons and kept their distance.[21]

Ostensibly, Johnson's disparaging remarks reflect his repulsion at the thought of free and unfree persons socializing freely. A closer reading of Johnson's diaries leaves room for other interpretations of his aversion to "darkey parties," which may have reflected a concern over moral standards, especially if he accepted the prevailing notion that enslaved women were promiscuous. To be sure, he was quite upset to find two of his apprentices fondling an enslaved woman. He knew that the possibilities of intimacy between young unmarried persons, free and unfree, were fraught with complications involving the crossing of legal boundaries. Free black persons were often not welcomed on plantations and ran the risk of humiliations, beatings, or worse by patrollers: designated groups of whites authorized to monitor the comings and goings of slaves after nightfall. Neither Johnson's diaries nor one kept by his daughter, Katherine, include anything about her thoughts regarding the "darkey parties" or the apprentices who attended them without her father's approval.[22]

In the absence of adult supervision, youth often satisfied their own whims, and there was enough potential for ill-mannered behavior and mischief making to go around among black and white children alike. For example, the Mississippi-born ex-slave Manus Brown told WPA interviewers in the 1930s that his owner's children put him "up to a heap o' meanness" and "would git [him] to do de things dey wuz scart to do." At the outset, it appears that Brown was a helpless victim; however, a careful reading of his testimony raises questions about the extent to which he was indeed victimized. He explained,

> I got kotched on fire one day when I wuz a little slave chile. I was acting de fool an' de white chilluns put me up to throwing some cartages **us** had in a fire **we** had built on the side o' the road way down from marse' house. Dey wanted de fun o' hearing em go off but wuz scart to throw em in.

It is clear that the children were knowingly treading on very dangerous ground when playing with fire and live ammunition away from the gaze of adults, but it is less clear what Brown meant when he said he was "**acting de fool.**"[23]

After emphasizing that the white children were visibly anxious, Brown added, "so's de fust thing **dey all knowed** I marched up to de fire an' throwed de whole bunch [of cartridges] in deir at once, it wuz a plumb hand full." Brown muddles his account. Was he acting on his own or upon the commands of the white children? Or, was this lack of clarity his effort to obfuscate what really happened as if he had second thoughts about casting white playmates in a negative light while recounting the story to a local white WPA interviewer in the 1930s? Nevertheless, the bullets "went to shooting 'fore I knowed it," said Brown, "Fire flew every which way an' I purt nigh got burnt up." No doubt, the black and white children learned a valuable lesson about playing with fire, literally and figuratively.[24]

Children, without regard for the circumstances—parental permissions, color, or class—often played together and learned from each other. Commonalities in the play of children of different cultures and national origins make it impossible to say definitively where an activity originated.

Many former slaves recalled their play days with fond memories, but it is fallacious to assume, even under the best of circumstances, that a consistent unknowing innocence or sense of equality prevailed among slaveowning masters and mistresses-in-the-making and the children they or their parents owned. It is often easier to note what appears to be an unfair act on behalf of white children toward black girls and boys than to explain the rationale for such behavior.

Launcelot Minor Blackford serves as one illustrative example out of many. He was very much aware of the status of enslaved persons and had contributed a small amount of money in 1849 for the welfare of ex-slaves living in Liberia whom his mother had emancipated. Yet, Blackford's treatment of the enslaved children who pulled the cart for Richard and Alice's ride was callous. He showed little sympathy when "one of the little black children fell down and hurt herself." He concluded that she "was of no loss as she was a hindrance to the rest . . . she could not keep up." His primary interest was in keeping the carriage moving efficiently and effectively. There is no mention of rewarding the little girl with a cart ride for her efforts.[25]

Casting enslaved children in the role of draft animals was not unique to Blackford. A comparable example is that of J. G. Clinkscales who received a small wagon as a present and decided to hitch Jack and Peter to it. According to Clinkscales, his "little sister did the riding," and he "did the driving." Writing long after slavery ended, Clinkscales recalled that he had cracked a whip "over the backs, and sometimes *on* the backs, of [his] two-legged horses." In compliance with role play, the enslaved boys delighted "the little queen who rode" and the driver when they "kicked and reared and snorted like real horses," wrote Clinkscales. Before long, Pete and Jack tired of the game and asked to end it. Clinkscales agreed and replaced them with calves. One must ask why was this an alternative rather than Clinkscales's first choice?[26]

When comparing the white drivers, Clinkscale was more sensitive than Blackford in that he honored Jack and Pete's requests for relief without grousing about it. Both Clinkscales and Blackford used black children as draft animals, but neither of the white boys wrote about switching places out of a sense of fairness.

Enslaved children did not have miniature carriages for their own entertainment but played "hoss" nonetheless. George Briggs explained, "Befo 'Cheney Briggs went to Arkansas he was our play hoss. His brother [Henry] was the wagoner and I was de mule." Henry, the smallest of the children "rid" the backs of the other boys, "sometimes." This account leaves no doubt about the nature of their representative play—games replicating real life situations—and the mutual decision about who would or would not ride the "hoss." Size rather than color determined that the smallest boy would ride the larger one's backs, sometimes. Since the children determined the frequency of privileging Henry with a ride, it is unlikely that George and Cheney would tire of the game as readily if they had no choice.[27]

It was not uncommon in representative play, for white children to hold power positions consistently and make decisions about the roles played. Note the play of a group of children on a Louisiana plantation who staged a mock funeral service in 1832 after a black boy found a dead chicken. Amelia Thompson Watts, who was among the group of children, provided the details. "The boys," she wrote,

> made a wagon of fig branches, and [used] four of them as horses. We tied a bow of black ribbon around the chicken's neck, and covered him with a white rag, and then marched in a procession singing . . . negro hymns, all the white children next to the hearses, marching two by two, and the colored children following the same order.

After the procession, the children stood by the grave where a white girl in the fold preached the sermon, "We must all die."[28]

This account raises questions about respect for social and gender conventions after the final preparations to lay the chicken to rest. First, was marching next to the hearses a privileged position? Why were the children separated according to color? And, why did the black children bring up the rear of the procession? These children appeared to know enough about funerals to use the appropriately colored shroud and black ribbon denoting the sorrowful occasion. They also seemed to know that social etiquette in the plantation South forbade the mixing of black and white mourners. It also follows that enslaved children would heed the directions of white slaveholding children.

A second set of questions regarding gender and color is equally poignant. Why did the boys act alone in building the hearse? Why did a girl assume the most important role in the game, delivering the eulogy? Why did the black boy who found the chicken not do so? What role did whiteness play in this decision?

Women did not preach sermons to mixed congregations within organized churches of the Old South, but it was not unusual for older women to make remarks at funerals. In this case of child's play, color, custom, and, possibly, age were the determining factors. If slaveholders did not object, enslaved blacks worshipped with white churchgoers and listened to white preachers. In other instances, slaveowners hired ministers to preach to their chattel in separate afternoon services. In these situations the ministers were often white men not unfamiliar to both black and white children. But what was less well known to white children is that enslaved persons often maintained "hush harbors" where they conducted religious services secretly and listened to black ministers. To come forward with objections based upon what they saw in their own community would subject participants in surreptitious church services to punishment. Rather than insist upon duplicating what they actually saw and did in their own secret church meetings, enslaved children accepted the prescriptive role for Maria as their preacher. This was in keeping with traditional expectations of southern race relations with whites, small and large, holding the upperhand, but it was not in keeping with gender conventions.[29]

The roles played by black and white children indicate that they were indeed aware of differences in their positions based upon color and status. An ex-slave described playing with white children whose attitudes of superiority were evident. In their games, "De whites was de soldiers an' me and de rest of de slave boys," he said, "was de Injuns." The "soldiers," who carried wooden guns, shot and scalped the Indians. Similar circumstances existed among a group of children in Virginia who played the game "Harpers Ferry" constructed from their understanding of John Brown's 1859 raid. A white child portrayed Brown, and his supporters were black. This is a significant example of representative play, for it captures a class attitude and shows that the children were aware of national events. Similarly, southern white boys played the "Federates," and the black played "Yankees." The Confederates always took the Union soldiers prisoner and threatened to slaughter them. When recalling the game in the 1930s, a freedman mused, "Guess dey got dat idea f'om dere fathers." On a more neutral note, during the Civil War another group of black and white children sat around a bonfire trying to "imitate the soldiers on picket."[30]

Games that required decisions about who filled a specific role were more open to race, gender, and age discrimination than games of chance or skill. Frederick Douglass recalled that black boys "could run as fast, jump as far, throw the ball as direct and true, and catch it with as much dexterity and skill as the white boys." Moreover, young blacks prided themselves on their agility. The slave-born Robert Ellett believed he had an unusual strength and claimed he "was the best of the young boys on the plantation" near West Point, Virginia.[31]

Obviously, some children observed rules of sportsmanship and did not let the slaveowner–slave relationship decide who won or lost. Ellett considered the "young masters" his pals, but he did not allow them to win at any of their games simply because of they owned him. And, Hilary Herbert, lawyer, author, and member of the house of representatives from 1877 to 1893, and secretary of the navy from 1893 to 1897, did not take advantage of the child he owned. Herbert reminisced about playing with his constant companion when they were nine or ten years of age. The black boy always asked, "Marse [Herbert], will you give me a white man's chance?" The question gives pause to the potential for unsportsmanlike conduct motivated by race and status. The boys had reached a moment of truth and recognized that racial and social differences existed between them. They also knew that the overarching structure did not demand that the black boy receive a "white man's chance." Herbert agreed to play fair and "always lived up to [the] contract." Theirs was not the ordinary slaveowner–slave relationship; it was something more. Herbert wrote, "We were friends."[32]

Frederick Douglass's recollections of his enslavement were mitigated by his association with Daniel Lloyd, the youngest son of the slaveowner Edward Lloyd. On occasions Daniel gave Frederick cake and protected him from the "bigger boys." When taken together, these acts were extraordinarily meaningful for Douglass who wrote,

> For such friendship I am deeply grateful, and bitter as are my recollections of slavery, it is a true pleasure to recall any instances of kindness, any sunbeams of humane treatment, which found way to my soul, through the iron grating of my house of bondage.

The "sunbeams of humane treatment" were rare for a child who ordinarily experienced hunger, cold, nakedness, and physical or sexual abuse.[33]

During the early stages of their lives, slaveholding and enslaved children were sometimes comrades in play despite differences in their color or status. Under more serious circumstances, white children have been credited with charitable acts toward their enslaved contemporaries. For example, Sam T. Stewart, born on December 11, 1853, said, "I would have been whipped to pieces (by the local constable) if it hadn't been for a white boy about my age by the name of Thomas Wilson. He told them I was his nigger, and they let me go." The incident is more significant than one child doing whatever was possible to prevent another child from suffering. It also raises a question about whether Wilson's word as a non-slaveholding white boy would have been sufficient to save Stewart.[34]

In all probability, the constable could have ignored the protests of any white child. But the official would not trample upon the rights of a white slaveholder. Regardless of the slaveholder's age, he could exercise authority to protect "his nigger," or chattel property, whom the authority promptly "let go." Slaveowners were literally free to brutalize their own property with impunity, but they did not yield that "right" to others.[35]

This is not to suggest that Wilson's interests in saving Stewart were entirely related to his association with the enslaved boy as a property owner rather than as a personal companion and friend. The relationship between the daughter of a well-known Alexandria, Virginia, slave trader and two enslaved girls that he owned is similar. The children enjoyed a friendly association. And, the trader's daughter succeeded in getting the sale of the young slaves postponed, but she could not prevent it permanently. The child did not own the girls—her father did.[36]

Regardless of who owned whom, an untold number of young enslaved boys and girls enjoyed amicable relationships and learned to read and write through the tutelage of slaveholding white children. The WPA narratives contain many such accounts. For example, Robert Glenn of Raleigh, North Carolina, remembered his owner's son, Crosby. The boy, he said

> . . . took a great liking to me. Once in an undertone he asked me how I would like to have an education. I was overjoyed at the suggestion and he at once began to teach me secretly. I studied hard and he soon had me so I could read and write well. I continued studying and he continued teaching me. He furnished me books and slipped all the papers he could get to me and I was the best educated Negro in the community without anyone except the slaves knowing what was going on.

The sense of pride and elevated self-esteem are evident in the statement. Glenn's recollections indicate that the two children knew their act would not meet adult approval. Note the words "undertone" and "slipped." Black and white children and youth ignored prohibitions and transcended the hurdles to black literacy.[37]

There are similarities in the way Susie King Taylor's white playmate, Katie, offered her lessons if she would not tell Mr. O'Connor, the girl's father. "On my promise not to do so," writes Taylor, "she gave me lessons about four months." Their agreement remained secret. Katie's mother was fully aware of the lessons since she had granted permission to Katy for them. Again, this account implies that the children knew their actions would not meet the approval of the white patriarch who could stop their interactions at will.[38]

Slaveholders of means provided for the education of their own children either by hiring tutors or teaching the children themselves, while others sent their children to local schools or those outside the community. The possibilities of slaveholding children teaching enslaved children were thus ever present.

This was also true in black households where owners held their own kin. For example, following the 1841 death of Susan Rapier, a free woman from Baltimore, the widower, James T. Rapier, bought the sixteen-year-old Lucretia to care for his four children. Over time, Lucretia gave birth to four children fathered by Rapier who attempted, unsuccessfully, to free them. Rapier's older children attended school in Nashville, and could have easily shared their literacy with their enslaved siblings. Ordinarily, slaveholders objected to slaves learning to write because they feared that their bondservants would forge travel passes or even freedom papers. This, of course, was not a concern of James T. Rapier.[39]

Whether they were literate or not, enslaved children, like enslaved adults, were expected to perform chores in a satisfactory and timely manner. Manus Brown explained the end of one phase of his life and the transition to another when he told the WPA interviewer in the 1930s, "I alwas' played wid de white chilluns til I wuz big enough to be put to wuk . . ." The number of slaves in a household often determined whether or not slaveholding children worked along with enslaved children. The children of white yeomen farmers probably worked with the few persons their parents owned. Sons of the prosperous freed mulatto William Ellison of Statesboro, South Carolina, worked in the shop making cotton gins with the skilled slaves their father owned. In larger more diverse households, it is less likely that slaveholding children would work alongside slaves. Rather, they would learn to supervise slaves.[40]

The workplace was often the contested ground upon which the paths of slave-holding and enslaved children diverged. Lunsford Lane, like Manus Brown, played with the white and black children on the North Carolina plantation where he lived until he was old enough to work. It was then, he wrote, "I discovered the difference between myself and my master's white children. They began to order me about, and were told to do so by my master and mistress." Their relationships were changing from those of childish equality to ones in which white children held power backed by parental authority over black children.[41]

Slaveholding parents often attempted to instill an awareness of differing status in both their children and those they owned. When introduced to her "young mistress," a young enslaved girl failed to internalize that message when she looked at the infant in her mother's arms and said, "I don't see no young mistress, that's a baby."[42]

At Hygiene, a small slaveholding household in Louisiana, the mistress Tryphena Blanche Holder Fox set a process into motion to foster unequal social relations between her daughter Fanny and the enslaved children owned by the Fox family. In a letter to her mother on January 1, 1860, Fox referred to her three-year-old daughter as "Miss Fanny" when speaking of the child in connection with the bondservants old or young. The title "Miss" denotes differences in their status and indicates that the blacks Fox owned, regardless of age, owed deference to the white toddler. Although Adelaide's response to the title is unknown, these two examples are illustrative in suggesting that slaveholding children learned to expect deference and enslaved children learned to pay deference at early ages.[43]

According to Fox, her "house pet"—Adelaide—was a good natured, "bright little negress—not very black" who was "quick to learn" with "tolerable quick motion." As a young mother, Fox managed "pretty well with Fanny by making Adelaide . . . come in & play with her." The six-year-old Adelaide, Fox wrote, was "quite delighted when . . . [called] 'to go wash her face & hands & come play with Miss Fanny.' "[44]

Perhaps Adelaide saw the invitation as an opportunity to play whereas her owner saw it as a chance to free herself of a modicum of childcare responsibilities. This is evident in Fox's letter when she wrote, "there are *no playmates* here for [Fanny] & she is sometimes very lonesome." In actuality, she meant there were no white children living nearby with whom Fanny could play. Adelaide's younger sister Margaret and brother Buddy, who were close to Fanny in age, were across the back yard in the cabin. In the meantime, Adelaide's job was to amuse Fanny and save the child's mother a few steps.[45]

Many enslaved children, like Adelaide, were responsible for "nursing" slaveholding children. Rather than giving full attention to their care, black children often rocked cradles, fetched toys, and attended to the personal needs of their charges. Louella Williams told a WPA interviewer that she was "kind of a nurse girl to Miss Lucy, even tho' I warn't any bigger dan her." Louella's job was to run alongside Lucy to pick up her bonnet and put it back on her head. The task of keeping the bonnet on the child's head was not a great one, but perhaps it served a purpose in teaching Louella her supposed role. Lucy may have shaken her bonnet off to entertain herself and create additional work for Louella in the meantime.[46]

Like Louella Williams, Harriet Jacobs was a caregiver for the three-year-old Mary Matilda Norcom, who inherited Jacobs when she was twelve years old. Their relationship was amicable during their formative years. The interactions between her brother John Jacobs and James Norcom, Jr., was a different story. Harriet Jacobs described Norcom as a mean-spirited boy with a penchant for listening to tales a younger sibling concocted about John. As "young master," Norcom decided to flog the high spirited Jacobs, a twelve-year-old with an aversion to the word master and the idea of being whipped. Jacobs, who had lived as a virtually free person until Dr. James Norcom purchased him, defied his "young master" and "fought bravely." Once when Jacobs defeated Norcom in a fight, Norcom was too stubborn to concede the loss to a slave. The "young master" attempted to tie Jacobs's hands behind his back but failed. It was not unusual for overseers or owners to restrain slaves by fastening their hands and feet or tying them at whipping posts and locking them in stocks. On occasions, persons administering punishment also commanded slaves who happened to be present to assist in floggings.[47]

"Young master" Norcom was accustomed to whipping "little" enslaved boys, but "was a perfect coward when a tussle ensued between him and white boys his own size," according to Harriet Jacobs. Rather than stand and fight, Norcom ran away. Comradery would have been more likely between James Norcom and John Jacobs had they grown up together. John Jacobs was ten years old when Dr. Norcom purchased him and gave him to his sons, who "had charge of me," wrote Jacobs.[48]

The differences in the relationships between the Jacobs and Norcom children had much to do with their age and gender. Although slaveholding women did use physical punishment upon slaves, it was generally less severe and less frequent than when applied by their male counterparts. At the outset, Mary Norcom was physically incapable of flogging Harriet Jacobs due to her age and size. The Norcom and Jacobs boys were close in size and age. Jacobs attributed his defiant spirit to his father, a skilled slave who taught his son to hate slavery but failed to teach him how to conceal it. The elder Jacobs's greatest desire was to purchase and emancipate his children. They had lived virtually free before entering the Norcom household; therefore, it was especially difficult for John to assume a subservient role at the behest of his white peers.[49]

James W. C. Pennington's comments about his relationship with white slaveholding boys in his autobiography, and his disdain is clear. He explained:

There is another source of evil to slave children, which I cannot forbear to mention here, as one which early embittered my life,—I mean the tyranny of the master's children. My master had two sons, about the ages and sizes of my older brother and myself. We were not only required to recognise these young sirs as our young masters, but they felt themselves to be such; and, in consequence of this feeling, they sought to treat us with the same air of authority that their father did the older slaves.

Pennington's experience in slavery supports Jefferson's observation.[50]

Young slaves who played more intimate roles in the household often experienced very different relationships than those described by Pennington. Eugene D. Genovese notes that the most long lasting relationships between slaveholders and enslaved persons were skewed in favor of special positions, such as personal servants. For example, Mary Matilda Norcom professed a long-standing love for her personal servant, Harriet Jacobs, but when the adult Jacobs fled to the North, the adult Mary Matilda Norcom Messmore insisted upon Jacobs returning to bondage in North Carolina or purchasing her own freedom. "But," wrote the mistress, "I should prefer having you live with me." Given the harassment Jacobs endured, it appears that financial reasons and interest in personal service motivated Norcom more than sentimentality.[51]

By contrast, the Virginia-born Charles L. C. Minor inherited Ralph, a child who was only a few years older than himself in 1808 or 1809, and was willing to emancipate him. Minor developed a fondness for his constant companion. In the opening lines of an 1832 letter informing Ralph that he had decided to free him, Minor wrote, "I am no longer your master, but I am still your friend, and as perhaps we shall never meet again, I have determined to give you this assurance of my esteem." Recalling their friendship through the years, Minor remembered his "playmate and nurse and the good will" Ralph showed to him. Returning wages that Ralph had earned as an artisan, Minor liberated him and urged him to emigrate to Liberia and remove himself from the grasp of slave traders. Minor bade his former servant well, and with the stroke of the pen, severed their legal relationship. "No more your master," he wrote, "but always your friend."[52]

Friendships spanning two generations in the William T. Barry household served as a reason for repurchasing an enslaved family. It was a financial sacrifice for the small slaveholding white farmer to do so, but Barry believed he could not afford to ignore the matter. The sale of the enslaved family had been "a source of infinite pain" to his wife. In the interest of his own domestic tranquility, Barry succeeded in buying the black family back in August 1829. He claimed his wife was "more gratified" than he had seen her in many years when the "faithful creatures" returned to their Virginia home. The black family seemed happy and appreciative. Beyond the mutual satisfaction, this reunion had deeper implications for the enslaved couple, Issac and Fanny, who could see their relatives and friends again. Their six-year-old son probably rejoined former enslaved playmates. Obviously, William Barry's son, Armistead, was "much pleased" with the boy's return to his family.[53]

The former slave Mary Reynolds told a WPA interviewer about her close relationship with Sara, a young white slaveholding girl. The bond between them was longstanding and more intricate than the one shared by the Barry family. Following the death of her mother, Mary Reynolds' mother served as a wet nurse for Sara and suckled the two girls in tandem. "It's a thing we ain't never forgot," yet, according to Mary, Sara's father, known only as Dr. Kilpatrick, did not approve of his daughter playing with a "nigger young'un" and thus sold Mary. Sara "pined and sickened" to the extent that Kilpatrick purchased Mary and brought her back to his home in the interest of his daughter's health. The children were more than delighted with their reunification.[54]

Manuscript sources left by prosperous freed mulattos William Ellison and his contemporary John Stanly of New Bern, North Carolina, tell virtually nothing about the personal relationships between their families and the slaves they owned, which were undoubtedly even more complicated than those described above. Certainly neither of the freedmen could ignore the presence of the slaves, who increased in numbers from two in 1820 to sixty-three in 1860 on the Ellison holdings, and from two in 1805 to over one hundred in 1830 on the Stanly plantations. Moreover, William Ellison's slave-born wife, Matilda, was at least twenty-one years of age and the mother of the five- or six-year-old Eliza Ann when he purchased and emancipated them. Stanly also purchased and freed his wife and several children by 1805. Kitty Stanly and Matilda Ellison were not so far removed from slavery that either freedwoman was oblivious to the trauma associated with the separation of mothers from their children. Accounts of how Stanly and Ellison bought, sold, worked, hunted for runaways, or thwarted efforts to purchase loved ones provide enough evidence to say both held and treated their black chattel with surprising indifference. The women set examples for their offspring to follow.[55]

Details about interactions between James Warner, also known as Okah Tubbee, and his black owners are better known than those of the Ellisons and Stanlys. The story began when Franky, also known as Frances, a woman owned by James McCary, a Pennsylvania-born cabinetmaker living in Natchez, Mississippi, gave birth to her third child, James Warner in 1810 or 1811. The boy's life became complicated in 1813 when McCary died and manumitted Franky along with her mulatto children Robert and Kitty, apparently fathered by McCary. His will made provisions for the biracial children to receive an education, property, and money. By contrast, the will stipulated that Warner "and his progeny were 'to be held as slaves during all and each of their lives' " for the benefit of Kitty and Robert.[56]

The sentence meted out to Warner was a reflection of McCary's disaffection with Franky and dislike for Warner, who was obviously not McCary's offspring. Growing up in a household with free siblings no doubt ignited Warner's desire for liberty. He must have been keenly aware of the differences in their status and his own. While Robert and Kitty had access to education, Warner learned a trade through an apprenticeship. Although illiterate, he was clever enough to concoct a plan to liberate himself once the apprenticeship ended by 1830. He argued that he was now free merely by completing the indenture.[57]

He distanced himself from blacks, free and enslaved, while creating a new personae that included a claim of being the kidnapped son of the Choctaw Indian chief, Moshulatubbe. This savvy tale appealed to a gullible public with a penchant for believing exotic tales about long-lost children. In the meantime, Warner, a talented itinerant musician began working as an entertainer on Mississippi River boats. An observer noted:

> Out of his fife, he can get more music, and get it longer and stronger, and more of it, and put more twists in it, and play lower, and go up higher, and give more octaves, and

crochets, ketches and sky-rockets, change the keys, and gingle them with better grace, imitate more partridges and young chickens, and come the high notes shriller and low notes softer, and take off his hat more gracefully while he is doing it, and look at the people while it is going on, on his fife, better than any other man living.

With talent and skill, he crossed the boundaries between bondage and freedom as the boats made their way from the deep South into free territory north of St. Louis. Ultimately, Warner not only changed his status from slave to free, he also changed his name from Warner McCary to Okah Tubbee and his race from black to red. In the process of recreating himself, Tubbee divested his mulatto owners, Robert and Kitty McCary, of their legacy.[58]

We can readily ascertain that Tubbee and other enslaved youth experienced some of the worst facets of bondage whether owned by blacks or whites. The exploitation of their labor and encroachments upon family integrity through sales were among the abuses they experienced regardless of their owners' color. Sexual exploitation is somewhat harder to trace because it is more elusive in the sources. Yet, available data related to the topic suggest that white slaveholding men of all ages exploited enslaved girls and women with impunity. Slaves, male and female, of all ages were chattel and without rights to their person or to defend themselves against sexual aggression from owners.[59]

Parallel accounts relevant to intimacy between black slaveholding and enslaved youth, if extant, are not readily accessible. This is not to say adolescents in black slaveholding households did not play out their youthful curiosities and sexual desires upon their enslaved contemporaries.[60] It is reasonable to think this did not occur within kinship circles because of the cultural taboo among Africans against intimacy among blood relatives. In other cases, intimacy may have occurred, but marriage between free slaveholding blacks of means and their chattel was unlikely. Owners of means were likely to marry persons within their own class.[61]

Ultimately, the factors governing relationships between enslaved and slaveholding children depended on the attitudes of adults who meted out punishment or assigned chores and, as Thomas Jefferson observed, set examples for their offspring to follow. Slavery was an economic institution grounded in the expropriation of another's labor. Within such a system, the greatest variation in slaveholders and the treatment of persons they owned are governed by familial relationships rather than by skin color. Certainly, far fewer blacks owned slaves than did whites. Of the black slaveholders, many owned relatives for benevolent reasons and treated them accordingly. Even so, both black and white slaveowners enjoyed economic benefits and a particular class status that accrued from slaveownership. Those benefits were of more importance to the slaveowners than the colors of their skin.

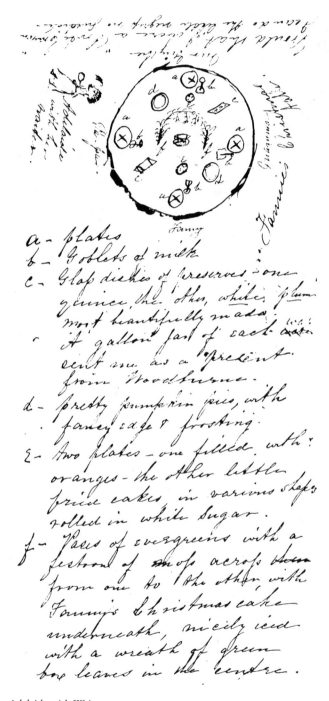

a — plates

b — Goblets of milk

c — Glass dishes of preserves — one
quince, the other, white plum
most beautifully made.
A gallon jar of each one
sent me as a present
from Woodburne.

d — pretty pumpkin pies, with
fancy edge & frosting.

e — Two plates — one filled with
oranges — the other little
fried cakes in various shapes
rolled in white sugar.

f — Vases of evergreens with a
festoon of moss across them
from one to the other, with
Fanny's Christmas cake
underneath, nicely iced
with a wreath of green
box leaves in the centre.

Figure 3   Adelaide with Waiter

Source: Mississippi Department of History and Archives, Jackson, Mississippi.

CHAPTER THREE

WITHIN THE PROFESSIONAL HOUSEHOLD: SLAVE CHILDREN IN THE ANTEBELLUM SOUTH

The feeding and clothing me well could not atone for taking my liberty from me.
—Frederick Douglass[1]

"You ought to have seen her *face & eyes* when I gave her the pretty white glass beads which I had bought for her," wrote the northern-born Tryphena Blanche Holder Fox in 1860 of Adelaide, an eight-year-old enslaved house servant. It was difficult to tell who was more delighted, the donor or recipient. By contrast, Harriet Jacobs, speaking of her difficult relationship with her owners when she was fourteen years old, recalled, "I resolved never to be conquered." Such comments illustrate that the nature of interactions between slaveowners and enslaved children varied widely in the antebellum South. Acknowledging differing experiences of enslaved children is essential to understanding both their personality development and socialization. As Willie Lee Rose pointed out in 1982, "few historians have stressed this aspect of slavery, or described it adequately." Since that time, this void has been partially redressed by Steven Mintz's *African American Voices*, which in the chapter "Childhood" recounts the experiences of three ex-slave men, and my own *Stolen Childhood: Slave Youth in Nineteenth-Century America*.[2]

The present study takes a further step toward a fuller picture of slave experiences by examining the lives of children in five professional households using critical factors suggested by Eugene D. Genovese to compare conditions and determine distinctions among slave children. These factors are (1) "day-to-day conditions," referring to food, clothing, shelter, and work environment; (2) "conditions of life" encompassing family situations, opportunities for independent social and religious life, and cultural development; and (3) "access to freedom and citizenship," meaning one's ability to own his or her person, work for fair wages, practice a religion of choice, pursue an education, form families, and to have the right to participate in the political decision-making processes both locally and nationally. Enslaved children in professional households experienced many of the same abuses suffered by their contemporaries elsewhere on plantations in the antebellum South. Yet their atypical position frequently put them in very different circumstances than their contemporaries living on plantations, thus their lives offer an insightfully differing perspective from the historian of enslaved children.[3]

Sources available for studying the lives of slave children vary greatly, from firsthand written accounts to secondhand correspondence, to oral family tradition. Adelaide, the young girl who received the beads, together with several siblings and her mother Susan, were owned by David Raymond Fox, a physician in rural Jesuit Bend, Plaquemines Parish, Louisiana. While neither Adelaide nor Susan kept any records of their lives, Adelaide figured prominently in the correspondence of the doctor's wife, Tryphena Fox, between 1858 and 1864.[4]

By contrast, in 1861 Harriet Jacobs published a detailed account of incidents in her life as a slave from 1825 to 1835 in the household of James Norcom, a medical doctor in the small town of Edenton in Chowan County, North Carolina. *Incidents in the Life of a Slave Girl*, written under the pseudonym Linda Brent, has received much attention by scholars of American slavery. Unlike other slave narratives, it does not recount Harriet's entire life but only specific incidents, particularly how she confronted sexual harassment and exploitation. Earlier scholars doubted the book's authenticity because of the pen name and its seemingly incredible claims, and reservations still have not subsided. In 1987, Jean Fagan Yellin documented much of Jacobs's story through the use of archival resources and by comparison with the account of John S. Jacobs, Harriet's younger brother, "A True Tale of Slavery," which appeared in the English journal, *The Leisure Hour*, in February 1861. Additionally, Yellin's *Harriet Jacobs: A Life* has appeared. When taken together these sources do much to dispel doubts associated with the veracity of Jacobs's story.[5]

The case of Cornelia Smith provides a glimpse into the lives of five slave children in the Orange County, North Carolina household of James Smith, a medical doctor and politician. Cornelia's birth was the result of her mother's brutal rape by James's son, Sidney. Thus, Cornelia's place in the household of the prominent doctor and state legislator was part of a tangled relationship that crossed color and class lines. Cornelia's story is told by her granddaughter, Pauli Murray, in *Proud Shoes: The Story of an American Family*. Murray blended historical research with personal recollections to shape the narrative of her own youth in the home of her maternal grandparents, where, as a young girl, Murray learned about the childhood of her slave-born grandmother Cornelia.[6]

Imogene and Adaline Johnson were the daughters of the Kentucky attorney Richard M. Johnson and his mulatto slave Julia Chinn. Johnson was an officer and veteran of the War of 1812 who served as a U.S. Congressman, and from 1837 to 1841 was vice president under Martin Van Buren. Most unusually, Johnson treated Julia as his wife; she was the mistress of his household, and he openly acknowledged paternity of their daughters. The story of Richard Johnson's slave family is told in *The Life and Times of Colonel Richard M. Johnson of Kentucky*, written by Leland Winfield Meyer.[7]

The final case concerns three brothers, Archibald, Francis, and John Grimké, sons of Nancy Weston, a mulatto slave woman, and Henry Grimké, a successful attorney in Charleston, South Carolina, whose union was apparently consensual. The children grew up in a quasi-free state, even after their father's untimely death, until Grimké's adult son Montague claimed them for his own house servants. Archibald and Francis resisted and eventually fought their way to freedom, becoming prominent American citizens. The account of the Grimké brothers' upbringing is part of the biography *Archibald Grimke: Portrait of a Black Independent,* by Dickson D. Bruce, Jr.[8]

Interviews collected in the 1930s by federal workers, known collectively as the Works Progress Administration (WPA) narratives, were used only peripherally in this study because they generally lack a sustained voice or discussion of youth in professional households comparable to those in Jacobs's *Incidents* or Murray's *Proud Shoes.* Admittedly, the resources used in this study are uneven and sometimes reveal more about slaveholders than their slaves, but nonetheless provide data for discussing a range of topics affecting nearly twenty children in several different households in the Upper and Lower South. While the sample is too small to be certain that it accurately represents the majority of slaveholding professional households, it does reflect the intricacies of bondage for slaveowners and their chattel outside the plantation context.[9]

The Fox correspondence reveals much about owning young slaves in the antebellum South. In late 1857, Dr. Fox's wife reported the purchase of Susan and her two children, five-year-old Adelaide and three-year-old Margaret. Fox deemed the $1,400 price as an excellent bargain, as Susan was pregnant. The February 2, 1858, birth of her son, Buddy, enhanced the doctor's investment. Tryphena Fox acknowledged that Adelaide and her siblings added to her cares, but "having invested so much in one purchase" it was in the Foxes' interest to see that they were "well taken care of & clothed and fed." Dr. Fox completed the transaction in January 1858, and the family moved to Hygiene, his home located in the sugar-growing region of Louisiana. His holdings increased over time as Susan gave birth to three additional children, and the doctor purchased another slave, the teenaged Maria, in 1860. The physical conditions under which the Fox slaves lived were adequate and probably better than those of many of their contemporaries. In 1858, Dr. Fox built a separate cabin standing several feet above the ground "with a *fireplace* on account of [Susan] having young children.[10]

Slaves increased in value as they matured. Children were initially valued as fractional hands such as one-quarter or one-half hands. These designations changed as a child's strength increased, and they learned to perform demanding physical chores comparable to the work of adults. Females in childbearing years added a welcomed dimension to ownership, as both production and reproduction were valued. "The extent to which the slaveowner consciously emphasized one or the other," historian Deborah Gray White posits, "ultimately depended on his need."[11]

The slaveholder's priorities also determined when enslaved children began to work and the chores they performed. Knowing that their offspring were subject to arbitrary authority, punishments, and possible separations, parents shielded their offspring by teaching them how to work satisfactorily and to survive within a slave culture. This process of adaptation can be seen in several of the case histories under study.

Adelaide, who began working in the Fox home when she was seven years old, was responsible for chores similar to those of her contemporaries in other slave-owning households. She ran errands, entertained the owner's child with games and toys, and also helped to feed the chickens and ducks. Adelaide also worked in Tryphena Fox's vegetable garden and probably assisted her own mother in the kitchen.

The Fox family's treatment of Adelaide and her mother Susan demonstrates how benevolence and cruelty could exist within the same household. Although none of her children endured physical punishment, Susan was whipped in June 1859 for disobedience. Adelaide, working inside the house, probably witnessed her mother's punishment. Slave children often tried to deflect lashes aimed at parents by running between the victim and the tormentor or by attacking the person meting out the reproof.[12]

Looking back on his childhood, the former slave Jacob Branch told the WPA interviewer that he witnessed his mother being punished and said he moved close enough to "take some dem licks" intended for his mother. Jacob Stroyer, another former slave who came of age in bondage, admitted running back and forth between the overseer and his mother until the beating stopped. The boys received whippings along with their mothers. It was especially painful for Stroyer because he held himself responsible since his mother's whipping resulted from protests she had made about his treatment.[13]

By contrast, Adelaide appears to have been an idle bystander. Susan's recalcitrance continued, and Tryphena threatened to complain to Dr. Fox. Without waiting for a second whipping, Susan ran away. Running away for brief periods after punishment was not unusual; Susan, who was pregnant at the time, probably intended to return when calmer tempers prevailed. But when Dr. Fox found her after a week's absence, he immediately sent her to Woodburne, a cotton plantation owned by his father James A. Fox, in Warren County, Mississippi. This treatment appears unusually harsh for a first offense, but it may have been prompted by Susan's constant agitation of the mistress, who was also pregnant.[14]

Adelaide, Margaret, and Buddy, who had already been permanently separated from other family members, did not know if or when they would ever see their mother again, and the separation must have frightened them. The Foxes ignored any emotional distress the children suffered from Susan's banishment; however, Tryphena simply commented, "Adelaide is old enough to take care of herself & does a great many useful errands around the house." The historian Nell I. Painter argues that slaves coped with abuses through family or community support and religious faith, but Adelaide, Margaret, and Buddy grew up in an isolated rural river community without access to education, religion, or familial sources of support. During their mother's five month absence, Ann, a slave woman hired from her owner by Fox, attended to the children's physical needs. Perhaps she comforted them.[15]

In addition to separation and physical abuse, sexual exploitation was also common in slave-owning households. As Molly Kinsey, who was ten years old when slavery ended, told a WPA interviewer, "I was so young I missed all the evil but chile I knowed about it." Kinsey's observation confirms Harriet Jacobs's assertion that even "the little child" became "prematurely knowing in evil things" before reaching twelve years of age. While Adelaide and Margaret were not sexually abused themselves, they must have been aware of their mother's experiences. Susan gave birth to several children after her purchase in 1858 and circumstantial evidence suggests that Dr. Fox may have fathered Susan's son born in 1860. If true, it helps to explain why she and Tryphena Fox shared such a stormy relationship.[16]

Harriet Jacobs, who figures prominently in the second case studied herein, became the property of the James Norcom family through an estate dispersal. In 1825, the North Carolinian Margaret Horniblow bequeathed the twelve-year-old Harriet to Mary Matilda Norcom, her three-year-old niece and daughter of Mary Horniblow Norcom and her husband. He purchased Harriet's brother, John, and owned scores of slaves housed on farms outside Edenton, North Carolina, but the Jacobs children lived in Edenton where Dr. Norcom practised medicine.[17]

The Norcoms made no special preparations when Harriet and her brother John came into the household. Dr. Norcom already owned their aunt, who also lived in his Edenton home. Harriet assumed responsibilities as a domestic servant that were appropriate for her age and, as she later recounted, "tried to merit . . . kindness by the faithful discharge" of her duties. She was partly responsible for the care given to her three-year-old owner. Jacobs loved Mary, who returned her affection. When Mary's mother intimated that her daughter's affection "proceeded from fear," it troubled Jacobs, who believed that Mary Norcom was jealous of the close relationship with her daughter.[18]

Because Harriet and John's mother had died, their only familial support came from their grandmother, Molly Horniblow, a freedwoman who owned a home in Edenton, North Carolina. Horniblow and her children were able to help meet Harriet and John's physical and emotional needs. Slaveowners commonly issued children one or two garments per year, often of poor quality, and sometimes children were forced to wear these clothes long after outgrowing them. Harriet's scanty wardrobe, primarily the linsey-woolsey dress, rankled her. She hated the garment not so much because it was uncomfortable but because it was a badge of slavery. Horniblow supplemented Harriet's clothing supply, which no doubt boosted her self-esteem. She also gave her granddaughter extra food from her bakery, a welcomed addition since, as Harriet later recalled, in the Norcom household "little attention was paid to the slaves' meals." Unlike many slaves, Harriet was literate, having taught herself to read. She read the Bible, although she did not write of any particular religious convictions in her autobiography. Because of their literacy and their opportunities to interact with freedpersons outside the Norcom household, Harriet and John Jacobs had a more expansive world than the children owned by Dr. Fox. This experience and knowledge encouraged their desire for freedom.[19]

John and Harriet Jacobs knew that their grandmother's father, a white planter in South Carolina, had made provisions to free her and two other siblings along with the children's mother at his death. According to family lore, they were prevented from leaving South Carolina and sold to different slaveowners. As an adult, Molly was restive as a slave and worked in her own time earning money to purchase her freedom and that of her children. Unfortunately, her owner reneged on the promise and kept $300 that Molly had saved toward their freedom. This chilling tale probably made the Jacobs children realize the value and fragility of freedom. Despite Horniblow's disappointments, she was eventually freed in April 1828 by Hannah Pritchard who had purchased the middle-aged Horniblow at a January 1, 1828, sale.[20]

Once freed, Molly Horniblow purchased her eldest son, although she did not manumit him. This was not entirely unusual, especially in situations where state laws required emancipated persons to remove themselves within a year. In order to prevent such separations, free persons often held family members in virtual slavery. According to John Jacobs, Horniblow did not emancipate her son, who lived as a free man, for reasons of economic security.[21]

Daniel Jacobs, Horniblow's son-in-law and the father of Harriet and John, remained the slave of Dr. Andrew Knox, who also lived in Edenton. John Jacobs attributed his abhorrence of slavery to their father, a man who chafed under bondage. "I could frequently perceive the pent-up agony of his soul," John remembered. "The knowledge that he was a slave himself, and that his children were also slaves, embittered his life." Harriet confirmed that her father, "by his nature, as well as by the habit of transacting business . . . Had more of the feelings of a free man than [was] common among slaves." When prohibited from hiring himself out as a carpenter, thus ending the possibility of earning enough money to purchase his children, Daniel Jacobs "sank into a state of mental dejection."[22]

Like Susan, Harriet Jacobs could not avert sexual aggression. By the time Jacobs was fourteen years of age, she wrote, "the war of my life had begun." Dr. Norcom attempted to seduce her with "unclean images such as only a vile monster could think of," but she resisted. Finally believing it was "less degrading to give one's self than to submit to compulsion," the teenager began a liaison with an unmarried white man, Samuel Tredwell Sawyer, rather than submit to Norcom's sexual aggression. Jacobs anticipated that an enraged Norcom would sell her because she favored another and fantasized about the generous lover she hoped would buy and eventually free her. "With all these thoughts revolving in my mind and seeing no other way of escaping the doom I so much dreaded," wrote Jacobs, " I made a headlong plunge." She did not condemn Sawyer, but said, "I knew what I did, and I did it with deliberate calculation."[23]

Harriet Jacobs made the decision out of a misguided sense of desperation. The fifteen-year-old girl was too immature to fathom the true nature of the power relationship she entered. Certainly, attention from the suave Sawyer, an attorney later elected to Congress, was flattering, but his intentions were no more honorable than those of James Norcom, and in any event, Norcom did not sell her. Sawyer fathered Harriet's two children, Joseph and Louise Matilda, who lived with Molly Horniblow. Norcom was furious when he first learned that Harriet was pregnant and threatened to beat her. "He did not fail," wrote Jacobs, "to remind me that my child was an addition to his stock of slaves." Norcom continued trying to seduce her after the birth of her child. When he learned that she was again pregnant, he "was exasperated beyond measure, and cut off all her hair. To add to Harriet's problems, Mary Norcom, erroneously suspecting an illicit relationship between her husband and Harriet, also badgered the girl. At twenty-two years of age, Harriet ran away and remained in Horniblow's unheated and unventilated attic for nearly seven years, hidden even from her children, before making her way North. Sawyer eventually purchased Harriet's children, though he did not manumit them. They continued to live as quasi-free persons with their great-grandmother.[24]

The third case history examined here is that of Cornelia Smith, who, in contrast to the Jacobs children, enjoyed a relatively privileged upbringing in Orange County, North Carolina. But the shadow of sexual abuse also hung over Cornelia, as her birth had resulted from Sidney Smith's brutal rape of Harriet Smith, a slave owned by his sister, Mary Ruffin Smith, in the home of their father, Dr. James Smith. He had given Harriet permission to marry Ruben Day, a free man, and she bore him a son, Julius. But within two years, James's sons Sidney and Francis began to abuse Harriet sexually, and it became impossible for Day to protect the integrity of his family. In fact, Day's last attempt to visit his wife and young son ended when the Smith brothers assaulted him with the "butt end of the carriage whip" and threatened to "shoot him on sight" if he ever returned.

Following a life-threatening fight between Sidney and his brother Francis over her, Harriet settled into a long-term relationship with the victorious Francis, a doctor who fathered her three younger children, Emma, Laura, and Annette.[25]

The Smith brothers remained unmarried and continued to live in their father's home, though the enmity between them never subsided. Their sister, who also never married, assumed maternal responsibility for Cornelia and the children of Harriet and Francis Smith. The girls lived within the Smith home while their mother remained in the slave quarters across the yard with Julius. They were estranged from their mother, and Mary Ruffin Smith and Harriet "shared a strange motherhood in which neither could fully express her maternal feelings." Under such circumstances, if the girls sang the old Negro Spiritual "Sometimes I feel like a Motherless Child," it was understandable. Cornelia had no difficulties with her owner. She performed domestic chores and acted as her aunt's chief assistant in the smoke house, poultry yard, and dairy barn, which she seemed to relish. She probably also helped her aunt with her young siblings' care, which although there is no mention of it, would not have been unusual for a child her age.[26]

The Smith girls were baptized in the Chapel of the Cross on the campus of the University of North Carolina (where their fathers attended school and Cornelia's granddaughter, Pauli Murray, delivered her first sermon after ordination as an Episcopal priest), but proximity to the school otherwise made no significant difference in their lives. Cornelia Smith appeared to have been only minimally literate, and her sisters probably received little, if any, schooling at the hands of their well-educated relatives. The Smiths' treatment of Harriet's daughters reveals their ambivalence toward them. On the whole, the children were kindly treated; as Pauli Muray wrote, "The Smiths were as incapable of treating the little girls wholly as servants as they were of recognizing them openly as kin." "At times," she continued, "the Smiths' involuntary gestures of kinship were so pronounced the children could not help thinking of themselves as Smith descendants. At other times, their innocent overtures of affection were rebuffed without explanation and they were driven away with cruel epithets."[27]

Although Francis Smith's children kept their distance and called him "Marse Frank," and he, in turn, "shrugged them off and treated them as part of the surroundings," Cornelia's relationship with her father was warm. Sidney Smith, an attorney and member of the North Carolina Assembly in 1846, showed affection openly, "gloried in her," and made the child his confidant. Acting as his personal servant, Cornelia drew close to her father while seeking acceptance and clarification of her own identify. She gained a reputation for being high spirited, outspoken, and hard to manage. Indeed, it must have been difficult for Cornelia and her sisters to maneuver through the tension-filled household. Emma, Laura, and Annette must have been aware of the affection Sidney showed toward Cornelia, while their older sister appeared to ignore the protection her father afforded her against the harsher facets of slavery. Never reconciled to her status as a slave, Cornelia explained repeatedly, "We were free. We were just born in slavery, that's all." Sidney Smith encouraged her to believe she was an octoroon and could marry either a white or black person. Besides, he told her that "one-eighth nonwhite ancestry was Indian instead of Negro."[28]

Imogene and Adaline Johnson, subjects of the fourth case study, were also the off-spring of a biracial union like the Smith children, but their mother appears to have been a willing participant in a long-standing relationship with the Kentuckian Richard M. Johnson. Julia Chinn, unlike Harriet Smith, assumed a prominent place in her owner's Kentucky household as the "chief manager of the domestic concerns," taking full charge of the household during Johnson's absence. On occasion, she was assisted by Thomas Henderson, a young white tutor at the Choctaw Academy on Johnson's plantation. In either case, Johnson was fully aware of the arrangements, and Chinn reported routine events to him in regular correspondence. According to family lore, Chinn became Johnson's mistress following his mother's objections to his intentions to marry outside their social class. Nevertheless, Johnson treated Chinn as his wife and did not deny paternity of her children.[29]

There is no mention of the work assigned to Imogene or Adaline Johnson. An observer noted that rather than have the girls live in the slave quarters or send them to a cotton field, Johnson treated them in a "kind and tender manner." In fact, he "unblushingly treated [them] as his daughters, placing them at the same table with the most honorable of his white guests." It was clearly understood by persons employed or owned by Johnson that the girls were not servants. If they performed chores, it was at the behest of their mother, who, as mistress of the Johnson household, delegated all work assignments. Clearly, Imogene and Adaline were not subjected to the kind of arbitrary authority their enslaved contemporaries often endured.[30]

Imogene and Adaline Johnson lived in their father's Kentucky home and enjoyed their parents undivided attention. Johnson, a Baptist known as a humanitarian among his contemporaries, indulged his daughters and provided for their education. The tutor at the Choctaw Academy "soon discovered . . . uncommon aptness" in the two children. "I want you to persevere in learning my girls," Johnson urged their tutor in late 1825. "Make them get a lesson [on Sundays] when they do not go to meeting." Imogene and Adaline Johnson received instruction "until their education was equal or superior to most of the females in the country."[31]

Richard Johnson, like Cornelia Smith's father, recognized his children and doted upon them. In fact the Kentuckian violated the unspoken rules of polite southern society when he insisted upon having the girls accompany him to public events. To help secure their future and that of their progeny, Johnson deeded parcels of his estate in Scott County, Kentucky, to them. The White Sulphur tract went to Imogene and her husband, while Adaline and her spouse, Thomas W. Scott, received the Blue Spring farm. There is no indication that the girls were not fully accepted in white society after they both married white men.[32]

In all probability Adaline and Imogene were phenotypically white based on the social and historical, rather than the biological, construction of race. As a result, it is possible for individuals of one racial designation to be defined as members of another race. The possibility of this happening to Adaline and Imogene Johnson was great since their father was designated as white and their mother, Julia Chinn, was described as a "mulatto" by Johnson's biographer. Aside from skin color, race may be determined by context, and choice in addition to court decisions such as *Hudgins v. Wright* (1809).[33]

The absence of uniformity in racial designations is evident in a compilation of "record linkage" in selected areas of Philadelphia from 1850 to 1880. The data indicate that approximately one-third of the sample received different designations over time. Twenty-six percent of those called "black" in 1850 received "mulatto" designations in 1860. A larger shift occurred when the census designated 47 percent of the persons considered "mulatto" in 1850 as "black" in 1860. The changes and lack of uniformity in designations give pause and raise questions about the significance of skin color in the eyes of the beholder.[34]

When Adaline died in 1839, her distraught father wrote, "She was a source of inexhaustible happiness and comfort to me. She was mild and prudent. She was wise in her counsel beyond her years & obedient to every thought & every advice of mine. . . . She was a firm & great prop to my happiness here, but she is gone where sorrow & sighing can never disturb her peaceful & quiet blossom."[35]

The circumstances surrounding the birth of Archibald, Francis, and John Grimké, the fifth family studied herein, were initially much like those of the Johnson children. They were the sons of the mulatto slave woman Nancy Weston and a successful Charleston, South Carolina lawyer, Henry Grimké. After an unsuccessful bid for a seat on the state supreme court in the mid-1840s, the widowed Grimké retired to Cane Acre, a rice plantation near Charleston where his biracial sons were born.

Grimké planned to move his family to Charleston after the birth of Nancy's third child, but he died unexpectedly during the typhoid epidemic in 1852. The pregnant Weston was left with Archibald and Francis, who were three and two years of age respectively. A codicil to Grimké's will stipulated that his biracial family would become the property of Grimké's adult son, Montague Grimké, an engineer for the Northeastern Railroad, later known as the Atlantic Coast line. Henry Grimké did not free his slave family because an 1820 state statute prohibited emancipations within the state.[36]

Following the estate sale, Montague allowed Weston and her children to live as "virtually free" in Charleston for several years. Although illiterate, Weston supported herself and built a house with her own earnings as a laundress. Her resources were meager, but with the help of free relatives, the impoverished family managed to eke out a respectable living. Henry Grimké's untimely death precludes speculation about the possibilities of a relationship with his younger children. The boys maintained a close association with their deeply religious mother, who worked assiduously to provide for their education.[37]

Any work Archibald and Francis performed was in their own interest and under their mother's direction, but this arrangement changed in 1860 when Montague Grimké and his new bride decided that the ten- and eleven-year-old boys should become their house servants. Having lived essentially free all their lives, Archibald and Francis strongly resented slavery in their half-brother's household. Although they bowed to their new mistress, they refused to greet her more courteously. Archibald worked slowly and inefficiently, often refusing instructions and feigning ignorance. Francis simply walked away from a job when so inclined. Their defiance was not unlike that of other enslaved persons who registered discontent through day-to-day resistance. Because of his unsatisfactory behavior, Archibald was beaten not only by Montague but also in the public workhouse, a Charleston facility that dispensed corporal punishment, at his half-brother's behest. In addition, he was confined to the stock with his hands attached to a pulley, his body stretched tightly while he was whipped. Far from being submissive, Archibald defiantly reminded his tormentor that the beating was all at the behest of his own half-brother. Before long, Montague sent Francis to the workhouse as well. Neither of the boys recanted or accepted the loss of their liberty.[38]

Archibald ran away when he was thirteen years old and stayed for a short time in the home of one free family before fleeing, with his mother's assistance, to the home of another free man, Thomas Cole. Archibald remained there until the February 1865 fall of Charleston two years later. Francis also fled from bondage a few months after Archibald and worked as a valet in the Confederate Army before he was discovered as a fugitive. Afterward, he was arrested and jailed for several months. During his incarceration Francis became seriously ill and was released to Montague for care. Rather than trying to "re-enslave" the youngster in his home after he recuperated, Montague sold the boy to a Confederate officer. Francis's term back in bondage was brief due to the Confederacy's surrendering soon afterward.[39]

Following emancipation, Archibald and Francis Grimké enrolled at Pennsylvania's Lincoln University where they came to the attention of their father's sisters, Sarah and Angelina. Sarah Grimké Weld declared that "her brother had wronged [the] children" and that "his sisters must right them." The two women, abolitionists and advocates of women's rights, established a cordial friendship with their nephews, who became prominent citizens. Archibald, an editor and author, later served as American consul to the Dominican Republic from 1894 until 1898. Francis Grimké was equally successful in pursuing his own goals as a Presbyterian minister. Their early years of freedom and subsequent enslavement made a lasting impression upon the brothers, leaving them fiercely independent and determined to achieve their ambitions.[40]

To return to Genovese's typology and the first of his comparative criteria, the day-to-day existence of the slave children in this study varied markedly. The Smiths and Johnsons children were treated well materially, far beyond the lot of most slaves. While the Fox family provided Adelaide with occasional gifts in addition to shelter and clothing, the Jacobs children received only parsimonious allotments of food and clothing that were barely adequate for their needs. As Tryphena Fox noted, supplying adequate clothing, food, and shelter was in the best interest of slaveholders. Healthy slaves were more productive, but providing more than basic necessities depended on the whims of the owners.

The living conditions and treatment of the children under study also varied widely. Adaline and Imogene were well treated as the favored children of the house.

They were well educated, inherited their father's property, and married men of their choice. Cornelia Smith was also favored by her father Sidney. The experiences of Cornelia Smith and her sisters are similar to those of the Grimké children—at least during their early years—in that their owners were ambivalent about their status as persons or property, family or servants. The Smiths generally treated Harriet Smith's daughters well, though little or no effort was made to educate them. Archibald and Francis Grimké were allowed to live virtually free during their early years, but their education came about through their mother's efforts rather than their owner's. Harriet and John Jacobs were self-taught. While Tryphena Fox sometimes treated Adelaide kindly, Adelaide and her siblings were never considered anything but household servants. Harriet and John do not appear to have had even that level of kindness, having instead an acrimonious relationship with their owners.

All of the children lived within a slave society where the physical abuse and degradation of enslaved persons were common. The Grimké children probably experienced the harshest physical punishment of the children in this sample since, after being forcibly returned to Montague Grimké, they were whipped by the jailer as well as their brother. Even in the usually benevolent Johnson household, when Julia Chinn reported to Johnson that most of the adult slave men were absent from the plantation one Sunday in December 1825, he called upon the tutor to "chastise them on their naked skins." Although Chinn, a slave herself, did not dispense the punishment, she contributed to its execution.[41]

Most of the children in this study were also exposed to sexual abuse in one form or another. Harriet Jacobs posited that "a sad epoch in the life of a slave girl" began when she reached her teens. Harriet experienced sexual harassment and exploitation at the hands of her owner and Samuel Tredwell Sawyer, who fathered her children, and dwelt emphatically on this aspect of her life in slavery in her autobiography. In the case of the Fox household, the father of Susan's mulatto son remains unknown. What young Adelaide, Margaret, and Buddy thought of the "fine mulatto boy" also remains unknown, but the birth of a child whose physical features differed from their own would not have gone unnoticed, either by the children or Tryphena Fox. As the southern diarist Mary Chesnut commented:

> Like the patriarchs of old our men live all in one house with their wives and their concubines, and the mulattoes one sees in every family exactly resemble the white children—and every lady tells you who is the father of all the mulatto children in everybody's household, but those in her own she seems to think drop from the clouds, or pretends so to think.[42]

While the Smith girls did not personally experience sexual abuse, as an adult, Cornelia Smith's "face saddened and she shook her head sorrowfully" when remembering her own mother, Harriet. "Sometimes she would break off in the middle of her tale and sigh as if to say what that poor woman went through was too painful to put into words," Cornelia's granddaughter Pauli Murray wrote. She would rock back and forth, "her eyes fixed on the red embers, as if she were caught in some strange ritual of memory." Perhaps she knew that her mother held a "silent smoldering hatred against [Sidney and Francis Smith] to the end of her days."[43]

Each of the households in which these selected children lived differed, yet few of them were free from encroachments upon their social development and family integrity. The complexities of slavery caused the lives of parents, children, and owners to intersect at so many points that the actions of one inevitably reverberated among the others. Harriet and John Jacobs, having already lost their mother, were abruptly removed from their childhood home when the Norcom family acquired them. Susan's children had been separated from their father and any extended family before David Fox purchased them. Although they were not directly in the "crossfire" between Susan and Tryphena Fox, Adelaide, Margaret, and Buddy could not escape the tensions created when their mother and owner quarreled, and faced the continual threat of separation from their mother as a result of this ongoing acrimony. In all probability, Adelaide's subdued behavior resulted from seeing the repercussions of such disputes.

We will never know the extent to which Imogene and Adaline Johnson viewed themselves and others around them. According to the tutor Thomas Henderson, "A stranger would not suspect [Imogene and Adaline] to be what they really are— the children of a colored woman." The contrast between Richard Johnson's and Sidney Smith's affection for their daughters and Francis Smith's indifference toward his children is striking. Yet, as Archibald and Francis Grimké discovered, even an indulgent father provided at best a tenuous security for his enslaved children.[44]

Further examples of slavery's complexities are evident in the lives of the majority of the children described herein. Among the more poignant ones is the apparent lack of a relationship in the Smith household between Julius and his father, Ruben Day, who had talked of buying his son before the Smith brothers forcibly cut him off from his slave family. Julius appeared to have had little interaction with his half-sisters since they did not live together. Even more poignant, Harriet Smith had little time for her son because of her work inside the main house. In addition, she was forced to maintain a relationship "barren of all communication save that of the flesh" with Francis Smith, who helped drive Julius's father away. Julius's woes were compounded at thirteen years of age when he lost his way in the woods during a snowstorm and was not discovered until exposure to the severe temperature had inflicted permanent physical disabilities.[45]

Regardless of their conditions and however well they were treated, slave children were shackled to a system in which they were defined by their mothers' legal status. Material well-being paled when compared to other facets of treatment. "The feeding and clothing me well," wrote Frederick Douglass as he remembered his childhood in bondage, "could not atone for taking my liberty from me." As slaves or "quasi-slaves," children observed or experienced corporal punishment, separation of family, and sexual exploitation.[46]

To help their children cope with the vagaries of bondage, enslaved parents, whether together or alone, assumed the major responsibility for teaching their offspring the behavior appropriate for a child and for a slave, and how to defer to whites while maintaining self-respect. The basic goal was to shield slave children from harm at the hands of hostile whites. Archibald Grimké once commented that blacks "learned early to pass much of their lives in an underworld . . . far removed from the white man's eyes and ears."[47]

Despite frequent fragmentation of the family unit, enslaved parents insisted upon filial allegiance and obedience. Harriet and John Jacobs's father, Daniel, demonstrated this demand when he scolded his son: "You are my child and when I call you, you should come immediately, if you have to pass through fire and water." John had responded to his owner rather than his father, and Harriet Jacobs attested to the confusion caused by simultaneous calls from her father and the doctor's wife. Daily experience taught slave children how to maneuver through the society, navigating sometimes conflicting demands of both parents and owners.[48]

No matter how skillfully a slave could handle his or her situation, the only way to escape exploitation and abuse was to obtain freedom. There are no accounts of the Fox slaves' desire for freedom, but absence of documentation does not mean the rebellious Susan did not kindle dreams of liberty in her children. Adelaide's fascination with trinkets such as Tryphena's beads was only a young child's response to an act of kindness. It says nothing about the hopes and dreams that she may have harbored.

Both Harriet and John Jacobs emphatically recorded their determination to escape slavery. When her distraught brother lamented, "We shall never be free," Jacobs rejected the notion vehemently. "We were growing older and stronger," she remembered. "Perhaps we might, before long, be allowed to hire our own time, and then we could earn money to buy our freedom. William [pseudonym for John] declared this was much easier to say than to do; moreover, he did not intend to *buy* his freedom. We held daily controversies upon this subject." Further, when Molly Horniblow's youngest son plotted to run away, he discussed his plans with Harriet.[49]

Gender was a factor whether slaves purchased freedom or ran away. Slave mothers were less likely to run away than childless persons due to both the extra hazards of taking children along and an unwillingness to leave them behind. Women had fewer opportunities to purchase their freedom than men: they mostly lacked the artisanal skills that sometimes allowed men to hire themselves out to earn extra money. But even Harriet and John Jacobs's father who was determined to buy his children's liberty, but he was never able to do so. Knowledge of this thwarted goal made a profound impression upon the children, who knew their father's ardent wish to liberate them, and their yearning for freedom did not subside.[50]

Harriet Jacobs never accepted bondage as a permanent state for herself or her children. As an adult Harriet Jacobs considered running away alone, Molly Horniblow said, "Nobody respects a mother who forsakes her children." The enslaved mother believed if she ran away her owner would grow tired of the children and sell them. "Stand by your own children," admonished the old woman and "suffer with them till death." Heeding the advice, Jacobs survived agonizing deprivations while hidden in the attic of her grandmother's home for nearly seven years. From her refuge Jacobs watched her children as they suffered from her absence while she was nearby. Jacobs also suffered from seeing her children endure the loss of a mother's comfort and love, yet she could not expose herself for fear of detection. The old woman suffered too. The burden of concealing her granddaughter, caring for the children under such conditions, and leading a life of deception caused unusual anxiety for Horniblow, but she did it willingly. Their suffering was a part of their intergenerational linkages. After all, Horniblow would never advise her granddaughter to do something that she herself would not live up to. Never forsaking the dream of freeing her children, Jacobs persevered. Fighting a psychological battle with her owner, the slave mother manipulated him into thinking she had fled to the North. From her "den" she orchestrated the sale of her children, arranged for her daughter to move to a free state, and finally succeeded in outwitting her owner. At last, she gained her freedom and that of her children.[51]

Like the Jacobs children of both generations, Archibald and Francis Grimké lived in an urban setting and interacted with free persons in Charleston, and had aspirations for their own freedom. Nancy Weston believed that Henry Grimké had made provisions for her protection and care following his death. In willing Nancy and her children to Montague, Henry Grimké expected him to treat them as family; instead, the young engineer viewed them as property. Although Montague allowed them to live as free persons for several years, supporting themselves, he had no compunction about reclaiming Archibald and Francis when they were old enough to be of use to him. The Grimké boys had thought they would be freed and believed that Montague had betrayed their father's confidence, which only strengthened their determination to escape slavery.

The Jacobs nor the Grimké children were content to wait for someone else to free them. Both Harriet and John Jacobs ran away to the North, gained freedom, and worked for the abolition of slavery. The Grimké brothers also ran away from slavery amid the turmoil of the Civil War. Afterward, they completed their education and went on to become prominent American citizens.

Although the children owned by Fox were younger than the Jacobs and Grimké's children, their opportunity for freedom came with the Civil War. Hygiene was a small isolated household in rural Louisiana along the Mississippi River south of New Orleans; therefore, in 1862 Dr. Fox moved his family, white and black, to a place of greater safety at Woodburne, a few miles from Vicksburg, Mississippi. Ten-year-old Adelaide must have wondered about her family's hurried move. When the other slaves owned by Dr. Fox ran to Union lines, Adelaide, her siblings, and her mother remained behind until July 1864. After emancipation, rather than returning to Louisiana, they went north to Memphis. They probably saw the war as a great liberating factor in their lives. Adelaide and her siblings were no longer subjected to arbitrary authority and abuses. Opportunities for independence social and cultural development were not as remote as before.

By contrast, the Civil War shattered the world with which the seventeen-year-old Cornelia Smith identified. Unlike many slaves who welcomed the Union soldiers as emancipators, Cornelia avoided them while helping her aunt bury the family's valuables. She remained loyal to Mary Ruffin Smith and stayed with her for several years before marrying the freeborn Robert Fitzgerald. As for the Johnsons, there is no evidence to suggest that Imogene and Adaline saw themselves as enslaved or persons of color; they did not appear to be concerned with their peculiar circumstances. They married white men and lived among whites.

The remnants of slavery disappeared slowly. It would require much time for ex-slave children, whether owned by planters or professionals, to divest themselves entirely of slavery's cruel legacy. As they matured and became parents of free boys and girls, they were now solely responsible for the care and treatment of their children, and even basic necessities were sometimes difficult to obtain. Most former slaves, even those favored like Cornelia Smith, had received only minimal education at best. The Johnson sisters were a rare exception. But, as Harriet and John Jacobs and the Grimké's found, while there were new difficulties, there were also new opportunities, educational and otherwise, for the former slaves as they and their children carved out places for themselves as American citizens.

Figure 4 Undated photograph

Source: Southern Historical Collection, Wilson Library, The University of North Carolina at Chapel Hill, North Carolina.

CHAPTER FOUR

NO BONDAGE FOR ME: FREE BOYS AND GIRLS WITHIN A SLAVE SOCIETY

"To-day school commenced," wrote the Philadelphia-born Charlotte Forten, who began keeping a journal May 24, 1854, shortly before her seventeenth birthday. Wednesday, September 12, 1855, signaled the beginning of classes and chances to reestablish the alleged camaraderie among schoolgirls. Rather than rejoicing over the renewal of acquaintances among classmates at the predominantly white Higginson Grammar School in Salem, Massachusetts, Forten was "most happy . . . to return to the companionship of [her] studies." Challenging academic assignments were her "ever . . . most valued friends."[1]

What caused the young girl to prize schoolwork more highly than her classmates? One feels thinly veiled despair and loneliness behind this hollow enthusiasm. As a free person of color in the slave era, Charlotte Forten was an anomaly. There were over 205,063 free blacks under twenty years of age in 1850 and 235,587 in 1860. Many of them did not feel at ease among whites or enslaved blacks. Northern prejudices based upon color thwarted uninhibited associations with whites, while customs based upon legal status prevented unrestrained interactions with slaves. Bondage was incongruent with the natural rights ideology of the American Revolution, yet slavery and freedom coexisted paradoxically in the United States. It has been commonly assumed that all blacks were free in non-slaveholding states, and that their contemporaries in slaveholding states were enslaved. This simplistic notion, as we shall see, falls apart under close scrutiny, and a far more complex picture emerges.[2]

What did it mean to be black and free in a country where the majority of blacks were not free? In 1832, the freeborn New Englander Maria W. Stewart, known as the first American woman to address a public gathering of women and men, lamented that the condition of this free population was "with few exceptions," she wrote, "but little better" than that of their enslaved counterparts. Stewart admitted the possibility of her statement being "very erroneous" because of unevenness in circumstances across regions, classes, and genders. In actuality, she was not far off the mark. Legal differences between enslaved and emancipated blacks were obvious, yet few free persons, male or female of all ages, escaped the furies of race-based discrimination in the workplace, judicial system, and school districts. Discrimination surrounded free persons of color, yet it did not dissuade all slaves from seeking liberty. The slave-born

Jermain Loguen was among them, and in a narrative of his life he recounted telling a friend, "All I live for now, is to get freedom, and if I can't get that, I don't care to live at all."[3]

This essay examines the conditions under which free girls and boys across geographical regions studied and worked. It also looks at their reactions to living in a hostile environment and how they responded to the movement to abolish slavery as they struggled to define their own liberty. A common African heritage linking emancipated and enslaved persons often proved strong enough to motivate free persons to join in the struggle to overthrow bondage for their enslaved contemporaries.[4]

When the federal government conducted the First Census of the United States in 1790, the number of free persons of African descent in all age groups had increased from several thousands in 1750 to 59,466. The free population constituted 7.9 percent of the 697,624 blacks in the United States at the time. The free population peaked in 1830 when its numbers reached 319,599, or 13.7 percent, of all blacks in the United States. After 1830, the percentage of free blacks fell to 13.4 percent in 1840, 11.9 percent in 1850, and to 11.0 percent in 1860. By that time, the free population had reached 488,070. Of that number, 240,921 males and females were less than twenty years of age.[5]

Free black girls and boys, living in urban and rural areas of the North or South, attributed their status to a variety of sources. Being born to a free woman, without respect for color, remained a constant source of liberty throughout the slave era. For example, Benjamin Banneker, born in 1828, was the offspring of an African man, Robert, and a free mulatto woman, Mary. Her mother, Molly Welsh, a white indentured servant had owned, freed, and then married an African known as Bannaka. Over time the spelling of his forename changed to Banneker and became the family's surname. Many freedpersons selected new appellations or added last names when emancipated, including Robert who had no last name that he could call his own. He chose his wife's family name, Banneker, as his own.[6]

Apart from natural increases, the Revolutionary War ideology that touted freedom, especially political and civil liberties, was responsible for the largest increase in the free population in the eighteenth century. In response to the philosophy, states north of Delaware either abolished slavery or made provisions to do so following the Revolutionary War. At first glance, it appears that this revolutionary spirit flowed generously from newly independent lawmakers to enslaved persons. For example, the preamble to Pennsylvania's 1780 emancipation bill recounted both the horrors of the nine-month occupation by British soldiers and the "grateful sense of the manifold blessings" upon the citizens when the Red Coats evacuated. "We conceive that is it our duty," declared the legislators, "to extend a portion of that freedom to others [slaves], which hath been extended to us, and a release from that state of thralldom." Acting upon this premise, the legislature passed a bill, effective March 1, 1780, which won the distinction of being the first of its kind in North America; however, it did not free anyone instantly. The state placed conditions upon emancipations: girls and boys born before March 1, 1780, prior to the ratification of the bill, remained in bondage while children born afterward became free at twenty-eight years of age.[7]

Between 1777 and 1804, other states in the region adopted measures for emancipation. New York granted unconditional emancipation to boys and girls born before 1799; however, girls born afterward were bound to service until they reached twenty-five years of age. Boys remained in service until they were twenty-eight years old. Similar laws in Rhode Island, Connecticut, and New Jersey granted freedom to children once they were at least eighteen years of age.[8]

Rather than destroying slavery completely within their own generation, revolutionary era lawmakers postponed its ultimate demise in the North for another generation. However, they did find opportunities to prevent its growth elsewhere. When drafting a proposal to organize the Northwest Territory, Thomas Jefferson recommended prohibiting slavery in the land north of the Ohio River and east of the Mississippi River. Congress failed to adopt this measure in 1784 but included it in the Northwest Ordinance of 1787. Similarly, during the Constitutional Convention in 1787, the founding fathers prohibited the African slave trade after 1808. They limited slavery in these ways but protected it in others. For example, the Constitution contains a clause covering persons "held to service or labor" who escaped to another state. Instead of liberty in their new locations, the Constitution required states to deliver fugitives "up on claim of the party to whom such service or labor may be due." Ambivalence of this sort has caused historians to describe the founding fathers loosely as "skittish abolitionists," and it reaffirmed the fears of free and potentially free blacks that their liberty was tenuous and always in jeopardy.[9]

Despite the niggardly course of emancipation, by the end of the 1840s few northern girls and boys remained in bondage. By contrast, slavery remained firmly entrenched in the South, but legal suits such as *Hudgins v. Wright* (1808), a Virginia case involving several women who won their freedom based on phenotypical features resulted in their freedom. Self-purchases and private manumissions also remained potential fonts of freedom. Between 1850 and 1860, one-fourth of the freed women and men in Washington, D. C., owed their liberty to self-purchases or purchases with the assistance of others. And, slaveowners eager to avoid the cost of maintaining young women in their childbearing years were three times more likely to emancipate teenaged girls than to free their male cohorts in Washington, D.C.[10]

Private manumissions were possible but sometimes went awry as was the case of two children, according to their ten-year-old cousin in Cincinnati. As an 1834 class assignment, children attending a newly opened school in Cincinnati were to write a composition in response to the question: "What do you think *most* about?" Of the five extant responses, written by children between seven and sixteen years of age, each mentions slavery. The ten-year-old wrote:

> I have two cousins in slavery who are entitled to their freedom. They have done everything that the will requires and now they wont let them go. They talk of selling them down the river.

Obviously anxious about the relatives, the child asked, "If this was our case what would you do?" The assignment ended with the child's plea for advice that would be helpful in removing the two children from bondage.[11]

An unknown number of enslaved persons escaped from bondage and melded into the free population. Historians John Hope Franklin and Loren Schweninger created the "Runaway Slave Data Base" (RSDB), containing more than two thousand advertisements for fugitives in five states from 1790 to 1816 and 1838 to 1860 to document the extent of flights by persons who thirsted for freedom. The authors used the RSDB to undergird the prize-winning study, *Runaway Slaves: Rebels on the Plantation*, which allowed them to say with accuracy that the greater majority of runaways were males between thirteen and twenty-nine years of age. They were either unmarried or, if married, had no children.[12]

Fewer females of all ages were among the successful runaways. In all probability, absconding females attracted more attention when traveling alone and were stopped or arrested before owners could place notices of their disappearances in the papers. Also, females in childbearing years often recoiled from fleeing if they had children who would prove too burdensome to take along, and mothers obviously were reluctant to leave their offspring behind. Regardless of gender, slaves committed "theft of self" most easily by escaping to nearby non-slaveholding northern states or melding into the general free black population of densely populated southern cities, such as New Orleans, Charleston, and Baltimore.

An unknown number of fair-skinned slaves quietly emancipated themselves by claiming to be white in a society where it was commonly assumed that whites were free and blacks were slaves. The social construction of race made this possible for persons without visible traces of African ancestry. However, the interest in designating a "place" for African Americans evolved over time in colonial America and served to interfere with the liberty of boys and girls entitled to legal freedom. In 1662 the Virginia Assembly enacted legislation declaring that "all children born in this country shall be held bond or free only according to the condition of the mother." The legislation was contradictory to English common law, which based status upon paternity, but it was in keeping with British ideas about property rights. The law relieved white men of financial and legal responsibilities for their mixed race offspring and relegated these biracial children of enslaved women to bondage for generations to come.[13]

The arresting question asked by the slave-born Elizabeth Keckley, a haute couture dressmaker for Mary Todd Lincoln and mother of a child of mixed parentage, highlights the meaning of the law. In her autobiographical narrative, Keckley asked: "*Why should my son be held in slavery?*" She explained:

> He came into the world through no will of mine, and yet, God only knows how I loved him. The Anglo-Saxon blood as well as the African flowed in his veins; the two currents commingled . . . *Why should not the Anglo-Saxon triumph*—why should it be weighed down with the rich blood typical of the tropics? Must the life-current of one race bind the other race in chains as strong and enduring as if there had been no Anglo-Saxon taint?

In short, why was her son and tens of thousands of others considered black and enslaved like their mothers rather than white and free like their fathers? Keckley's word choices could be interpreted in several different ways: her rhetorical denigration of "the rich blood typical of the tropics" very well may have been ironic; her quip about the "taint" of Anglo-Saxon blood certainly turns the racist ideology of the day on its head.[14]

Regardless of the manner in which children acquired their liberty, they were anomalies in North America. Even more of an aberration among them were the "virtually free" boys and girls who were enslaved legally but lived, worked, and behaved as if they had been emancipated. As a youngster in the 1910s, Pauli Murray heard much about the complexities of slavery from her grandmother. "We were free," declared the biracial North Carolina slave Cornelia Smith, born in 1844, when speaking of herself and her three younger sisters growing up in the home of their paternal grandfather, a white medical doctor in North Carolina. The girls enjoyed the comfort of a planter's home while their mother and older half-brother, fathered by a free black man, lived across the yard in a humble cabin. "We were just born in slavery," she added, "that's all".[15]

The early childhood of Amanda America Dickson, daughter of David Dickson, a wealthy Georgia merchant, who earned a reputation as an agricultural reformer with a penchant for growing experimental crops and testing scientific methods, was strikingly similar to the Smith girls. Aside from his business acumen, David Dickson was described as the "foremost" of "agriculturalists and the man above all others who had contributed most to the development of the farming interest" in Georgia.[16]

Amanda's mother, Julia Frances, was a thirteen-year-old slave girl playing in the meadow in February 1849 when Dickson, a man twenty-seven years older, rode past on his horse, swooped her up, and continued on his way. There are no accounts of Julia Dickson's reaction to this incident, which resulted in the November 20, 1849, birth of her daughter, Amanda. This child slept in her paternal grandmother's bedroom and came of age in a household where she enjoyed an amicable relationship with white relatives and all of the privileges money could buy, yet legally, she remained a slave.[17]

The biracial children John, Henry, and James, born between 1808 and 1827 to the Virginia-born slave, Sally Thomas, did not enjoy such opulence as did Amanda. They did, however, live as virtually free persons after 1818 in Nashville, Tennessee, where Thomas established a home-based laundry business and earned her own money. Her intent was to save and purchase the children's freedom, and the two older boys contributed to this effort. By the time he was eleven years of age, John worked as a waiter and poll boy on a river barge owned by Captain Richard Rapier, and Henry earned money by running errands for local white gentlemen.[18]

The Thomas family managed to save $350, but it was not necessary to spend the money toward the older children's liberty because Captain Rapier purchased and manumitted John in 1829, and Henry ran away. Sally Thomas used the money to buy her youngest child, James, born in 1827. Since slaves could not technically own property, real or personal, Thomas asked Attorney Ephraim H. Foster to execute the transaction and hold her son in trust to avoid complications with ownership and to evade the Tennessee law requiring newly manumitted slaves to leave the state. Although James remained technically enslaved, Foster had no interests in the child as his own chattel.[19]

As a virtually free child, James lived with Sally Thomas, his mother and titular owner, in downtown Nashville where he contributed to her business by assisting with making soap, heating water, and delivering laundry. He also attended school, studied the fundamentals of reading, writing, and arithmetic. Afterward, James served as an apprentice and learned the skills of a barber. His life as a virtually free person did not differ from that of other children in his position except he lived in the home of his enslaved mother and was legally the property of a white person without familial connections.[20]

Other virtually free children, including Suzanne Metoyer, born 1768 in Louisiana, daughter of the French gentleman Claude Thomas Pierre Metoyer and the enslaved woman Marie Thérèze, nee Coincoin; Imogene and Adeline, the Kentucky-born daughters of the Kentucky politician Richard M. Johnson and the enslaved woman Julia Chinn; and Maria Ann Ellison, daughter of an unnamed enslaved woman and the wealthy freedman William "April" Ellison, a South Carolina cotton-gin maker who purchased his teenaged daughter in 1830. They were hobbled by the absence of legal documents declaring them free. While this is true, they suffered no interferences from owners, relatives and others, who did not threaten them with sales, arduous labor, or corporal punishment. Only the absence of legal documents made them chattel. "That's all," Cornelia Smith said, that was keeping her from freedom.[21]

Legal documents, including manumission papers, bonds, registration certificates, or tax receipts, assured the most fundamental right to one's own person and his or her offspring along with the right to marry legally and own property. Free blacks could also sue and be sued, establish businesses, and keep their earnings. Furthermore, they could pursue an education and worship in churches of their choice. Despite legal differences between enslaved and emancipated boys and girls, free blacks were subjected to the loss of liberty if they could not prove their status, ran afoul of laws, or fell victim to kidnappers. Additionally, few free persons, including Charlotte Forten and Benjamin Banneker, escaped the torments of race-based discrimination in schools, churches, marketplaces, and public accommodations.[22]

Draconian legislation in the South against free persons of color was widespread during the slave era. The Alabama legislature passed a dozen laws affecting free blacks in 1852, including one that forbade sojourners from entering and remaining in the state for more than thirty days. Other codes forbade literate persons from writing passes for slaves. Laws affecting free persons were especially stringent in South Carolina, which required payment of an annual capitation tax for free persons. The penalty for ignoring the 1792 law was enslavement. Additionally, the state demanded that newly freed persons leave the state, and in 1822 the legislature passed a law prohibiting free persons from reentering the state upon the penalty of enslavement.[23]

Proslavery advocates complained that free persons were lazy, set bad examples for slaves, and encouraged them to resist bondage. After examining these reasons, it was easier to accept the theory of George Fitzhugh, a southern apologist for slavery and author of "What Shall Be Done With the Free Negro," published in the Fredericksburg, Virginia, *Recorder* in 1851. Fitzhugh wrote: "Humanity, self-interest, [and] consistency, all require that we should enslave the free negro." But, was it legal to take away the liberty of free persons and enslave them for life?[24]

Arkansas was the first of the slaveholding states to enact harsh legislation against free blacks in response to agitation by whites. In July 1858 the *Arkansas State Gazette* published the circular "To the People of Arkansas" from a twelve-member committee claiming to represent the citizens of Little Rock and Pulaski County. The circular was a litany of complaints against the "evil among us," free blacks, who

> instinctively take the side of those [slaves] under [the] government [of slaveowners] console with them when they complain, harbor them when they escape, tell them they

are entitled to be free, and encourage them in insubordination and to pilfer and defraud if not to commit offense more serious, and do acts more dangerous still.

The committee railed about free persons interference with slaveowners ability to make their chattel submissive and loyal based on the conviction that "servitude to a higher race" was the slave's "natural condition." The committee called for a law to expel the free black population.[25]

In 1859 the Arkansas legislature required free Blacks to either leave the state by the end of the year or choose "masters" who would "give bond not to allow such negroes to act as free." The legislature declared that "any free Negro in the state by January 1, 1860, would be reenslaved." Following Arkansas's lead, other southern states entered debates about similar legislation. Persons with the wherewithal to flee did so while others suffered a cruel fate.[26]

Given these circumstances, even the schoolgirl Charlotte Forten remained amazed that African Americans were not misanthropes as a result of living amid racial hostilities and facing routine acts of injustice. "Surely," she wrote in 1855, "we have everything to make us hate mankind." Kind and cordial classmates on school grounds ignored her when off campus. She responded with indifference considering the incidents as "trifles" when compared to the great public wrongs against her people in bondage. When considered within the historical context and juxtaposed against bondage, the insults were easier to endure. Yet, Forten admitted that the "trifles" were "most wearing and discouraging" to persons who experienced them.[27]

Charolotte' Forten's contemporary Maritcha Lyons had firsthand knowledge of such behavior but was not inclined to ignore it. The sixteen-year-old girl moved from New York to Providence, Rhode Island, in 1854 where she attended school after her mother appealed to the governor to assure her admission. Under the circumstances, "if any girl tried to put 'on airs,' " wrote Lyons, "I simply found a way to inform her of my class record." She flaunted her academic superiority as a way of saying to classmates that she too was entitled to an education and to show that blacks could excel academically if given a chance.[28]

Many free black children in the North enjoyed access to education. Among them was the slave-born but freed mulatto John Mercer Langston who moved from Virginia to Ohio with his older brothers following the death of their parents. Langston attended a school within walking distance of his guardians' home, and his autobiography does not record any negative experiences during his school days. Barriers to literacy in the South, such as the closing of black schools and the enactment of statutes against teaching blacks to read and write following the 1831 rebellion led by literate preacher Nat Turner, did not exist in the North. Educational opportunities, however, were not always ideal. Some school systems in the North prohibited black children altogether while others, Philadelphia, for example, maintained segregation. Rosetta Douglass, daughter of the famous slave-born abolitionist, Frederick Douglass, felt the impact of racism in Rochester, New York, where public schools remained closed to black children until 1857. Meanwhile, Rosetta attended the private Seward Seminary until Frederick Douglass learned that she received instructions in a separate room from the other students.[29]

Ordinarily, protests brought no positive results. In 1853, the freeborn Robert Purvis, president of the Pennsylvania Anti-Slavery Society, protested the payment of school taxes for which his children had no access. The complaint resulted in Joseph P. Butcher, Bucks County, Pennsylvania, tax collector, relieving Purvis of paying the tax, but the schools remained segregated.[30]

When confronted with segregation in Boston's public schools, Benjamin Roberts took a different stance. He sued the city of Boston on behalf of Sarah, his five-year-old daughter, who walked past five white elementary schools before reaching the overcrowded and badly deteriorated Smith Grammar School for blacks. At the center of the Roberts's case was an 1845 statute saying children who were excluded unlawfully from the city's schools were eligible for relief. The well-known Charles Sumner along with Robert Morris, the first African American lawyer to try a case before a jury, represented the plaintiff in *Roberts v. City of Boston* (1849). The Supreme Judicial Court of Massachusetts headed by Chief Justice Lemuel Shaw heard the case in which Sumner argued that attending a separate school was disadvantageous to Sarah and that white children were also harmed by segregation. "Their hearts, while yet tender with childhood, are necessarily hardened by this conduct," said Sumner, and "their subsequent lives [will], perhaps, bear enduring testimony to this legalized uncharitableness."[31]

Shaw, a former member of the Boston School Committee, disagreed and maintained that segregation was for the good of both black and white children. In his opinion, the School Committee which supported "separate but equal" was solely responsible for the operation of the city's schools. Roberts did not win relief through the court, but it was not for the lack of support from the black community and the legal team.[32]

Nevertheless, the negative decision precipitated a massive petition and publicity campaign over the next few years. The black community seemed to believe that equal access to educational opportunities was the key to freedom. In all probability acceptance of the adage, "Knowledge is power," and that it could be used to uplift the race, helped to sustain black Bostonians until 1855 when the state legislature heard their pleas and voted to end segregation in Boston's public schools.[33]

In the face of segregation elsewhere, parents and guardians sought alternatives. Frederick Douglass once hired a private tutor for his daughter, Rosetta. The wealthy Philadelphia sail-maker James Forten, Sr. objected to the segregated schools in the "City of Brotherly Love," and his granddaughter, Charlotte, received private tutoring before attending school in Salem, Massachusetts, between 1853 and 1856. In Salem, she boarded with John and Nancy Remond who had relocated from Salem to Newport, Rhode Island, in the mid-1830s so that their son, Charles, and daughter, Sarah, "might not suffer from the discriminatory practices found in the high schools of Salem."

While Charlotte Forten was in Salem, the conditions in Pennsylvania hardly changed. In 1856, her cousin Harriet Purvis wrote to a friend that she had been tutoring her younger siblings at home since "there was no school [in Bayberry, Pennsylvania] . . . for them except a **Public School**" where they had to sit by themselves "because their faces are not as white as the rest of the scholars." The seventeen-year-old Purvis said it made her "blood boil" just to think of the unfair treatment. When her own private tutoring ended, Purvis attended Eagleswood, a New Jersey boarding school run by abolitionists Theodore D. Weld, his wife Angelina, and her sister Sarah Grimké. At Eagleswood, Purvis mingled with the children and grandchildren of white abolitionists. Although living away from home caused anxiety and feelings of disengagement, Hattie Purvis established meaningful relationships with white classmates including Ellen Wright, who eventually married William Lloyd Garrison.[34]

The curricular offerings at public and private schools included traditional reading, writing, arithmetic, geography, and spelling courses. At Philadelphia's Institute for Colored Youth, a classical high school founded in 1837 by the Society of Friends, pupils had a greater variety of courses. The freeborn Sarah Mapps Douglass, a stellar teacher in charge of the Girl's Department at the Institute, enrolled in medical classes at the Ladies Institute of Pennsylvania Medical University between 1855 and 1858 in order to introduce new subjects, including physiology, into the Institute's offerings.[35]

Based on comments about her final examinations, H. Amelia Loguen, daughter of the slave-born Jermian W. Loguen, an African Methodist Episcopal Zion Bishop, studied an expansive curriculum. On April 10, 1862, she wrote:

> Spring has brought with it as usual, the ever dreaded, yearly school examinations, *dreaded* because they are so *very tedious*. Monday I thought of nothing but Chloride of Sodium, Nitrate of Silver detection of arsenic, uses of Zinc etc etc; Tuesday, Parlez-vous français? Comment-vous appelez-vous? and Je me porte tres bien, yesterday oh! terrible thought Plane Trigonometry; do you wonder then that last night I dreamed of being in France . . . trying to show that Chemistry is one of the most useful and interesting studies imaginable and lastly I was alone in some queer place trying to accertain [*sic*] the height of a "fort on a distant hill inaccessable [*sic*] on account of an intervening swamp." O! how refreshing on awaking this morning to know that all *such* is for a time past and that vacation is close at hand.

Loguen's curriculum was broad and seemingly free of gender-bound notions suggesting that girls were not suited to study the sciences.[36]

Unlike Loguen, James Forten, Jr. did not leave specific written accounts chronicling the details of his education, but manuscripts related to the Forten family indicate that he exuded an interest in the humanities and social sciences. He was also interested in chemistry, astronomy, and philosophy. Forten's father, James Forten, Sr., encouraged the educational development of his sons and daughters, and the elder Forten could well afford to hire private tutors and maintain an extensive family library for his children's intellectual growth and development.[37]

How free boys and girls gained literacy varied widely across regions and classes. In the absence of suitable public schools, persons with the financial wherewithal hired private tutors, sent their children away to school, or relocated entire families. Others were self-taught or received lessons from family members, as did Benjamin Banneker whose grandmother introduced him to the fundamentals. Before moving to Ohio, John Mercer Langston said his father, a white slaveowner, used "his own efforts and influence" to introduce Gideon, John's older brother, to a "thorough English education, with general information and mental and moral improvement, as to make him a useful man." Their father held "recitations . . . the year round, at five o'clock in the morning."[38]

Indeed, Langston's situation was unusual and not representative of the whole, but just one indication of the many ways in which free black children in the South gained literacy. It is somewhat remarkable that any of them succeeded in the absence of an open and accessible public school system.

Racial discrimination also made it difficult for many northern children to acquire an education, but it was never illegal to teach them to read and write as in several of the southern states following the 1831 uprising led by Nat Turner. Although prohibitions existed, many states did not enforce such laws uniformly; therefore, all avenues to literacy were never completely closed. Thomas McCants Stewart, born December 28, 1853 in Charleston, South Carolina, to George Gilchrist and Anna Morris Stewart, attended the privately operated Morris Street School, which was open to free and enslaved children alike. In fact, the slave-born Archibald and Francis Grimké were in regular attendance there.[39]

Francis Grimké's autobiographical writings mention attending the Morris Street School in the 1850s. However, he wrote nothing about its curricular offerings, class assignments, or his early musings about using his education for his own empowerment or that of his people.[40]

By contrast, letters written for an English class by Grimké's contemporaries who attended the *Ecole catholique pour l'instruction des orphelins dan l'indigence* in New Orleans provide a virtual cornucopia of data about their grasp of historical occurrences in their midst. The boys, primarily between twelve and seventeen years of age, used the writing assignments to demonstrate their knowledge of geography and political events. When combined with their language skills and vivid imaginations, they created their worlds anew within the parameters of the school which promised them a practical, moral, and religious education.[41]

In a study of the letters written in the 1850s and 1860s, the historian Mary Niall Mitchell argues that the assignment served to educate the children to the possibilities of establishing themselves and prospering far away from New Orleans. Knowledge of black migration from the United States after the passage of the Compromise of 1850 and its threatening more stringent fugitive slave clause made Haiti and Mexico their destinations of choice.[42]

Once in Mexico or Haiti, albeit in their minds' eye, the boys discussed the practical nature of farming and considered the climate and soil. They also concerned themselves with business arrangements of interest to merchants, shippers, or planters. Business deals, even imaginary ones, allowed the students to use their math skills to solve problems related to wages along with "the exchange of specie for dry goods and . . . promissory notes."[43]

The written exercises of the schoolboys in New Orleans were more sophisticated in character than the compositions of the school children in antebellum Cincinnati, yet in each case the children had opportunities to express their anxieties about the present and hopes for the future. To be sure, this was a vital part of their education as they grew into mature men and women.

Aside from studying at local elementary or secondary schools, a limited number of black adolescents attended schools of higher education at institutions founded specifically for African Americans. The oldest of these institutions was Ashmum Institute, Oxford, Chester County, Pennsylvania which began on January 1, 1854, under the auspices of the Presbyterians and later changed its name to Lincoln University. The following year, the Cincinnati Conference of the Methodist Episcopal Church founded Wilberforce University. Although these early institutions incorporated the word college or university in their official names, they traditionally admitted students in their upper adolescence to preparatory classes before admittance into the college departments.[44]

Lincoln and Wilberforce were founded especially for African Americans, but several white institutions including Rhode Island State Normal School, Harvard University Medical School, and the University of New York, admitted blacks. Young black men interested in the ministry could study at the Theological Seminary of Gettysburg, Pennsylvania; the Theological Seminary of Charleston, South Carolina; and the Dartmouth Theological School, Massachusetts.[45]

Oberlin Collegiate Institute (now Oberlin College), near Elyria, Ohio, had enrolled nearly one hundred black males and females by 1865. Although they made up only 2 to 5 percent of the student body, the historian Carter G. Woodson said Oberlin "did so much for the education of Negroes before the Civil War that it was often spoken of as an institution for the education of the people of color."[46]

Most females at Oberlin enrolled in the "Ladies' Course," which unlike the college department, did not require Latin, Greek, or higher mathematics. If students did not meet the college's prerequisites prior to enrollment, they could enter the preparatory department. It was considerably smaller than the college department because many students never entered the upper division. What happened to them is not entirely clear. Many probably believed their educations were sufficient and left or enrolled at other institutions.

What happened to "Wildfire," the daughter of a Chippewa Indian woman and African American man, who entered Oberlin in 1859, is very well known among historians. School officials promptly changed her name to Mary Edmonia Lewis. This reflected the desire to make Native Americans assimilate into the dominant culture or as they sometimes said, to "walk the White man's road." After Lewis completed the preparatory courses, she entered the liberal arts program but left without graduating.[47]

Afterward, Edmonia Lewis earned an international reputation as the first major sculptress of African American heritage. Her bust of Colonel Robert Gould Shaw received accolades from Harriet Hosmer, a neoclassical sculptor, who praised the work and said it was "finely moulded." Lewis financed a trip to Europe for further study through the sale of plaster copies and other pieces. Over time she shifted from sculpting white abolitionists to creating pieces representing African Americans. Lewis's *The Freed Woman and Child* portrays the subject kneeling in prayer after learning of her emancipation and that of the child in her arms. The artist said she received the inspiration for the work from her father's people and her attempt to recognize them in her own way.[48]

Among the male students who attended Oberlin in the mid-nineteenth century, the children of Alan Jones, a North Carolina blacksmith, deserve note. Between 1849 and 1859, four of the Jones children graduated from Oberlin. The first, James Monroe, completed requirements in 1849 and migrated to Canada where he worked as a gun-maker. Another brother, John, graduated in 1856 and became a school administrator in British Columbia. William, the third son of Alan Jones, ended his college career at Oberlin in 1857. He later practiced dentistry in British Columbia. Elias, the last of the four, graduated in 1859. He migrated to British Columbia where he worked as a gold miner.[49]

The fact that the four young men emigrated from the United States reflects their desires to remove themselves from a potentially threatening environment for educated blacks in the South. The timing of their emigration coincides with the flight of other free persons to Canada and Liberia because of the enforcement of the Fugitive Slave Act of 1850, which jeopardized their freedom. A career as a school administrator would have been less problematic for John Jones in British Columbia than in North Carolina in the 1850s.

A great number of free black boys and girls, especially those who were economically deprived, did not attend schools of any kind regularly. Instead, many of these children entered bound service to persons who agreed to provide food, clothing, and shelter along with domestic and educational training in exchange for their labor. In general, free black girls and boys entered service younger, received less educational training, and remained bound longer than their white contemporaries. As a result, the black youngsters spent most of their formative years performing manual labor outside their own homes.[50]

Ordinarily, agreements of indenture were gender specific and had few if any variations. Girls received training associated with housewifery, while boys learned the business of farming. In all probability persons holding indentures would use both boys and girls for agricultural work if there was a need for additional labor.

The talented Robert S. Duncanson, born in Seneca County, New York, completed an apprenticeship that differed from most free black male apprentices. Born into a family of carpenters and house painters in 1821, Duncanson and three of his four brothers gained skills and work experience as apprentices during their adolescence. The Duncansons migrated to the commercial boomtown, Monroe, Michigan, on Lake Erie, and on April 16, 1838, Robert and a friend, John Gamblin, placed an advertisement in the *Monroe (Michigan) Gazette* announcing the establishment of "A New Firm" and solicited business as "painters and glaziers." Their ads appeared consistently throughout the year.[51]

It was possible to earn a living in the paint and decorating business, but Robert Duncanson's creative talent and interest in fine art led him into a career as a painter in the Hudson River and Ohio River Valley school traditions. In order to follow his ambitions and develop his talent more fully, Duncanson moved to Cincinnati, a thriving cultural center with a relatively large free black population.[52]

By his twenty-first birthday, Duncanson had completed "Portrait of a Mother and Daughter," probably a commissioned work featuring a stylishly dressed white child lovingly embracing a seated woman. In 1842, Duncanson entered three paintings, "Fancy Portrait," "Miser," and "Infant Savior," in a Cincinnati art show. Two of the paintings were copies of other creative works, which was not unusual at the time. As he grew more firmly into adulthood, he matured artistically and became known as the best landscape painter in the West.[53]

Unlike Robert S. Duncanson and Edmonia Lewis whose artistic talents and skills served as the basis of their livelihood, the majority of free boys and girls worked at unskilled or semiskilled jobs. Many girls gained domestic skills in food preparation and laundering clothes. Since these tasks were too demanding for most young girls, they ordinarily assisted adults. The autobiographical writing of Nancy Prince, a Massachusetts-born free African American, reveals the tedious nature of her work in 1814 as a fourteen-year-old domestic servant in a family of seven, including a patient suffering from a fever complaint and another from consumption. Prince recalled,

> Of course, the work must have been very severe, especially the washings. Sabbath evening I had to prepare for the wash; soap the clothes and put them into the steamer, set the kettle of water to boiling, and then close in the steam, and let the pipe from the boiler into the steam box that held the clothes. At two o'clock, on the morning of Monday, the bell was rung for me to get up; but, that was not all, they said I was too slow, and the washing was not done well; I had to leave the tub to tend the door and wait on the family, and was not spoken kind to, at that.

The teenager remained on the job only three months before it took a great toll on her health.[54]

The autobiographical fiction *Our Nig*, the first novel published in the United States by a black woman, Harriet E. Wilson, is also illustrative in this regard. *Our Nig*'s well-developed plot focuses on Frado, a six-year-old girl who became an orphan when her African-born father died, and her white mother, abandoned her. The young protagonist worked for an abusive white family in New England before the Civil War. The author wanted to show that racism existed in the North, and that Frado's life as a servant was not vastly different from her enslaved contemporaries in the South. The conditions under which Frado and Prince worked were more exacting because they lived under the watchful eye of employers.[55]

By contrast, when laundresses and other self-employed women, assisted by young children, worked in their own homes they experienced some reprieve and did not assume the "humble pose." At early ages, emancipated or enslaved children learned how to present a self-effacing posture or pay deference to whites publicly while privately maintaining their self-respect. The much-discussed "mask," a protective device for disguising personal convictions and steeling the psychic, facial expressions, and body language, was a significant facet in maintaining associations with whites whose patronage was critical to their economic survival. Scholar Sharon G. Dean, attributes the expression "a humble pose" to Frederick Douglass in reference to black businessmen who catered solely to a white clientele and displayed deferential behavior or business facade to woo and maintain white customers.[56]

Given these circumstances, it is not surprising that free persons preferred occupations in which both a source of livelihood and a degree of autonomy were possible. Women and girls found such jobs in the needle trade, in which they developed skills well beyond simple sewing. Without readily accessible and affordable manufactured clothes, dressmakers fashioned garments for black and white clients. Young girls often assisted dressmakers and gained marketable skills as they matured.

Many free black children worked on farms owned by their families or persons to whom they were indentured. Their jobs involved any tasks that were appropriate for their ages, such as planting and weeding. As a youngster, John Mercer Langston performed general farm work with a hoe and light plow. He also learned to drive a horse drawn cart. Until girls and boys were old enough to assume agricultural chores equivalent to those performed by adults, they assisted older workers.[57]

Regardless of the conditions under which they worked, free black children and adults held a highly precarious position in antebellum American society, and many tread carefully to avoid social and economic repercussions. But, they could not ignore the discrimination they faced nor could they forget the conditions of the boys, girls, men, and women who remained in bondage. As a result, some free persons, young and old, linked the fight against race-based discrimination directed at free persons with the abolition of slavery. The manner in which boys and girls were sensitized and articulated their understanding of these issues varied. For example, when free black school children in Cincinnati were asked to write a composition on the subject "What you *think most* about," mentioned above, their responses reflected an awareness of slavery and the movement to abolish it. In the form of a letter, a seven-year-old child wrote to schoolmates promising to be a good boy and become "a man to get the poor slaves from bondage." Another child wrote, "Bless the cause of abolition—bless the heralds of the truth that we trust God has sent out to declare the rights of man." An older and more articulate pupil explained that the children were studying "to try to get the yoke of slavery broke[n] . . . the chains parted asunder and slaveholding [to] cease for ever." Perhaps the children were familiar with fugitive slaves and the operations of the underground railroad in Cincinnati and knew the consequences of making a choice between reticence and activism regarding the abolition of slavery.[58]

Other girls and boys, especially those whose parents and other relatives supported the abolition of slavery, often joined in the struggle. Certainly, this is evident with the children of James Forten: his four daughters, four sons, and grandchildren were all imbued with this legacy and passed it from one generation to another. In fact, one of Forten's sons publicly encouraged parents to "fit your children in your domestic circles, for public life." In many free black families one can trace an individual's social consciousness back to childhood experiences in homes where adults recognized ills within the society and attempted to eradicate them.[59]

The James Forten family spanned three generations of activists who assisted in founding, financing, and nurturing six abolitionist societies. More specifically, Charlotte Forten, along with three of her daughters, were among the founding members of the Philadelphia Female Anti-Slavery Society in 1833. Charlotte Forten's granddaughter, Charlotte, adopted the family tradition. Her insights about racism among her peers when a schoolgirl are reflections of her background, growing up in an anti-slavery household.[60]

Much is known about the Forten family, but there were other free families who never joined formal organizations yet fought against racial inequality and slavery. The domestic inculcation of these values helps to explain an 1847 incident involving a group of women led by the prominent Bostonian Nancy Prince. They successfully thwarted a slave-catcher seen at a Smith Court home. According to one report the men were away at work, but "there were those around that showed themselves equal to the occasion." With a dramatic flair, the report said before the kidnapper "could fully realize his position she [Prince], with the assistance of the colored women that had accompanied her, had dragged him to the door and thrust him out of the house." The commotion drew a large number of women and children who pelted the would-be-kidnapper with stones and other missiles as Prince ordered. Not only did the women and children stone the empty handed villain, they also chased him away.[61]

The spontaneity of the crowd is not surprising. Free persons, young and old, knew that they were vulnerable to kidnapping and sale into slavery. They also knew that slave catchers grabbed blacks, whether fugitive or free, and carried them into the slave South. To avoid the seizure of runaways and free persons alike, crowds gathered quickly to thwart any such attempts.

Parallel data about free boys and girls in the South are largely absent. The lack of empirical evidence suggests that free black families were not at liberty to express their sentiments in an area where pro-slavery whites abhorred their very existence. Whites feared that free persons would have an unsettling influence upon slaves and stimulate their desire for freedom.

To avoid repercussions, many free persons toed the line, ostensibly. In reality, an untold number of unheralded individuals assisted slaves to gain their liberty. Without fanfare or membership in antislavery organizations, they helped to destroy slavery whenever the opportunity arose. It was incumbent upon them to do so since few free persons in the South could not claim a relative or friend who remained in bondage.[62]

Persons robbed of their freedom received surreptitious assistance from family and friends, but they did much to help themselves. The narrative of Polly Crocket, who came of age during slavery, a time in her life that she considered a dismal abyss, is the epitome of a freedom struggle. Crocket's daughter, Lucy Delaney, published the autobiographical *From the Darkness Cometh the Light, or Struggles for Freedom*, which presents the family's quest to regain and maintain its freedom. Delaney remembered that her mother "never spared an opportunity" to tell her children to seek liberty "whenever the chance offered."[63]

Delaney, and many other enslaved children, grew up knowing that slavery was the antithesis of the natural state of being: freedom. Through constant vigilance, Delaney and her family regained their liberty before the Civil War. The slave-born poet Phillis Wheatley, whose owner emancipated her in 1773 when she was approximately twenty years of age, described a familiar restiveness when she wrote, "In every Breast God has implanted a Principle, which we call Love of Freedom, it is impatient of oppression and pants for Deliverance." Free boys and girls could not enjoy their liberty until they were free from oppression and their enslaved contemporaries were delivered from bondage.[64]

Part II

CELEBRATION OF THE ABOLITION OF SLAVERY IN THE DISTRICT OF COLUMBIA BY THE COLORED PEOPLE, IN WASHINGTON, APRIL 19, 1866.—[SKETCHED BY F. DIELMAN.

Figure 5 Celebration of the Abolition of Slavery in the District of Columbia by the Colored People, in Washington, April 19, 1866—[Sketched by F. Dielman]

Source: Library of Congress, LC-USZ62-33937.

CHAPTER FIVE

"Dis Was atter Freedom Come": Freed Girls and Boys Remember the Emancipation

"Atter freedom"[1] did not necessarily mean the post–Civil War period. Quite to the contrary, some girls and boys were freed through a variety of measures long before the December 1865 ratification of the Thirteenth Amendment. In the Revolutionary War era (1770–1781), states north of Delaware either abolished slavery or made provisions for its gradual demise, and by 1850 slavery had disappeared there. In the interim, private manumissions, self-purchases, and the "theft of self," account for the liberty of many former slaves. In the meticulously researched *Runaway Slaves: Rebels on the Plantation*, historians John Hope Franklin and Loren Schweninger present compelling data about these fugitives and make it abundantly clear that persons enslaved on plantations did not lead an idyllic and carefree existence as portrayed by the historian Ulrich B. Phillips in his Pulitzer Prize–winning *Life and Labor in the Old South* (1929). Had Phillips been closer to the mark, fewer enslaved men, women, and children would have remained "contented" in their "places." Franklin and Schweninger estimate that if one-half of the planters and 10 to 15 percent of other slaveowners experienced only one runaway per year, the total number of fugitives would have exceeded 50,000 annually by 1860.

Finally, a series of emancipations affected children and adults in the Civil War era such as the Contraband of War Act, May 1861; First Confiscation Act, August 1861; the Second Confiscation Act, July 1862; the Emancipation Proclamation, January 1863; abolition in Washington, D.C., April 1862; abolition in U.S. territories, July 1862; abolition in Maryland, 1864; General Benjamin F. Butler's military families order; and, the Thirteenth Amendment, December 1865. These acts freed nearly four million blacks from bondage. Ultimately, the United States freed more slaves than all the other New World countries combined.[3]

Emancipation by whatever means opened the way for a new and different way of life. This essay seeks to examine how children experienced and were affected by emancipation. Did boys and girls experience independence differently? What difficulties did they face upon attaining freedom? What role did their families and the government play during the transition from slavery to freedom? What new opportunities were available to the children? And, did childhood, a special time in which children were sheltered from adult responsibilities, exist for newly freed children in the immediate aftermath of the Civil War? The objective of this essay is to answer these questions.

The sources for satisfying these inquiries are uneven at best. If enslaved persons were literate none recorded or published narratives about their experiences in bondage while still a child. A number of slave narratives, such as Frederick Douglass's *The Narrative of the Life of Frederick Douglass, an American Slave* (1845), and Booker T. Washington's *Up From Slavery* (1901), include discussions of early childhood, but the authors were adults when these autobiographies appeared. Similarly, the bulk of the testimony about enslavement comes from former slaves who were interviewed by Works Progress Administration (WPA) agents in the 1930s. The majority of those interviewed were less than twenty years of age when emancipated in 1865, but by the 1930s they were at least eighty years old. As a result, the slave narratives whether published before or after 1865 do not provide the voice of a child but their recollections of childhood.

As with any sources, care must be exercised when using the WPA narratives as evidence not only because of the great lapse in time but also because former slaves occasionally hedged when talking to white interviewers and responded according to what they believed interviewers expected to hear. This was especially true if interviewers were descendants of ex-slaveholders in the local area. In that same vein, Booker T. Washington, an accommodationist in twentieth-century race relations, was not likely to say or write anything for public consumption that could be construed as criticism of white society past, present, or future. Despite flaws, these sources cannot be dismissed out of hand.[4]

To be sure, this is a difficult task, but it is not insurmountable. When viewed together the collective narratives supplemented by other sources indicate that the ways freed children experienced the transition from slavery varied enormously. Civil War measures affected the greatest number within the shortest window of time, and much has been recorded about enslaved persons' responses to the Emancipation Proclamation that President Abraham Lincoln issued September 22, 1862, following a decisive Union victory at Antietam. The Proclamation, effective January 1, 1863, declared freedom for all slaves in states or designated parts of states in rebellion against the United States.[5]

Brigadier General Rufus Saxton, Commander of the Department of the South, a military territorial organization, primarily responsible for recruiting blacks for the 1st South Carolina Colored Volunteers, observed that slaves of all ages anticipated the coming of freedom with great delight and awaited the official reading of the Emancipation Proclamation, January 1, 1863. As a result, Saxton issued an order inviting all black children and adults in the vicinity to assemble at the Headquarters of the 1st Regiment of South Carolina Volunteers to hear the Emancipation Proclamation read. Afterward, he asked those under his command "to indulge in such other manifestations of joy as may be called forth by the occasion." He added:

> It is your duty to carry this good news to your brethren who are still in Slavery. Let all your voices, like merry bells, join loud and clear in the grand chorus of liberty—"We are

free," "We are free"—until listening, you shall hear its echoes coming back from every cabin in the land—"We are free," "We are free."[6]

In actuality the Emancipation Proclamation, penned by President Abraham Lincoln was "a fit and necessary war measure" for suppressing rebellion, but did not free anyone. Lincoln directed it at enslaved children and adults within states or parts of states in rebellion. Therefore, it affected only persons in the Confederate States of America where the U.S. Government could not enforce the measure and ignored others in locations over which the U.S. government had control. Within slaveholding areas under Union control, the U.S. Constitution protected the rights of individuals to own other human beings. Lincoln's intent was to uphold the constitution and maintain the loyalty of southern Unionists while undermining slavery in the Lower South.[7]

According to the 1860 census, there were 225,483 slaves in Kentucky and 114,931 in Missouri. Maryland's enslaved population was considerably less with 87,189, and Delaware had the smallest number of slaves in any of the border states with 1,798 slaves out of a population of 20,000 blacks in 1860. When adding these numbers with those enslaved in cities, counties, and parishes within states under Union control, the figures escalate further. For example, the Proclamation exempted the state of Tennessee, thirteen Louisiana parishes, and forty-eight Virginia counties designated as West Virginia along with seven additional counties in Virginia. These combined totals of children and adults reach more than 750,000 in Union holdings, thus outside the range of the Emancipation Proclamation.[8]

The intricately nuanced wording of the Emancipation Proclamation probably escaped the youngsters, but it kindled the hope of freedom and assured millions of slaves, 56 percent of whom were under twenty-one years of age, that the Union no longer ignored matters related to their legal status. Despite conflicting interpretations of the Emancipation Proclamation, many slaves marveled at the coming of freedom and repeated the same to WPA interviewers. As word of the Proclamation spread, Susie Melton, who was a ten-year-old living in Newport News, Virginia, at the time, remembered:

> We done heared dat Lincum gonna turn de niggers freed. Ole missus say dey warn't nothin' to it. Den a yankee soldier tole someone in Williamsburg dat marse Lincum done signed de'mancipation . . . ev'ybody commence gittin' ready to leave. Didn't care nothin' 'bout Missus . . . An' all dat night de niggers danced an' sang . . . [9]

The Missourian Mary A. Bell, who was a teenager in 1861, told the WPA interviewer in the 1930s that her father, a slave-born Virginian, Spottswood Rice, "read de emancipation for freedom to de other slaves, and it made dem so happy, dey could not work well, and dey got so no one could manage dem when dey found out dey were to be freed in such a short time."[10]

The Proclamation brought responses ranging from joy to ambiguity or even disdain, the age and education of the listener often affecting the reaction.

For example, the freeborn Charlotte Forten, granddaughter of James Forten, a wealthy Philadelphia sailmaker and abolitionist, declared that Thursday, New Year's Day, 1863, was "the most glorious day [the] nation has yet seen." She had witnessed the reading of the Emancipation Proclamation to large numbers of slave-born blacks in South Carolina. John Greenleaf Whittier, the well-known poet and Forten family friend, had encouraged her to move to St. Helena Island, South Carolina, to teach newly freed children.[11]

In September 1862, Forten applied for a teaching position under the auspices of the Port Royal Relief Association, a Philadelphia-based philanthropic organization founded March 1862 and dedicated to assisting former slaves in Port Royal, South Carolina. An estimated 10,000 slave-born children and adults in the area had come to the attention of northern reformers after Union forces gained control of Port Royal and the coastal islands between Charleston and Savannah in November 1861. The slaveholding white population had fled leaving their slaves behind. The Port Royal Relief Association sponsored teachers who relocated to South Carolina to assist the blacks in making the transition to independence and citizenship. It is not surprising that Forten, who had joined the Salem Female Anti-Slavery Society in 1855 shortly before her eighteenth birthday and begun her teaching career in 1856, sought such a position or that the association accepted her application. She had come of age in a family of abolitionists and had a deep sense of social responsibility toward her people.[12]

Forten arrived in late October 1862, and had settled into her job by the date of the official program at the Headquarters of the 1st Regiment in keeping with General Saxton's orders. Colonel Thomas Wentworth Higginson introduced the South Carolinian Dr. William H. Brisbane, a former slaveholder turned abolitionist, who read the Emancipation Proclamation to a crowd of girls, boys, women, and men whose faces beamed with anticipation. Based upon her experiences as a freeborn educated woman, Forten understood the contrast between her life and that of her enslaved contemporaries along with the magnitude of the imminent change in their status. She noted the occasion in her journal at the time but believed herself incapable of describing the scenes accurately.[13]

If it rendered her speechless, what did it mean for persons who never experienced the advantages of freedom as enjoyed by Forten during her formative years? The slave-born Susie King Taylor, who was thirteen years old when the Civil War began and among the crowd at Camp Saxton, agreed with Forten's assessment. "It was a glorious day for us all," Taylor wrote, "and we enjoyed every minute of it." She remembered the soldiers singing and shouting "Hurrah!" and recalled that fun and frolicking overflowed throughout the camp until taps sounded. The occasion was personal, meaningful, and without gendered constraints upon her behavior as a maturing young woman.[14]

By contrast, Pick Gladdney, born May 15, 1856, remembered the January 1, 1863, "speeching" in Maybinton, South Carolina, where he climbed a tree in order to see and hear better. He listened attentively but could " 'member nothin' what de man say." He recalled, "At dat time I was so young dat all I cared about on dat day, was the brass band what let out so much music." It was the first band he had ever seen and did not see another until World War I. "Bands charms me so much dat dey just plumb tickles the tips of my toes on both feets," he said. His tender age and fascination with the melody more than the message also suggest why he said "being free never meant nothing to us chaps, cause we never had no mind fer all such as that nohow." Gladdney's response reflects his experiences in bondage. He, like many boys and girls, had not yet endured the harshest realities of bondage—arduous labor, physical and emotional abuse, or separations from families before the general emancipation.[15]

At the time of her interview, an eighty-two-year-old South Carolina-born Violet Guntharpe was living near her birthplace and the descendants of her former owner. She remembered the emancipation well but did not exude enthusiasm about it. In the WPA narrative, Guntharpe recounted seeing white women weeping silently and black ones not knowing what to do when hearing about freedom. Of the children Guntharpe said, "de piccaninnies [were] suckin' their thumbs for want of sumpin' to eat." She attributed their miserable condition to "de Yankees" who upset daily routines and customary expectations. "Honey us wasn't ready for de big change dat come!" she said, and explained:

> Us had no education, no land, no mule, no cow, not a pig, nor a chicken, to set up house keeping. De birds had nests in de air, de foxes had holes in de ground, and de fishes had beds under de great falls, but us colored folks was left widout any place to lay our heads.

These well-formulated remarks were hardly those of a youngster in the midst of the monumental transition from slavery to freedom but the memory of an aged former slave who in retrospect, understood the circumstances, and put the disadvantages they faced in perspective. The situation was dire, in her opinion.[16]

Booker T. Washington, a well-known educator, founder of Tuskegee Institute in Alabama, and spokesperson for blacks at the behest of whites, was less vitriolic in his remarks made long after the emancipation. Guntharpe's education, standard of living, and recognition by whites contrasted sharply with Washington's. However, the essence of his comments are similar to Guntharpe's. Within a few hours after the reading of the Emancipation Proclamation, Washington remembered that "the wild rejoicing cease[d]" in lieu of "the questions of a home, a living, the rearing of children, education, citizenship, and the establishment and support of churches." The absence of resources to secure their physical, economic, and emotional well-being prompted him to ask "was it any wonder," he asked, "that . . . a feeling of deep gloom seemed to pervade the slave quarters?"[17]

To be sure, many former slaves experienced foreboding anxieties about what lay in store for them and recognized their dependent condition, but they never uniformly advocated or clamored for the reinstitution of slavery. Despite anxiety about the future, newly freed persons understood that the minimum of food, clothing, shelter, and medical care provided while enslaved was not an equitable exchange for their labor. Beyond the labor demands, they were subjected to family disruptions, arduous chores, sexual exploitation, and physical punishments in addition to denials of religious freedom, education, and citizenship.

Given the circumstances under which Violet Guntharpe and millions of other former slaves lived in addition to their general poverty when interviewed by WPA agents during the Great Depression, her comment "All us had to thank them [the Union soldiers] for, was a hungry belly, and freedom" is understandable. Most ex-slaves faced a bleak reality; emancipation jettisoned them into freedom and they had to find their own way in the world without any previous experiences of independence.[18]

Education, land, homes, and self-support were crucial; however, at the top of their immediate list of priorities was family reunification regardless of the time of emancipation. Parents sought their offspring while children searched for their mothers and fathers. Freedom without loved ones was incomplete. Many newly freed males and females, without regard for age, engaged in a massive, sometimes impossible, relocation effort. Several months after the Civil War ended, John Dennett, a reporter, met a freedman in search of his children and wife. He had walked from Georgia to North Carolina, more than 600 miles, in hopes of finding them. Fully a generation after the Civil War, black newspapers still published advertisements in an effort to locate persons whom slavery had separated from families and friends. Time and distance did not erase hopes of being together.[19]

When Will Adams freed the seventeen-year-old Missouri-born Mary Armstrong in a private 1863 manumission, she lost no time celebrating. "Away I goin' to find my mamma," said Armstrong, meaning she left immediately to locate her mother from whom she had been separated since early childhood. William Cleveland, Adams's father-in-law had owned Armstrong's mother but had taken her to Texas and sold her. With papers bearing "big gold seals" and money provided by her former owner, Armstrong traveled alone from St. Louis down the Mississippi River to New Orleans where she boarded a second boat to Galveston before embarking upon yet another vessel for the final leg of her journey up Buffalo Bayou to Houston.[20]

Armstrong did not find her mother in Houston and left for Austin within a few days. Afterward, Charley Crosby, whom Armstrong described as a "legislature man," told her about a "slave refugee camp in Wharton County." By then she had no money to continue the search but found work in Austin to support herself. Once the war ended, "I starts to hunt Mama again," she told the WPA interviewer. Armstrong located her mother in Wharton County, Texas, after nearly two years upon the circuitous odyssey. In her own vernacular, Armstrong described their joy: "Law me, talk about cryin' and singin' and cryin' some more, we sure done it."[21]

Armstrong's quest is unusual in several ways. During the "transportation revolution," which lasted from the turn of the nineteenth to the middle of the century, it was not uncommon for men to travel widely. By contrast, women were thought to have delicate constitutions and unable to endure travel over rough roads in stagecoaches, crowded rail cars, aboard river boats, or on horseback. Moreover, few white women were willing to ignore social conventions and damage their reputations by venturing far away from home alone.[22]

Armstrong did not have the same concerns as those of an elite white woman, but she was vulnerable to conditions that white female sojourners were not subjected.

As a young, black female traveling alone in the deep South before the general emancipation, Armstrong had no protection against abuses. In fact, at one point, a slave trader in Austin detained and attempted to sell her, but she produced the manumission papers and escaped unharmed.[23]

As an autonomous teenager at liberty to make choices, Armstrong's primary focus was on finding her mother, and she eventually succeeded. Armstrong's victory over the odds sets her apart from the many ex-slaves who endured forced separations and never rejoined loved ones as well as the many ex-slaves who located them but left no records to chronicle their successes.[24]

The extent to which parents or children would go to be with loved ones was boundless. Letters from Spottswood Rice, a private assigned to the U.S. Colored Troops, and father of enslaved children in Missouri, are illustrative. Rice, who ran away from his owner, enlisted in the Union Army February 9, 1864, and believed his military service would be instrumental in winning his children's freedom. On September 3, 1864, he wrote:

> My Children I take my pen in hand to rite you A few lines to let you know that I have not forgot you and that I want to see you as bad as ever now my Dear Children I want you to be contented with whatever may be your lots be assured that I will have you if it cost me my life on the 28th of the mounth. 8 hundred White and 8 hundred blacke solders expect to start up the rivore to Glasgow and above there thats to be jeneraled by a jeneral that will give me both of you when they Come I expects to be with, them and expect to get you both in return. Dont be uneasy my children I expect to have you.

Before ending the letter, he reaffirmed a wish to see his offspring and said "Spott and Noah," his older sons who had also joined the Union army, "sends their love to both of you."[25]

The letter would reassure Rice's daughters and raise their expectations for freedom and reunification. In all likelihood, they never received his correspondence. It is possible that Kitty Diggs, the owner of Rice's daughter, intercepted his missive that probably arrived at the same time as Rice's September 3, 1864, to Diggs. No doubt, awareness of imminent freedom for his children had empowered him.

Without any semblance of deference to Diggs, Rice indicated that one of his children had written to him saying she had accused him of trying to steal them. He chided the slaveholding woman:

> Now I want you to understand that mary is my Child and she is a God given rite of my own and you may hold on to hear [her] as long as you can but I want you to remembor this one thing that the longor you keep my Child from me the longor you will have to burn in hell and the qwicer youll get their.

As if assured that the army would support his individual effort, Rice wrote: "My Children is my own and I expect to get them and when I get ready to come after mary I will have bout a powrer and autherity to bring hear away and to exacute vengencens on them that holds my Child."[26]

Like Spottswood Rice, the mother of the slave-born Virginian Kate Drumgoold was adamant, once the Civil War ended, about trying to reunite with her children whom she said were scattered "all over in different places." In her autobiography, *A Slave Girl's Story*, Drumgoold claims that reports of their deaths did not dissuade her mother, who vowed to dig for their remains. That was not necessary since the children were indeed alive. Annie L. Burton's mother was no less adamant when their former owner in Alabama refused to release Burton and her siblings after the Civil War. The woman "threatened to set the dogs" upon Burton's mother when she attempted to take her offspring away. She remained unmoved by the threats and managed to "steal" her own children from their former owner whose sons tried to take Burton and her two siblings from their mother. "My mother refused to give us up," Burton remembered. The woman insisted that she and the former owner should go to "Yankee headquarters" to see if the children were indeed free.[27]

When comparing Rice's letter to the verbal protests of the Burton and Drumgoold women, his words were more threatening. Yet, the parents, male or female, made it clear that they intended to gather their children around their own hearths. No doubt the parents' fortitude in reunifying families made an indelible impression upon their offspring.[28]

Long after slavery ended, Rice's daughter Mary Bell, who was twelve years of age when her father wrote the letters, told the WPA interviewer, "Slavery was mighty hard." She remembered the stress on her family when several slaveholders owned her parents and siblings. Besides, her father's defiant behavior and determination to runaway complicated their circumstances, yet Bell admired him. "I love a man," she said, "who will fight for his rights and any person that wants to be something."[29]

Many newly freed parents were also "fighters" for the right to maintain the integrity of their families. Some searched for loved ones without assistance from others. By contrast, many located their children with assistance from the Bureau of Refugees, Freedmen, and Abandoned Lands, commonly called the Freedmen's Bureau, an official agency created by Congress March 1865 under the auspices of the War Department. The ideas of the abolitionist and reformers Samuel Gridley Howe, James McKaye, and Robert Dale Owens served as an impetus for the bureau that functioned as a relief and social agency responsible for dispensing food, clothing, and fuel to persons sorely affected by the Civil War. Congress committed the Freedmen's Bureau to the "control of all subjects" related to the newly freed children and adults.[30]

One of the most important of "all subjects" to former slaves whether in the years before or after the general emancipation in 1865, was locating loved ones and the reunification of families. They often wrote letters and made personal appeals to bureau agents for assistance. Agents responded and occasionally interceded, if needed. Sometimes, the agents and parents encountered the unexpected when children, who had been separated from their parents at early ages, had grown attached to owners and balked at leaving them. Certainly, this was the case with the North Carolinian Sarah Debro who lived in her owner's home in order to learn to be a "house maid." The impressionable child was fascinated with a bountiful supply of food, "even ham," and carriage rides with the woman of the house. Debro admitted that she "loved Mis Polly an' loved stayin at de big house." Debro's mother nonetheless succeeded in taking her away from the former owner.[31]

Other obstacles to reunification and the enjoyment of their childhood were apprenticeships for black children mandated by local courts, justices of the peace, and the Freedmen's Bureau. As early as November 2, 1864, whites in Maryland loaded black children indiscriminately into "ox carts, waggons, and carriages" for trips to local courts where they effected apprenticeships. In Maryland and elsewhere, thousands upon thousands of children were subjected to lengthy indentures. Court and bureau agents were quick to apprentice youngsters if they came from families with children fathered by different men. At other times, officials declared children "orphans" if their parents were not married legally or immediately at hand. Children were also bound out if officials decided parents were not capable of providing financial support for them.[32]

The criteria for apprenticeships teem with insidious motives designed to prey on circumstances over which former slaves had no control. For example, the absence of parity in gender ratios in many slaveowning households reduced slaves to coupling with persons owned by someone else in "abroad marriages." Slave marriages, whether abroad or within the same owners's household, had no legal standing. Consequently, from a legal perspective children born into these unions were "bastards" and potential charges upon the local community or state.

Further complications were attendant to the propensity of slaveowners to sell men more readily than women in their childbearing years. In all probability, such decisions were motivated by calculations regarding the mothers' potential reproductive value and the notion that women were the natural nurturer of dependent children. Ultimately, owners' decisions to break up families put additional distance between parents and their progeny. Once separated, some women and men united with other partners and formed new families. As soon as the Civil War ended, states across the South promulgated "black codes," draconian laws requiring gainful employment of able-bodied adults. The codes reduced unemployed parents to vagrants and deemed them incapable of supporting their offspring. Vagrancy laws and absent parents were tangential to apprenticeships. In retrospect, newly freed children—whether "bastards," "orphans," "indigents," or members of reconstituted families, were vulnerable to indentures or apprenticeships.[33]

Court and Freedmen's Bureau agents acted in *loco parentis* for children alone and bound them out, primarily to white men and women. Ostensibly, the agents were attempting to prevent homeless orphans from becoming vagrants or public charges. This action by agents appears to be a disregard for the rights of black parents and ignorance about a facet of their culture embracing the concept of extended families and fictive kin who render assistance to others in need regardless of blood relationships. That black "kinfolk" could have provided for these children may appear a moot point at this juncture; however, it must not be lost amid the roughshod actions of agents and others who relegated boys and girls to years of involuntary servitude.[34]

The practice of binding out poor, illegitimate, and free black children dated back to colonial times. Intent and precedent notwithstanding, the terms of indentures for newly freed boys and girls were reminders of slavery since many of the children were bound to persons who had owned them before 1865. Many ex-slaveowners regained control of freed children's labor and held them for lengthy periods while promising to feed, clothe, shelter, and provide them with medical care. The ages of the children and the extent of their service confirm that the apprenticeships were ploys to fill voids in the labor force created by the general emancipation.[35]

Whether the terms of post–Civil War indentures were printed on standardized forms or formulated by agents in the presence of concerned parties, they were essentially the same. Children were not to gad about at night but to work industriously, serve faithfully, and to obey the lawful commands of persons to whom they were bound. In addition to basic necessities, persons receiving the boys and girls often agreed to teach them to read, write, and according to one indenture, "cipher to the Single Rule of Three." Written agreements in Louisiana after the Civil War included a clause saying apprentices were "to attend church once each sabbath day & . . . receive Sixteen weeks schooling during each year."[36]

Ordinarily, there were slight differences between the indentures for boys and those for girls across the post–Civil War South. The two most obvious exceptions were in the lengths of service, cash, and other contributions upon release. In some instances, indentures bound boys and girls until they reached twenty-one years of age, but girls more often remained in service for a shorter period of time. In North Carolina and Missouri, the service of girls tended to end at eighteen while boys remained until twenty-one, and in Louisiana when girls reached fifteen years of age they were free to go but boys remained until they were eighteen years old. No explanations for these differences existed in the public records.[37]

At the completion of indentures in post–Civil War Missouri, apprentices were to receive a new Bible, two new suits of clothes, and cash. The allotment for the boys' clothes was $60 but ranged from $25 to $50 for the girls' wardrobes. The apprentices were to receive the same amount of cash, twenty dollars, without regard for gender, color, or service.[38]

In North Carolina, black female and male apprentices received differing sums of money and "such articles as are required by the laws of North Carolina to be given white apprentices" when they reach a specified age. For example, in 1866, Redding Luten indentured Naty Davis, a six-year-old black girl until she reached eighteen, and promised to give her $20 at the end of her service. The 1866 terms agreed upon for the eight-year-old Dorkass Williams were identical to those made for Davis, although she was two years younger and would remain in service longer than Dorkass, which was inconsequential. Each of the girls would receive $20, but Hardy, a six-year-old black male bound in 1868 to Calvin Perry was to receive $25 when he reached twenty-one years of age. Was it reasonable to assume that boys remained in service longer and worked harder at the "art and mystery of farming" than girls who were often "household servants?" Did boys deserve a larger sum since it was assumed boys would perform more physical labor? Or, did the practice simply reinforce gender conventions?[39]

According to the indentures, more often than not, girls were to receive training in the "business of housekeeping" or as a "house servant" while boys were to concentrate on the "business of farming." Although the terms reflected gender distinctions in the children's work, it is unlikely that anyone who indentured these children would refrain from putting both girls and boys to work in fields, if needed.[40]

Many parents, relatives, and friends protested the terms of indentures. Persons concerned about the children's welfare viewed the agreements as labor contracts designed to place newly freed children in a state of "neo-bondage." Apprenticeships, like bondage, severed sentimental relationships between children and parents and undermined parental rights. The indentures also dispossessed parents of their children's labor, which was vital to many as they struggled toward economic independence. Consequently, intense fights between parents or relatives and white employers ensued. The Freedmen's Bureau often served as a third party in these conflicts because of its responsibility to assist in the negotiation of contracts.[41]

Freedmen's Bureau records are replete with accounts of parents demanding nullification of contracts and claiming rights over children for whom they could provide. An Alabama judge said few black parents were "willing to bind their children whether they can support them or not." There were bureau agents who agreed with the judge based upon their own experiences with the parents of children who were bound out. The objections from parents and the disaffections of children knew no geographical bounds. Some children ran away to parents, who refused to return them. Other children, including the twelve-year-old Gloster and the thirteen-year-old, Jason, invoked their rights as freed persons and made complaints to a Freedmen's Bureau official in Arkansas on their own.[42]

Complaints lodged with the Freedmen's Bureau by children or adults were not uncommon because of its role in assisting freedpersons when negotiating labor contracts and overseeing apprenticeships. In terse language, the agents recorded complaints along with the actions taken. According to the Arkansas Freedmen's Bureau agent, Jason appeared before him in March 1867, the boy was nearly barefoot and in rags. The child's appearance was a reflection of his state of well-being. He complained that Bob Folley, his white employer, had abused him because he was not physically able to lift a log. The agent sent the boy to work elsewhere until he could investigate the alleged abuse. In the meantime, Jason's mother went to the bureau office and argued that Jason "should be cared for" and took him home.[43]

Like Jason, Gloster, a former slave, made two complaints on his own. First, he charged that his employer, Mrs. Moore, had beaten him over the head and arms with a fire shovel. Second, he claimed that she had not paid him for the work performed in 1866. After Gloster made his initial complaint, his mother confirmed that the child had not received any compensation for his services. On March 23, 1867, the agent referred Gloster's case to three disinterested parties. An April 12, 1867, entry in the register of complaints regarding Gloster says the referees, or disinterested parties, refused to act. Two weeks later, the agent noted, "On coming to trial today, Hudgens proposed to pay the woman [possibly Gloster's mother] $9" and costs. This was apparently agreeable to Gloster; therefore, the agent noted, "The case was so adjusted."[44]

In a rather unusual complaint to the bureau, the seventeen-year-old South Carolinian, Adam, appealed to the local agent with a request to keep the wages earned for himself. Adam said his mother was dead and claimed that he was "a bastard." Furthermore, he saw no reason to share money with a man, referred to as his "so called father," whom the teenager claimed did not treat him well. On July 4, 1866, the agent granted Adam approval to "select a guardian." Ironically, on the anniversary of the thirteen colonies declaring themselves independent from England, Adam received "independence" from his "so called father," but he was not completely free of the bureau's paternalistic hand since it could still oversee Adam's labor contracts and adjudicate relationships with his guardian, if needed. Obviously, the agent had decided the seventeen-year-old was not yet independent, or mature, enough to be an emancipated adult. Guardians were not necessary for independent adults.[45]

Adam, who had been freed by the Thirteenth Amendment, claimed a new meaning for his liberation and made his complaint through the proper channels, which as a free person was within his rights. Similar to Adam, James Warner, who was born a slave in Mississippi in 1810 or 1811 despised the treatment meted out to him by a parent, his mother, an emancipated woman. Unlike Adam, James had no legal rights as a slave and could not seek redress from federal authorities. Both boys were articulate, could explain their grievances, and wanted relief from an overbearing parent. The differences in results are attributed to the periods of time in which James and Adam lived and their legal status. James took matters into his own hands: he ran away from slavery and changed his identity by claiming to be an American Indian. Adams received relief without resorting to such drastic measures. The absence of slavery made the difference in the boys' actions.[46]

Girls and boys experienced added measures of freedom once the act of binding out subsided with the outlawing of the black codes and passage of the 1866 Civil Rights Act along with the United States Supreme Court striking down Maryland's apprenticeship law in 1867. Furthermore, the North Carolina Supreme Court decision *In the Matter of Harriet Ambrose and Eliza Ambrose* (1867) signaled the death knell for apprenticeships in that state.[47]

The end of apprenticeships for newly freed black children in North Carolina was linked to the treatment of several children. In September 1866, two minor children of Lucy Ross were taken from her home at gunpoint by their former owner Daniel Lindsay Russell, Sr. The children were jailed in Brunswick County before the magistrate apprenticed them to Russell, a planter, judge, and state legislator. Russell argued that he had a right to indenture the girls because their mother was not married. North Carolina's statutes permitted county courts to indenture the children of unmarried black women without parental consent.[48]

Rather than pursue the case in the interest of the Ross girls with their mother as the plaintiff, bureau agents found a similar case involving Wiley Ambrose, a freed black man with legal rights, and encouraged him to sue Russell. In December 1865, Russell had apprenticed Eliza, John Allen, and Harriet, without the consent of their parents, Wiley Ambrose and his wife Hepsey Saunders. Russell had owned the

Saunders and Ambrose family. The parents complained about the apprenticeships to the local Freedmen's Bureau. In June 1866, upon orders of the Freedmen's Bureau, Saunders entered Russell's property and retrieved her children. Russell in turn managed to apprentice the children a second time, and Saunders removed them from his possession again. General O. O. Howard, head of the Freedmen's Bureau supported Saunders and Ambrose and encouraged them to seek legal redress. Russell's actions were in violation of the Civil Rights Act of 1866.[49]

When the North Carolina Supreme Court heard the case, *In the matter of Harriet Ambrose and Eliza Ambrose* (1867), the Freedmen's Bureau lawyers on behalf of the Saunders Ambrose children entered two arguments. The first asserted that the girls were a part of a legitimate household and not subjected to apprenticeships as dependants who were orphaned or not connected to legitimate families. The second argument was linked to the children's rights as citizens. The Court decided that the children's rights had been violated and concluded that all persons involved in the negotiations, including the children, must be present at the time of binding to constitute a legal contract. Russell had violated the rights of the children, and the indentures, according to the Court, were null. The ruling recognized the rights of children and meant the cessation of binding North Carolina's former slave children in the manner as had proceeded following emancipation.[50]

The Court's decision along with the effort of parents protected their childhood from involuntary servitude that snatched away any protected time the children may have had before assuming work responsibilities on their own. Newly freed parents were not opposed to their offspring working outside their own homes, but they demanded the right to make decisions about the conditions under which their children toiled, the amount of compensation they received, and the duration of their services.

Under optimum conditions, parents with agricultural backgrounds preferred working for themselves with their children's assistance. However, without land of their own, they sought work in labor units made up of families and friends. For example, on July 22, 1865, 175 ex-slaves constituting forty-two families, headed by men as well as women in Dougherty County, Georgia, agreed to remain on the plantation of their former owner and work for shares of the crops they produced. The seventy-six children under eighteen years of age were now under the direction and care of family members rather than a white employer.[51]

There are many examples of families working together in postwar labor units and labor contracts often list the names of boys and girls along with their signs, "x," to indicate that they were integral parts of the agreements. The Wake County, North Carolina planter Alonzo T. Mial, who produced a bountiful crop in 1859 with fourteen hands, "mostly women and small boys and girls," entered a January 29, 1866, agreement with twenty-seven workers. The contract required that they

rise at day break & attend to all duties preparatory to getting to work by Sun rise, and work till Sun Set, and when ever necessary even after Sun Set to Secure the crop from frost, or taking up fodder or housing cotton in picking Season after the days work is over, or any other Small jobs liable to loss by not being attended to the night before.

Among those signing the edict to work faithfully and behave respectfully were eleven males twenty-one years of age or younger. Three of the six females were eighteen years of age or less.[52]

Mial provided monthly rations and wages in exchange for their labor according to gender. For example, Seaton Hinton, an eighteen-year-old male was to receive fifteen pounds of bacon, one bushel of meal, and ten dollars in wages each month. The compensation for Elizabeth Alston, also eighteen years old, was twelve pounds of bacon, one bushel of meal, and five dollars. The differences in compensation for two fifteen year olds are similar. Stellar Alston, probably Elizabeth's sister, was to receive twelve pounds of bacon, one bushel of meal, and four dollars while her contemporary, Rheubin Miles, would have twelve pounds of bacon, one bushel of meal, and six dollars each month.[53]

Two fourteen-year-old boys received the same compensation in cash and commodities. In only one instance did a girl, eleven-year-old Rebecca Miles, receive more money, three dollars, than a boy of her age or near her age. The twelve-year-old Alex Miles, probably an older sibling, received two dollars per month. Otherwise their compensations were the same.[54]

The Mial contract contains several implicit assumptions. Among them is the recognition of adults at eighteen years of age when cash earnings and food allocations reached the maximum allowed. Also, the compensation for adult males outdistanced women, but more arresting is seeing boys between fourteen and seventeen earning more than women over eighteen years old. Aside from these disparities in wages, the food allotments varied by gender. It appeared that Mial assumed Elizabeth and Stellar needed less meat than Seaton and Rheubin. This is probably related to the assumption that men's work was more labor intensive and demanded more energy. While this may be true of plow hands, it is unlikely that other general fieldwork exacted more from men than women. Mial made specific differences in compensations, yet all workers, regardless of age and gender, signed the same labor agreement.[55]

Disparities aside, families working together provided some protection of their offspring's childhood and against sexual exploitation, a concern of many parents. Especially poignant is a letter written by a freedman living in Ohio who considered returning to the South to work for his former owner but hesitated before finalizing any labor contract without some assurance of "safety" for his young daughters. Although the concerned father is not specific in mentioning the sexual exploitation of his older daughters, he is clear in asserting that he will not tolerate any violation of his younger daughters. In fact, he claimed to be willing to remain in Ohio and starve to death rather than subject his family to this kind of abuse that was endemic during slavery.[56]

After emancipation the number of black females laboring in southern agriculture declined much to the dismay of white planters who had assumed they could depend upon them as they had during slavery. Whites accused women of "female loaferism" and "playing the lady," meaning acting like white women who did not work in fields. The decisions to withdraw from the labor force had little, if anything, to do with any inkling to imitate white women. The gross disparities in wages for women and girls must have been a significant factor. Furthermore, the women and girls' desire for freedom from abuse, whether it was sexual exploitation or harsh labor conditions were important considerations as were concerns about fulfilling their own ambitions, including working for themselves.[57]

Some freedpersons were able to acquire their own land, but the majority did not have the wherewithal to do so. A viable alternative was working in family units as tenants or sharecroppers. Fewer women heads of households perfected sharecropping arrangements because of the demands for heavy labor that they alone could not provide. Consequently, their households depended upon the labor of children more than others. In situations where the children were too young to render assistance on farms, women found other forms of employment based solely upon their own labor.

Despite the need for their labor in securing a family's well being, there was enough reprieve for many boys and girls to attend school, a childhood expectation. On a basic level, education would instill the ability to reconcile accounts and negotiate labor contracts which was necessary in establishing an economic foundation leading to independence from perpetual servitude. In short, literacy offered some protection against malevolent whites intent upon cheating ex-slaves out of wages and recapturing much of the labor they once owned.[58]

On occasions before emancipation, the freeborn teacher Maria W. Stewart said "Knowledge is Power." Could this multitude of blacks empower themselves and their communities through education? Were they mentally capable of undertaking this challenge and fulfilling a social responsibility to their people? Prevailing stereotypes suggested that blacks were innately inferior and less capable than whites intellectually. Since the majority of black Americans were enslaved, they had virtually no opportunity to contest racist illusions about their capacities. Yet, an estimated 5 percent of slaves were literate in 1860. They succeeded by teaching themselves, learning from other blacks, and selected whites. The actual numbers remain unknown. Admitting literacy might have been an admission to violating plantation rules or legal restrictions, especially after the 1831 insurrection led by the literate preacher Nat Turner; therefore, some slaves pled ignorance when questioned about their ability to read and write.[59]

Once slavery ended along with the formal and informal prohibitions against literacy, freed boys and girls showed extraordinary interests in acquiring an education. A large number of children gathered for instruction in Louisiana after General Nathaniel P. Banks issued Order No. 38, March 22, 1864, to create a Board of Education in the Department of the Gulf, southern states under Union control, with the authority to establish schools, hire teachers, and develop curriculums. Between March 1864 and January 1866, 14,000 children enrolled in nearly 150 schools staffed by 265 teachers.[60]

The Department of the Gulf schools operated daily from 8:45 AM until 2:30 PM with a one-hour recess at mid-day for all children under twelve years of age. Their school days began with roll call followed by "either the singing of an appropriate melody, the repeating of the Lord's Prayer or the reading of a selection from the Bible." If boys and girls were not learning to read or practice their reading, they were to perform suitable exercises on their slates. Children who did not toe the line were subjected to modes of punishments that did not "differ in any respect from those employed in white schools."[61]

When threatened with closing schools in the Department of the Gulf, a flood of petitions poured into the state legislature. One petition, thirty feet long, contained 10,000 signatures and "x" marks. Persons signing indicated that they would willingly help pay for the education of their children. Education was more meaningful than simply learning to read and write. To be sure, it freed the mind of ignorance, but it did much to create independence in decision making for individuals, families, and communities.[62]

Other efforts at teaching the freed children came from black communities, benevolent organizations often called freedmen's aid societies, and associations linked to major religious denominations along with the Freedmen's Bureau, which assumed the responsibility of coordinating educational efforts in seventeen states and the District of Columbia. As a result of these combined efforts, a myriad of schools ranging from elementary, secondary, and normal to collegiate emerged. The Congregationalist missionary and first General Superintendent of schools established by the Freedmen's Bureau, John W. Alvord, observed the "thirst for knowledge among the negroes" concomitant with large numbers of teachers who volunteered to instruct them. Within this context Booker T. Washington's comment "It was a whole race trying to go to school" becomes more meaningful.[63]

As of January 1, 1866, there were 90,589 black students under the tutelage of 1,314 teachers in 740 schools across the South. The best schools, according to Alvord, were those in large towns. Virginia led in terms of the numbers of children, 12,898, enrolled in ninety schools, and a teaching staff of 195. The throngs of children gathered for instructions in places that defy the traditional idea of a "schoolhouse." The teacher Elizabeth Bond described her school as a "rough log house, thirty feet square and so open that the crevices admitted light sufficient without the aid of windows." The children sat on "undressed plank benches without backs" An "old steamboat stove" found in the river heated the room.[64]

The structure and condition of the schools were of less importance than what the pupils were to learn and how well they would use their educations. Students received the basic fundamentals in addition to much encouragement to improve home life and family conditions. Teachers challenged them to work intelligently, cultivate habits of thrift, and acquire property within the community. The underlying message fostered the idea that if blacks avoided sloth, immorality, intemperance, and indifference, whites would eventually accept them as worthy citizens of the community.[65]

The ages of the pupils and conditions of their clothing were inconsequential to the males and females who gathered in night schools, day schools, and Sunday schools. Their enthusiasm for education outdistanced the resources for hiring teachers and constructing buildings.[66]

John Alvord's semiannual school reports often lacked specificity regarding the curricular offerings. An exception came in his detailed report about the progress in

Alabama. Alvord wrote:

> The progress made by the majority of the scholars is truly surprising. The school opened in May, 1865 and now there are classes in all the different readers, from the Pictorial Primer to the Rhetorical Fifth Reader. One class is now in fractions of Robinson's Arithmetic; one class in intellectual arithmetic, reciting in reduction; other classes are well advanced in English grammar and geography.

The Alabama report differed from those coming from other states only in details. There were general comments about children receiving a common education or specific references to reading, writing, geography, and English grammar. The Superintendent mentioned "industrial schools" more than once in his first report; but, he did not comment about the objectives.[67]

Ordinarily, industrial training was highly gendered with girls receiving specific instructions in matters considered relevant to housekeeping and domestic affairs while agricultural and mechanical training were the reserve of boys. By January 1868, the Superintendent's report delineated facets of industrial training including sewing, knitting, and straw braiding along with the cutting, making, and repairing garments.[68]

Six months later Alvord's report contained lengthy commentary saying the "trace of feminine delicacy" was nonexistent among former bondswomen due to the burdensome work they had performed, the absence of family integrity, and subjection to gross passions during slavery. The conditions under which the enslaved woman lived had degraded and "forced her back to the stupor and brutality of the savage state." To alleviate this situation, Alvord wrote, "we must, with a just appreciation of the causes of this ruin, lay plans of recovery." Schools associated with the religious denominations had already incorporated lessons in their texts, which stressed manners and morals within a Christian atmosphere for the elevation of the race. No doubt Alvord's intent was to order training and behavior for girls and boys that was acceptable and fit within the parameters of current social conventions.[69]

If children could not attend regular classes, many persevered and went to school after the workday ended. Booker T. Washington explained the quandry he faced when his stepfather insisted that he work in the salt mines. Although disappointed, Washington arranged a workable alternative. "These night lessons were so welcome that I think I learned more at night than the other children did during the day," he wrote. Freedpersons who remained illiterate were generally unable to attend school because of pressing economic circumstances, lack of schools in their vicinity, or racial intimidation.[70]

Many whites did not support the ex-slaves' drive for education; therefore, it was not uncommon for them to burn schools, threaten teachers, and frighten children. Each of these vile acts encroached upon an idyllic childhood of schoolboys and girls. A witness testifying before the Joint Select Committee on Reconstruction, created by the Thirty-Ninth Congress, which met in December 1865, stated that blacks in Surry County, Virginia, were afraid to carry books although they were eager to learn to read, and there was no school in the area. The environment was far from conducive for learning, especially knowing local whites "would kill any one who would go down there and establish a colored school."[71]

Although intimidation and violence created an atmosphere of fear and encroached upon their childhood, they did not snuff out the thirst for education among many black boys and girls. Knowledge empowered individuals and communities. George Briggs never learned to read or write and was exasperated. "Dar is times," he said, "when I gets lost fer not knowing. I can't keep up. kaise I cannot read."[72]

The expansion of civil rights into the political arena by state legislation and the Fifteenth Amendment was significant in the creation of black manhood grounded in education and economic independence. Although women and children did not participate actively in electoral politics, they benefitted from male political participation and perhaps learned about the political process by attending political events or discussion at home.

Political participation was a shared activity by families and communities since its consequences fell upon voters and nonvoters alike. Such a situation made children and adults, aware of responsibilities not only to themselves but also the community. Commonalities in their heritage and previous conditions of servitude remained at the base of their political consciousness.[73]

Just as many whites objected to the access to education for black children, there were those who objected to black involvement in a new political order. As a result, some instituted a new kind of vicious intimidation and violence that was unknown prior to the Civil War. To be sure, enslaved women and girls were raped by owners and others, but following the general emancipation in 1865 the violence perpetrated by rowdy gangs of white men and organized secret societies used rape as an instrument of terror. Intent on punishing freedpersons who deviate from the expected norm as established in slavery, whites violated civil rights and liberties with abandon.[74]

Newly freedpersons looked to local law enforcement agencies for relief from this terror but were often dismayed with the results. Yet, they managed to survive through their religious conventions that a higher power would reward the steadfast and punish the vile. Others migrated to protect themselves and to provide their offspring with a childhood free from terror. They realized early on that freedom was not the idyllic stuff of dreams. It was up to them to forge it to their liking and make it meaningful. Indeed, that was possible once they reunited with families, secured a home of their own, acquired an education, and had the financial means to support themselves.

Margrett Nillin, who had worked as a personal servant in Texas before emancipation, reflected upon the change in her status. "In slavery I owns nothin'," remembered the ninety-year-old Nillin who emphasized the futile possibilities of claiming possessions of her own when she added, "[I] *never* owns nothin'." By contrast, Nillin, who was twenty-one years at the time of her emancipation, explained the changes over time when she said, "In freedom I's own de home and raise de family." According to the freedwoman, "All dat cause[d] me worryment." She did not have comparable frustrations in bondage, but as a free woman she could make vital decisions about her own time, labor, and life as well as that of her children. Moreover, she was in a position to protect her offspring from anything that could encroach upon their childhood. When given a choice between remaining enslaved and being emancipated, "I takes freedom" Nillin said without hesitation. Similarly, Victoria Adams, one of Nillin's contemporaries remembered the early years of her life and said, "I like being free more better."[75]

Figure 6   New arrivals including Eva Shawnee in 1900

Source: Courtesy of Hampton University Archives, Hampton, Virginia.

CHAPTER SIX

BLACK AND RED EDUCATION AT HAMPTON INSTITUTE: A CASE STUDY OF THE SHAWNEE INDIANS, 1900–1925

Hampton Normal and Agriculture Institute, founded by General Samuel C. Armstrong, son of American missionaries in Hawaii and a Union commander of black soldiers in the Civil War, opened its doors for newly freed blacks in 1868. Hampton has a long tradition of educating students of African descent; however, a significant but less well-known facet of the institution's history is its role in defining the education of native Americans between 1877 and 1923. Hampton Institute sought to educate the two peoples in academics, industrial trades, and manual training, along with Christian education. David Wallace Adams's study of the education of Arizona's Hopi Indians between 1887 and 1917 reveals similarities with Hampton's system: in both cases, administrators appeared more interested in "civilizing" and "Americanizing" the "oldest" Americans than providing well-rounded academic instruction. The implied objective was to force Native Americans to give up their customs. Integral to this process was the abandonment of their traditional names, clothing, and religion. Although a number of scholars have included discussions about Indians at the institution in larger studies, others, primarily ph. d. dissertations and m. a. theses, have remained unpublished. Donal F. Lindsey's *Indians at Hampton Institute, 1877–1923* is the seminal publication on the subject. This study, by contrast, focuses on an even smaller facet of Indian education—that of the "Shawnees," eight black students designated as Native Americans. The success of Hampton Institute's Indian program may be measured by studying these students, six of whom participated in programs "for Indians only" while the other two were classified as "Negroes" and integrated into the general student body of African Americans.[1]

Beyond the apparent desired cultural transformation within a highly regimented environment, students learned to speak and write English, acquire knowledge of American history, and gain a basic understanding of science, mathematics, and geography. After studying the Hopi schools, Adams concluded that "if instruction in academic subjects was an important aspect of the Indian's education, it was clearly secondary to instruction in manual and vocational trades."[2]

Hampton Institute's curriculum differed in that it combined academic and vocational training in an attempt to prepare students for teaching once they returned to their local communities. The preponderance of Hampton's early students lived in areas where schools were few and had short terms. As a result, the teachers' earnings were meager; therefore, Hampton encouraged its teachers-in-training to own land and have industrial and agricultural training as a means of support when not teaching.

An agreement between General Armstrong and Richard H. Pratt, the U.S. army captain responsible for seventy-five American Indian prisoners at St. Augustine, Florida, resulted in their enrollment at Hampton. The Indians had been incarcerated because of their participation in the Plains Wars. Pratt had accompanied the prisoners to Florida and while there, they learned the fundamentals of reading, writing, and arithmetic. Once the government decided to release them, Pratt believed they would be better served if they continued their education in the East rather than returning to their homes in the West. Pratt corresponded with Armstrong about their matriculation at Hampton Institute, and the general's initial reluctance gave way once he learned that several of the Indians had earned thousands of dollars selling their crafts. Enrolling Indians at Hampton Institute had the potential for bringing additional income into the school.[3]

Education for Native American took on greater importance in 1870 when Congress allocated $140,000 with increases totaling nearly $2 million by 1900. As early as 1872, Armstrong toyed with the possibility of educating Indians at Hampton Institute. In a June 5, 1872, letter to his wife, Emma, he wrote,

> I am on the track of some more money—it will be necessary to prove that the darkey is an Indian in order to get it, but I can easily do that you know . . . Keep dark about it & send me your thought on the identity of the *Indian* & *darkey* same thing arn't they?

Armstrong showed a missionary spirit and desire for pecuniary benefits when he concluded, "Tis a hopeful tree to bark up."[4]

Armstrong's initial interest in Native Americans perhaps came through Edward Parmelee Smith, a member of the Hampton Institute board of trustees. Smith, the corresponding secretary of the American Missionary Association received an appointment as commissioner of Indian Affairs in 1870. Aside from knowing Smith, Armstrong's father was a missionary in Hawaii where young Samuel had lived, and he seemed to meld the missionary-type interest in educating newly freed slaves with the Indians. Armstrong believed the institute could indeed educate and change the lives of both African Americans and Native Americans. The benefits of educating the students was evident in the improvements in their lives and that of their offspring. Beyond that, the school would receive money for the federal government for its part in educating Indians.[5]

Fifteen American Indians arrived at Hampton Institute under military escort on April 13, 1878. By October, Secretary of Interior Carl Schurz notified Armstrong that Congress would appropriate $167 annually for each of the students enrolled up to a total of 120. The allotment paid for their board, transportation, and clothing. Students agreed to remain for three years and spend the summers on an "outing," or work assignment, in the Northeast with selected white families where they could acquire domestic and agricultural skills besides earning money to defray expenses during the upcoming year.[6]

Between 1878 and 1923, 1,388 students from sixty-five different Indian Nations attended Hampton Institute. The Institute's administrators soon realized that the annual appropriation was not "easy money." There were constant struggles to get the bill passed each year. Hampton Institute became a microcosm of matters relating to the social, educational, economic, and religious welfare of American Indians.[7]

Educating African Americans and Native Americans together on the Virginia peninsula caused an untold amount of apprehension. Harvard professor and minister Francis Greenwood Peabody described this anxiety in his study of Hampton Institute, *Education for Life: The Story of Hampton Institute*, when he wrote, "Friends of the Indian intimated that the noble Red Man would be degraded by association with the Negro." Critics complained that Hampton Institute would become "a reformatory for Indian criminals," and others feared that the two "would fall in love with each other."[8]

If Armstrong harbored such anxieties, he kept them to himself and asserted that the experiment had reciprocal benefits. "Our colored students . . . furnish the best practical conditions for building up wild Indians in ideas of decency and manhood," he declared. Additionally, Armstrong said black students would be "richer and stronger for doing a good part for the Indian, and the exchange of ideas is better education as it is a greater power for good." To learn English and "civilized" customs faster, the original group of American Indians petitioned the administration for black roommates.[9]

The Institute experienced an anomaly in educating Native Americans when the first of eight "Shawnees" enrolled in 1900. Eva, Lafayette, Julia, Emaline, Lydia, Rebecca, Myrtle, and David were children of William Shawnee, a runaway slave, and Julia, a freed Creek woman. The Shawnees had captured and adopted William, hence his family took the surname "Shawnee." One Hampton official said the family was "colored" and "not Indian at all." He explained Julia's racial designation: "All Creek Freedmen and women are Negro pure and simple." Although descendants of Africans, the Shawnees enjoyed all rights and privileges of American Indians. Hampton's faculty, staff, administrators, and students regarded them as Native Americans. Moreover, the government allotted $167 per year for their education.[10]

If the Shawnees were indeed "Negro[es] pure and simple," why did they enjoy the privileges of Native Americans and government support at Hampton rather that the status of African Americans? Armstrong did not have the Shawnees in mind when he made the cryptic remark about the necessity of proving that the "darkey is an Indian." Born in Maui, Hawaii, in 1839 where his father, Richard, was a missionary, Samuel Armstrong arrived in the United States in 1860 to attend Williams College but left and managed to secure a commission at the outbreak of the Civil War. He rose to the rank of Brevet General after commanding the Eighth and Ninth Regiments of United States Colored Troops. Armstrong saw people of color as "backwards," inferior to Anglo Saxons, and in need of religious and educational training to uplift themselves and their peoples whether they were Hawaiians, African Americans, or Native Americans. In his eyes, there were finite differences but in general they were indeed the "same thing."[11]

By looking at race this way, perhaps Armstrong intuited the current understanding of race as a social and historical construction based upon illusions, theories, contexts, chances, and choices rather than a biological entity. The Shawnee students fit into a group united by historical contingents, shared history, social interactions, and context. Their father's adoption by the Shawnee provided the social setting and historical context for the children's "racial identity." Their mother, a Creek freedwoman, was apparently the offspring of a man of African descent and a Creek woman. If the status of such children followed that of their mother, they were considered Creek regardless of the father's nationality. The Shawnee children, whether among American Indians because of their mother's birth or their father's adoption, were at home among people, who accepted them as members of their cultural community. The Shawnee family exercised a choice in remaining among the Native Americans once slavery ended and William Shawnee's refuge was no longer a concern. The Shawnees may have been "Negroes pure and simple," but they were recognized, albeit temporarily, as Indians at Hampton.[12]

The Shawnees were not the first Indian students of mixed parentage at the Institute. Among their predecessors were descendants of Caucasian, Africans, and Native Americans. Students who were seventh-eighths Caucasian did not need special permission to attend Hampton and were eligible for government support, but those who were fifteen-sixteenths white needed verification of the Native American cultural heritage. In 1910, the sixteen-year-old Leta Meyers entered Hampton and created a sensation when her father paid her fees "all in one lump sum." This was clearly different from the majority of Indians who were too impoverished to support themselves and depended upon the government subsidy.[13]

Leta Meyers was one-sixteenth Indian and proved to be "unsatisfactory, proud, quick tempered, self-centered, and impertinent," according to Hampton's officials, she often criticized the Institute and told students there were other schools as "good or better." Hampton Institute's administrators concluded that she was a "disturbing element" and did not fit in culturally. In short, "real" Indians were less likely to challenge authority or articulate disaffections with the Indian program. Hampton did not tolerate "disturbing elements" and planned to dismiss her but found it impossible due to a clerical error.[14]

Rather than sending a letter informing Meyers of her dismissal, she received correspondence saying the government had withdrawn its yearly allocation for Indian education. Meyers responded to Hampton's missive saying, "The appropriation being stoped [sic] does not interfere with my plans" to return. She added, "My parents and myself think it best that I should continue my studies there." Eager to return, she asked, "When should I report?" The Institute had failed to properly notify Meyers and was obliged to permit her enrollment. However, George Phenix, an administrator, advised Meyers that the decision was conditional provided that she had a "different spirit" and that her family agreed to keep her return train fare on deposit in the treasurer's office.[15]

More than twenty students of African and Indian descent attended the Institute and received government funding between 1881 and 1923. Culture rather than color was the criteria for admission. If a student's mother belonged to a government-recognized and funded Indian nation, he or she was eligible for federal support as an

Indian. Adoption or incorporation into a tribe also made students eligible for admission. If a student did not qualify for federal support as an Indian, he or she could be admitted as an African American and qualify for financial assistance from private donors.[16]

Eva, the first of the Shawnee family to register, had attended a government school located near her home for nine years. Local Hampton alumni encouraged her to matriculate. Mary E. Williams, superintendent of the Absentee-Shawnee School, recommended Eva as a bright, industrious pupil, taught by the "best teachers" in her school "without prejudice." She was anxious about Eva's social adjustment since the girl had not associated with local "colored people," deemed as an "inferior order" by Williams. She wondered whether Hampton's white administrators and faculty would view Eva as red or black. How would American Indians from ex-slaveholding families perceive her? To alleviate any possible discomforts, Williams suggested that she enter the institution as an Indian student and live "among her own people until she learns that the Negro race can be respectful and respected." Williams claimed, "The peculiar circumstances of her life and surroundings give her no settled place in life."[17]

Eva and five of her siblings lived among Native American students, not because the superintendent requested it or due to a lack of respect by blacks, but because the government classified the Shawnees as American Indians and the institution had no qualms with this designated ethnicity. Between 1900 and 1912, the Shawnees and other African American students did not intermix. The Shawnees interacted only with American Indians, the very group the government and critics prohibited from associating with African Americans. This raises questions about the flexible nature of Hampton Institute's interpretation of cultural identity especially when it considered admitting Lydia Shawnee as a "Negro" in 1906, if the Indian quota were filled. Would the school house her among African Americans temporarily and then relocate her to the Indian dormitory as the quota changed?[18]

For a brief period, Native American and African American students may have interacted freely, but the racial climate in the late nineteenth and early twentieth centuries made this situation untenable. Hampton Institute segregated the students by color and claimed to do so in order to "fulfill an agreement with the . . . government" and for "reasons of diet." One historical study of the Institute suggests that "tensions . . . forced the creation of separate living facilities for Indians." "They were organized into separate military companies, ate in different dining rooms, took their recreation separately" and "racial blocks" existed in seating arrangements for religious services at the school's chapel.[19]

Further separations existed. Hampton built a dormitory, the Wigwam, for American Indian men in 1879 and partitioned off parts of Cleveland Hall until Winona Lodge could be built for the women. American Indian basketball teams played whites while African American teams only played other blacks. Local white churches invited Native Americans to worship at their regular services but did not extend invitations to black students.[20]

Conditions within Hampton Institute's grounds were a microcosm of those in the local community. Multicultural education at Hampton Institute was fraught, according to historian Robert Engs, with "all of the absurdities, hypocrisies, contradictions, and injustices inherent in American racial attitudes." School officials claimed students segregated themselves "naturally," and that racism on the part of the school did not exist. Probing through school records, letters, and publications suggests otherwise. Yet, Hampton Institute did relax racial barriers when expedient and when it was clearly in its best financial interests to do so.[21]

African Americans and Native Americans ate in different dining rooms until segregated rooms gave way to separate tables in a common dining room. These changes reflected declines in Native American enrollment and the Institute's fiscal interests. This reorganization upset social conventions in 1910 when the "Indian table" did not have enough chairs to accommodate all of its students. One Native American assigned to the "colored table . . . refused to go there." She ate only when another American Indian was absent. This "musical chairs" arrangement among the students reflected notions about their own identity and unwillingness to break bread with students who differed from themselves. This "problem" of color pride or prejudice was serious enough to warrant administrative action. After several faculty meetings where they discussed the issue, the student reversed her position and sat where she had been assigned.[22]

What such a decision meant to the student's emotional well-being is unknown. And, it is unknown how the African American students responded to the stranger, who had already registered her displeasure in having to dine with them. Perhaps the Native American complied under duress and the African Americans also conformed to the wishes of the school's administration. Students, black or red, male and female, learned early on that they either toed the line established by Hampton Institute and remained in good standing, or they faced possible disciplinary action and expulsion.

Fiscal constraints were often behind moves toward further integration. When the Institute's physician recommended closing the Indian hospital and treating students, without regard for color, together, the principal agreed. This decision escaped commentary in the school newspaper, *The Southern Workman*, and the Indian newspaper, *Talks and Thoughts*.[23]

As a routine matter, Hampton Institute encountered racial attitudes among students already enrolled or those considering matriculation. In 1880, Captain Pratt told the Commissioner of Indian Affairs that several potential students refused to attend school with blacks. Perhaps they had formed biased opinions based on conversations with students who had attended Hampton Institute and returned to the reservation. Nevertheless, no amount of persuasion on Pratt's part at Standing Rock could overcome prejudices against American Indians attending school with African Americans. A decade later, Helen W. Ludlow, author of *Ten Years' Work Among the Indians at Hampton, Virginia*, said "prejudice of color has been shown occasionally by some students from Indian territory, where Indians have held slaves." While at Hampton, the administrators considered the comfort level of their environment and recommended that no new Indian girls be admitted in summer 1914 while the other Indian students were away on outings, because "It would be killingly lonely . . . besides prejudice is too strong." Obviously, Ludlow believed the racial climate was inhospitable and that any new students would be more subjected to it. Besides, they would not have the companionship of other Native American students until they returned from working at their summer jobs in the North.[24]

Hampton Institute never ceased trying to educate student across class and color barriers, including former slaves and former slaveholders. But creating a racially integrated environment was not its top priority. Administrators even went so far as to instigate racial antagonism between blacks and Indians possibly in a deliberate effort to generate academic competition. Nevertheless, Armstrong urged Indians to imitate blacks because they exemplified habits of "study and labor . . . obedience . . . and general decency." Another administrator agreed that Indians were the "gainers" when studying with "select negro [*sic*] youth" who were "not too far advanced as most white boys would be, to sympathize with the difficulties which their red brethren . . . encounter."[25]

The September 1884 issue of *The Southern Workman*, read widely by students, alumni, and white philanthropists, summarized the black–red relationship succinctly:

> The Negro has in many respects a vast advantage over the Indian, and the contrast between the future of the two races, even should the latter be given every possible chance, is so overwhelmingly in favor of the strong sinews and sound lungs of the Negroes, that in common fairness he should hold out a helping hand to his less fortunate brother, who has even more unjustly than he, been sacrificed to the interest of the white man.

The paper acknowledged gingerly that "some delicacy in the mingling of races" existed at Hampton.[26]

Tension and uncertainty about racial identity were evident among the Institute's students. In her study of Hampton's Indian program, Margaret Muir argued that "each race felt superior to the other in some way and inferior in others. The words and actions of both blacks and Indians show a sense of condescension and superiority at some times, humility and shame at others."[27]

Although the Indian students received federal funding, it was insufficient to support them entirely. As a result, the student made appeals to potential benefactors. Uncertainty is evident in Eva Shawnee's letter to her scholarship donor when the young woman wrote, "Maybe you will be disappointed when I tell you I am not an Indian." She explained that her father, a fugitive slave was adopted by the Shawnee nation. A letter from Rebecca Shawnee to her scholarship sponsor calls attention to her identity as a black woman defined as a red one. She described selected school activities in this manner:

> The best part of New Year's day was the emancipation proclamation observation at which many of the colored students brought out the improved conditions of their people by telling how they are buying homes and becoming more civilized and more responsible for holding important business offices, also being ministers . . . teachers in their own schools.

Rebecca Shawnee anticipated the Indian Citizenship Day ceremony in which Indians would discuss improvements "*their* people have made and are making." It is never clear to which group of "their people" she felt that she belonged.[28]

Each member of the Shawnee family at Hampton Institute explained his or her racial identification differently. David claimed his father, a Cherokee descendent, had migrated to Oklahoma. Julia portrayed herself as one-quarter Indian, while Eva admitted that she did not see herself as an Indian.[29]

When Emaline considered matriculation at Hampton in 1909, her older sister Eva tried to dissuade her based on her own experiences and was confident enough about her actions to reports the same to Elizabeth Hyde, an administrator at the school. "I have talked to Emmeline [*sic*] and told her of the embarrassment she will no doubt undergo, but she has decided what is best for her to do," Eva wrote to the white administrator. Emaline disregarded Eva's warnings and enrolled at Hampton Institute where she remained until 1912.[30]

In 1909, four of the Shawnees were enrolled at Hampton. Lafayette and Julia were also at the Institute while Lydia studied nursing at nearby Dixie Hospital. When David enrolled several years later, many of the school's administrators, faculty, and staff who had known his sisters and brother were still employed at the Institute. David said his first year there was like "coming home since so many of my kindred came before me." Eva was far more isolated when she enrolled in 1900.[31]

The school classified the earliest of the Shawnees to enroll as "Indians." They lived in Winona Lodge or the Wigwam; participated in Dawes Day celebrations, events marking Native American independence as defined by the Dawes General Allotment Act of 1887; joined the Christian Endeavor Society, an uplift organization for Native Americans; and the Josephines, a literary society for Indian women. School officials contributed items about the Shawnees to *Talks and Thoughts* and filed their academic records among those of other American Indians. While this is true, administrators noted the difference in the Shawnees and other Indians by writing the letter "B" for black in red ink on the Shawnees' correspondence. The red letter identified them from other Indians and mulattoes.[32]

Six of the Shawnees participated in summer outings and their experiences were similar to their contemporaries. Lydia complained about low wages and accused her employer of being cross and uneducated, thus a justification for not respecting her. But the feelings were mutual. At summer's end, the employer told Hampton officials, "I had rather try an *Indian girl* another year." Hampton granted her wish.[33]

Other Shawnees had complaints about the outing. Julia and Emaline worked together in a boarding house cooking and cleaning for twenty-five guests. Their respective salaries were $2.50 per week for the first two months and $3.00 per week afterward. Mrs. R. F. Troy, owner of the business, accused Emaline of "shirking, moodiness and a bad disposition." The capstone came when Troy demanded an earlier than usual breakfast and Emaline refused. After an intense argument, Emaline left and obtained new employment.[34]

Troy confessed distress when she wrote, "I never had anyone talk to me as Emaline did. If Emaline talked to you as she did to me and left . . . I don't think you would let her walk back in just when she chooses to . . ." This was not a "normal" relationship between a white employer and black employee. Ordinarily, white women received deference from less assertive black servants. The delicate tone of Troy's letter suggests that she really did not want Emaline to return. Emaline refused to let the matter perturb her and did not report it to the school administrators responsible for arranging the outings. When questioned, Emaline maintained an imperial stance and retorted that the whole incident was "not worth while."[35]

There are no records in Emaline Shawnee's file to indicate that Hampton reprimanded her for a display of rude behavior. Certainly the young student's actions, open disrespect for a white employer and "quitting" a job without permission from school officials, were not condoned. An unsigned memorandum in Emaline's file, probably written by the administrator responsible for coordinating the outings, saying the employer had promised the student that the work load would be lighter in September, ends with "but." Without explaining further the note indicates that Troy had failed to honor her promise of less work at the end of the summer. The boarders planned a fishing trip on Labor Day, the first Monday in September. Emaline was working within the agreement as she understood it.[36]

Hampton Institute was usually paternalistic regarding students and the outings, yet it allowed some latitude whenever students or employers requested changes. Hampton also proved forward thinking in Emaline's situation. Although the school did not openly condone her behavior, it did not demand that she return to the campus after leaving the Troy's home. Furthermore, Emaline remained at her newly acquired position, one that she had negotiated on her own, until the end of summer.[37]

Emaline's negotiations for employment proved more successful than those involving her siblings and the federal government regarding their land allotments. Land ownership, according to the founding principal Samuel Chapman Armstrong, was essential to economic independence for newly freed women and men. Furthermore, owning property within one's own community showed an interest in accepting the responsibilities of citizenship. Following Armstrong's death in 1893, the New Englander Hollis B. Frissell, an 1874 graduate of Yale University who had studied at Union theological Seminary and served as the chaplain at Hampton Institute since 1880, became the school's second principal. Frissell believed the legal and business aspects of private land ownership were beyond the ken of American Indians and said the reservation system had no interest in teaching them commercial or licit methods. To bridge this gap, Hampton Institute established a business department, and the administrators assisted students with legal matters.[38]

Frank Thackery, superintendent of Indian Affairs at Shawnee, Oklahoma, learned that several claimants said they held deeds to land owned by the Shawnees. Although the Shawnees were of African descent, their family had been adopted by the Indians and considered as Indians. Under the circumstances, they too were entitled to land allotments. Certain of fraud, Thackery informed Lafayette Shawnee that L. J. Burt and R. Shaha, attorneys in Sapulpa, Oklahoma, could clear their titles for $25.00 per case. In consultation with Frissell, the Shawnees agreed to hire them. Several weeks later, the lawyers demanded forty acres of land from each client. The superintendent was confident in the lawyers and wrote, "They believe they will win, if not they get nothing." He advised the Shawnees to get "oil and gas leases on 120 acres" of land to offset expenses and requested an immediate reply from the students.[39]

Frissell refused to act hastily and began correspondence with Attorney Thomas Sloan, a Native American alumnus of Hampton Institute. "It seemed to us that if the property is valuable and has oil on it," he explained, "the payment of forty acres each . . . is altogether too great" in view of the original agreement. By this time, Frissell had lost confidence in Burt and Shaha. Lafayette Shawnee shared his anxiety with the principal. The lawyers, he wrote, "may choose the best [land] and leave me the cheapest, they seem rather anxious." Frissell continued to advise and assist the Shawnees in what developed into a long and complicated legal battle.[40]

Less than a year after the litigation began, the Shawnees returned to Oklahoma, fired their lawyers, whom they believed deliberately "started a lie" about the land, and initiated their own investigations. Lafayette Shawnee, weary of waiting, "let his land go for $250 to $300." Julia fared worse. She entered a "paper" transaction to prevent further entanglements, but her partner sold the land located "right in the heart of oil country." Its value was about $2,000.[41]

Emaline and Lydia took different approaches. Lydia cleared her land by August 1912. Emaline tried to convince the person holding a deed to her property that the land was worthless. The "owner" of her land, a former Hampton student whom she described as "the darkey Taylor from Oklahoma," did not agree, but she was determined not to give up without a fight. Hampton Institute's last notation of the matter was in 1916. It simply said "Still at law," meaning the court had not settled the matter, and the students were not willing to let the land go to someone else. The Shawnees did not return to Hampton as planned but remained in Oklahoma to fight for their land.[42]

It is ironic that they ended their education at Hampton the same year Congress voted to terminate support of Indian education at the Institute. The Democratic control of the sixty-second Congress did not serve Hampton Institute well. Furthermore, the new chair of the House Committee on Indian Affairs, John H. Stephens was unsympathetic to the Indian program at Hampton. When the bill came up for renewal in 1912, opponents argued that it was too expensive to send Indians to Hampton rather than to western schools.[43]

Samuel W. McCall of Massachusetts said that John H. Stephens, chair of the hearings, opposed the bill for other reasons. Those reasons became obvious when Stephens asked, "Why humiliate the Indian boys and girls, our wards and dependents, by educating them in the same school with negro children?" He proposed that Indians be raised to the level of white men rather than degraded and humiliated by "sinking . . . to the low plane of the negro race."[44]

This discussion prompted Hollis B. Frissell, Hampton's principal; Booker T. Washington, Hampton's most famous graduate; and J. D. Eggleston, superintendent of public instruction for Virginia, to seek lobbyists. Representative William A. Jones defended Hampton with statements from presidents of major universities. Jones told the congressmen that "Woodrow Wilson, when president of Princeton University, endorsed the Hampton school in terms of commendation and praise scarcely less strong" than his colleagues at Harvard and Johns Hopkins Universities.[45]

During the floor debate Jones addressed the real issue, race, which prevented the continuation of funding. He argued that American Indians at Hampton, a school founded for African Americans, "never objected to the presence of negroes" in the student body. Additionally, Virginia never withheld land grant money because "Indians and negroes met together in the lecture halls and shops on the experimental farms."[46]

In the final ten minutes of debate, Representative Charles P. Carter, a Chickasaw from Oklahoma, said whites had carved the great American republic exclusively from lands owned by Native Americans, without "adequate considerations." He joked that Native Americans met white aggression with "cruel and relentless war" until whites retaliated with "benevolent assimilation," the "steam roller." The House responded with loud applauses and raucous laughter. Carter also recounted how Indians had conceded land, religion, and treaties. "Mr. Chairman, the white man has demanded and the Indian has conceded until he has nothing left but his self-respect," he continued with this line of reasoning, "Now you come to him with Hampton school and ask him to surrender that self-respect by placing his children on a social equality with an inferior race, a level to which you yourself will not deign to descend." His speech continued to amuse the congressmen who again responded with a "loud applause." Afterward, the committee chair called for a vote, and Hampton lost its funding by sixty-five to thirty-three ballots.[47]

Those who argued so bitterly against racial education and integrating the two peoples at Hampton were not aware of the Shawnees' presence in the student body, their color, or that they were among the Indians who petitioned Congress to continue funding the program. Hampton Institute recoiled from a fight because it "might be interpreted unfavorably in the South along social lines." Hampton officials sacrificed federal support for the sake of harmonious social relations. The school capitulated to racism publicly, but the faculty said privately, "We have long felt there should be no distinction made between our Negro and Indian students . . ."[48]

There were remarkable efforts to keep the program alive without federal support, substantial outside funding. Frissell transferred money designated for other purposes to the few remaining Indian students. Myrtle and David Shawnee enrolled between 1917 and 1923 and their family paid all expenses. By the time David entered, the school no longer separated student records by color, and his files are housed along with other black students rather than with his "Indian" siblings.[49]

Unlike other Shawnees at Hampton, David experienced difficulty in accepting the school's strict rules. One is left to wonder about his social adjustment in a school where six Shawnees were treated as Native Americans and the other two as African Americans. School personnel and rules remained basically unchanged between 1900 and 1923. David and Myrtle must have studied under some of the same teachers as their older siblings, which raises concerns about whether the teachers viewed all Shawnees as Native Americans or African Americans, and if the faculty continued to make distinctions as federal appropriations ended? Even more poignant is knowing if the faculty were of the same opinion as Samuel Chapman Armstrong about the racial identity of blacks and Indians being "the same thing."

As the number of students from western reservations dwindled, the Institute relaxed its racial barriers. It was too costly to maintain segregation. One teacher praised the few remaining American Indian women for their "lovely spirit and great pluck," saying "nothing has brought them out and done as much for them as placing them on the same basis as the other girls." She said they were "loyal and brave and coming out stronger than under the old regime." Six of the Shawnees had no opportunity to interact on the "same basis" with black students at Hampton. The youngest Shawnees were on the same basis as "other" students. They were the other students, indeed.[50]

After 1912, only Lafayette and Rebecca maintained continuous correspondence with favorite teachers and officials at Hampton Institute. Lafayette eagerly reported his progress. During the Great Depression, he suffered from economic downturns just as other Hamptonians, but he handled the misfortunes poorly when he learned that his 1912 academic diploma did not qualify him for state certification despite years of successful teaching, administrative, and agricultural demonstration work in Oklahoma. Economic insecurity, deprivation, and the realization that his credentials were barely equivalent to a high-school diploma exerted a tremendous amount of pressure on an otherwise strong man. He blamed Hampton Institute for much of his distress.[51]

By 1935, Lafayette's financial condition had not changed. He begged that his credits be upgraded to college work. Hampton's officials patiently adjusted his transcript for every conceivable credit to the extent that a Bible study class became "ancient history." Despite this, Lafayette complained, "I am a reputable graduate and deserve consideration." Seemingly, he failed to understand that the registrar simply could not alter high-school transcripts to make college courses.[52] Unlike Lafayette, his sister Rebecca weathered the depression admirably. She claimed that feat was possible because of the education she received at Hampton Institute. She lived by a motto, "Freely ye have received, freely give," learned there. Crop failures and devastating grasshoppers in 1936 did not change her positive attitude. Her last letter to the Institute exemplifies her sentiments: "Best wishes to all [,] [I] shall pray God's blessing on Hampton [,] my home by the sea."[53]

When assessing the education of Native Americans who attended government supported schools, the comments of Don Talayesva, a Hopi, are of interest. After several years of study, he reported:

> I could talk like a gentleman, read, write, and cipher. I could name all the states in the Union with the capitals, repeat the names of all the books in the Bible, quote a hundred verses of scripture, sing more than two dozen Christian hymns and patriotic songs, debate, shout football yells, swing my partners in square dances, bake bread, sew well enough to make a pair of trousers

and, he added, "tell 'dirty' Dutchman stories by the hours."[54]

An assessment of the skills and knowledge gained by the Shawnees reveals that they were reasonably well prepared for lifelong careers. An assessment reveals that the skills and knowledge gained by the Shawnees prepared them reasonably well for lifelong careers. They did not "return to the blanket," which in the eyes of the Hampton Institute officials was a true measure of progress, nor did the Shawnees follow the traditional jobs of many American Indians, subsistence farmers, and housewives. Eva taught in Shawnee, Oklahoma, Elizabeth City (NC) State Normal School, and at Langston University, Oklahoma. Lydia, a successful nurse, was also partner in her husband's mortuary business. Evelyn Twoguns who also attended Hampton Institute, said Lydia and her husband, owned an "automobile ambulance hearse for their trade." Twoguns made it clear that Lydia worked and contributed "her money to buy all those modern things." Only one of the Shawnees, Rebecca, returned to Oklahoma, married an American Indian, and worked a land allotment, thereby continuing to live among their people.[55]

Hampton's keen interest in fulfilling federal requirements in return for annual appropriations, and its penchant for avoiding controversy prevented six Shawnees and many other American Indians from interacting with African American students. Racism in the U. S. House of Representatives was largely responsible for the loss of funding for the Indian education program at Hampton. To be sure, the enrollment had dwindled over the years when potential students decided to attend schools closer to their homes in the West. Attending Hampton Institute without federal funding was not economically feasible.

Rather than viewing the demise of the Hampton Institute Indian education program as a failure, it may be useful to think that Hampton Institute was also a victim of its own success. A great number of the Indians who had attended Hampton returned to their homes in the West and became teachers. As representative models of the Institute and its multicultural program of education, the Hampton alumni and returned students (nongraduates) could educate boys and girls without removing them from their families. Certainly, Hampton Institute had provided the Shawnees with a fundamental education that could serve them well whether they were considered red or black.

Figure 7 Hattie Lee Cochran and Friends
Source: Courtesy Alvin R. Hunter.

CHAPTER SEVEN

WHAT A "LIFE" THIS IS: AN AFRICAN AMERICAN GIRL COMES OF AGE DURING THE GREAT DEPRESSION IN URBAN AMERICA

Throughout 1931, fifteen-year-old Hattie Lee Cochran recorded methodical summaries of her daily activities in a slim clothbound volume. The "Ready Reference Diary" contained a cornucopia of data ranging from details about the Boy Scout Movement to judging distance by sound. The diary featured helpful tidbits of information printed at the bottom of each blank page. Yet, these dry factoids pale in comparison to the wealth of information conveyed by Cochran's writings that fill the pages above them. Her daily entries reveal a tremendous amount about the life of an African American girl who came of age in urban America during the Great Depression.[1]

The 1931 diary serves as the centerpiece of this essay in its attempt to investigate the impact of the Great Depression upon Hattie Cochran's adolescence along with the extent to which these years were like or different from those of her contemporaries in Cleveland, Ohio.[2]

The diary contributes to a greater understanding of childhood and adolescence in urban America during this period; however, it is important to note that Cochran's experiences may not have been representative of black girls across class and region during the depression. Even a cursory review of several dozen interviews collected in 1986 under the rubric "Preserving African-American Culture" by the Sadie J. Anderson Missionary Society of St. James African Methodist Episcopal Church in Cleveland reveals significant differences in experience among persons in Cochran's East Cleveland neighborhood in the 1920s and 1930s.[3]

Furthermore, publications by and about Cochran's contemporaries Pearl Bailey (1918–1990), Billie Holiday (1915–1959), Lena Horne (1917–), Elizabeth Catlett (1919–), Margaret Walker (1915–1998), Dorothy Height (1912–), and Florence Kennedy (1916–), provide different coming-of-age stories. These well-known women spent their adolescence in cities such as Brooklyn, Washington, D.C., Birmingham, Richmond, and Kansas City, during the 1920s and 1930s.[4]

Several examples will suffice. By the time the Virginia-born Pearl Bailey was in her teens, she was working outside the home. She earned extra money cleaning houses on Fridays for Jewish families in Philadelphia and was clear when saying, "Mama didn't send us; it was my ambition to work, so she said okay." By the time she was fifteen years old, Bailey was attracted to the world of entertainment through her brother, Willie, who was earning a "big reputation in show business as a tap dancer." Once she landed a job that promised to pay thirty dollars per week, she had no interest in babysitting for her older sister and admitted that "School suddenly lost its charm." Pearl was far more interested in the entertainment world and made her way into it.[5]

Lena Horne's entry into the entertainment world also came at an early age. Having grown up in a prominent middle-class family in New York, Horne attended a school of dance and received voice and dramatic lessons. By 1934, Lena Horne had made her debut in the famous Cotton Club. The *Amsterdam News* reported, "Miss Lena Horne is a woiking goil but earning her bread does not interfere with the business of getting an education." The youngest member of the new revue at the Cotton Club attended Wadleigh Night High School and she earned twenty-five dollars per week for three shows each night of the week. Horne, like Bailey, seemed delighted with having her own money, and it appears that each of the young entertainers worked because of their own interest rather than economic necessity.[6]

The life of the Alabama-born Margaret Walker differed dramatically from that of Bailey, and Horne. Walker's father was a Methodist minister and her mother was a music teacher. Both parents were also educators at a college in New Orleans where she enrolled. By the time Walker was sixteen years old, she had begun to write poetry and received encouragement from Langston Hughes. After graduating from Northwestern University in 1935, Walker remained in Chicago where she pursued her literary ambitions. Unlike Bailey and Horne, Walker became an educator.[7]

The experiences of Bailey, Horne, and Walker were uniquely their own. The narratives about their lives demonstrate that the experiences of blacks girls in urban America during the Great Depression varied greatly.

Hattie Cochran was born on September 9, 1915, on a 150-acre farm in Daleville, Mississippi, near Meridian, the county seat and second largest city in the state. Like hundreds of thousands of other African Americans, between 1890 and the end of World War I, Cochran's family migrated from the rural South to the urban North. But, unlike many young black men and women who fled southern economic deprivation and racial intimidation unaccompanied, Perry Cochran, Hattie's father, migrated from Lauderdale County, Mississippi, to Cuyahoga County, Ohio, with his wife, Mary Banks, and their five children in 1915. The Cochran's oldest son, Arenzia, had already migrated to Cleveland.[8]

Concomitant with Lauderdale County's general population decline, Cuyahoga County's population expanded.[9] Hattie, a two-month-old infant at the time of her family's move, did not return to Mississippi until 1992 when she looked at her place of birth with eyes anew. She came of age in Cleveland where the population was approaching the one million mark in 1930. No doubt Perry and Mary Cochran's basic reasons for migrating northward had to do with the possibilities of improving the family's well-being.[10]

According to the 1910 census, Perry Cochran engaged in "general farm" work, but family lore maintains that he was a teacher. It is possible that he combined the occupations since school years for black children in Mississippi were relatively short and would not have interfered with the growing season for subsistence crops. Once in Cleveland, again according to family lore, Cochran was relegated to manual labor because his academic credentials were insufficient for teaching there. By 1930, he was working at Kelly Seed Merchants and Peanut Products.[11]

Whatever the veracity of the stories about Cochran's occupation, they do confirm that all too often the North was not the promised land that many southern migrants believed it would be. Despite many less than desirable conditions and the relatively inhospitable winter weather, the trek northward still proved more advantageous for the Cochran children than would have been the case had they remained in the South. Hattie and her brothers and sisters enjoyed greater educational opportunities in Cleveland, a model city of the Progressive era. Daleville's schools paled by comparison.[12]

Cochran attended Central High School. Founded in 1846, Central was one of fourteen secondary schools in the city in 1931 and touted itself as being the first free high school west of the Allegheny Mountains. Furthermore, Central High School offered college preparatory course, according to Roy Roseboro, one of Cochran's contemporaries who graduated from the school in 1924.[13]

Another of Hattie's contemporaries, Benjamin O. Davis, Jr., president of the student council who graduated in 1929, remembered Central High School fondly. He recalled that it was a "racially mixed" school with a "healthy cross section of Cleveland's population in attendance—white, black, Italian, Polish and several other nationalities." Roseboro said blacks constituted only 5 percent of the student body. Ironically, Cochran never made references to the color or ethnicity of any of the students or teachers. The differences in race consciousness exhibited by the Central alumni may be attributed to their ages at the times of their testimonies.[14]

Hattie Cochran's diary, like the short story "Two Offers," by Frances E. W. Harper, the most prolific black woman writer in the nineteenth century, had a cast of colorless characters in terms of skin tones. The social construction of race may lead readers to think that Cochran's friends were also African American, but it is just as reasonable to assume that they were not. The Cochrans were faithful members of the Church of God, which had an all black congregation in Cleveland; but, they attended mixed services at the church's headquarters in Anderson, Indiana. Finally, the communicants at the Church of God's annual weeklong camp meetings held at West Middlesex, Pennsylvania, were racially mixed.[15]

Regardless of the colors of her pals, Hattie Cochran "had gangs of fun" at Central High School where she enrolled in history, biology, art, gym, and English. She also mentioned "rhetoricals," perhaps a facet of her English class. To round out her 1930–1931 curriculum, Cochran was in a domestic science course that divided its time between cooking and sewing.[16]

Hattie Cochran, who had declared that "education is my aim" in 1929, never mentioned her academic progress; yet she appeared to be a conscientious student who stayed up late nights to complete assignments, work on a biology notebook, or to prepare stencils for school. Claude Sharpe, a frequent visitor at the Cochran home, made a special trip to her home one evening in early October. Afterward, Hattie wrote, "I helped him with his Algebra lessons." Not only did she complete her own homework in a timely manner, visit the local library for references, and assist others, Cochran appeared mature enough to accept extra responsibilities at Central High School.[17]

On September 14, at the onset of the 1931–1932 school year, she wrote, "I am in charge of some 7B boys in Study Hall." The next day, she was "in charge of some girls." When or why she incurred those duties and how long they lasted remain a mystery, yet it is evident that she had a positive relationship with someone in authority who believed she was capable of fulfilling the tasks. Perhaps, it was one of her instructors.[18]

Curiously, Cochran never praised her teachers beyond the assessment "pretty fair." Even more surprising was her lack of commentary on March 4, 1931 when Blanche Ondracek, a teacher, died unexpectedly. Cochran's cryptic—"Dry Day," noted the occasion. By contrast, Benjamin Davis, Jr., remembered his instructors with fondness, especially his homeroom teacher, Helen Chesnutt, the daughter of the well-known African American poet Charles Chesnutt. She taught Latin and won the admiration of Roseboro also. Cochran was in Miss Bein's English class and never mentioned knowing or having a class with Miss Chesnutt.[19]

The diary's sparse and often terse comments suggest that Cochran wrote out of a self-imposed sense of duty rather than because she savored chronicling the details of her daily existence. Certainly, the diary did not serve an introspective function for the extraverted young woman. She only included those things that especially delighted or annoyed her. For example, on March 27 she enjoyed the rhetoricals because of the "swell history pageant." Another time the class merited her attention, but it was only "pretty good." She was more enthusiastic about her art class and looked forward to the first lesson in soap carving.[20]

Furthermore, she eagerly anticipated a January 13, 1931 class trip to the Cleveland Museum of Art, but Miss Scroggs, who had been absent the day before, postponed the outing. In Cochran's view, this made the instructor a "big Sap." By all accounts, the label was the most stinging invective leveled against any person without regard for age or position during the entire year. What warranted such a response? The class was not going on just any ordinary field trip but to a world-class exhibit. The students were to see the Guelph Treasure on display from January 10 through February 1, 1931.[21]

No doubt, Miss Scroggs had prepared the students for the visit since the exhibit was the most dramatic event at the museum since opening. It is also possible that they had learned about the collection through the newspapers since it was the most widely advertised event in the museum's history to that point. The *Cleveland Plain Dealer*'s January 11, 1931, edition featured a page of photographs of pieces selected from among eighty objects in the valuable collection. The paper's description of the eleventh-century Guelph Cross of "gold studded with pearls and precious stones, and enriched with filigree and enamel" was enough to rouse the interests of the most lackluster teenaged art enthusiasts.[22]

Perhaps the Museum of Art also informed the public about the Guelph Treasure via one of Cleveland's six radio stations. In 1930, 48.1 percent of the 221,502 households in the lakefront city owned radios. The Perry Cochran family was among the 4,008 black families (22.8 percent) who reported having a set in their homes. It was not unusual for Hattie Cochran to listen to the radio as a routine activity.[23]

Whether she had gained a deep appreciation for fine art or simply wanted a diversion from a routine school day, Cochran appeared sorely disappointed in not seeing the sacred relics from the St. Blasius Cathedral in Brunswick, Germany, as originally scheduled. The pieces, valued at $5,000,000, had belonged to the Houses of Hanover and Brunswick for eight or nine centuries before financial stress caused them to sell some of their possessions. It is unlikely that Cochran contextualized the Great Depression as a global occurrence affecting rich and poor alike. Moreover, one must wonder if she and her classmates sympathized with the owners because of their financial distress.[24]

Hattie Cochran's diary leaves a void in the discussion about the Guelph Treasure. Why had Scroggs postponed a learning experience of certain historical value and cultural enrichment for the art class? What was the significance of the young girl's January 12 entry that reads, "Had a good time in Art today Cause Miss Scroggs was absent?" Did having a "good time" mean she and her classmates behaved in some way that was different from what routinely happened during the teacher's presence?[25]

The diary also leaves readers wondering why Hattie Cochran did not accompany the students to the museum January 19, 1931. Did this have anything to do with her "good time" during the teachers' absence? The answers are unknowable, yet all is not lost. The museum purchased nine ecclesiastical objects for its permanent collection at a cost of $570,000. In all probability, Hattie Cochran, viewed those artifacts on July 5 when she and "a crowd" of her friends went to the Museum of Art.[26]

Interactions with her friends in school or afterward was an added dimension to Cochran's existence. Although her family had a telephone in the home, Hattie rarely mentions receiving or making calls. This suggests that most of her friends did not have phones or that they preferred more personal contacts. The dense population on Cleveland's eastside and the closeness of houses put youngsters within easy reach. Living in rural Mississippi would have made regular visits more difficult.[27]

Hattie Cochran's "bum" and "ho hum" days were invariably those when she remained home, mostly on Saturdays when she shampooed her hair and completed household chores. Of more significance, these were days when she had no visitors. The absence of boys and girls coming into or going out of her home was rare for the fifteen-year-old whose routine contacts with friends spilled over from the classroom to the long walks home from Central High School some twenty blocks away, into the evenings, weekends, and summer vacations. Hattie's friends maintained a virtual foot patrol to and from her home. When they were not parading in or out, she went in search of them.

Two examples illustrate the point. One Saturday in January, she wrote:

> Worked all day around the house. X called. Went down to Anna's house. She came over and went with me to buy some Shoes. Claude came over. To bed at 2: A. M.

On a mid-July Saturday, she explained:

> Daisy came up this morning for a while. Went to the clinic Came back by Clara Boyce and Daisys house. Pauline, Ann, and Albert Turner was up to night. Went down to Ann's house. To bed about 2. A. M.

Neither rain, snow, nor the summer heat stopped the pedestrian traffic in and out of 2228 East 78th Street. Boys and girls visited and revisited, and Cochran seemed to relish their company.[28]

Had she lived and worked on a farm in the rural South her patterns of visiting, sleeping, and waking would have been untenable. Cochran did not work outside her home and seemed to have a great amount of leisure time. In fact, she, like some teenagers then and now, made her activities, her friends, and herself the center of her universe.[29]

Extracurricular and after school activities consumed a tremendous amount of her time. She sang in a choir of 150 voices and went to school activities in the city's state-of-the-art auditorium. Cochran, a sports enthusiast, admired the talents of Jesse Owens, a friend from her neighborhood, but basketball and baseball were her favorites. She attended games in the high school gym and the neighborhood Y.M.C.A. (77th and Cedar Avenue) and listened to the Indians' games over the radio. Moreover, the radio broadcasts of "true stories" held her attention rather than the "Amos 'n' Andy" show. Late night music filled the air waves and her ears. Cab Calloway's "Minnie the Moocher," and "Kickin' the Gong Around" were familiar tunes as were Russ Colombo's "Prisoner of Love" and "Save the Last Dance." She went to the carnival and movies, or read novels. When she finished "Silver Slippers," Cochran wrote, "Its good and how." James Weldon Johnson's *The Autobiography of an Ex-Coloured Man* won her unequivocal approval. In her opinion, "It was 'real good.' "[30]

Cars, or the "machine" in Cochran's vernacular, fascinated her. On inclement days, she received occasional rides home from school with her girlfriends whose fathers saved them of the long walk home. At other times, cars driven by young fellows transported her far away from her eastside neighborhood. Sunday, May 30, 1931, serves as an example. Cochran wrote, "Robert Jackson came by for me at 2 O'clock and we went to Garfield Park. Left the P.R. about 3:30. Came back home in the Rumble Seat." In the meantime, "It Rained down real hard," but that did not dampen her spirit.[31]

The highlight, or "spring of hope," in Hattie Cochran's year was the family's trip to the Church of God campground in West Middlesex, Pennsylvania. Preparations related to the weeklong church meeting included buying stockings along with having her hair cut and "dressed." To be sure, she readied herself for a religious revival, but she and her teenaged friends turned the camp meeting into a grand social occasion. The day of departure finally arrived as Cochran explained:

> We left home about 4:30 [AM] Arrived at W. M. S. at 9: o' clock Saw a gang of kids I knew. Bill, Major, Jay, Adair, Mittie, George S. and Parker, Daisy and my self went to Sharon [Pennsylvania], to Mitties house. Daisy & I went with Pleas Arkanas & another fellow to W. M. S. C. B. & George sat on the porch & talked to Daisy & [me] a long time.

She slept a great part of the next two days, visited friends, played golf, took a walk through the woods, stopped by the spring, arrived back at the campgrounds too late for dinner, but declared that she "had a pretty fair time after all."[32]

August 19 was more exciting; Johnny Cannon arrived. "I wore his 'class ring' tonight 'and—How'—oh my," wrote Hattie. A few days later she "Met a new Boy . . . 'Morris Harris' from Detroit." "He is a chum," she admitted. In the next sentence, Hattie added, "Daisy and I sat in Johns car tonight also *Gene*." Finally, on August 21, "Issac Williams and some other boy [were] up from Pittsburg," and she "had a gang of fun." Her comment, "What a pleasant life this is," speaks for itself.[33]

Hattie Cochran was steeped in the teen culture of her time, and she appears no different from the young people whom she befriended. She enjoyed her age group and interacted well with other boys and girls. Certainly, friction existed among her peers, but Hattie remained aloof and enjoyed it from a distance. For example, when she walked home from school January 6, she "Saw a tough fight upon Central [Avenue]," which demanded the emphasis, "and how." She labeled it "a chicken Scrape" and never mentioned it again. If a conflict involved her directly, she appeared unaffected as in the situation with Louise who "tried to act mad all day." Whatever disturbed Louise did not merit further commentary from the young diarist, and Hattie dismissed the girl's disaffection with a simple "Ho. Hum." Peer pressure in this case was of little consequence to Cochran.[34]

If Louise did not literally and figuratively "come around," it is unlikely that Cochran would worry since she was popular among the teen crowd and had interests of her own. If guidance or advice were needed, her parents and siblings were at hand.[35]

In fact, much of the support and advice regarding life plans came from relationships between siblings in their late adolescence and early adult years. Hattie got along well with her brothers and sisters. Moreover, sibling rivalry among the Cochran children appeared nonexistent. The only hint of dissatisfaction with a sibling came October 2 when Hattie worked on a biology notebook after a full day in school and preparing the family's dinner. Apparently, it did not go as well as she had expected because "a gang of Marie's noisy friends" were in the house that night.[36]

Hattie Cochran was surrounded by her family and grew up in a God-fearing fundamentalist Christian home with two loving parents, yet she never mentioned her father. There is no evidence to suggest that she, like other children of the Great Depression, was disappointed in her father's financial wherewithal to support the family. The absence of data about this father–daughter relationship does not mean the two were estranged or that anything was amiss. The diary is in the hurried hand of a girl "on the move" whose time fostering comradery is spent with persons her own age.[37]

In that same vein, the Cochran mother–daughter nexus defies explanation. Current scholarship focusing on mothers and their adolescent daughters often unravels questions about self-esteem, gender role identity, and body image (dress size, eating disorders, and clothes). Cochran's interests were not those of contemporary children in that she only mentioned her own clothes once and talks about shopping for shoes three times. There is nothing to suggest that she was ill-clad or unshod. Moreover, the absence of discussion about clothes may be less related to her family's economic status than to its membership in a church that frowned upon the use of cosmetics, jewelry, and conspicuously stylish clothing.[38]

With reference to eating, many children of the depression were preoccupied with food, but in all probability, their interests were in having enough to sustain them. They were not distressed about ingesting too many carbohydrates, an overabundance of sugar, or a majority of fatty foods. Adolescent eating disorders and the link to obsession with body images are relatively recent phenomenons.[39]

Cochran mentions cooking or helping to prepare meals more than fifty times during the year. There were no explanations as to why nor is there any pattern to suggest that she was pitching in because her mother had taken employment outside the home. Hattie never writes of being hungry nor does she say what she prepared for dinner or ate, with few exceptions.

By contrast, two frequently mentioned food-related topics actually have greater meanings beyond mere sustenance. First, the Cochrans' were regular participants in "the fish fries." Economically depressed families often took creative measures to staying afloat. As a result, they sometimes took in lodgers, laundry, or organized gatherings where they charged a small admission price, sold food, and created a festive environment. The latter, dubbed "House rent parties," provided entertainment and helped defray routine expenses. In all probability, "the fish fries," which the Cochrans held alternately with the Bostons and Godbolds, members of the Church of God, were events designed to raise money for their ministry, or to offer support to impoverished members.

The second group of food-related diary entries referred to "The Barbeque Stand," which held a gripping attraction for Hattie Cochran. She visited the establishment eleven times between May 18 and June 19, 1931. After a lapse of nearly three months, entries about the barbeque stand resumed. Between September 10 and 23, 1931, there were ten notations. Enough evidence exists to posit that the teenager, who celebrated her sixteenth birthday September 9, 1931, frequented the business because it was a "hangout" rather than because she was hungry and went to buy food.[40]

The duration of Hattie's visits lasted from "a few minutes" or "a little while" to several hours. She went there one afternoon at 5:30 and did not leave until 11:00 PM Another time, she stayed until midnight. Her friend, Daisy, and sister, Willa, accompanied her once, otherwise she went alone. What she did at the barbeque stand or who she saw there remains unknown. Without notice of anything being amiss, Hattie's trips to the barbeque establishment stopped.[41]

It is possible that her parents ended her outings that may have precipitated a conflict especially if the young girl went to the popular Bama's Barbecue at 8609–8611 Cedar Avenue, located in the midst of Cleveland's eastside nightspots. Along the way to Bama's Barbecue was "Val's in the Alley," a nightclub on 86th and Cedar Avenue, where dancing was a routine occurrence, and the musician Art Tatum was a featured attraction. The "Greasy Spoon" was next door, and the "Douglass Social Club" was only a few steps away at 7919 Cedar Avenue.[42]

The intersection of Cedar Avenue and 79th Street was a high traffic area with speakeasies, dancing, and music. These activities deviated sharply from the conservative teachings of the Church of God. It is possible that the elders would have also disapproved of Hattie reading "True Confessions" magazines, seeing movies, and riding around in cars with boys. Hattie's other activities appeared innocuous because of the crowds of teenagers, including her own siblings, around her. But, going to the barbeque stand so frequently on school nights, especially when she had examinations the following day could not escape the notice of caring parents.[43]

If they read the *Cleveland Plain Dealer* they could not ignore the many stories about children getting into trouble. For example, the paper reported that several girls were detained by the court for frequenting a "liquor flat" after school hours. The owner of the house promised to give them "drinks" if they were "nice" to gentlemen customers. Maybe they read about the police finding a fourteen-year-old boy chained to his bed, by his parents, because he had stayed out until 10:00 PM with his friends.[44]

If Mary and Perry Cochran intervened in their daughter's activities, questions are in order. Did Hattie respond with the typical adolescent protest, or did she capitulate? There is nothing in the diary to indicate that Hattie Cochran was a willfully disobedient girl prone to quarreling with her mother and father. But, the diary's entries suggest that something had transpired to cause her level of enthusiasm for life to dip along with a change in her routines. She no longer wrote of having gangs of fun or, in her words, "feeling forte." In fact, she noted the change in herself when she wrote, "Rather quiet for me before adding 'Ho. Hum.' " The young girl was home more and on September 25, she went to bed at 8:00 PM.[45]

This was such a drastic deviation from her routine, Cochran asked, "What is going to happen?" Something had happened, but it is not clear if this had anything to do with the barbeque stand or if her responsibilities increased. Her older brother Arenzia's wife had given birth to their third child, and Hattie began taking care of the couple's two young daughters in addition to going to school "as usual," and cooking supper for the family. There was little if any time for her friends. Furthermore, the weather was rainy and disagreeable. In exasperation, she wrote, "What a life this is."[46]

At one point, it appeared that she "had everything before" her, but now it looked as if nothing lay ahead other than the routine of school, cooking, and caring for someone else's children. Her "spring of hope" was gone, and the "winter of despair" had set in. Only a month earlier, she had written "What a pleasant life this is" but now she lamented, "What a life this is."[47]

"Doom and gloom" hovered above, but it was not related to the worsening state of the Great Depression. In actuality, Hattie Cochran seems unaware of the economic conditions around her. She writes about having film developed and going to the "beauty parlor," albeit infrequently, yet it is evident that she had access to money for nonessential purchases. Furthermore, she did not work outside the home.[48]

Observers have said that the depression meant little to blacks because they were already in a state of economic depravation. This does not appear to be true in Hattie Cochran's case. In fact, her 1929 autograph book contains witty sayings written by her friends at Central High School on October 21, 1929. Her peers professed their friendship until "the cows come home," "until Hungary fried Turkey in Greece," or until they screamed ice cream. They, too, were oblivious to the changes in the stock market not because of their color but because of their youth and their interests.[49]

In that same vein, when Hattie lamented "What a Life this is," she was unhappy about the changes in how she spent her leisure. It was disconcerting, and she seemed to resent it.[50]

Fortunately, Cochran reclaimed her leisure time as soon as her sister-in-law resumed the full care of her own children. The remainder of the teenager's year was relatively uneventful, and on December 31, 1931, she declared:

> The year as a whole has been pretty fair to me, but hope that the next year (1932) will treat me still better. I will try [to] make some resolutions that I think will do others good as well as myself will try to be friendly with every one I come in contact with and have a real success thro out the year "1932"[51]

A review of Hattie L. Cochran's 1932 diary makes it possible to determine if the new year was indeed better than the old one. In many ways, they were very much the same. She continued to balance meal preparations and cleaning chores at home with reading novels and true stories. Her school days were filled with attending classes, completing assignments, and endless chats with friends. Selected events, especially the extra-curricular or after school activities garnered more attention and received insightful comments. Such was the case in January 8, 1932, when she wrote: "Noble Sissle entertained us at School this morn." The well-known musician, and Central High School alumnus, had distinguished himself with the 369th Regiment Band said to have "filled France with jazz" during World War I. Cochran noted, "He is really good." The April 1, 1932, dramatization by the Western Reserve students received only a "good" evaluation while a musical at the nearby Y.M.C.A. two days later failed to win her approval. Cochran remarked, "couldn't expect any more than I Saw."[52]

On Wednesday, June 8, Cochran appeared exasperated when she sighed, "The last day of School–What a relief it is." Such a comment leads readers to believe that the year has been less than satisfying, but a closer examination of her school's culminating activity which mentioned that "Boys & girls Danced in the gym" demands a reevaluation. This is especially true, in view of her confession, "I think that I really have had my share of 'fun' this TERM," also written June 8, 1932.[53]

Cochran's share of fun seemed to spill over into the summer as she went to carnivals, movies, and resumed trips to the barbeque stand. Her fascination with the establishment was constant as indicated by the frequency of her visits, sometimes twice in one day, and the varied spellings including "Barbeque Stand," "Bar B-que Stand," "the Bar. Beque Stand," and the "B.Que. Stand," a demonstration of her lexical flexibility.[54]

Obviously, the barbeque stand offered a form of entertainment, but Cochran was certain to remain home and close to the radio some evenings in order to hear the broadcast of sports events. On June 21, 1932, she "Listened to the world championship fight between Jack Sharkey and Max Schmeling." As a true fan of the Cleveland Indians, she was delighted July 14, 1932, when the "Indians won game from N. Y-11-3." Her enthusiasm escalated further July 27, and she wrote, "Listened to Double header between Indians & Yankee's. *Cleve won both.*"[55]

Of course the highlight of her summer in 1932, like the summer of 1931, was her family's trek to West Middlesex, Pennsylvania, for the annual Church of God camp meeting. They arrived Sunday, August 14, at 9:15 AM, and Hattie began immediately to renew friendships with girls and boys whom she had met in years past, especially Alberta and Janie Hunter along with their brother Rufus. She also initiated fast associations with newcomers.[56]

To be sure, the West Middlesex camp meeting was a religious gathering, but Hattie did not write about its sacred dimensions in 1931 or 1932. Instead, she focused on her own activities. "Daisy & I," she wrote, "went for a ride with Rufus Hunter & Johnnie Warner in a Roadster." The following day, she lolled about with a "gang" of her friends on the riverbank. As the week neared its end, they rowed across the river for a corn roast at the Cannon farm where they had a "wonderful time." Ordinarily, Cochran had little or nothing to say about food, but she made an exception. It was, she wrote, "the best corn I ever tasted in my life."[57]

The next afternoon, she and a "gang" of friends returned to the Cannon farm, which she described as a "lovely place," where they rode horses, ate pears and apples, and enjoyed the homemade cider. Of the refreshing drink, she confessed, "It sure was good." The social aspect of the "camp meeting" prompted her to add, "Kinda hate to leave." Had she written "What a life this is" on August 20, 1932, its meaning would have been as clear as her August 21, 1931, comment "What a pleasant life this is." On both occasions she was surrounded by friends in a bucolic setting.[58]

Parting from her friends was somewhat sad, but she had "made pictures" of them and recorded the most significant events in her diary. Both would serve as pleasant reminders of what was ahead of her in August 1933 when the family would again travel to West Middlesex, Pennsylvania. In fact, the camp meetings remained an integral part of her life. Afterward, she married Rufus Hunter, and they continued going to West Middlesex until she died May 26, 1994, a few months short of what would have been her seventy-ninth camp meeting. She had missed only one, and that was due to the August 14, 1941, birth of her daughter, Joyce.

Among the most salient features of this brief glimpse of an African American girl, based upon her personal diaries, is the fact that her life as a happy, well-adjusted teenager in a working-class family differs from the historical portrayal of what millions of children, black and white, encountered during the Great Depression. Certainly, Hattie Cochran may have been guilty of dissembling, but it does not appear that she had anything to hide.

The consistency with which she made daily entries in 1931 and summarized the year is replicated throughout her 1932 diary. On December 31, 1932, she was retrospective and could truthfully say she had fulfilled the 1932 resolution to "be friendly with every one" whom she had contact. Of the successes in 1932, Hattie Cochran's education, unlike that of many of her contemporaries throughout the United States, was not interrupted by the Great Depression. Moreover, she was making progress, with above average grades, toward the completion of requirements for graduation from Central High School.

As 1932 came to an end, Cochran remained optimistic about what life held in store for her. On December 31, 1932, she wrote:

> This is the last day in the year. It is some what sad to see it depart But perhaps next year will bring prosperity. Let us hope. Things that I know that I should have done, and didn't do I will try to fill them next year. Sincerely hoping that next year will be one of the best we have had.

The Hattie L. Cochran diaries contain many silences, yet her voice comes through enough to know that she enjoyed an adolescence in the midst of the greatest depression ever experienced in the United States. Cochran had leisure time and spent much of it with her friends listening to the World Series on the radio, attending basketball games at the Y.M.C.A., strolling through the city's parks, or attending the Church of God retreats in West Middlesex. She admitted to having "gangs of fun" in a special period of time unencumbered by the adult responsibilities such as earning a living. It is also clear that living in urban America offered far more educational and cultural opportunities than would have been the case had her family remained in Mississippi. Hattie Cochran's friends in Cleveland appeared to have had the same advantages as she. Certainly, those routinely mentioned in her diary were involved in similar activities whether at school, church, or home.

Figure 8 Theodore Roosevelt and Gold Dust

Source: Washaw Collection of Business Americana—Soap Archives Center, National Museum of American History, Behring Center, Smithsonian.

CHAPTER EIGHT

THE LONG WAY FROM THE GOLD DUST TWINS TO THE WILLIAMS SISTERS: IMAGES OF AFRICAN AMERICAN CHILDREN IN SELECTED NINETEENTH- AND TWENTIETH-CENTURY PRINT MEDIA

In late September 1954, Kay Kits, a Springfield, Illinois, company, advertised the "cutest" apron ever seen in the *American Home*, a popular magazine. The craft company's illustrated advertisement promising easy-to-follow directions for the apron that appears on a page along with ads showing hanging lamps, folding banquet tables, aluminum awnings, fringed tablecloths, adhesive backed tile ashtrays, and a food chopper guaranteed to prevent tearing when slicing onions. Instead of a general run-of-the-mill product advertisement, Kay Kits drew protest from the National Association for the Advancement of Colored People (NAACP). Rather than complaining directly to the company, the NAACP's executive secretary, Walter White, addressed his complaint on behalf of the civil rights organization to the advertising agency. "We are inexpressibly shocked," wrote White, to see that *American Home* would accept and print such an advertisement.[1]

Ordinarily, there was nothing unusual about a precut ready-to-sew piece of protective covering, but this apron trimmed with white and green rickrack featured "a wide-eyed pickaninny," stereotypical image of a black child, ogling "over a luscious pink slice of green watermelon." The melon covered a significant portion of the lower part of the apron, and the little pickaninny's "kinky head," partially buried in the melon, functioned as the apron's pocket.[2]

The executive secretary surmised that an uninformed person on the magazine's staff was responsible for the faux pas. He told the editor that a number of concerned citizens had voiced strong objections and requested that the NAACP convey their displeasure to the Madison Avenue corporation.[3]

Thousands of stereotypical caricatures of black children cast as pickaninnies, such as that found in *American Home*, designed to appeal to a mass market, appeared in the print media from the turn of the twentieth century well past the middle of the century, against which the NAACP waged a lengthy campaign. Since its founding in 1910, the NAACP had protested against racism in all media.[4]

Figure 9   Postcard #2CH291

Source: Lake County (IL) Discovery Museum, Curt Teich Postcard Archives.

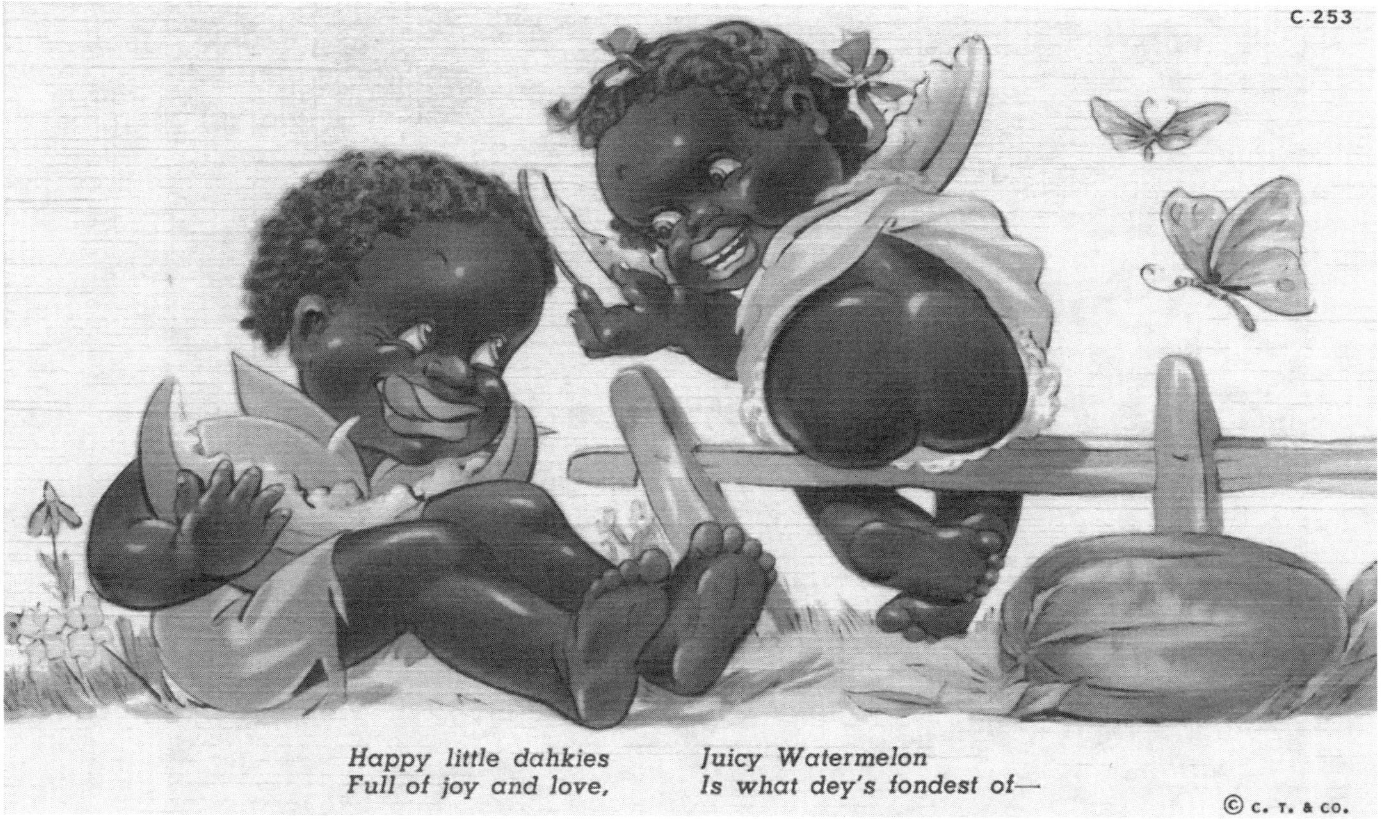
C.253
Happy little dahkies
Full of joy and love,
Juicy Watermelon
Is what dey's fondest of—
© C. T. & CO.

Figure 10 Postcard #7AH2676

Source: Lake County (IL) Discovery Museum, Curt Teich Postcard Archives.

Figure 11 "Got Milk" Campaign advertisement

Source: Courtesy Bozell Worldwide, Inc., agents for National Fluid Milk Processor Promotion Board, New York, NY.

This essay focuses on the derogatory characterization of black children in certain forms of print media, especially postcards, occasion/greeting cards, trade cards, and newsprint advertisements. It attempts to answer questions about the origins, appeal, and impact of such imagery along with how and why it changed over time. The chapter also attempts to examine why this imagery, mostly derived from the minstrel tradition of the late nineteenth and early twentieth centuries, endured for so long.[5]

Unkempt black children with wide toothy grins, rolling white eyes, shiny dark faces, and uncontrollably kinky hair are typical in these images. These characters engaged in foolish behavior or simplistic acts and often comment about them in an exaggerated dialect. Supportive props—watermelon, bales of cotton, and alligators— are also common accessories. The more vicious scenes devalued black children's lives to the extent that entrepreneurs claimed they were "dainty morsels" appropriate "free lunches" or "gator bait" for carnivorous reptiles.[6]

The exaggerated features and minstrel-like scenes presented by professional photographers, artists, or illustrators contrast sharply with those of well-dressed well-mannered seemingly intelligent white children amid pleasant surroundings. Frederick Douglass railed against stereotypical representations of African Americans in photographs, a new medium that attracted his attention. Douglass also criticized naturalists, ethnographers, and phrenologists for the biases displayed in their work. He wrote, "The European face is drawn with the most scrupulous regard to excellence in harmony with the highest ideals of beauty." By comparison, "The negro is pictured with featured distorted lips exaggerated forehead low and depressed and the whole countenence [sic] made to harmonize with the popular idea of negro ignorance, degradation and imbecility." Presentations of this nature permeated the notion that "beautiful" subjects represent "civilized" whites and "ugly" ones represented "uncivilized" black. Harriet Beecher Stowe's descriptions of the children, Topsy and Eva, in Uncle Tom's Cabin, are full enough to lend support to the stereotypical images found in many nineteenth- and twentieth-century advertisements.[7]

Racism and segregation sustained these stereotypical symbols, designed to sell manufactured products and entertain consumers. By casting blacks as buffoons, servile laborers, or contented children, card manufacturers relegated them to a marginal place and eliminated any hints of competition or agency that might threaten whites. Popular accordion-style postcards featuring local attractions along with young smiling watermelon-fed cotton pickers conveyed sentimental or humorous messages that sought to portray blacks as happy and nonthreatening.[8]

A "Greetings from DIXIELAND," a single accordion-type packet of cards, produced by Curt Teich & Company, Chicago, Illinois, with a 1937 copyright, contains eighteen color photographs printed on the front and back. Black children appear in one-third of the cards that were readily available from street vendors, gift shops in train depots or bus stations near tourist attractions. On one card, "Sitting Soft in Dixieland," is the photograph of a young girl relaxing cheerfully in an overturned cotton basket in the midst of a cotton field. Another card, "Sportsman in Dixieland," captures the smiling face of a young boy with the day's catch—two very small fish. The title sarcastically contrasts with the unsportsmanlike conduct of the child for keeping such tiny fish. "Working hard for the family dinner," another in the series, derides the children who are lolling around on a pier. Despite the long string of fish one youth has, which indicates patient persistence, fishing with a pole or rod generally carries connotations of leisure rather than providing sustenance. The faces of children in "A Busy Day in the Cotton field" are solemn, but those eating watermelon are made to look ridiculous in contrast.[9]

Aside from the melon, alligators, and cotton, several other characterizations appear repeatedly to perpetuate the racist portrayal of African Americans as credulous promiscuous thieves with insatiable appetites. Exaggerated facial expressions imply that black children were easily frightened and incapable of understanding simple concepts. These characterizations appear in trade cards that were used by merchants in the post–Civil War era to advertise their goods. The child-centered scenarios on cards often have no real connections to the advertisements.

Of six advertisements for the turn-of-the-century Clarence Brooks & Company, manufacturer of fine coach varnishes, only one includes a carriage. The New York-based company's illustrations are reminiscent of Currier & Ives prints; however, all individuals are black and shown hunting, preparing for Christmas dinner, or celebrating July 4. A placard advertising the company blends into the background or appears on roofs, doors, walls, samplers, and fence posts.[10]

At first glance the illustrations appear innocuous, but closer examination reveals cynicism. Children in the ad "The First Ulster in Blackville" appear frightened at the sight of a man, bearing a slight resemblance to the "grim reaper," striding through the snow dressed in a long blue belted coat. The children are wearing jackets or heavy sweaters; however, they appear startled as if they have never seen an overcoat. In any case, there is no correlation between the ad and the product.

Even more ludicrous is "The 'Small Breeds' Thanksgiving," another Clarence Brooks's ad. The artist depicts a large family, replete with an elderly woman—perhaps a grandmother, gathered around a table spread with a bountiful selection of foods as a young man enters the doorway. He is tall, handsome, and well dressed with a hat placed jauntily on his head. The family appears happy and thankful. A portion of the caption reads, "Return of the first-born from college." Standard English gives way in the remainder of the caption, "Bress his heart! Don't he look edgecated?" The malapropisms serve specifically to ridicule the family and African Americans in general. Aside from the varnish company's name on the doorway and a sampler, there is no apparent link to the product. The intent is to advertise varnish and entertain consumers at the expense of African Americans.

Similarly, one trade card advertising cigars features a small black barefoot child against a stark background with a pull toy in tow wondering aloud "Do they miss me, at home?" Without any response to her question, the advertiser's caption reads "Smoke Clayton's Happy Thoughts, Pure Havana." The child's finger and not a cigar dangles from her mouth. The subliminal message says a pure Havana offers euphoric relief, "happy thoughts." How this disturbing image of a lost child is related to "happy thoughts" is unclear. Only in a deeply racist context could this image be construed as amusing or, connected to the product.[11]

Humor of this sort is present in the advertisements of Everette H. Dunban, dealer in fine boots and shoes for gentlemen, located at 71 Monroe Street, Lynn, Massachusetts. His card used images of two children, one black and the other white, to sell his merchandise. The innocent-looking white boy is wearing a highly polished blue boot while skipping rope. The illustration suggests that his properly aimed foot was swift enough to "boot" the black boy into orbit without missing a step. The black child's oversized top hat is airborne and his swallow-tailed coat lofts upward to expose his ample backside and well-shod feet high above the ground. Shoes and boots are central to the advertisement, but why one child must kick the other in the seat of the pants to sell footwear is unclear.[12]

Three manufacturers, Merrick, J. & P. Coats, and Clark, also used caricatures of black children to advertise thread. To indicate the strength of its product, the Merrick Thread Company's ad showed a barefoot black boy hanging by the seat of his ragged pants over the gaping mouth of an alligator. A single durable thread keeps the child out of harm's way. He teases the alligator, "Fooled dis time, Cully," he said, "Dis cotton aint gwine to break." The Coats Company touted the dye as its strength. An ad features a dark-skinned child sitting astride a huge spool of black thread while surrounded by larger than life ravens. The caption, "We," refers to both the animate and inanimate objects, "never fade," explains why the brilliant sun in the background radiates a sad face. The black child's skin, like the ravens' black feathers and the thread are all lumped together, thereby dehumanizing the child.[13]

Aside from employing racialized jokes about skin color, these trade cards also reinforce the stereotypically servile position of laborers in white households. The "Gold Dust Twins," stock trade symbols for N.K. Fairbank and Company's Gold Dust Soap Powder depicted two black children. Introduced in the 1880s, the twins, "Goldie" and "Dustie," all-purpose cleaners like the detergent they sold, appeared on trade cards, and in newspapers and magazines, washing, scrubbing, and scouring in tandem.

These small black boys with banjo-shaped eyes happily performed housekeeping chores ordinarily undertaken by servant girls and women. The exotic boys wore stiff skirts, much like the imagined grass skirts of "native" Africans, but did not wear shirts. The half-naked boys thwarted gender conventions in their appeal to millions of women, who, according to the advertisement, used Gold Dust as a time saver in washing dishes, scrubbing sinks, scouring stoves, cleaning kitchen utensils, and polishing enamel ware. Deprived of their masculinity, the Gold Dust Twins appeared in newspaper and magazine ads across the country. The Chicago-based soap manufacturer promulgated the racist idea of black boys as effeminate and servile, fit only for menial tasks usually assigned to women.[14]

The degraded status of the boys is clear in a rhyming advertisement that uses the product name as an acrostic:

G—Stands for Gold Dust,
Of cleaners the prize,
All folks who use
Praise it up to the skies.

O—Is for oilcloth
On tables or shelf;
Keep bright with Gold Dust,
Apply it yourself.

L—Is for laundry
Place clothes in a tub
Gold Dust will clean them
With scarcely a rub.

D—Is for dishes
Cleaned three times a day
Use Gold Dust and drive
Half the labor away.

D—Is for dirt,
Likewise dust and decay,
With Gold Dust it's easy
To keep them away.

U—Is for utensils
Pot, kettle and pan;
In a second with Gold Dust
They're made spik and span.

S—Is for scrubbing
Woodwork, door and floor;
Gold Dust works like lightning—
Your back won't be sore.

T—Is for Twins,
Ne'er known to shirk;
Make housework so easy—
Let them do your work.

No distinction is drawn between the two boys and the soap powder; not only does that ad make the boys appear servile, but it dehumanizes them by reducing them to a mere commodity.[15]

Consumers could learn more about the boys and the soap from the pamphlet "Who are We?" written to amuse and tell about the boys' mission on earth. The partially hidden twins peek shyly out from its cover. Inside, readers find pages of testimonials about the qualities of the Gold Dust Soap Powder and what the twins do with it. The boys clean and brighten everything they touch. The pamphlet concludes with the twins making a personal appeal to readers: "If you have not yet availed yourself of our services, lose no time, but summon us through your nearest grocer and 'let us do your work.' " The ideally cloned boys, "signed" themselves—"Your servants, The Gold Dust Twins."[16]

In addition to its advertisements in the print media, Fairbank and Company displayed what many consumers called the "greatest commercial poster ever placed on a bill-board" in any major American city. The 1910 billboards coincided with Theodore Roosevelt's return from an African safari. Uncle Sam stands in the foreground and the Statute of Liberty rises high in the background to welcome the big game hunter and his minions, the Gold Dust Twins, ashore. The bill-board's bold caption, "Roosevelt scoured Africa" and "The GOLD DUST TWINS Scour America," links the ex-president's captivating adventures in Africa with possibilities of what the twins will conquer in America—dirt, grease, grime. Roosevelt's mission is completed and his hands are empty. By contrast, his foot servants, who have much work to do in the future, are weighed down with the Roosevelt's baggage, gun, and the carcass of a tiger. Despite their heavy loads, the twins balance boxes of Gold Dust soap on their heads. Ultimately, their presence is in keeping with the Fairbank's motto, "Let the GOLD DUST TWINS do your work." The little black boys, like their African forbearers, were in America to perform arduous labor for white capitalists.[17]

While Fairbank and Company used other racialized images of children in its advertising, the Gold Dust Twins were among its most recognized trademarks. The company produced Fairy Soap, described as "dainty, refined and delicate in perfume," which had the "appearance, odor and performance of a high-class product." The Fairy Soap ad includes a fully dressed white girl, with curly-hair showing beneath her hat. The child is perched atop an oval-shaped cake of soap, with an accompanying motto, "Have you a little 'Fairy' in your home?" It is apparent that when Fairbank wanted to associate a product with luxury and refinement, the company used an image of white femininity. When it wanted to sell a product that would act as a "humble servant," it used an image of the servile, emasculated black boys.[18]

Another of the Fairbank's ads incorporated the picture of a fair-skinned white girl at play with a black contemporary. In all sincerity the nonplused white child asks her ragged barefoot playmate, "Why doesn't your mamma wash you with Fairy Soap?" The purpose was to amuse consumers by playing on the ostensible innocence of a white child who saw dark skin as dirty but failed to understand that no amount of Fairy Soap would change her friend's color.[19]

Other soap companies, including Kirkman's Wonder Soap, and Pearline Soap, used similar advertising tactics. Pearline trade cards avoided coy questions, as asked by the Fairy Soap girl, and simply use a caricature of a black woman washing a child's face with its product. The "clean" side of his face is white, but the unwashed side remains black. "Golly!" the woman exclaims, "I b'leve PEARLINE make dat chile white." In that same vein, the mother of the "two little nigger boys" who disliked bathing has no doubts about Kirkman soap and offers a testimonial, "It's true, as I'm a workman— And both are now completely white. Washed by this soap of Kirkman."[20]

The paint and varnish advertisements also used the trope of turning black children into white ones. Trade cards produced for the Elliott Paint and Varnish Company illustrate a black boy painting his companion white in keeping with the slogan: "See how it covers over black." Using the same black caricatures, the Norfolk Paint Company's caption declared that its product "Covers Black with One Coat."[21]

The claims of such transformations were intended as humorous advertising tactics not to be taken seriously by white consumers. None of the soap or paint companies spent dollars to convince buyers that white children could or should be colored in the same way for they were already "clean." Fairbank had no interests in claiming it could change the Gold Dust Twins into white boys or employing images of white children as servile laborers. Only black children were subjected to these degrading depictions.[22]

Likenesses of black children similar to those on trade cards and in newsprint appeared on postcards, but often surpassed them in crudeness and viciousness. For nearly a century the Curt Teich Company, a Chicago-based business, printed the largest volume of scenic and advertising cards of any company in the world. Many of its cards featuring black boys and girls have an erotic subtext depicting children as unwitting participants in inappropriate behavior. At the time, the red dresses, wraps, aprons, kerchiefs, ribbons, and bonnets worn frequently by black girls represent a lack of modesty or morals. Sexual overtones are also implied in the postures of children devouring luscious red watermelon.[23]

Perhaps the most notable of the Teich postcards bringing the color and fruit together is one printed in 1952 showing a young child wearing a clinging red dress with matching accessories while standing alone in a watermelon patch. She is obviously pregnant and as rotund as the melons at her feet. The illustration carries a subliminal message related to warm climates, natural fertility, and promiscuity. As if oblivious to her condition, the wide-eyed grinning girl responds to an unseen inquisitor, "Oh—I is not!" she retorts, "It must be sumpthin' I et!!" Her flushed red cheeks suggest embarrassment, the "glow" of pregnancy, or pride. The card clearly infers that black children are lascivious at an early age. The card's purpose is to amuse consumers and imply that blacks were not only promiscuous but credulous as well.[24]

Another Teich Company card printed in 1942, also sexualizes an image of a black child. A bucolic landscape features sugar maple trees growing amid the lush green rolling hills. Wooden pails hang on the tapped trees. A small black boy, sans-culotte, stands half-hidden behind a tapped tree while a matronly black woman wearing a red bandana stands looking at him at a different angle from the viewer. She is amazed at the sight and exclaims, "Lawsy me! What a pe-culiar little boy." The spigot in front of the tree suggests that the boy is urinating through it. The card plays upon stereotypical notions of hypersexualized black males with oversized genitalia.[25]

Base humor surfaces in other Teich postcards as little black boys and girls display physical attraction toward one another reinforced by the sexual innuendo in the captions. One among several is a 1937 card showing a half-naked boy and girl who are too amorously distracted to see an agitated boy standing nearby. The caption, "Ah's bout as mad as ah can be / Yo' all can't go an' two-time me," explains his emotional state. The distraught boy aims a loaded slingshot at the loving couple. The card moves beyond innocent amusement and suggests the boy's growing hostility is due to the girl's "infidelity." Sadly, the illustrator makes the girl into a "Jezebel," the stereotypical depiction of black women as promiscuous and unfaithful.[26]

Such an attempt at humorous advertisements continued between 1937 and 1952 as the Teich Company produced series of postcards featuring black boys and girls wearing shirt, blouses, and pinafores, but without any skirts, pants, or underwear thus putting their exaggerated buttocks in full view. Depictions of blacks with oversized buttocks may be traced to Sara or Saartjie Baartman, a young South African also known as "The Hottentot Venus." To Europeans, Baartman became an icon of black female sexuality in the nineteenth century because naturalists were fascinated with the greater than "normal" amount of fatty tissue in her "pronounced steatopygia." Widely circulated ethnographical illustrations added to the curiosity about her physique and reinforced stereotypes about black female sexuality.[27]

Perhaps Teich illustrators picked up on this visual tradition, often using the device to create visual puns. In addition, the caricatures' buttocks are heart-shaped when the card is inverted. Nevertheless, illustrations on two postcards are appropriate for discussion herein. One card printed in 1952 shows a young girl sitting wearily on a red stool at a lemonade stand where she has reduced the price from five to four then to three cents. Her complaint, "There's 'barely' any business at all," completed the pun.

Yet, her arched back and exposed buttocks along with her red lips and red ribbons suggest a disturbing sensuality.[28]

Viewers are likely to ask what is the child actually selling? Teich illustrators did not portray white females, regardless of age or class, in this manner. The card " 'She Sells Sea Shells' in Florida" is a useful comparison. It features the photograph of a young girl and the lettering on her sign replicates a childish handwriting. While both depict youthful entrepreneurs, the similarities end there. The white child is dressed appropriately in beachwear and the black one has her buttocks exposed. How can one account for the stark differences in the two images?[29]

In what historian Nell Irvin Painter calls "the panorama of American racist caricature," black females are often defined only in terms of their sexuality. But, says literary scholar Hazel Carby, "Identifying and cataloguing the perpetrators of racist stereotyping . . . [do] not reveal how ideologies actually worked to construct racial and sexual referents."[30]

In other words, the caricature of the libido-driven Jezebel, dating back to the initial contact between Europeans and Africans took on a life of its own. European ignorance of African culture led to the misinterpretation of traditional African dress, dance, and marriage as lascivious or lewd. Moreover, the general nudity of enslaved girls and women in North America as they worked, were punished, or sold reinforced the notion that they were libidinous. This sort of sexualized racism functioned as a rationalization for the exploitation of black girls and women across time and regions.[31]

Popular literature propagated this notion of oversexed black females well before the Teich Company put its cards into production. One of the earliest testimonials to their alleged lewd behavior appeared in a 1777 poem that claimed "sooty dames [were] well vers'd in Venus' school / Make love an art, and boast they kiss by rule."[32]

The second card, also printed in 1952, shows two young children, a girl and a boy, in a meadow as colorful butterflies hover overhead. The children are eating watermelon. The boy reclines on the ground while the girl sits on a split rail fence. Her back is turned toward him; therefore, her exposed buttocks are at his eye level. He is drooling, licking his lips, and gazing upward lustily. Although the caption reads, "Happy little darkies / Full of joy and love / Juicy Watermelon / Is what dey's fondest of," it is unrealistic to assume his attention is directed solely at the fruit in his hands.[33]

The Teich Company used illustrations of children in a line of cards fitting into the "potty" joke genre. Toilets, outdoors and indoors, or chamber pots, large and small, are integral parts of the messages and travel scenes. Defecation and urination, normal bodily functions, are not usually subjected to the public gaze, but the company made them integral to several cards featuring the images of black children. One example shows a boy sitting on a chamber pot, flatulently, declaring, "You'll be hearin' from me soon." Another features a girl struggling to get into the toilet stall. She exclaims, "I can't hold back any longer—Sure do miss you." Yet another shows a boy who has fallen into a toilet, lamenting, "You all can see without a guess / Dat I is in an awful mess! / Don' frame dis pos' card, lawsy me / Lak somebody's gone 'n done t' me." The Teich Company nor its competitors put white children into such humiliating situations.[34]

That such cards were in poor taste did not seem to dissuade boosters of certain cities or regions from using them as advertisements. One card with a child wearing only a top hat sitting on a chamber pot in view of the waterfront with sailboats in the distance reads the message: "You're invited here, Galveston, Texas for the BIG BLOW OUT!" Another card advertising the beauty of the Old Southwest is similar in style and wording; it only changes the scenery. No connection to black children is apparent. One might speculate that the cards sought to portray blacks as harmless buffoons so as to comfort potential white tourists coming from areas without sizable black populations.[35]

Consumers, mostly women, purchased postcards for themselves and their families primarily because of the humorous or sentimental pictures or captions. The message written by senders with rare exceptions, had nothing to do with the pictures or captions. An illustrative, but hardly representative example is that of the March 6, 1909, card mailed by Eulah in Oakland, Indiana, to her cousin Anna Carlisle in Terre Haute, Indiana. The card features a photograph of a young barefoot African American boy and girl locked in a dance pose. On the reverse side, Eulah asked, "Why don't you ever write to me?" The simple question has no connection to the card's caption, "I'd Rather Two Step than Waltz." Another message from Eulah, dated May 20, 1909, to Anna is more revealing. The caption below the photograph of a young smiling African American girl wearing a ragged dress while holding a tambourine above her head asks, "Is Everybody happy?" The question has no link to Eulah's plans to spend the day in the country and suggestion that Anna bring the paper dolls when she joins her.[36]

Like trade and postcards, occasion or greeting cards capitalized on stereotypical characterizations of black children. Greeting cards often used similar imagery that differed in fundamental ways. Occasion cards for birthdays, anniversaries, holidays, health, and friendship often used humorous or sentimental characters on the cards to convey the sender's wishes. They did not stoop to the same base level of humor as postcards, yet black characterizations were often still negative. The Hallmark Card Company produced stereotypical images of barefoot black children in pigtails, representations of "pickaninnies." The children speak in ungrammatical dialect as they conveyed birthday wishes or other sentiments. A perky little black girl appeared on the front of one greeting card announcing, "De sun do shine / De sky am blue / Eb'ry time dat I'se wif you / But now dat yo is gone away / It rains and po's de livelong day!!" A get-well-card with a dejected looking boy on the front declares, "Jes' because you's feelin' porely / Don't be sad and blue / *Yo'* has miseries / *Ah* has miseries / *Ev'ybody* do!"[37]

It is unlikely that many black children purchased the cards with such derogatory imagery. Yet, as a widespread part of the popular culture it would have been difficult for blacks of any age to avoid them, especially in areas frequented by tourists. The negative characterization and parody of black children's phenotypical features, language, or behavior must have had an impact on their self-esteem. It was not unusual for organizations founded by blacks to encourage the general black population to avoid any behavior, including wearing colorful clothing, that would prompt unfavorable comments from whites. What did black youth have to say about the comic and sentimental illustrations found in the print media?

Studies developed by Kenneth and Mamie Clark, founders of the Northside Center in Harlem, offer insight into the psychological effects of racism and segregation on children. In the 1940s the Clarks developed "the doll test," which they administered to African American children between three and seven years of age. Using four identical dolls, two white and two brown ones, the professional psychologists asked the girls and boys to select the doll they preferred in response to a series of questions soliciting perceptions about a doll's color, looks, and character. White dolls were the choice of the majority of children who also showed preferences for white skin in coloring tests also devised by the Clarks. The abysmally low level of self-esteem disturbed the Clarks, but their findings did not differ substantially from those of Maria J. Radke and Helen G. Trager who also tested children for color preferences.[38]

Based on his expertise as a psychologist, Clark provided the NAACP with data for its *Brown v. Board of Education* (1954) brief, which argued that "segregation tends to create feelings of inferiority and personal humiliation in black youngsters, whose sense of self-esteem is soon replaced with self-hatred, rejection of their racial group and frustration." If the Clarks reached those conclusions based on studies and tests using identical dolls, what would be the results had the social scientists asked children about their preferences based on choices between paper dolls representing the Gold Dust Twins and the Fairy Soap girl or the Norfolk Paint and Varnish caricatures?[39]

The racial stereotypes of black children in trade, occasion, and postcards did nothing to build the self-esteem of black children who may have viewed cards showing alligators dining on black youth or being kicked skyward. Such racial stereotypes knew no bounds. Even the Mother Goose rhyme "Ten Little Nigger Boys" chronicled devastating erasures. Aside from learning to count, children are likely to "learn" that little black boys are rambling lazy gluttons who blunder into beehives or animal cages. Otherwise, they fall victim to the raging sea, blazing sun, or holy matrimony.[40]

Indeed, the negative images probably affected many psychologically and took a devastating toll on the emotional well-being of black children who saw such depiction. What impression would the postcard featuring an alligator and child make upon a child who read its accompanying ditty:

I'm just as scairt as I can be / I'm afraid this 'gater is goin' to get me / Oh, mammy come and get me soon / Or you won't have no little coon?

Parents and concerned citizens protested against such images on behalf of children as did Mildred H. Lanser who complained to the NAACP about the stereotypical drawing of a black child on the organization's letterhead for "The Children's Activities" newspaper. "I thought their advertising stunt was revolting," she wrote and questioned whether an organization, "which permits the perptuation [*sic*] of this slanderous characterization can offer my 7-year- and 4-year-old boys the kind of reading material and other information which will help them develop into the kind of citizens which I would like them to be—citizens free from vile racism, discrimination and bias." In all probability, many black parents shared Lanser's values.[41]

Parents and others, including organizations such as the NAACP's youth chapters, voiced concerns on behalf of children, and occasionally, children themselves initiated their own protests. The New Yorker Adrienne Ashby, describing herself as a "school student," wrote to complain about the song "Ma Curly-Headed Babby." Although copyrighted in 1926, the April 1954 *Hit Parader* printed the lyrics:

> Oh, ma babby, ma curly-headed babby
> We'll sit below de sky, an' sing a
> song to de moon
> Oh ma babby ma little nigger babby,
> Yo' daddy's in de cotton field,
> A-workin' for de coon.

Ashby said this "could cause much embarassment [*sic*]" because her "fellow students don't hesitate when they get the chance to heckle one another." The schoolgirl does not give any details about her fellow students' age or color, but she was confident that the NAACP would not let the matter "go unheeded."[42]

Some white and black consumers did wage protests against racism in the media by boycotting products, protesting directly to the offending company, or by bringing the offender to the attention of the NAACP. Once the NAACP received complaints from concerned citizens about caricatures of black children on greeting cards, shoe polish advertisements, or caricatures of black children on business stationary, or some other media, the office followed up with a formal letter of protest and requested discontinuation of the offensive imagery.[43]

The case of the Boston-based company, Contemporary Arts, Incorporated demonstrates how the NAACP proceeded in these circumstances. The company had included "Darky Cherubs" among its 1953 decorative specials for Christmas. According to the print ad, these "cutest ever" angels had "black features with yellow robes and gold wings," coming in six different styles. "The kids love 'em all year round," said the blurb. Herbert L. Wright, youth secretary of the NAACP informed Contemporary Arts that the NAACP's Division of Youth had received "many complaints from youth and adult members around the country" about the "Darky Cherubs." He considered the "stereotyped material" an affront and asked the company to remove the offensive items from its product line.[44]

Alan Fox responded on behalf of Contemporary Arts. After acknowledging receipt of the NAACP's complaint, Fox registered a protest of his own. "This is the kind of letter that we think does more harm in the field of minority effort," he wrote, "than professional minority workers seem to realise." Fox asked for specificity in terms of the nature and the numbers of complaints received. Of greater importance, he wanted "some suggestion specifically as to what your [Wright's] letter [had] in mind on the problem of 'affront.' " Fox claimed that it was "a little different for pre-conditione[d] people to receive this type of letter" while wondering about the "effect of arrogant generalities as read by a complete outsider." Fox seemed to marginalize the NAACP's protest.[45]

His imperiousness did not dissuade Wright from sending a second letter charging that selected print materials such as that distributed by Contemporary Collection, Incorporated did "much to cement many of the stereotyp[ical] attitudes which bigoted individuals have about racial and religious minorities in this country." Wright urged Fox to give his protest and others careful consideration and take responsible action to use "more objective and democratic standards" in its advertising. Finally, Wright informed Fox that he was mailing a copy of his own letter to the president of the Boston NAACP "for appropriate action," meaning that the local chapter would continue pursuing this matter.[46]

From its beginning, the NAACP maintained continued vigilance against racial stereotyping. One of its earliest protest campaigns was against D. W. Griffith's film "The Birth of a Nation." A dogged persistence characterized most of the NAACP's protest campaigns. It also took up cases in which ordinary citizens did not receive satisfaction from their own complaints. For example, an April 4, 1954, letter from Sidney Jackson complained about the Hollywood Shoe Polish company's use of a black Raggedy Andy doll caricature to advertise its "Skuf Shine." The black doll endorses the product's ability to deodorize, clean, and polish children's shoes that "get hard wear." A white Ragged Ann doll claims "Skuf Shine" renews, cleans, and restores shoes to the original finish.[47]

Irving Sternberg, a company agent, responded to Jackson's protest in a less than respectful tone, accusing Jackson of being colorblind in mistaking blue print for black and letting his "imagination run away" before urging him to have his eyes examined. No doubt Jackson saw Sternberg's reply as adding insult to injury; therefore, Jackson asked the NAACP for assistance. Henry Lee Moon, director of NAACP Public Relations, responded:

> We feel that Mr. Jackson quite properly referred to the design of your package as a "Negro caricature." We fail to see the importance of whether the color used on your "ragged boy" is black or dark blue. The point is that the dark hue of this character can and will be associated with members of the Negro group. Mr. Jackson's reaction is substantiation of this condition.

Perhaps Moon made an association with Irving Sternberg's name with the intent to show that prejudices were not confined to any one ethnic or religious group when he added, "Certainly you would not use in your advertising a representation of a hook-nosed individual and pretend on a technicality that it was not the classic caricature of the Jew." Moon, and other NAACP officials, ended letters by assuring recipients that the organization was opposed to discrimination against any people regardless of race, color, religion, or national origin.[48]

Some company representatives, like Sternberg, resented the NAACP's tactics, but others responded graciously. Walter White's September 22, 1954, letter to the *American Home* Magazine Corporation regarding Kay Kits's apron brought a hasty reply from the corporation's Market Place editor, Helen De Motte. She acknowledged receiving correspondence about the apron from readers, many of whom were African Americans. "I am distressed," wrote De Motte, "to find that I have offended even one of them." De Motte claimed not to know that the ad could be interpreted as disparaging before promising to "be on guard to see that this does not happen again."[49]

Among the protests related to negative characterizations about African Americans were those directed at Hallmark Cards, a company that produced the lion's share of America's occasion cards. Henry Moon registered a January 11, 1954, complaint on behalf of the NAACP with reference to "two offensive cards." One of the Valentine cards carried the caricature of a smiling black male of an indefinite age who asked, "Is you is?" The figure holds a large heart near his chest. It was sheer irony, said Moon that the company used the motto "Send a Hallmark [card] when you care enough to send the very best" but produced cards representing "the worse kind of taste and thought." He asked the company to withdraw them from circulation.[50]

Neither Hallmark nor other greeting card companies limited themselves to stereotypical images of any single ethnic group. Cards showing Scots and Native Americans were among the cards produced by Rustcraft, a company that merged with Norcross in 1981. Of the 461 different types of ethnic cards produced by Rustcraft between 1927 and 1959, 42 percent replicated illustrations of black children, 30 percent contained caricatures of Scots, and 6 percent featured drawings of Native Americans. Regardless of the company or ethnic group, stereotypical language and images prevailed. The words put into the mouth of a Native American on the front of one card read, "Heap long time / No See / No Hear / No nuthin' / ugh!" A birthday card showing a Chinese boy reads, "Confucius say / Wise man enjoy himself / He not suppress a single yen / Because he know a year must pass / Until his birthday come again." Finally, a black character on a birthday card says "Ah's uncertain of the date / But Ah disremembers when it is / but somehow I allo it positively jes / cain't be / So very far from now."[51]

As the NAACP reacted to consumer protests, John A. Boppart, managing editor at Hallmark Cards, responded and assured Moon that it was not their intention to publish anything that reflected badly on any group. Moreover, Boppart admitted that the company printed "many humorous" cards depicting various ethnic groups in "humorous situations," but the greater number of the cards represented whites, according to Boppart. Without apologizing, he wrote, "There was no intention to offend any one in designing the two Valentine cards" and declared that it was impractical to attempt to recall them but would be "extra careful in planning" future cards.[52]

The Hallmark response was much like that of the *American Home* editor. But the NAACP protest prompted Hallmark to follow up with a February 10, 1954, meeting with NAACP officials. The company's New York representative, M. L. Finch, and R. V. Breen, a public relations consultant, agreed that "certain of the cards were obviously offensive and would not be reproduced . . . for future distribution." Moreover, the Hallmark representatives also agreed to discontinue the use of dialect and to consider the matter of "multiple pigtails" on the children—stereotypical pickaninnies—and their general lack of shoes.[53]

Finch conveyed what appeared to be a sincere interest in improving their cards. Moon suggested that Hallmark consult someone who was familiar enough with the black community to review their cards as a way of gauging reactions to black characterizations. Finch promised to forward Moon's suggestions to the company's editorial department for future reference.[54]

It seems that Hallmark was indeed interested in "improving" its cards featuring black illustrations. Nonetheless an August 12, 1955, letter from Louis Marcus to Hallmark mirrored the Moon's protest about Valentine cards more than one and one-half years earlier. The card in question, a black child asking "Is you is or is you ain't my Valentine?" The illustration was the same but carried different identification numbers. Obviously, Hallmark had continued producing the same or virtually the same, offensive cards.[55]

Following the NAACP's success in *Brown v. Board* (1954, 1955), and the emergence of the modern Civil Rights and Women's Rights movements of the 1960s, a new level of consciousness about racial stereotyping developed and precipitated a decline in blatant degradation of African Americans in the selected print media. With increased political consciousness came increased consumer awareness when buyers saw the efficacy of direct action in economic boycotts. Merchants, large or small, were fair targets by insulted consumers who objected to racist products, marketing techniques, or sales associates. As a result of the boycotts and pressure from the NAACP, variety stores and pharmacies began withdrawing objectionable cards from routine sales.[56]

Larger numbers of black entrepreneurs created occasion cards extolling blackness and sold them through mass marketing techniques. Major card companies, interested in remaining competitive, began altering their products to eliminate potentially offensive images and language. A writers' manual produced by the Rustcraft Company delineated several taboos saying, "We never use colored dialect, or cards portraying any nationality or racial group by which we might be prompting an insulting stereotype." Religious subjects were not to be treated in a "frivolous or sacrilegious manner." It was safest not to mention religion in humorous or contemporary cards, said the manual. It also urged writers not to mention potatoes, pigs, drunkenness, or the color green in St. Patrick's Day cards produced by Rustcraft. This escalated sensitivity to the representation of "others" is evident elsewhere in the occasion card industry.[57]

Stereotypically derogatory images disappeared from routine sales in selected print media, with few exceptions. Reproductions of vintage cards are stock items in New Orleans' French Quarter while original postcards are available in memorabilia shops, trade shows, and antique markets. "Yuletide," a rare edition postcard of the Gold Dust Twin Santas dressed in fur-trimmed hats and skirts and carrying a bag filled with boxes of soap may command more than $200 from collectors.[58]

The Hallmark company has created "Mahogany," a special division of greeting cards featuring African Americans. The images of black children are markedly improved.

The 1909 billboard featuring the servile soap powder boys is a sharp contrast to the "Got Milk?" billboards graced by Venus and Serena Williams in the late 1990s. The "milk moustache," an identifiable trademark, "worn" by the seventeen and nineteen-year-old tennis champions is no different from that seen on the upper lips of other celebrities who encourage milk consumption. The caption, "Make ours doubles," puns on their tremendous tennis success.[59]

As partners, the sisters won the U.S. and French Opens in 1999 and at Wimbledon in 2000. "We hate to lose," say the two before adding "nutrients, that is." Milk contains nine essential nutrients for active bodies; therefore, the sisters declare, "It's the only thing we serve." Perhaps children seeing the popular ads will make the connection between drinking milk, healthy bodies, and athletic prowess. Furthermore, the confident posture of the teenagers, who earn millions of dollars in product endorsements, make it clear that they are not unwitting ploys for the print media to depict them as anything other than what they are—champions.[60]

Figure 12 Large crowd looking at the burned body of Jesse Washington, eighteen-year-old African American, lynched in Waco, Texas, May 15, 1916

Source: Library of Congress, LC-USZ62-35348.

CHAPTER NINE

African American Youth Face Violence and Fear of Violence in Nineteenth- and Twentieth-Century America

The scale of this carnage means that, on the average, a black man, woman or child was [lynched] nearly once a week, every week, between 1882 and 1930 by a hate-driven white mob.

—Stewart E. Tolnay and E. M. Beck[1]

It would be disingenuous to say that violence and the fear of violence pervaded the lives of many African American children, but it is not presumptuous to say little is known about how terror impacted upon these children or how they responded to it. Over time, intimidating challenges to their mental and physical well being such as sales, threats of sales, and indiscriminate corporal punishment, subsided. By contrast, other forms of physical violence, especially rape and arbitrary killing or lynching, became even more serious threats well into the twentieth century.

The words rape and lynch are gendered and colored to the degree that many persons readily conjure up images of "white women" at the pronouncements of "rape" and think "black men" when they hear the word "lynch." Furthermore, conventional wisdom has suggested that black females are promiscuous and cannot be raped; therefore, white society placed little legal value upon sexual violations of these women but made the sexual abuse, real or imagined, of white females by black males capital offenses.[2]

The late-nineteenth- and early-twentieth-century media did much to popularize and maintain the farcical relationship between the "black-male-rapist" myth and lynching. Historical data do not support sexual assault or the allegations thereof as evident in the cases of thousands of children and adults—black, white, and other—who died at the hands of mobs for charges of murder, murderous assault, accessory to murder, complicity in murder, poisoning, and arson. Other reasons, including unwise remarks, writing insulting notes, knowledge of theft, and mistaken identity, were the bases for taking lives. Furthermore, race prejudice as a cause for lynching illustrates the rash behavior of white men and women who rushed to snuff out the lives of persons they deemed guilty of an offense, racism, which they also harbored. Despite the array of reasons other than rape or allegations of rape, the fear of losing one's life for intimacy, real or imagined, with white women remained constant threats for southern black males throughout much of the twentieth century.[3]

One of the most poignant realities of what it has meant to be a black male accused of sexual impropriety occurred in 1955 when Emmett Till died a tortuous death at the hands of white Mississippians. They lynched the fourteen-year-old boy for allegedly whistling at a white woman. Few of Till's contemporaries articulated their reactions to this tragedy as graphically as did Anne Moody when she wrote:

> Before Emmett Till's murder, I had known the fear of hunger, hell, and the Devil. But now there was a new fear known to me—fear of being killed just because I was black. This was the worst of my fears. I knew once I got food, the fear of starving to death would leave. I also was told if I were a good girl, I wouldn't have to fear the Devil or hell. But I didn't know what one had to do or not do as a Negro not to be killed.

Moody's commentary gives pause and raises questions about the extent to which other black children over time have wondered what they had to do or not do as African Americans to remain alive and free of physical danger.[4]

This chapter examines acts of physical violence, especially rape and arbitrary killing or lynching, against black girls and boys to illuminate their reactions and the resulting impact over time. The intent herein is not to argue that these heinous acts are comparable but to direct the focus upon black children who suffered as primary and vicarious victims of such violence.

Although mobs formed and lynched persons accused of violating community mores prior to the emancipation, few of the victims were enslaved because of slaveowners' interests in power and profits. However, there were instances in which enslaved children were touched by or witnessed the violent death of another slave. Such was the case with Joe, a ten-year-old boy, who was present during the August 27, 1827, stabbing of Gilbert, a man owned by Andrew Jackson, at the hands of Jackson's overseer, Ira Walton. The unfortunate incident occurred at the Hermitage, General Jackson's plantation near Nashville, Tennessee, when the overseer attempted to chastise Gilbert, a thirty-five to forty-year-old slave whom he considered recalcitrant.[5]

The overseer testified at a coroner's inquest that Gilbert, a strong-willed muscular man, had a penchant for running away. In fact, a Mr. M'Callough had brought Gilbert, with his hands tied, to the Hermitage, the night before his death. Although Walton claimed Jackson had indulged Gilbert's past behavior, it is clear from Jackson's correspondence to Egbert Harris, another of his overseers, that his indulgence was not without a toll. With reference to Gilbert's April 1822 flight, Jackson wrote, "I have only to say, you know my disposition, and as far as lenity can be extended to these unfortunate creatures, I wish you to do so." Of great significance in his instructions, Jackson added, "Subordination must be obtained first, and then good treatment." Jackson decided to sell Gilbert, and Walton's task was to deliver him to a Nashville trader the following day. But, in keeping with Jackson's philosophy regarding the management of slaves, "Subordination must be obtained," he asked Walton to take Gilbert out to a field where other slaves were working and to whip him moderately.[6]

Joe accompanied the two men.[7]

Gilbert, with his hands still tied, must have suspected something was afoot as they headed toward a field where slaves were working. Once Walton ordered Joe to climb a hornbeam sapling and break off several branches, his intent to whip Gilbert was clear. While the overseer diverted his attention to the boy, Gilbert, according to Walton, untied his hands and assaulted him. "I have no doubt," testified the overseer, that he would "have killed me had I not drawn my dirk and stabbed him." After several thrusts with the knife, Gilbert knocked the weapon from Walton's hand.[8]

Seeing this intense life-threatening struggle must have been disconcerting for Joe, but the simultaneous commands from the overseer and enslaved man to retrieve and hand over the knife probably exacerbated the child's confusion. No doubt the boy must have asked himself whose demands he should obey. As he hesitated, Walton ordered him to stab Gilbert. Joe obeyed and plunged the knife into the fleshy part of Gilbert's thigh. Walton then ordered Joe to stab Gilbert in the side. When the boy approached, according to Walton, "Gilbert threw out one of his feet against him . . . by the violence of the blow, [Joe] was thrown off to a considerable distance and fell." Gilbert swore, testified Walton, that he would kill Joe if he did not "keep off."[9]

Walton had placed the child in the awkward position of first gathering the instruments of terror and then demanding that he assist in subduing Gilbert. It is not clear if Joe feared the loss of his life based upon Gilbert's threat or if he dreaded the possible consequences of not obeying the overseer. Nevertheless, he handed the knife over to Walton and watched him stab Gilbert in the stomach before cutting a deep gash in the back and side of his neck. Walton tried to sever an artery. The child became alarmed and ran to the nearby field for help. Upon his return, General Jackson had reached the scene. He called for a doctor to treat Gilbert, but it was no use.[10]

Afterward, Andrew Jackson dismissed Walton and asked for a coroner's inquest along with an indictment for manslaughter. Jackson declared that he had no wish to try Walton other than as "guardian" of his slave. "It is my duty to prosecute the case so far as justice to him may require it," said Jackson. The slaveowner's paternalism turned upon the belief that Gilbert's hands remained tied and Walton inflicted the fatal wound in Gilbert's back as he ran away from the scuffle. Jackson showed interest in "justice" for Gilbert, yet he exuded no visible concern for Joe and the impact the killing had upon his emotional well being.[11]

Unlike Anne Moody, Joe left no extant record about his reaction to Gilbert's death. As a result, it will remain unclear about whether he lamented about his role in the fatal struggle or asked himself about differences in the consequences had he given the knife to Gilbert rather than to Walton. No one will ever know if Joe were as sure as Andrew Jackson that Gilbert died of a wound in his back rather than the one he inflicted. Questions will remain about how Gilbert's death influenced Joe's perception of the overseer who replaced Ira Walton and if the child feared the possibility of another overseer–slave confrontation and another death. In short, Joe did not know what one had to do or not do as an enslaved child to remain alive and well.

The slave-born Frederick Douglass wrote about a remarkably similar incident that occurred when he was a child on the Maryland plantation owned by Colonel Edward Lloyd. Douglass's description does not provide details about what preceded the confrontation between the overseer, Austin Gore, and Bill Denby, described as an "unmanageable" slave, but Douglass wrote clearly about Gore shooting and killing the man. Afterward Gore, like Walton, faced criminal prosecution but was not indicted for manslaughter.[12]

Colonel Lloyd, unlike General Jackson, did not fire the overseer. "His very presence was fearful," wrote Douglass, "and I shunned him as I would have shunned a rattlesnake. His piercing black eyes and sharp, shrill voice ever awakened sensations of dread." It is reasonable to think that Joe's opinion of Walton would not have differed greatly from Douglass's, especially after being a part of the deadly conflict between Walton and Gilbert.[13]

To be sure, some enslaved males as well as females died at the hand of whites, but as chattel property they represented an economic asset; therefore, it is unlikely that slaveowning capitalists with an eye on profit margins would destroy or permit the destruction of economic investments with abandon. In 1800, the cost of a prime hand in Georgia was $450 but had risen to $1,050 in 1851. Less than ten years afterward, the price of a prime hand had risen to $1,650. Damage or destruction to slaves translated into economic losses for owners. Consequently, slaveholders were likely to prosecute others, such as Walton and Gore, if they were responsible for the physical impairment or death of another's slave, a prime capital investment. Legislation existed against the wanton killing of slaves.[14]

By contrast, there was not a shadow of protection for enslaved girls or boys against sexual violence. According to Harriet Jacobs, it could be inflicted upon them by "fiends who bear the shape of men." Enslaved females, especially, were subjected to rape by men, black, white, enslaved, and emancipated. Much of the sexual abuse directed at them by white males was linked to the stereotypical notion that black women were naturally promiscuous. As a result, this erroneous idea provided a ready rational for the sexual abuse of black females.[15]

The historian Eugene Genovese claims that married slaves "did not take white sexual aggression lightly and resisted effectively enough to hold it to a minimum." Many white men, he argues, avoided "resistant women and dangerous men" by directing their attention toward "single girls by using a combination of flattery, bribes and the ever-present threat of force." It is unlikely that these "resistant women and dangerous men," especially the mothers and fathers of "single girls," would take sexual aggression toward their children lightly regardless of the perpetrator's color.[16]

There are examples of families and friends who acted individually and collectively to shield enslaved girls from sexual exploitation whether it was at the hands of owners or others. One readily available account is that focusing upon Solomon Northrup's observation of an enslaved woman who learned that her daughter, a mulatto, would be offered for sale in the "fancy trade," business arrangements designed especially to provide enslaved concubines for white men. In the eyes of the trader the child was highly valued as a "fancy girl," a female used primarily for the sexual pleasure of an owner, and could earn him as much as $5,000 on the New Orleans market. To the "absolutely frantic" of a mother, her daughter was priceless. But, no amount of pleading dissuaded the trader from selling the child away from her.[17]

Eliza failed to save her young daughter from that dreaded fate, but Paul Edmondson was successful in keeping his daughters, Mary and Emily, from being sold on the New Orleans market in the 1840s. The fifteen- and thirteen-year-old Washington, D.C.-born sisters were among a group of seventy-five slaves aboard the schooner *Pearl* when they attempted to escape from bondage. Their flight was unsuccessful due to adverse weather and betrayal by a disgruntled slave. Several slaveowners marshaled forces, overtook the *Pearl*, and returned the fugitives to custody. In the meantime, the slaveowner sold Emily and Mary to Bruin & Hill, a slave trading business in Alexandria, Virginia. They set an unusually high price on the young girls because they "had those peculiar attractions of form, of feature, and complexion, which southern connoisseurs in sensualism so highly prize."[18]

The traders expected to earn a handsome sum for the girls in New Orleans but decided not to remain there and expose them to the current ravages of yellow fever. The girls' plight might have easily escaped public notice without the national attention given to the trial of the *Pearl*'s captain. Newspaper editors who opposed slavery publicized the trial and linked the children's name with that of the fated ship. It was to the girls' good fortune since the case drew national coverage and gave Paul Edmondson time to involve the New York Anti-Slavery Society in their case. He worked along with the antislavery society, local churches, and the well-known minister and abolitionist Henry Ward Beecher, to raise enough money to buy and free his daughters.[19]

Mary and Emily Edmondson were fortunate indeed to be free from the foreboding abuse, and there is no accurate count of the number of other children who escaped sexual exploitation while enslaved. To be sure, many slaves were abused, but there is no accurate way of knowing the number of children who resisted the aggression. Neither is the extent to which they would go to protect themselves from abuse known.[20]

One of the most dramatic and unusual cases of sexual abuse, resistance, and violence involves Celia, an enslaved teenager, in antebellum Missouri. The recently widowed white Missouri farmer, Robert Newsom, bought the girl at an 1850 auction in Audrain County, Missouri. There is no evidence to suggest that she behaved like the proverbial Jezebel and lured the sixty-year-old man into an intimate encounter while in route home from the sale. Nevertheless, he raped her. Newsom's aggression continued until 1855 when Celia allegedly killed him and burned the body in her fireplace.[21]

Charged with a capital crime, and entitled to a jury trial along with court-appointed counsel, Celia, a pregnant nineteen-year-old mother of two mulatto children, stood trial. Her defense team resorted to a clever argument based upon an 1845 Missouri statute against coercing "any woman unlawfully against her will and by force, menace or duress . . . to be defiled." The court asserted that the statute did not protect Celia. Such a safeguard against sexual abuse in Missouri, or elsewhere in the slaveholding South, would have given Celia and millions of other enslaved females legal rights to defend themselves against all sexual aggression.[22]

On the surface, the argument appears a sincere effort to defend a client. On another level it seems to have been a mere exercise in jurisprudence designed to pacify antislavery advocates more than to convince a jury containing white slaveholders of the black teenager's attempt to shield herself against sexual abuse. After all, was it reasonable to expect an all white male jury to find Celia, a black female, innocent of killing their neighbor, and perhaps their friend, to avoid sexual exploitation? Celia was Newsom's legal property, and he was within his rights to determine the nature of their relationship, even if it included rape.[23]

Harriet Jacobs wrote about sexual abuse in her autobiographical *Incidents in the Life of a Slave Girl*. Jacobs declares that "the war" of her life began at age fourteen when her owner's father, the medical doctor James Norcom initiated an unrelenting period of sexual harassment. Jacobs's word choice to describe the power relationship with Norcom is revealing. To suggest that the two of them engaged in "war" illustrates that she was not a helpless victim nor could she be accused of willingly engaging in an illicit affair with him. Jacobs's narrative destabilizes the idea of a morally bankrupt black woman who gives definition to the mythical "Jezebel," a timeless construction of a naturally promiscuous woman capable of seducing innocent men.[24]

Norcom's attention did not flatter Jacobs. Instead, she claimed enslaved girls, such as herself, lived in an environment filled with fear. She understood the licentious nature of many associations between slaveholding men and the women they owned. In her opinion, "the profligate men who have power over [them] may be exceedingly odious."[25]

Perhaps the enslaved Texan Rose Williams thought of her owner, Hall Hawkins, forcing her to marry Rufus " 'gainst her "wants" as an odious abuse of power by a profligate man. Calling herself an "igno'mus chile," Williams had no idea that as a married woman she was to do more than "tend de cabin for Rufus." When he insisted upon sleeping with her, the seventeen-year-old literally kicked him from the nuptial bed and defended herself with a fireplace poker. To her dismay, she soon learned that the "de Marster's wishes" were for the couple to bring forth "portly chillen."[26]

Rose Williams compelled herself to live with Rufus to avoid corporal punishment. Besides, she said, "I thinks 'bout massa buyin' me offen de block and savin' me from bein' sep'rated from my folks." Rose was in a precarious situation and expressed exasperation when she asked, "What am I's to do?" On the one hand, she knew if she refused to be a wife to Rufus, Hawkins would punish or even sell her. On the other hand, Rose had the temporary assurance that her parents were nearby, the sole mitigating factor in her decision to be a wife to Rufus.[27]

The former enslaved Virginians, Louisa and Sam Everett, like Rose and Rufus Williams, had been forced into marriage by their owner who encouraged indiscriminate mating. This was indeed odious to Sam and Louisa Everett. She told the WPA interviewer:

> Marce Jim [McClain] called me and Sam ter him and ordered Sam to pull off his shirt— that was all the McClain niggers wore—and he said to me; "[Louisa] do you think you can stand this big nigger?" He had that old bull whip flung acrost his shoulder and Lawd, that man could hit so hard! So I jes said "yassur, I guess so," and tried to hide my face so I couldn't see Sam's nakedness, but he made me look at him anyhow.

Louisa Everett did not provide their ages, but Sam's garment was the ordinary clothing of a child not yet old enough to complete the chores of adult men, such as plowing. Perhaps he was twelve or thirteen years of age at the time.[28]

The licentiousness of the forced arrangement was extraordinarily humiliating to Louisa Everett. Her mortification reached a devastating plateau when the owner told the young couple "what they must get busy and do." Everett added, "And, we had to do it." "To do *it*" meant that she and Sam were to engage in sexual intercourse while Jim McClain gazed upon them. What were the alternatives and costs for Louisa and Sam? Despite the perverse arrangement under which they consummated their "marriage," they shared a common exploitation and remained together. "Sam was kind to me," said Louisa, "and I learnt to love him."[29]

By contrast, Rose Williams hated Rufus, whom she considered a bully. Her testimony suggests that he was more mature than she, understood the marital arrangement, and behaved as if he were "entitled" to a wife to fulfill his sexual desires. Although Rose Williams did not articulate the concept of marital rape, she felt oppressed and betrayed by Rufus who reported her obstinacy to their owner's wife.[30]

Rose detested Rufus immensely and was equally adamant about Hall Hawkins. Once emancipated, she freed herself of Rufus and vowed to never have "any truck [association] wid any man" saying one " 'sperience am 'nough." Long after slavery ended, Rose Williams remembered "Master Hawkins" and declared that she would "always hold it 'gainst him" for "w'at he done."[31]

The marriage to Rufus affected Rose deeply, and she put it into her distant past. She preferred to rear her two children, one of whom was born after emancipation, without Rufus. Ultimately, the children would suffer from the results of forcing their parents into a marriage with individuals they did not choose or love.

The testimony from Rose Williams and Louisa Everett reveal intimate details about their private lives. Beyond the lucid expressions of fear of separation from loved ones or the searing whip, their testimony lapses into vagueness about their own sexuality. Williams refers to "*w'at* he done" and Everett uses "*it*" as tropes. Similarly, Harriet Jacobs and Elizabeth Keckley, authors who published narratives about their enslavement, also spoke gingerly about their sexuality. That they divulged any personal information in print or privately is somewhat unusual. Ordinarily, sexually abused persons submerge themselves in a culture of dissemblance and remain silent or resort to codes.[32]

If licentiousness were as prevalent as Jacobs and Everett suggested, whether one talked about it or not, it is not likely that the behavior was confined to any age, region, or gender. In fact, the historian Norrece T. Jones, Jr. maintains that "there is no reason to assume . . . [homosexual] slaveholders were any less predatory than their heterosexual counterparts." The historian Nell Painter suggested "that about 10 percent of [slave] masters . . . slept or wanted to sleep with their enslaved men and boys, some mistresses possibly also regarded their female slaves as objects of desire." Similarly, Orlando Patterson believes homosexual assaults upon slaves were not unknown. The scholar suggests that homosexuality has existed in every known human society with an estimated 3 to 6 percent among whites Americans who, writes Patterson, found "themselves with total power, and no risk of arrest, over fine-looking slave boys, it is a reasonable assumption that they would have exploited them in some cases." Furthermore, Patterson concludes, "Southern culture was highly honorific, with a considerable degree of male bonding and homoerotic male play." Based upon his study of the literature about honorific societies, Patterson added, "They tend to have a higher than normal proportion of homosexuals." Considering the foregoing, it is reasonable to conclude that homosexuality existed in selected relationships between slaveowners and enslaved persons.[33]

Perhaps Harriet Jacobs was referring to homosexual or homoerotic behavior when she wrote about a slaveholder's treatment of Luke, an acquaintance. The young slave "became a prey to the vices growing out of the 'patriarchal institution' " and endured frequent beatings, according to Jacobs. Luke's owner "took into his head the strangest freaks of despotism; and if Luke hesitated to submit to his orders," wrote Jacobs, the owner authorized the constable to whip him. Jacobs provided no specifics about what transpired between Luke and his owner that caused such commotions in the household when writing "Some of these freaks were of a nature too filthy to be repeated." There are no clues about what Jacobs considers "vices" and "freaks." She provides no explanation as to why Luke's owner, whom Jacobs described as a "mere degraded wreck of manhood" chained the slave to his bedside. Finally, an understanding of the criteria upon which Jacobs constructed the idea of "manhood" would be useful in determining the relationship between Luke and his owner.[34]

The subject of sexual exploitation in the slave era needs additional research since its major focus is upon the heterosexual exploitation of enslaved women by white men to the virtual exclusion of homosexuality. Until recently sexual behavior considered deviant from what the majority population believes is "normal" has received little historical attention. Other disciplines have been less reticent and have provided useful studies. For example, Wainwright Churchill, a clinical psychologist and one of the founders of Philadelphia's Psychoanalytic Studies Institute, investigated male homosexuality cross-culturally and concluded that "homosexual responsiveness is far more frequent among males than females" in all societies. Churchill's data reveal that homosexual contact is most frequent and characteristic of relationships between older and younger males rather than between equally mature men.[35]

Many homosexuals construct "double lives" for their own convenience if exposing their sexual preference, identity, and choice will jeopardize their economic, social, or physical well being. "Discreet" behavior does not draw unwanted attention or harassment from family, friends, neighbors, or complete strangers. If secrecy were important to gay slaveholders, what better way was there to protect one's identity and exercise privileges than to engage in homosexual activities with enslaved persons? After all, to whom could enslaved males and females complain and what would be the costs of their complaints?[36]

The slave narratives do not contain testimony about sexuality that might be construed as homosexual or homoerotic, but this silence does not mean the absence of either occurrence. Instead, it is more likely that the subject was not open for discussion because it did not conform to the dominant or accepted pattern of sexuality. Although dissemblance is considered peculiar to female culture, it is not unreasonable to think males also resort to dissemblance in situations where they experienced shame or wished to avoid questions about their own manhood.[37]

Once slavery ended, parents no longer feared the licentiousness associated with the wishes of profligate owners, yet their children were not completely free of potential sexual abuse. A former slave articulated concerns about protecting his daughters when considering returning to work for his former owner in Tennessee. "Please state," Jourdan Anderson wrote, "if there would be any safety for my Milly and Jane." The young girls were coming of age and pretty, according to their father. "You know how it was," Anderson chided, "with poor Matilda and Catherine." Anderson does not define "it" or explain what happened to "poor" Matilda and Catherine, but the inference is clear when he continued saying he prefers remaining in Ohio and starving rather than have his young daughters "brought to shame by the violence and wickedness of their young masters," if the family returned to Tennessee.[38]

Anderson exerted his right as a free man to protect Milly and Jane from harm. His older daughters and many other enslaved girls, including Harriet Jacobs and Elizabeth Keckley, suffered from the "violence and wickedness" of men empowered by the institution of slavery. The Thirteenth Amendment, ratified December 1865, ended slavery, but "violence and wickedness" in addition to "licentiousness and fear" remained. In actuality, some historians have argued that violence against blacks intensified after emancipation. Once slavery disappeared, slaveholders, like Andrew Jackson, no longer had any interests in protecting former slaves or their offspring. Without pecuniary and ostensibly benevolent reasons to circumvent violence against African Americans, mayhem and murder prevailed.[39]

The heightened hostility against blacks began during the Civil War, and freedpersons knew immediately that new and significantly more savage dangers faced them. As a result of fundamental changes in civic and political conditions, black females were now subjected to a kind of violence that was unknown heretofore. White men used rape as an instrument of terror to destroy pride and confidence accrued through freedom. It was also a way for the men to regain and solidify power and privilege lost through the abolition of slavery.[40]

Congressional Reports and Bureau of Refugees, Freedmen, and Abandoned Lands papers are replete with testimony about violent acts, sometimes called "outrages" inflicted with impunity upon blacks in the postwar era. The WPA narratives also contains eyewitness accounts of the brutality. The slave-born Millie Bates, a resident of Union, South Carolina, described what she defined as "de worsest time of all." As if the horrendous event had just occurred, Bates told the interviewer about "de Ku Klux":

> We wuz little chilluns a playin' in Dans house. We didn't know he had done nothin' ginst de white folks . . . when something hit on de wall. Dan, he jump up and try to git outten de winder. A white spooky thing had done come in de doo' right by me. I was so scairt dat I could not git up.

Her fear intensified when the "white spooky thing" shot and killed Dan. Bates managed to scramble under a bed. "When I got dar," she said, "all de other chilluns wuz dar to, lookin' as white as ashed dough from hickory wood."[41]

Remembering the terror prompted Bates to remark, "Ain't no bed ebber done as much good as dat one." Unfortunately, there was nothing to protect her afterward from seeing Dan's body hanging "to a simmon tree," and knowing that "Dey [whites responsible for the murder] would not let his folks take him down." According to Bates, "He jus stayed dar till he fell to pieces." The psychological toll upon Bates and the other children was immeasurable. She placed its permanent dimension within the historical context when she added: "It still makes de shivvers run down my spine and here I is ole and you all a sittin' around wid me and two mo' wars done gone since dat awful time."[42]

The treatment of newly freed girls and women during the 1866 riots in Memphis was also devastating. "The crowning act of atrocity and diabolism," according to one Congressional report, was the "ravishing" of an unknown number of black women. Sixteen-year-old Lucy Smith was present during the 1866 Memphis riots when four "fiends in human shape" beat and raped the crippled ex-slave Frances Thompson. Smith testified before a House Select Committee that the men drew their weapons, threatened to shoot, and burn the house if she and Thompson did not "let them have their way." One man seized and choked Smith before raping her. The teenager escaped further violation because, as one man said, "she was so *near dead he would not have anything to do with her.*" That did not stop him from striking her "a severe blow upon the side of the head." Smith's neck injuries prevented her from speaking for two weeks.[43]

Black females, without regard for age, who endured such violence at the hands of whites had no husbands, fathers, uncles, brothers, or sons who could completely shield them from the vehemence. Black men were as vulnerable to white mobs as the women during this reign of terror when a new double standard governing interracial sex emerged.

Before slavery ended, black males had not uniformly endured violent retribution for sexual intimacy with white females. The prevailing stereotypical notion that it was poor white licentious females who chose black lovers absolved them from retribution. Society's devaluation of the women's worth rendered their selection of black men of little or no social consequence. The poor white women were assumed to be promiscuous and exhibiting a predilection for debauchery while elite white women, accorded to the typecast, represented southern ideals of purity.[44]

Furthermore, in instances where black males were accused of rape or attempted rape before the emancipation, they received trials and often escaped capital punishment. In more than 150 cases of alleged rape of white women in Virginia between 1800 and 1865, almost one-half of the condemned blacks avoided execution. Once slavery ended, "white anxiety and alarm over black male sexuality reached an unprecedented level of intensity," according to historian Martha Hodes. The value of those previously denounced poor white women rose as freed blacks began exercising newly gained civil rights in heading families, earning a living, and making other decisions about their lives. As citizens, this was in keeping with the rights and privileges extended by the Thirteenth and Fourteenth Amendments.[45]

Additionally, the Fifteenth Amendment guaranteed that the men's right to vote would not be interfered with based upon previous conditions of servitude. This combination of civil and political rights along with hopeful aspirations of economic independence projected black men beyond the old parameters of white control. To curtail black potential as politically conscious citizens, whites sought ways to reinstitute social controls. Whites feared that politically conscious blacks would demand social equality, which in their minds, would lead to miscegenation. As a result, laws criminalizing what previously passed as relatively innocuous behavior, including black intimacy with white women, proliferated.[46]

In writing about the shifts in black–white relationships, historian Joel Williamson noted that between 1889 and 1915 several states in the lower South "internalized the 'Radical mentality' and reformed their institutions to radically reduce black people educationally, judicially, politically, and materially, and to remove them generally further away from the sources of power." In the meantime, whites argued that the black population would destroy itself due to improvidence, disease, and the general inability to compete in a free society. Until those erasures occurred, whites resorted to disfranchisement, segregation, and lynching as measures of political and social control.[47]

Such an environment fostered the creation of the mythical "beastly black rapist" from the loveable servile and equally mythical Sambo. Sex, or allegations of sex, between black males and white females was now more risky than ever and could lead to a ritualistic death at the hands of a white lynch mob. Few of the thousands of African Americans lynched between 1880 and 1980 were children, but that does not mean they did not suffer vicariously from the extralegal killing of their fathers, uncles, brothers, and male playmates, or mothers, aunts, sisters, and female playmates across geographical boundaries.[48]

The literature on lynching illuminates diversity according to the age, background, and culture of its authors. Many white historians, even those who specialize in southern culture, refrain from writing about lynching while black scholars note and contextualize it as a prominent occurrence in American history. Joel Williamson commented about the absence of such discussions in his historical reflections, "Wounds Not Scars: Lynching, the National Conscience, and the American Historian." David Levering Lewis, who reviewed the Williamson essay before it appeared in the March 1997 *The Journal of American History*, March 1997, responded:

> The situation here is rather analogous to the familiar plaint of a generation of Germans about knowing nothing of the Holocaust. Repression, conspiracy of silence, genteel protocols among WASP scholars during the long night from *Plessy* to *Brown* is a more authentic way of assaying what wasn't being talked about. Finally, of course, there is no "silence" about lynching in the press, white or black.

Neither is there "silence" among black scholars. Rayford Logan's *The Negro in American Life and Thought* (1954) captures the essence of the period in which the majority of lynchings occurred.[49]

Differences in historical accountings aside, lynching was so much a part of southern history that its culture and literature brim with it. Indeed, few of its citizens in the late nineteenth and early twentieth centuries have no awareness of its occurrence. "The scale of the carnage between 1882 and 1930," write the scholars Stewart E. Tolnay and E. M. Beck, "meant, on the average, a black man, woman or child was lynched every week by a hate-driven white mob."[50]

Lynchings were often festivals of violence when large crowds of white children and adults gathered to witness the ghoulish summary executions. Sterling Brown's "Old Lem" says repeatedly, "They don't come by ones / They don't come by twos /" instead, "they come by tens." In actuality, they came by the hundreds and sometimes the thousands to participate in dispensing of what they considered as "justice." It was not unusual for onlookers to bring weapons, fire rounds of ammunition at the corpse, chat with bystanders, collect souvenirs of bone fragments or teeth, pose for photographs with the victim's mutilated remains, and use picture postcards to announce the occasion to family or friends not in attendance.[51]

Claude McKay's "The Lynching," describes the ugly orchestrated scenario of a victim's spirit ascending to heaven amid the smoke from the blaze that smothered out the life. The poet noted the dawn afterward when a mixed crowd came to view the charred remains of the accused. "The women," wrote McKay, showed no sorrow in their "eyes of steely blue." Even more arresting, the "little lads, lynchers that were to be / Danced round the dreadful thing in fiendish glee." Photographs of white children and adults in the crowds lend credibility to McKay's notion that some whites were not at all disturbed by this torturous violence. The placid looking and sometimes smiling spectators posed for photographs with what they dubbed the "negro barbecue."[52]

Several "little lads" capitalized upon the May 15, 1916, lynching of Jesse Washington in Waco, Texas, by selling souvenirs. A jury found the seventeen-year-old Washington guilty of murdering and raping Lucy Fryer, a fifty-two-year-old white woman, May 8, 1916. A group of spectators in the courtroom seized Washington and proceeded toward a site where local citizens were building a bonfire. The mob stabbed and hanged him before hoisting his body above the fire where it remained for nearly two hours. A horseman removed the charred body and drug it through primary streets of the town. In the process, the head separated from the body. Several young boys, perhaps from the local school, who spent their lunch hour at the lynching, retrieved the head "extracted the teeth and sold them for five dollars apiece." Whatever they earned was profit since the enterprise had cost them nothing. They merely seized an opportunity to provide souvenirs to an eager clientele.[53]

The entertainer Billie Holiday's rendition of "Strange Fruit," based upon the lyrics and melody written by Lewis Allen, calls attention to bucolic southern scenery and the sweet scent of one of its most representative flowering trees. Within this hospitable environment, abnormally inhospitable events, lynchings, occurred with frequency. Holiday sang about the cacophony in the wind when black bodies swayed in the breezes and scents of magnolia trees mixed with burning flesh. Whether artists protested lynching through poems or songs, their outpourings politicized the popular culture. They and millions of other Americans lived in a society that cultivated mean soil and knew liberal applications of hatred and acts of inhumanity produced bitter results.[54]

Hearing about the summary execution of another person was chilling but what was it like to witness such events unfold? Mary McLeod Bethune was only twelve years old in 1887 when she saw a noose tightened around the neck of a black man, a potential candidate for lynching, because he refused to blow out a match upon the command of a drunken white man. The incident exemplified the height of man's inhumanity to man and terrified Bethune. Fortunately, calmer heads prevailed and halted the lynching. Whether the execution continued or ceased, it left an indelible impression upon her.[55]

Three years after Bethune's brush with terror, several white boys, thirteen years of age or less, in Richmond, Virginia's East End had conflicts with blacks in the neighborhood and decided to kill them. The "little lads, lynchers that were to be," had murder in mind and only needed to find an appropriate object of their venom. A twelve-year-old black boy became their moving target but escaped the youthful mob's stones by taking refuge in a white woman's house. The local African American newspaper, *Richmond Planet,* lamented that the frequency of lynchings had provided an awful example for children to imitate. That boys so young would embrace lynching as a way of solving problems with peers speaks volumes about their understanding of mob rule, the criminal justice system, and the sanctity of another's life. The miserable soil upon which the boys grounded their ideas had the potential for bearing "strange fruit."[56]

The event involving the youngsters in Richmond ended without deadly consequences, but another that also began as a conflict in 1931 between black and white youth resulted in a horrendous nightmare after nine young black males, known as the "Scottsboro Boys," hitched a ride on a freight train from Chattanooga, Tennessee, to Paint Rock, Alabama. Clarence Norris, who was eighteen years old at the time, argued that he was only guilty of stealing a ride on the train as did the "mean, prejudiced crackers." The black and white "hobos," began a fight in which the blacks won. According to Norris, "We threw their asses off the train in a fair fight and they went running to the nearest sheriff to report a pack of uppity niggers."[57]

Ordinarily, a case of vagrancy and possibly assault would not have become an international *cause celebre.* But, this was no ordinary case since Ruby Bates and Victoria Price, two white women on the train, claimed the black youth had raped them. The women saved themselves from arrest as vagrants while relegating the black youth to a very dangerous position. Norris admitted, "I was scared before, but it wasn't nothing to how I felt [while awaiting trial] I knew if a white woman accused a black man of rape, he was as good as dead." The case of the nine, minimally educated and unemployed, black youth ranging in age from thirteen to twenty years old is instructive in showing how the accusation of rape and specter of death intersected. The Scottsboro Boys escaped a lynching but remained incarcerated for a combined total of 104 years despite evidence to prove their innocence.[58]

The Scottsboro case should be read in conjunction with the 1958 Monroe, North Carolina, case evolving from a "kissing game" played by three white girls and two black boys. The kissing case is an excellent study of radical racism associated with suggestions of interracial sex. The eight-year-old David E. "Fuzzy" Simpson and his ten-year-old pal, James Hanover Thompson, soon learned the implicit danger of innocent play with white girls. As white imaginations ran amok, a mob formed, and threatened to lynch the boys for their "offense." When the eight-year-old Sissy Sutton's mother learned that a black boy had kissed her daughter, she declared repeatedly that she "would have killed Hanover" had the opportunity arisen.[59]

The local police arrested the children ostensibly to protect them. While in custody, law officials beat and badgered the boys unmercifully. On October 31, the officers draped themselves in sheets and terrified the children into thinking the Ku Klux Klan had broken into the jail to lynch them. The children were probably more intimidated by the police than by the mob outside. After six days of incarceration, and without benefit of counsel or seeing their parents, a judge reviewed the case charging Thompson and Simpson with assault and molestation. He sentenced the children to an indefinite term at the state school for delinquents. In the meantime, the court mentioned something about good behavior and possible release before they reached twenty-one years of age.[60]

Similar to the Scottsboro case, the kissing case received national and international press coverage and attention from the National Association for the Advancement of Colored People. The International Labor Defense, the legal arm of the American Communist Party, assisted the Scottsboro Boys in winning their freedom while the Southern Workers Party, an offshoot of the American Communist Party, gave support for Thompson and Simpson's releases. The cases are comparable in showing how allegations and illusions of sexual misconduct could have deadly consequences.[61]

The seventeen-year-old Cordie Cheek of Maury County, Tennessee, was as innocent of the sexual impropriety as the nine youths in Scottsboro, Alabama, and the two boys in Monroe, North Carolina, but he died at the hands of a white lynch mob in 1933 when "Lady Ann" Moore, an eleven-year-old white girl accused the black teenager of rape. The background for the homicide originated with a dispute between Cheek and Lady Ann's nineteen-year-old brother, Henry Carl. Cordie and Henry were well acquainted since they lived near each other, and Cordie's mother, Tenny, had worked as maid, midwife, and cook for the Moores over the years and was not opposed to her son completing chores for them. Henry Moore was a prime mover in the killing of his former playmate, who was two years younger.[62]

Clearly, Henry had outgrown Cordie and cared nothing about his life or what the loss of it would mean to the Cheeks. They had befriended him when his mother died and his father committed suicide. Any good will that existed between Cordie and Henry evaporated when Cordie asked for wages the Moores owned to him and his mother. To the young white teenager, Cordie had stepped out of his place. To further complicate their relationship, Cheek had gotten the better of Moore in a fistfight. Moore did not take it well and developed a plan to rid himself of his old friend, without paying him.[63]

In mid-November 1933, Cordie Cheek chopped wood for the Moores and carried it inside. As he walked past Lady Ann, the jagged edges of the wood snagged her dress. Following the accident, Cheek talked with Ann's older sister about his chores for the next day and left. There was no fuss about the ripped dress until Henry allegedly encouraged Lady Ann to say Cheek had attempted to assault her. Henry gave her one dollar for agreeing to tell the lie. Once he had her consent, Henry quickly notified a local merchant who telephoned friends and neighbors. As a crowd gathered at the grocery, a black employee understood its intent and warned the Cheek family.[64]

Cordie Cheek managed to escape the ensuing mob but was later arrested and spent several weeks in the Nashville jail before a grand jury decided not to indict him. Deemed a free man by law officials, Cheek left the jail. This was tantamount to delivering him to a lynch mob smarting over the delay in parceling out "justice" to a black man who was "too biggity." A group of whites seized Cheek, December 15, 1933, from the home of relatives living at the edge of Fisk University's campus. As they drove through the campus with Cheek, Henry Carl Moore stood on the running board of one of the automobiles brandishing a handgun. Two coeds watched as the cars sped through the campus.[65]

The terror gripping Cordie Cheek probably escalated as the men drove him to an isolated site, telephoned invitations to friends, then waited for the mob of men, women, and children to assemble before executing him. Cheek's distress was probably matched by that felt by James L. Garrett, a black teenager, who happened to be driving a truck past the lynching site with two white passengers, his employer and the employer's son. The mob stopped Garrett. He remained in the truck with his employer's son while the older man joined the lynch mob. From the truck, Garrett saw that Cordie Cheek's hands were "tied behind his back with a strong rope and . . . a rope around his neck. It was a big rope." According the Garrett, "They [the mob] had the rope up on a limb on the tree and a step ladder about four feet high under the limb of the tree." Garrett and the white boy watched as the mob castrated Cheek, led him up the ladder, pushed it from underneath his feet away, and fired round after round of ammunition into the lifeless body. Indeed, as in Claude McKay's poem, Cheek's "father, by the cruelest way of pain / Had bidden him to his bosom once again." It is reasonable to ask if James L. Garrett, like Ann Moody, did not know what to do or not do as an African American to avoid a similar fate.[66]

Garrett granted an interview afterward in which he was asked, "What was Cordie doing?" Garrett responded, "He was standing there trembling." Cheek did not cry, struggle, or speak. According to Garrett, "He was just trembling." No doubt Garrett also trembled as he watched his peer being blindfolded, led up the stepladder, and hanged. He also saw the men as "they passed the pistols around and lots of people shot at him [Cheek]."[67]

Once the mob satisfied its thirst for violence, the cars, 247, according to Garrett's count, began leaving. His employer returned to the truck, and they continued their journey as if nothing had happened. When asked if the whites "sitting by you said anything?" Garrett answered, "No Sir, except they said you don't need to drive so fast." He had noticed a car following him that appeared to slow down and sped up when he did. "You are all right," said the employer, "Nobody's going to hurt you." Garrett was not convinced.[68]

It was impossible for the employer to understand the extent to which the youngster had already been "hurt." To be sure, witnessing the brutal murder was traumatic. In a July 13, 1943, interview with Dr. A. E. Barnett, who was gathering information about the crime, Garrett's parents said for weeks after the lynching their son "was very nervous," had trouble sleeping, and "would wake up screaming." Moreover, he was reluctant to talk about the lynching. How the youngster coped with the immediate stress and its long term effects upon his emotional well-being remains unknown.[69]

As word of the lynching spread, students at Fisk University were particularly troubled. Among those enrolled was the nineteen-year-old John Hope Franklin, president of the student government. He recalled making "loud noises and protests to the mayor, the governor, and even President Franklin D. Roosevelt." No amount of protests, verbal or written, could relieve the students' pain and anguish nor could it bring Cordie Cheek back. Franklin was disillusioned with the president of the university and the President of the United States in their responses or absence of responses regarding the lynching.[70]

Violence of this sort terrorized some youngsters and adults into inertia. When remembering the Emmett Till murder, a Mississippi-born, woman commented about a "suspicious" death within her own family. In the 1940s, a group of white men summoned the help of her grandfather in identifying a man whom they had discovered on the railroad track in her small town. To the older man's horror, it was the mangled body of his own son. In all probability, the death was no more "accidental" than it was "coincidental" that the men, or mob, needed help identifying the "unknown" black man. Memory of her uncle's death melded into her reaction upon hearing about Till. Only one word, "scared," could describe her emotions as a teenager.[71]

No doubt, many black youth, across time and regions, were "scared" by violent acts committed around them, yet some assisted in the attempts to eliminate violence as a result of their own experiences. Examples abound but several will suffice. Lucy Smith's testimony before the 1866 select committee did not result in the arrest of the perpetrators of violence. Instead, it helped several state and national measures to extend protection to blacks during Reconstruction. The nineteen-year-old Angelina Weld Grimké collected signatures in 1899 for the passage of a national antilynch bill. Congress never endorsed such legislation, but the petition campaign helped publicize the evil associated with summary executions.[72]

Even more poignant is the link between Robert F. Williams witnessing violence as an eleven-year-old child in Monroe, North Carolina, and his civil rights activism as an adult. Until he died October 15, 1996, Williams told and retold an account of seeing Sheriff "Big" Jesse Helms kicking, beating, and dragging a black woman off to jail as if it had just happened. In actuality, it was in 1936 when Helms grasped the woman's dress and held it above her head as he pulled her prostrated body across the pavement. It was disturbing for Williams to see Helms's inhumanity to another human and terrifying to hear the woman's screams as her flesh scraped against the cement. It was just as humiliating for the boy to hear the white men, who watched the dastardly act laugh, while the black men, who saw the same thing, remained transfixed in silence.[73]

The incident haunted Williams, and his biographer asserts "that moment marked his life, and his life marked the African American freedom movement in the United States." Williams, one of America's most "dynamic race rebels," was instrumental in using his ingenuity to galvanize the press, local supporters, and national organizations to pressure the local, state, and national government into intervening on behalf of Thompson and Simpson in the kissing case. Perhaps, Williams identified with the two boys who were near his own age when he saw Helms abuse the woman. Whatever the case, he managed to help free the children while calling national and international attention to the case.[74]

Thompson and Simpson did not lose their youth in legal detention for an imaginary violation. By contrast, the mythical abuses of Ruby Bates and Victoria Price robbed the Scottsboro Boys of their freedom and made serious inroads into or snuffed out the remainder of their youth. Norris was on death row five years and sentenced to the electric chair three times. "Living that way, waiting, wondering and hoping is hell," he wrote. Once eligible for parole in 1944, he violated it by leaving the state and was returned to prison. Norris received a second parole in 1946 and promptly left the state again.[75]

For thirty years Norris lived as a free man in the North and avoided extradition to Alabama. In the meantime, he married and had a family. As he reached retirement age, Norris recognized some positive changes in the racial climate of the United States as a result of the Civil Rights Movement and the Civil Rights Act of 1964. Alabama was also changing; therefore, he believed it a propitious time to clear his name. Of more importance, "My kids were growing up and they didn't even know who I was," he admitted. It was important to him that they not learn he was a convicted rapist without knowing his version of the story. "I had to fight for my rights," wrote Norris, so the children would have "the courage to fight for theirs."[76]

Based upon a review of the case in August 1976, the Alabama attorney general recommended a pardon for Clarence Norris. Governor George Wallace approved and signed the unconditional pardon exonerating Norris of the alleged crime. After nearly half a century, Norris emerged from the bitter ordeal with a clear name and his humanity in tact. He had one message for everyone, especially his children. "Always fight for your rights," he advised, "Stand up for your rights, even if it kills you."[77]

Figure 13   Civil Rights Demonstrations, St. Louis NAACP

Source: Courtesy of the St. Louis Post-Dispatch, St. Louis, Missouri.

Chapter Ten

Emmett Till Generation:
African American Schoolchildren
and the Modern Civil Rights
Movement in the South, 1954–1964

In the midst of the Civil War, an elderly man told a bystander, "I'se berry ol massa, but de little ones—dey'l see it; dey'l see it yit." The old gentleman was shaking and trembling with the "spirit of freedom" as he watched Union soldiers drilling before going into battle in 1862. The gentleman had grown old in bondage and was now witnessing the foundations of slavery disintegrating around him. Grounded in his knowledge of the gloomy past, he linked his aspirations for a bright future to the younger generation. A century later, Martin Luther King, Jr., also tied his hopes for a better world to the younger generation and dreamed of the day when children, even his own, would not be judged by the color of their skin but by the content of their character.[1]

In each case, adults made wishful projections for their progeny's future. It is appropriate to ask what, more specifically, were these children to see and what roles would they play in bringing their elders' predictions to fruition. In doing so, this essay focuses on schoolgirls and boys in the South who participated in the modern Civil Rights Movement, and it seeks to determine how and why these children made the transition from scripted actors to viable activists. Scripted actors were children such as Ruby Bridges who admitted that when she was six years old the Civil Rights Movement came knocking on her door. She accepted the role at the behest of her parents and played it well. Several years later, Martin Luther King, Jr., assured the parents of black teenagers in Birmingham, Alabama, that their children, read activists, would be safe if they participated in the Children's Crusade May 2–7, 1963. In fact, King asked parents not to "hold them back if they want[ed] to go to jail." At this juncture, the children, according to King, were "doing a job not only for themselves, but for all of America and all of mankind." He added, "Somewhere we read, 'A little child shall lead them.' "[2]

This essay interrogates reasons for changes in the views of Civil Rights organizations regarding the use of children as active participants in mass demonstrations that exposed them to violence accompanying the massive resistance tactics of segregationists. Of equal significance is assessing the effectiveness of the youngsters' contributions once they became active agents for civil rights. An examination of the impact of a Supreme Court decision and the circumstances surrounding the deaths of several black children are illustrative.

At first glance, these events appear disparate, but they are cojoined by time and racial hatred. The first, *Brown v. Board of Education, Topeka* (1954, 1955), represented hope for the future for nine-year-old Linda Brown and millions of other black boys and girls who attended America's public schools. The second is a reminder of the aborted hope for growth and development due to the brutal August 27, 1955, murder in Money, Mississippi, of Emmett Till and the September 15, 1963, killings in Birmingham, Alabama, of Addie Mae Collins, Denise McNair, Carole Robertson, and Cynthia Wesley, along with Johnny Robinson and Virgil Ware. Defining moments, including the murders, affected black youngsters to the extent that many of them became "warriors" for equal rights in public places and schools across the South.[3]

Once slavery ended, a most pressing and prevalent interest of newly freed blacks was access to education. As an enslaved child Booker T. Washington fantasized about going to school and equated it to entering "paradise." Freedom created opportunities for Washington and millions of other former slaves to make that dream a reality. Ideally, an education would provide students with an adequate foundation for self-support along with the wherewithal to recognize social ills and identify solutions for those problems. Additionally, the education should prepare its recipients for making creative use of their leisure time.[4]

In the post–Civil War years, black parents, community leaders, and other interested persons, often with the assistance of the Bureau of Refugees, Freedmen, and Abandoned Lands, commonly called the Freedmen's Bureau, an official agency created by Congress March 1865 under the auspices of the War Department, and religious denominations, built schools, hired teachers, and enrolled children. The ex-slaves' excitement and greed for literacy was infectious regardless of their age or gender. By contrast, many white southerners preferred that newly freed blacks not gain educational access because, they believed, it would disturb the established social and economic order thereby eradicating the chasm that separated ex-slaveholders from ex-slaves. Mean-spirited whites harassed children, threatened teachers, and destroyed schools.[5]

Access to a quality education for black children opened one of the greatest battles over contested terrain in American history. To further exacerbate the situation, the U. S. Supreme Court upheld racial segregation in *Plessy v. Ferguson* (1896) through its "separate but equal" decision. The case involved transportation initially but spilled over into many facets of American society, including educational institutions. Throughout the nation separate but *unequal* schools, with inadequate curricular offerings based on ethnocentric notions, prevailed. America's children of color suffered the academic, economic, and social consequences of legalized segregation for more than a century.[6]

With the passing of time, rising levels of expectations among black Americans made mere access to education less and less satisfactory. African Americans, without regard for geography or gender, began demanding an education of the same quality as that received by whites under ordinary circumstances. The National Association for the Advancement of Colored People (NAACP) responded to their demands and began initiating suits for equal education in professional schools prior to the *Brown* decision. The NAACP followed the "Margold Rule" or "Margold Bible," a guiding principle initiated by Nathan Margold, which asserted that the New Deal climate favored appeals for equal opportunities rather than demands for integration.[7]

By the end of the 1940s, it was clear that the NAACP abandoned the Margold principle in *Brown v. Board of Education* (1954) and asked for the integration of schools. Brown, a class action suit, included five cases appealed to the Supreme Court on behalf of children in Kansas (*Brown v. Board of Education, Topeka*), South Carolina (*Briggs v. Elliott*), Virginia (*Davis v. County School Board of Prince Edward County*), Delaware (*Belton v. Gebhart*), and Washington, D. C. (*Bolling v. Sharpe*). The Supreme Court agreed with the argument saying "To separate them from others of similar age and qualifications solely because of their race generates a feeling of inferiority . . . that may affect their minds and hearts in a way unlikely to ever be undone." With this reasoning, fortified by sociological studies, the Supreme Court declared *Plessy v. Ferguson* unconstitutional in its May 17, 1954 decision. The following year, in *Brown, II* the Court said school districts were to desegregate with all "deliberate speed." Many schools eliminated racial barriers through busing, pupil placement plans, and freedom of choice alternatives. Others offered mass resistance and maintained segregation.[8]

Without regard for how quickly or slowly school boards reacted to the *Brown* decisions, the Court ruling impacted upon millions of black and white American children in kindergarten through twelfth grade. Schoolgirls and boys did not initiate the action. Rather, it was on their behalf yet they were very much at the center of the desegregation struggle in public schools across the nation. Once the action began, the children were the only ones who could enroll, attend the classes, and integrate the schools.

The graphic image of the fifteen-year-old Elizabeth Eckford, walking with books in hand amid an angry mob of hateful whites gathered outside Little Rock's Central High School September 4, 1957, shouting racial epithets and demanding a lynching while Arkansas's National Guards stood by with raised bayonets in defiance of the Supreme Court, remains an indelible imprint in the minds of all who saw the events unfold on television or viewed the photograph in the print media. Equally poignant is Norman Rockwell's 1965 painting, "The Problem We All Live With," which depicts a small black girl with books and ruler in hand while surrounded by federal marshals as they all walked past a stark granite wall dripping with the fleshy particles of a blood-red tomato that some unseen protester had smashed upon the wall slightly below the scrawling word "NIGGER."

At base, the images are similar. Both schoolgirls were "tender warriors" on the battlefield for educational equality. One, a teenager, was quite grown up. Her school board had decided to begin integration at the high school level and the other, a six-year-old, was not so grown-up. Her school board had decided to begin integration at the elementary level. Despite differences in their ages and grade levels, both children exemplified dignity and serenity as they walked calmly past mobs of angry segregationists, male and female. Neither child looked to the left or right but kept her sights fixed on a higher goal directly ahead of her. The similarities end here. One student walked alone and faced hostile authority with fixed bayonets intent upon defying the federal law while the other had the comfort of knowing armed men dedicated to upholding the federal law walked along with her.[9]

Although Rockwell's "The Problem We All Live With" is generally said to represent Ruby Bridges who attended New Orleans' William Frantz Elementary School in 1960, a spokesperson for the Norman Rockwell Family Trust claims the painting was a general representation of school desegregation at the time. If this is true, the photograph of "The Problem" is well placed on the cover of Melba Pattillo Beals's *Warriors Don't Cry*, which commemorates the fortieth anniversary of integration at Central High School, Little, Rock, Arkansas.[10]

In the initial days of integration, no one could fathom the extent of the danger they faced. Years later, Beals wrote, "As I watch videotapes now . . . I wonder what possessed my parents and the adults of the NAACP to allow us to go to [Central High School] in the face of such violence." A white teacher in Clinton, Tennessee, also pondered about the school crisis in 1957 and wrote, "I often think, how can they [black students] stand it? I couldn't let my little boy go through what those children face every day." Ernest Green, one of *those children*, at Central High School, said "I didn't have any sense of the danger that occurred. I figured it would be uncomfortable, but I could deal with the discomfort in relationship to what I was as the bigger picture."[11]

Neither parents, pupils, teachers, school administrators, civil rights activists nor the federal government had any precedence upon which they could uniformly gauge white reaction to school integration in the 1950s. In some instances, including several Arkansas communities as early as 1954, desegregation proceeded without notable turmoil while in others places, campuses turned into virtual battlegrounds with distractions ranging from the burning of an effigy to explosives, police, national guards, federal marshals, paratroopers, and detectives along with the potentially violent mobs of cheerleaders for segregation. It was against this mixed background that the young son of twenty-eight-year-old Louise Gordon of Clay, Kentucky, asked why he could not go to the school nearest their home rather than to one eleven miles away. Gordon admitted, "I'd never even thought of it," but she responded: "If you have the guts to go: I got the guts to take you." The young mother admitted that she died a thousand deaths each day until 3:00 PM when classes ended and she knew that her son was safe.[12]

Leaders of the NAACP believed desegregation in Little Rock Nine, perceived to be a moderate city, would not be tumultuous. But on September 4, 1957, when the Little Rock Nine, Minniejean Brown, Melba Pattillo, Gloria Ray, Ernest Green, Thelma Mothershed, Elizabeth Eckford, Terrance Roberts, Jefferson Thomas, and Carlotta Walls, approached Central High School, they saw the Alabama National Guard and State Police under the direction of Governor Orval Faubus, seemingly without the consent of Mayor Woodrow W. Mann, preventing them from entering the school. Chaos reigned supreme and was replete with racial epithets, threats of lynchings, and physical assaults. President Dwight D. Eisenhower evaluated the crisis and deployed more than 1,000 soldiers from the 101st Airborne Division to Central High School to enforce the law and end segregation. Helicopters and bayonets added to the show of force.[13]

Governor Faubus responded to the crisis in a September 26, 1957, televised address and told viewers, "We are now an occupied nation." In asking for calmness, the governor reminded his audience of the supremacy of the U.S. army when used, he said, against "a defenseless state." Faubus charged that the federal government had made a "grave and grievous" error in deploying the troops to enforce peace. The governor vilified the soldiers when he warned that an "impetuous or thoughtless act [by] a white student could result in the penetration of a bayonet." Faubus did not shift his mantle of concern to the black students who braved the gauntlet inside and outside the school. In situations where black children faced hostility from vicious white mobs, they made the transition from the role of scripted actors to nonviolent activists.[14]

Beals's *Warriors Don't Cry*, based in part upon a diary she kept in 1957, describes days at Central High School as nothing short of hellish. "I got up every morning," she wrote, "polished my saddle shoes, and went off to war." Clearly, this was not the paradise Booker T. Washington had envisioned. Beals's catalogue of abuses ranged from fellow students stepping on the backs of her shoes, to throwing a caustic substance into her eyes, squirting ink on her clothes, bombarding her in the toilet with burning tissue tossed over the petitions, to threatening to lynch her.[15]

Ernest Green described the guerilla tactics used by some white students, male and female, as "hand-to-hand combat . . . trench warfare," that tested the mettle of black students entering previously all-white schools in Little Rock and elsewhere. Once enrolled, peers, parents, organizational leaders, and the African American public expected the school children to shoulder the responsibility of peacekeepers. Beyond that, the nation's eyes were upon them. Theirs was an awesome assignment, and the youth knew that responding to abuse in kind was certain to bring trouble, perhaps expulsion.[16]

Vivian Carter Mason oversaw the orientation for the small group of black students entering Norview High School, Norfolk, Virginia, in the 1950s. She acknowledged that the students had to grow up and leave their childhoods behind. Black students were to ignore anything "aimed at them in a detrimental and provocative manner" while applying "themselves with great vigor on the job of mastering the academic work required of them." Finally, according to Mason, the black students were to respond positively to white students who were friendly toward them. The black students had, said Mason, "accepted the role of pioneer." Beals acknowledged that she and her eight friends paid for the integration of Central High with their innocence and youth.[17]

The harassment of the "Little Rock Nine" was not vastly different from what other blacks in previously all-white resisting schools faced elsewhere in the South. The Kentucky-born Margaret Anderson, a white teacher in Clinton, Tennessee, during its throes with school desegregation in 1957–1959 wrote:

> The few Negro children, trying to learn under fear, and sustained by a great American courage, in their more than two years in our school have endured every possible form of torment from the smallest harassment to threats of murder. "If you come back to school, I'll cut your guts out!" could be heard in the halls. Eggs smashed on their books, ink smeared on their clothes in the lockers, knives flourished in their presence, nails tossed in their faces and spiked in their seats. Vulgar words constantly whispered in their ears.

Anderson continued and recounted an especially vitriolic incident, in a study hall when 150 white students created such a threatening commotion the lone black student left the auditorium. When she rose to go, the white students "applauded as if they had scored a great victory," said Anderson.[18]

The incident disturbed the teacher to the extent that she could not sleep and berated herself. She asked, how "I [could] call myself a teacher, knowing that a child, any child, had been persecuted under my supervision." Following a telephone conversation with the student, whom the teacher identified only as "Victoria," the two of them discussed the incident. The black girl related how the white children had barraged her with filthy names, which she said "I could take that," but the defining moment came when a white boy looked as if he "was going to touch me," she said. The teacher apologized for her own behavior and "told her how ashamed [she] was" of her own failure to control the situation the previous day. Victoria, truly the triumphant one here, responded: "I understand. I don't want to cause no trouble."[19]

Minnijean Brown, the most controversial of the "Little Rock Nine," was far less retiring than "Victoria." According to Melba Pattillo Beals, Brown was prone to saying "exactly what she was thinking as though she weren't afraid of anything or anybody." Brown was not ordinarily disruptive but exuded an air of "confidence-slash-arrogance," which white students labeled as "an attitude." In either case, her demeanor was annoying to the white students who vilified Brown in an attempt to justify their own rude behavior. One of the white students at Central High School in 1957 remembered Brown well and said, "She walked the halls *as if she belonged there*."[20]

The choice of words used to describe Minnijean Brown reveals discomfort with the young woman who had presence and defied expectations. Brown was an ordinary teenager who wanted a "normal" high school experience. There was nothing "normal" about the bullying harassment from white peers who realized that Brown, unlike the other black students, was prone to react to their goading.

For some students, the presence of Minnijean Brown and the others among the "Little Rock Nine" disrupted their lives and interfered with their opportunities to have a glorious academic year filled with football games, pep rallies, sock hops, and business as usual. Other white students were not disturbed particularly by the "Little Rock Nine," if "*they*," read black students, stayed in their "*places*." Trouble came when the black students acted "*badly*," meaning protested the violation of their rights, or behaved as if they "*belonged*" there. Few, if any, of the white students actually conceded openly that the "Little Rock Nine" or any other black student had a right as taxpaying American citizens to an education equal to that received by white boys and girls in the public schools. Most whites saw Central High School as their school and believed it belonged to them exclusively.[21]

Central High School, a massive state-of-the-art structure containing 100 classrooms, opened in 1927 with nearly 2,000 students. The imposing building, selected by the American Institute of Architects as the Most Beautiful High School in America, had cost $1.5 million to construct. The building's architectural style, complete with a water fountain and dual staircases presented the picture of an academic sanctuary. The classical statues high above the triple arched front entrance signified "Ambition, Opportunity, Preparation, and Personality." The expansive curriculum and high quality programs prepared students to achieve their ambitions. In short, Central was "*THE*" high school to attend, consequently any number of white students from outside the city moved into town, lived with host families or relatives, paid tuition, and enrolled. Being there gave them a sense of importance because Central High School had a fine academic reputation, respected athletic programs, and its students excelled.

The differences in the size and condition of the physical facilities, curricular offerings, and instructional materials at Central High School and the all-black Paul Laurence Dunbar High School, located a relatively short distance away, were stark. Many students who attended Dunbar High School lived closer to Central High School, which is located in a racially mixed neighborhood. Central High School's location had nothing to do with the white students' sense of privilege.

Benjamin Fine, a *New York Times* education reporter, who comforted Elizabeth Eckford after the guards prevented her from entering the school, witnessed the reaction of several white girls when they realized the black students had indeed entered Central High School September 4, 1957. Fine wrote:

> The crowd let out a roar of rage. "They've gone in," a man shouted. "Oh, God," said a woman, "the niggers are in school." A group of six girls, dressed in skirts and sweaters, hair in pony-tails, started to shriek and wail. "The niggers are in *our* school," they howled hysterically. One of them jumped up and down on the sidewalk, waving her arms toward her classmates in the school who were looking out the windows, and screamed over and over again: "Come on out, come on out." Tears flowed down her face, her body shook in uncontrollable spasms . . . Hysteria swept from the shrieking girls to members of the crowd.[22]

Many white students believed they alone were entitled to attend Central High School and did whatever, with reference to badgering, harassing, or other threatening behavior, they could get away with to assure that the "Little Rock Nine" did not share in *their* entitlements. White students who disagreed with the segregationists were generally too intimidated to speak out in support of integration or to call a halt to their peers' offensive behavior. As a result, the "Little Rock Nine" were moving targets for hostile actions.[23]

It appeared that Minnijean Brown's threshold for suffering abuses in silence was lower than the other black students at Central High School. Following a series of ugly incidents, in and out of the school cafeteria, and a suspension, the school board voted to expel Brown. For the segregationists, this was a sweet victory. Of the decision, Elizabeth Huckaby, a Central High School administrator wrote:

> So Minnijean was out. It was an admission of defeat on our part, I felt. But I was sure that Minnijean's continued presence in Central High would have been a hazard to the other Eight. Her suspension, dated February 6, read: "Reinstated on probation January 13, 1958, with the agreement that she would not retaliate verbally or physically to any harassment but would leave the matter *to* authorities to handle . . ."

A name-calling and purse-throwing incident was not sufficient to expel a student, but, according to Huckaby, "Minnijean . . . was our difficulty. It was just that she and our impossible situation would not mix." Minnijean Brown was expendable.[24]

As the student body learned of Brown's expulsion, the racists began the "One down, eight to go" campaign with highly vocal support from the avowed segregationist Sammie Dean Parker, a junior, which subsequently led to her own expulsion.[25]

With regards to Brown's expulsion and the other abuses suffered by the "Little Rock Nine," the memories of black and white students are poles apart. White students are inclined to say the black students exaggerated incidents that were nothing more than "boys-being-boys" or simple acts of "making mischief." While this may be true, they did not direct their venom at other white students. Whites who where opposed to blatant actions by the segregationists were probably called "Nigger lovers" and endured some wrath from the dominant group. But, the fact remains that white students responsible for the harassment of black and selected white students were not behaving with camaraderie in mind.[26]

The "boys will be boys" supporters were not without a distaff side. It was girls who set fire to the toilet tissue and tossed it into the restroom stall occupied by Melba Pattillo Beals. Furthermore, photographs of "twisted scowling faces with open mouths jeering" belonged to white girls as they harassed Elizabeth Eckford. In fact, the expressions of hostility catapulted Hazel Bryan into the "poster girl of the hate generation" position. By contrast, Elizabeth Eckford became the "poster girl of passive resistance." The Yin and Yang of racial sentiments raise questions about the origins of diabolical behavior exuded by one adolescent and the dignified actions of another.[27]

Acceptable behavior and peaceful actions were key to survival for black children at Central High School and any other school in the midst of contested terrain for integration. To garner any semblance of a normal high school experience, most of the black children did whatever was necessary to avoid attracting attention. Ostensibly, they accepted rejection by white classmates along with exclusion from extracurricular activities. As if oblivious to their surroundings, black students maintained quiet nonconfrontational postures.[28]

The experiences of Ruby Bridges, the first African American child to enroll at William Frantz Elementary School in New Orleans, differed from those of black children in Little Rock, Arkansas, and Clinton, Tennessee, since she was the lone black student in a school that, ordinarily had an enrollment of 576. The majority of whites boycotted the school with the encouragement of the state legislature, and only a handful of white children attended Frantz school during the 1960–1961 school year. A noisy crowd of angry segregationists protested as the black first grader entered and exited the school each day.[29]

At one point, the little girl misinterpreted the mob's shouts and flying missiles as Mardi Gras activities. Bridges's age and innocence did not prevent her from incorporating the chant "Two, four, six, eight, we don't want to integrate" into her rope-jumping rhymes after school. Despite this childish immaturity, the sight of a black doll in a small coffin held by an adult surrounded by white children terrified her. Bridges did not misconstrue the taunts of the pallbearer or the woman who promised to poison her each day as she entered the school. The threats frightened Bridges to the extent that she had some difficulty sleeping and refused to eat lunches her own mother prepared.[30]

Once inside the school, Bridges had no classmates, no recess, and no meals in the cafeteria. She was the proverbial "outsider" inside but, unlike the "Little Rock Nine," she did have a openly concerned teacher. The teacher extended herself to the child and greeted her daily "with a compliment about how nicely she was dressed to help make her feel special," wrote Barbara Henry, "as she was, and to make her feel more welcome and comfortable." A mutual friendship developed between the teacher and pupil. Henry explained: "I grew to love Ruby and to be awed by her. It was an ugly world outside, but I tried to make our world together as normal as possible." Henry's efforts were successful and the child responded by imitating the teacher, Boston accent included.[31]

The atmosphere within Henry's classroom was as normal as possible for this curious form of segregation within a supposedly integrated school. Ruby Bridges remembered that she and Barbara Henry did "everything together, reading and word puzzles, spelling and math. We sang songs and played games. Since I could'nt go outside, we pushed desks out of the way and did jumping jack exercises" in the room.[32]

Before the end of the school year a few white children returned to Frantz where they met Ruby Bridges who still had trouble understanding what was occurring around her. The moment of realization came when a little white boy said, "I can't play with you" and explained his mother forbade it because Bridges was "a nigger." It was the catalyst to understanding that the brouhaha outside was about the color of her skin. The "Little Rock Nine" knew from the outset that the chaos enveloping Central High School was related to color.[33]

Without regard for the students' age, gender, grade, or location, there were commonalities among them, including family support and religious beliefs. The faith of Ruby Bridges came to the fore one day as she approached the crowd of hecklers, stopped, faced them, and appeared to speak. When Henry asked what she had said to the mob, Ruby explained that she had maintained a daily ritual before and after school. She prayed for the people who harassed her. On the morning in question, the child had forgotten to say her prayer and stopped to do so. From the teacher's window, it looked as if she were speaking to the crowd. Instead, Bridges prayed:

> Please, God, try to forgive those people.
> Because even if they say those bad things,
> They don't know what they're doing.
> So You could forgive them,
> Just like You did those folks a long time ago
> When they said terrible things about You.

The prayer was meaningful for Bridges whose mother helped her to cultivate a belief in its efficacy.[34]

Melba Pattillo Beals claims she survived the tumult at Central High School because of support from her loving family, a strong faith in her God, the assistance of the NAACP, and a white classmate, known only as "Link." Additionally, reading a book by Mahatma Ghandi, a gift from her grandmother, added a new dimension to her confidence needed to survive the 1957–1958 academic year at Central High School. She employed passive resistance tactics and played "mind games" to gain control of negative circumstances created by tormentors.[35]

Regardless of their sources of sustenance, the children involved in school desegregation frays across the South fought their battles collectively and individually, with dignity, and won praise. Indeed, they were the tender warriors on the battlefield for equality and eventually received recognition as such. Of course, the "Little Rock

Nine" have received more national attention because of federal intervention, media coverage, and the Congressional Gold Medals for their actions in 1997.[36]

With or without publicity or medals, the children became self-styled activists and employed weapons of the weak. They prayed, engaged in passive resistance, and stared down tormentors. As they did so, the warriors within gestated. Melba Pattillo Beals described the metamorphosis when she wrote, "The warrior growing inside me squared my shoulders and put my mind on alert to do whatever was necessary to survive." Fighting for survival became so much a part of her, it pushed Beals into the sorrowful lament, "Please God, let me learn how to stop being a warrior. Sometimes I just need to be a girl." Other children not involved in school integration plans also became warriors, or fighters for civil rights, because of spontaneous moments such as the Civil Rights Movement knocking on their doors or external forces such as the murder of the fourteen-year-old boy, Emmett Till in 1955.[37]

After seeing the *Jet Magazine* containing a photograph of Emmett Till's mutilated body, Joyce Ladner, a Forrest County, Mississippi, youngster, asked her sister Dorie "How could they do that to him?" "He was only a boy," one of the girls exclaimed. In actuality, he was not *only* a boy, he was a boy their ages. Joyce said she was eleven or twelve and her sister was older. Deeply affected by the August 27, 1955 lynching, the sisters empathized with Till's family and worried about the safety of their brother, father, and themselves. Despite the tremendous fear of foreboding danger, the children made a hasty daily jog to a local store in Palmers Crossing, their hometown, near Hattisburg, Mississippi, for a copy of the *Hattiesburg American*. The youngsters, who seemed to know of the killing almost immediately, had to know more about what had happened to the boy affectionately called "Bobo" by relatives and friends. Gender and geography separated the Ladners from Till, yet they identified with him because he was their age.[38]

The widespread media coverage of Till's funeral made it impossible to claim that the murder was an illusion. Unlike the families of other lynch victims, Mamie Bradley, Till's mother did not grieve privately. She included the public by authorizing a four-day memorial service complete with an open casket viewing so the world could see what the lynchers did to her son. More than 10,000 mourners paid their respects and an even larger segment of the population saw graphic photographs of events in newspapers and magazines. Afterward, a public hungry for more details about the child's death followed the trial through the newspapers across the nation. The Till murder and trial were the first major media events of the modern Civil Rights Movement. It served to publicize as well as to politicize the lynching.[39]

Till's death ignited the inspiration for many black children of his generation to fight the discrimination surrounding them in the 1960s. Tommie Lee Hudson, who was twelve years old at the time of Till's death, said, "It put fire in you." Joyce Ladner maintains that the Till murder

> served as a grave incident that showed people how intractable a problem could be and how difficult a solution would be. So when the spark came in Mississippi to sit in the public library, for example, people who participated had been incensed by the Till murder. The Till incident was the catalyst.

For Ladner the linkages between Till's death and emerging activism by young blacks were clear. In fact, she coined the phrase "The Emmett Till Generation" as an expression of that belief.[40]

Young activists of the 1960s included persons who associate the inspirations for their actions with the Till murder. Others had vague or no recollections of the murder but joined the Civil Rights Movement as it came to their neighborhoods or towns. This was probably the case with the six-year-old child who marched May 3, 1963, in Birmingham's Children's Crusade and was arrested. It is appropriate to ask about the extent to which such young children understood the circumstances surrounding them and the consequences of their actions. Did the young black boys and girls in Mississippi during Freedom Summer (1964) who greeted civil rights volunteers with the salutation, "Hey freedom!" understand that they were in the midst of a social and political revolution?[41]

To be sure, some children were only aware of the Civil Rights Movement when it was within their environment; however, it is important to mention that local NAACP youth council chapters existed in the South following World War II. As a result, an organizational structure was already in place that could channel the activities of boys and girls who were sensitized by Till's death. Children outside these organizations moved more spontaneously into the activist role as the movement spread, or as they heard about atrocities, such as the bombing of the Birmingham church and the beating of two teenagers who staged a 1963 "sit-in" in Selma, Alabama.[42]

During the years that lapsed between the *Brown* (1954, 1955) decisions and passage of the Civil Rights Act (1964) a decade later, thousands of black children participated in mass demonstrations, boycotts, and/or school integrations. An estimated 70,000 persons, without regard for age, color, or gender, participated in mass demonstrations in 1960 alone. Nearly one-half of that number was arrested and some spent time in jail. Time served in jail became a badge of honor for them to wear proudly. Brenda Travis, a teenager from McComb, Mississippi, is only one example of a youngster who seemed to put interests in equal justice before personal ambitions. She participated in a lunch counter sit-in, was arrested, dismissed from school, and sentenced to one year of detention in a center for juvenile delinquents. Although released after serving only six months upon the condition that she leave McComb, the reprieve was not enough to make Travis relocate or refrain from future participation in the movement. When asked if she would join other protests, she responded, "Of course."[43]

Black teenagers, such as Brenda Travis, were far less likely than their parents and other elders to accept segregation and remain in their "places" as blacks had done for generations. "Parents," wrote a reporter for *The Saturday Evening Post*, "measure how far Negroes have advanced since World War II: the[ir] child measure how far they have yet to go." Differences in perceptions of progress help to explain the contrasting behavior of the older and younger generations of blacks. The media coverage of the Civil Rights Movement along with its coverage of independence movements in fourteen West African countries gave pause. If blacks the world over were gaining their freedom, why could it not be done in the United States? Inspired by the changing times and angered by a negative comment from a young white acquaintance, one young black reacted and said, "I have an obligation to act, to protest, to demand equal rights." Even more poignant are the words of a thirteen-year-old African American boy in Mississippi who wrote, "We are trying to get freedom . . . because slavery is the next thing to hell . . . we want our freedom now . . . If I have to die[d] for freedom I don't mind."[44]

Ironically, the adult leaders of the struggle for civil rights in McComb, Mississippi, were reluctant to include children because they did not wish to alienate parents who objected to "using" their offspring. Also, civil rights leaders were troubled by the possible results, violence, school expulsions, incarcerations. Indeed, black teenager civil rights demonstrators from McComb's public schools were expelled and incarcerated. Once released, they could not return to the local school but were compelled to complete their education in a special program established for them at Campbell College in Jackson more than fifty miles away. Despite these realities, children in the movement served as an incentive for other teens and adults.[45]

By Spring 1963, the movement's initial reluctance to use children gave way to a new philosophy of incorporating boys and girls as a significant entity in the fight for civil equality. This decision came in Birmingham, Alabama, after weeks of ostensible failures to integrate public places. Mass demonstrations led to mass arrests and raised important questions. If civil rights leaders languished in jail, who would lead the movement? If fundraisers were in jail, who would raise money to post bails? Clearly, leaders and fundraisers were indispensable and needed outside assistance to carry on business as usual rather than languishing inside locked cells. Who, then, were suitable candidates to fill their places in jail? The most vulnerable to physical danger but least susceptible to economic and political pressures were children.[46]

After considerable debate, the civil rights leaders in Birmingham agreed that juveniles should be among the demonstrators. After all, children were participating in the Civil Rights Movement in increasing numbers with or without consent from parents and civil rights leaders. In fact, children were highly visible in civil rights campaigns in Mississippi and Georgia. With the endorsement of the civil rights organizations, high school, junior high school, and some elementary school children in Birmingham, Alabama, joined in the Spring 1963 mass marches, dubbed the "Children's Crusade," as wave after waves of demonstrators left area churches, especially the Sixteenth Street Baptist Church across the street from Kelly Ingram Park.[47]

The use of young girls and boys in mass demonstrations ultimately served a duel purpose. First, children filled the need for more troops who protested, were arrested, and filled the jails. Their actions called attention to the plight of blacks, young and old, within a highly segregated society. More than 2,500 protesters of all ages participated in the May 7, 1963, demonstration in Birmingham. Before the children went back to school in September, more than 3,300 blacks, varying in age, had been arrested. Second, to see the willing participation of youth and the brutal treatment of young demonstrators at the hands of the Birmingham police generated a media frenzy and further politicized public opinions about law enforcement officials who aimed high-powered water hoses at demonstrators or threatened them with trained attack dogs. Television viewers watched as sheets of water lifted and tossed demonstrators about. Equally as graphic was a chilling photograph of a dog attacking fifteen-year-old Walter Gadsden. Although he was not a civil rights demonstrator, the photograph carried no such explanation. Viewers would only see the dog lounging at the youngster. A story in *The Atlanta Constitution* summarized events of May 3, 1963:

> Snarling police dogs chased away crowds of Negroes and fire hoses flattened youthful demonstrators Friday as hundreds of Negroes tried to stage antisegregation marches.

Five Negroes reported they were either bitten by the leashed dogs or injured by water hoses which a fireman said had pressure of 50 to 100 pounds. Whether using hoses or dogs, the treatment of the youthful demonstrators precipitated national outrage.[48]

Several days after the Children's Crusade began under the auspices of the Alabama Christian Movement for Human Rights and the Southern Christian Leadership Conference (SCLC), Fred Shuttlesworth and Martin Luther King, Jr. announced that Birmingham's officials had agreed to a desegregation plan for the city. The Children's Crusade figured importantly in the negotiations. Historian Glenn T. Eskew, author of *But for Birmingham*, posits "the children's crusade broke the stalemate in local race relations [and] broke the stalemate on the national level as it forced the president and Congress to draft legislation that ended legal racial discrimination" with the passage of a civil rights act the following year.[49]

Rather than a joyous and peaceful aftermath of the Children's Crusade and the end of racial discrimination in Birmingham, a September 15, 1963, dynamite blast at the Sixteenth Street Baptist Church opened a gaping hole in race relations. The explosion occurred as the congregation was preparing for its annual Youth Day Celebration. Three fourteen-year-old girls, Addie Mae Collins, Carole Robertson, and Cynthia Wesley, died along with their eleven-year-old friend, Denise McNair.

Confusion, panic, and hate erupted. Spontaneous rock-throwing fights broke out between blacks and whites as they learned of the children's deaths. The police attempted to break up one fight and ordered the sixteen-year-old Johnny Robinson, an African American allegedly involved in throwing rocks at whites, to stop. He failed to halt, and the police shot him in the back. Finally, the thirteen-year-old Virgil Ware died from a gunshot wound inflicted by sixteen-year-old Michael Lee Farley, a white Eagle Scout, who had attended a segregationist rally earlier that afternoon. The boys had not met nor had they engaged in any confrontations. Ware was riding a bicycle with his brother when Farley, riding a motorized scooter, fired at the two brothers in passing.[50]

The tragedies surrounding the bombing redirected the world's gaze at Birmingham. The Honorable John Lewis, who headed the Student Nonviolent Coordinating Committee (SNCC) in 1963, admitted that the bombing murders was a "very, very dark moment for the civil rights movement," but it galvanized the movement and caused civil rights advocates to intensify their efforts. Martin Luther King, III, son of Martin Luther King, Jr., who was only a child himself at the time, remembered how disturbing the event was for his father. "It evoked sympathy and empathy across the nation," said King. Mark Potok, spokesperson for the Southern Poverty Law Center, concluded that the bombing at the Sixteenth Street Baptist Church was a watershed in the Civil Rights Movement that awakened the "conscience of white America, a conscience that had been sleeping for a long time."[51]

Indeed, in a letter to the *Birmingham News*, Marjorie Lees Linn, a thirty-three-year-old white woman, who had spent the greater portion of her life in Birmingham asked, "How can responsible, clear-thinking white people possibly believe that there is any excusing such acts or for that matter any excusing their own prejudice against the colored race?" Linn's criticism of the dastardly act was tantamount to breaking ranks with other whites, including the segregationists, whether she supported them or not. Certainly, it was a moment of reckoning for her when she realized there was "no way to avoid looking into the monstrous face of prejudice and bigotry."[52]

What could interested persons, black and white, young and old, do about looking into the monstrous face of prejudice and bigotry? After the funerals of the children killed in the church bombing, members of SCLC and SNCC gathered and talked with Martin Luther King, Jr. The overarching question was what could they do to continue the fight for civil rights. The group eventually decided to "turn up the heat . . . in Selma [Alabama]" and to stage freedom votes in Mississippi.[53]

Mass demonstrations had already begun in Selma. The day following the Birmingham church bombing, black teenagers picketed the Dallas County Courthouse, "the first such open defiance" writes John Lewis, in the city's history. By the end of Freedom Summer in Mississippi, 1964, and the passage of the Civil Rights bill, hundreds, if not thousands of black children had participated in the various facets of the Civil Rights Movement. Moreover, many had gained a deeper comprehension and appreciation of the concepts of liberty and equality. As the old gentleman had said nearly one hundred years earlier, "De little ones—dey'l see it; dey'l see it yet." The evasive yet effervescent "it" was something that many of the girls and boys were experiencing thus they could give deeper meaning to the greeting "Hey freedom" as if they were reacquainting themselves with a long-lost friend.[54]

AFRICAN AMERICAN CHILDREN IN CONTEMPORARY SOCIETY

More than four hundred years have passed since the first Africans stepped ashore in English-speaking North America. The status of the majority evolved from indentured servitude to chattel slavery in the 1660s and remained as such until the general emancipation in 1865. As they made the transition from slavery to freedom, newly liberated persons assumed that the rights and privileges denied to them in bondage would be available in freedom. Unfortunately, many were disappointed with the paucity of opportunities for economic and political independence in the hostile post–Civil War South. Additionally, for nearly a century their access to an equal public school education was not forthcoming. Despite disillusionments, many African Americans remained hopeful about what the future would bring for them and their progeny.

At the turn of the twenty-first century, it is appropriate to inquire about the status of young African Americans. A special feature in the June 7, 1999, *Newsweek* proclaimed:

> Black employment and home ownership are up. Murders and other violent crimes are down. Reading and math proficiency are climbing. Out-of-wedlock births are at the lowest rate in four decades. Fewer blacks are on welfare than at any point in recent memory. More are in college than at any point in history. And the percentage of black families living below the poverty line is the lowest it has been since the Census Bureau began keeping separate black poverty statistics in 1967.

What is the actual state of welfare for the majority of America's black children? How much consideration is given to them in public policy debates related to health, welfare, gun control, substance abuse, and pornography on the internet and airwaves? The range of issues require selectivity; therefore, commentary will be limited to black children and the issues related to their educational opportunities, well being, and freedom from harm.[1]

Following court ordered desegregation in 1954–1955, students throughout the nation attended schools with more diverse student bodies. Questions arise regarding the success of integration and if equal access closed the achievement gap between majority and minority students? There are no systematic ways to answer these questions; however, a recent study of student progress at Cleveland, Ohio's Shaker Heights High School provides insight about one of the nation's best high schools. Shaker Heights High School has a nearly equal number of black and white upper-middle-class students.

The achievement levels of the African American students is of concern to the administration. Blacks represent less than 10 percent of the high achievers, and reasons for the disparity varied. Economic disadvantages and test biases are not mentioned. Instead, the perceptions of teachers and parents are among the indictments. Teachers seem to impose less rigorous standards on black students and their parents' tend to accept mediocre grades as better than their children being guilty of substance abuse or unacceptable behavior, according to the report. This finding reflects reasons for the achievement gap at Shaker Heights High School only and does not represent the whole. But, it does indicate attention to shifting expectations.[2]

In addition to concerns about differences in academic achievements by children of color is the retreat from *Brown* (1954). The idea that court orders are no longer necessary combined with Supreme Court decisions limiting desegregation are responsible, in part, for the new trend. As court orders end and school districts phase out desegregation plan, resegregation follows. Segregation in today's public school is not only defined by color but by class as well. The enrollment of poor children of color is prevalent in public schools of New York, Los Angeles, Chicago, Philadelphia, and Detroit. The same is true of school systems in Houston, New Orleans, Washington, D. C., and Miami. "Segregation due to economics rather than the intentional separation of the races," wrote scholars A. Reynaldo Contreras and Jessica E. Stephens, is "commonplace near and within many American cities." Gary Orfield and John T. Yun, authors of "Resegregation in American Schools," agree. Resegregation of the 1990s is likely to be as devastating as segregation of an earlier period if school districts do not provide a quality education.[3]

In an effort to improve America's public schools, President George W. Bush signed the No Child Left Behind Act (NCLB) into law January 8, 2002. The bill requires the accountability of a school's instructional program based on assessments of students' performances on standardized tests. The NCLB will be effective in 2005–2006 for reading and math exams in grades three through eight. The law provides sanctions against schools or districts receiving Title I funds if they fail to reach the state's Adequate Yearly Progress (AYP) objective. It is too early to know what impact NCLB will have upon black children.

As American school boards struggled with complying or retreating from court ordered desegregation, changes occurred in curricular offerings that reflect greater diversity among students. As a result, authors, editors, and publishers have done much to fill demands for multicultural resources.

Among the recent scholarship focusing on African Americans and designed for young readers is *To Make Our World Anew* by historians Earl Lewis and Robin Kelley. The authors assert that it tells the story of the nation while placing the struggles and achievements of blacks in a larger international framework. The single volume text followed the appearance of Kelley and Lewis's eleven-volume series, *The Young Oxford History of African Americans*. Books in the series span the years from 1502 to the 1970s and address topics about the trans-Atlantic slave trade, Revolutionary War concepts, Civil War, New Deal, and Civil Rights Movement. A comparable sixteen-volume series, *Milestones in Black American History*, edited by Darlene Clark Hine and Clayborne Carson in 1995, addresses many of the same subjects. Each texts emphasizes events within a ten-year period.[4]

The Young Oxford and *Milestones* texts stand in sharp contrast to those of the 1950s that gave little attention to African Americans or touted slavery as a benign institution. *The Growth of the American Republic*, a popular text published in 1950 and used in American history courses in many colleges and universities, the training ground for America's public school teachers, noted the presence of slaves with the statement: "As for Sambo, whose wrongs moved the abolitionists to wrath and tears, there is some reason to believe that he suffered less than any other class in the South from its 'peculiar institution.' " The authors, Samuel Eliot Morison and Henry Steele Commager, continued, "The majority of slaves were adequately fed, well cared for, and apparently happy . . . Although brought to America by force, the incurably optimistic Negro soon became attached to the country, and devoted to his 'white folks,' " concluded the authors.[5]

Historians continue to assess the nature of relationships between enslaved men, women, and children and their owners. On one hand, energetic scholars may find much evidence to support the notion of slavery as a benign institution while on the other hand, equally energetic scholars may uncover data to refute the idea that slavery was indeed benign. Even a cursory review of the recent literature on slavery suggests that the debate about the nature of slavery will continue. The resounding benefit resulting from this historical argument is the cornucopia of scholarship on the subject. Children and adults have a great variety of publications from which to choose.[6]

A major watershed for changing the historiography occurred in the 1960s as a result of the Civil Rights Movement, Black Arts Movement, urban unrest, and a general increase in black consciousness. New interpretations of American history emerged and emphasized the unsung men and women on the lower rungs of society for a bottom up approach rather than a top down treatment. Through the next generation, much of the scholarship incorporated race, class, gender, and regional analyses thereby providing more balanced treatments in scholarly studies.[7]

Interest in the presentation of balanced views about African American history and culture in fiction and nonfiction predates the 1960s. On December 20, 1945, Walter White, an official at the National Association for the Advancement of Colored People's (NAACP) national office in New York, responded to a letter from Rev. E. Martin Lewis concerning *Little Black Sambo*, a popular children's book. White wrote:

> The question of reading matter in schools which can be considered derogatory to the Negro has long been one which concerns the Association. This is especially true when children of a tender age sometimes intentionally, sometimes by pure accident, come in contact with reading matter which tends to make for the placing of certain minority groups in so called "traditional" aspects.

As the NAACP received complaints about negative images or characterizations of African Americans in the print and electronic media, it entered a formal protest with the responsible parties. It also encouraged the branch organizations to address such matters on the local levels.[8]

An increased number of protests about *Little Black Sambo* began appearing in scholarly journals in the 1940s and deserve attention. Critics raised questions about the characterization and illustrations of people of color. Little black Sambo, replete with dark skin, kinky hair, and red lips, came to life in 1898 when the well-read

Helen Bannerman created the tale about a garishly dressed boy who outwitted several vicious tigers intent upon devouring him. Sambo bartered his red coat, blue trousers, green umbrella, and curled-toed purple shoes in exchange for his life. When wearing the child's garments each of the predators proclaimed himself the grandest animal in the jungle. Ultimately, they chase each other into oblivion, rather near oblivion. The tigers turned into the butter that Sambo and his family poured over the huge stacks of pancakes they enjoyed at mealtime.[9]

Little Black Sambo is an incredible story designed to amuse young children. It contains the necessary components for success including an interesting plot, admirable protagonist, and a satisfying ending. The basic narrative remains consistent in the many editions printed throughout the world, but the illustrations in selected volumes assumed regional flavors and biases. A major concern of anxious adults focused on how young readers perceived the images, and they questioned the impact the book had on the readers' well-being.

The appearance of the popular little book in the United States prompted many readers to associate Sambo with blacks of African descent. It did not matter that tigers, integral characters in the story, are indigenous to Asia rather than Africa. The child's name, Sambo, a respected appellation in Africa, served as a derogatory trope for passive generic blacks in the United States. In the hands of biased illustrators, Sambo became a racist stereotype rather than an innocuous caricature. In the process, Mambo, the boy's mother assumed the mammy-like characteristics of southern plantation folklore in the 1908 version published by Reilly and Britton. Illustrations in the 1917 edition by Cuppes and Leon transform Mambo into a minstrel character. Ultimately, many African American readers deemed *Little Black Sambo* offensive and inappropriate for children, black and white.[10]

Among those worried about the negative impact of *Little Black Sambo* upon impressionable children were librarians familiar with literature for young readers. In 1971, Augusta Baker, librarian at the Harlem branch of the New York Public Library, said:

> The depiction of a black person is exceptionally important in books for children. An artist can portray a black child—black skin, natural hair and flat features—and make him a stereotype and a caricature. The black child who sees the picture which ridicules his race may be deeply hurt, feel defeated, or become resentful and rebellious. The white child who sees the stereotyped presentation of the black person begins to feel superior and to accept this distorted picture or "type."

Another librarian asserted that the publication of *Little Black Sambo* was a "dark and backward step in publishing history" for African American children.[11]

A defender of the text appears to cast aspersions at those who found the book offensive because of literal interpretations when in actuality, the observer wrote:

> The Sambo adventures . . . happen to never-never people in a never-never land that is neither India nor Africa nor—certainly—the American South; alas for Anglo-Indian Mrs Bannerman, her head full of perfectly real exotic scenes, and real snakes and tigers, innocently colouring her figures black to suit the story.

Little Black Sambo is fantasy and appeals to children between five and seven years of age, many of whom may be too young to discern fact from fiction. It is likely that they will understand that tigers chasing each other will not turn into butter. But, is it as likely that they will know all blacks do not have exaggerated physical features, hanker after bold colors, or eat gargantuan amounts of food?[12]

By the 1970s, shifts in realities and fantasies were significant enough to demand that *Little Black Sambo* be less accessible to impressionable children. The small book containing the delightful story of a little black boy and "derogatory" illustrations had become too controversial for the comfort of many teachers, librarians, and parents. The popularity of the book faded, but its plot remained intriguing.[13]

In the 1990s, acclaimed author Julius Lester teemed up with illustrator Jerry Pinkney to render a new telling of *Little Black Sambo* in *Sam and the Tigers*. The biggest challenge for Lester and Pinkney was to produce a book free of any hint of racism and cultural baggage that would satisfy all readers. To alleviate any objections about the protagonist's name, Sambo, Lester changes it to Sam. In fact, all characters in this version of the story are called Sam. To eradicate confusion about the location of events, Africa or India, as in *Little Black Sambo*, Lester sets the story in the "never-never" land of "Sam-sam-sa-mara" where animals and people live in harmony as if it is an ordinary occurrence.[14]

The narrator uses current jargon to describe Sam's walk in the jungle, and it does not interfere with Sam's creativity. When one tiger fails to see the utility of the green umbrella and threatens to eat him, the child declares, "If you do, it'll send your cholesterol way up." The fantasy surrounding *Sam and the Tigers* is clear, and the illustrations are free of derision. To say the innocuous *Sam and the Tigers* differs dramatically from many older versions of *Little Black Sambo* is an understatement. For many readers, *Sam and the Tigers* is a welcomed change.[15]

Another welcomed addition to the literature for children is the six-volume American Girl series about Addy Walker. The imaginary adventures of the nine-year-old girl help young readers understand that many enslaved persons suffered the worst facets of bondage, including separations from loved ones, and physical abuse. Addy Walker, the heroine, and her mother run away from a North Carolina plantation to avoid the possible sale and sexual exploitation of the child. The pair make their way to safety in Philadelphia while a younger child remains in the care of fictive kinfolk. The family is eventually reunited in Philadelphia where Addy goes to school.[16]

Addy Walker, like Sambo, is a fictional character, but her story is told through carefully chosen dialect with realistic illustrations and attention to historical events. The "Peek into the Past," a section at the end of each book provides historical data about many of the subjects discussed. The delineations between fact and fantasy are clear enough for children to learn about American history and culture during the Civil War era.

The debut of Addy Walker, the storybook character along with hundreds of dollars in accessories related to her adventures, was not without controversy. Some critics questioned the motives of a successful white-owned company and its production of an enslaved character. Many Americans, said detractors, were ashamed of the fact that their ancestors were enslaved or slaveholders; therefore, the books would be offensive. Historian George Fredrickson declares that more than 135 years after its abolition slavery remains "the skeleton in the closet." Why would anyone create a doll representative of this shameful period in history? Some Americans preferred to forget the past while others wanted to celebrate it. One newspaper reporter wondered if Addy Walker could "facilitate racial harmony today?" Regardless of one's status in America before 1865 or stance on race relations, the fact remains that the majority of blacks in America were in bondage while the majority of whites in the country did not own slaves. Less than 25 percent of whites owned slaves in 1860, yet they held the majority of unfree people of color. The remainder of the slaveholders were free African Americans, a source of embarrassment for some and amazement for others.[17] Additionally, a relatively small number of Native Americans also owned slave.

Connie Porter, author of the Addy series, acknowledged the challenge in creating "a positive, universal character in Addy without sugarcoating the hardships of her life." Porter was careful not to portray Addy and her family as completely victimized by an inherently evil system. Author of children's books and winner of the John Newberry Medal for children's literature, Virginia Hamilton praised Porter's tasteful treatment of the bondage in "spare concise language." Hamilton recommended that the historical tale be read by all children, and Dorothy Height, president of the National Council of Negro Women added to the accolades when she said,

> Addy's story is a great way to celebrate the history, rich heritage and traditional values of the African-American family . . . Addy reminds us that now more than ever, children need that historical strength, love and care [of a family].[18]

The appearance of *Sam* and *Addy* reflect corporate interests in meeting demands for books and toys that celebrate African American life and culture. During the 1990s Mattel, Playskool, and Tyco manufactured products to satisfy discriminating consumers interested in their children playing with toys or reading books that influence their ideas "about beauty, who they are and what they can become." Darlene Powell Hopson, author and child clinical psychologist, noted the importance of children embracing "images that represent themselves and reinforce self-esteem and racial identity."[19]

Today's black children have more positive print and electronic media images with which to identify than they did generations ago. Positive reinforcements are much needed as children face physical challenges to their well-being that differ in scope from those faced by children one or more generations ago. The number of lynchings in the United States declined greatly after the 1930s, but a significant number of blacks died at the hands of whites during the Civil Rights Movement of the 1960s.

Almost none of the whites charged with the murders of blacks were found guilty and sentenced to terms in prison. However, in 1977 a jury found Robert Edward Chambliss guilty of the September 15, 1963, dynamite blast that killed Cynthia Wesley, Addie Mae Collins, Denise McNair, and Carole Robertson. He died in prison in 1985 after serving seven years of his sentence. Attorney General Janet Reno reopened the case in 1997 when new evidence surfaced. In an exceptional turn of events in May 2000, a grand jury indicted Bobby Frank Cherry and Thomas E. Blanton, Jr., for their roles in the crime committed nearly forty years ago. Both men were primary suspects in the case each of the four times it was reopened. They surrendered to the Jefferson County, Alabama, sheriff while maintaining their innocence. A May 2002 jury found both men guilty of murder, and they are now serving life sentences. A fourth suspect, Herman Cash, died in 1994 before being indicted and tried.[20]

Several other cases involving crimes committed against civil rights activists in the 1960s have been reopened as a result of the dogged determination of some local, state, and national justice officials who are not willing to allow this violence-filled chapter to remain closed. Since there is no statute of limitations on murder, it is possible that other cases will be reopened as social and political climates shift in favor of doing so.[21] Certainly, this is true of the June 2005 conviction of Edgar Ray Killen, a former Klansman, found guilty of manslaughter in the 1964 deaths of three civil rights activists.

Since the 1960s the sporadic killings of blacks by whites continue to occur, such as the Ku Klux Klan orchestrated March 21, 1981, murder of nineteen-year-old Michael Donald in Mobile, Alabama. More recent summary executions are likely to be called "hate crimes" rather than lynching as in the June 7, 1998, dragging death of forty-nine-year-old Texan James Byrd. Regardless of the name given to the murder, James Byrd, father of three children, suffered a tortuous death at the hands of Shawn Allen Berry, John William King, and Lawrence Russell Brewer. The men were arrested and tried for the murder.[22]

Many questions related to Byrd's death were answered during King's trial in which he received the death sentence; however, the June 16, 2000, hanging of seventeen-year-old Raynard Johnson in Kokomo, Mississippi, remains shrouded in mystery. Family members believe the teenager's death "was motivated by the fact that Johnson and his brother were friends with two 17-year-old white girls." Johnson's death and the swirl of questions regarding the hanging are reminiscent of times when associations, real and imagined, between black males and white females led to the death of the males. During the height of lynching, persons responsible for the deaths willingly draw public attention to the "events" and themselves rather than cloak their deeds in darkness.[23]

Although the rate of violent crimes is down, the number of Americans victimized by murder, aggravated assault, rape, sexual assault, and robbery in the 1990s was exceptional. Moreover, African Americans were more vulnerable to serious violent crimes than others. The September 1997 United States Department of Justice Report covering a three-year (1992–1994) study notes that blacks constituted 12 percent of the American population but were 51 percent of the nation's murder victims. Ten percent of those killed were between eighteen and twenty-one years of age. The report does not include statistics for children under twelve years of age. This does not mean they escaped the violence. No doubt they suffered as a result of the victimization of their relatives and friends.[24]

Perhaps, the most horrific of crimes involving a black minor occurred October 2002. Few children or adults in metropolitan Washington, D.C., or its surrounding area, could escape from the twenty-three-day reign of terror at the hand of the "beltway snipers," John Allen Muhammad and Lee Boyd Malvo. That Malvo, a juvenile, was intricately involved in murdering ten and wounding three innocent persons without regard for color, gender, or age, raised unanswerable questions about the boy who supposedly believed he was on a secret undercover mission for the U.S. military and appeared to be pleased with himself as he claimed "he never missed a shot." Initially, he declined to provide details about the shootings fearing that "someone else would copy them." It is unlikely that any clear-thinking teenagers would be willing to imitate Lee Boyd Malvo and languish in the criminal justice system for the remainder of their lives or cause someone else to become a vital statistic.[25]

The statistics indicate that one in eighty-nine females between twelve and twenty-four years of age was a rape/sexual assault victim. The serious nature of rape and sexual assault of African American females continues to be defined ambiguously by many black Americans. The highly publicized 1991 case in which a black teenager, Desiree Washington, accused prizefighter Mike Tyson of rape, revealed sharp differences in perceptions by leaders and lay persons in the black community. To some, "Iron Mike" was the "victim" of "rape" by the media that portrayed him as a brutal sexual predator. One writer described Tyson as a *"walking keg of testosterone."* Others suggested that he was not capable of separating his actions as a fighter inside the ring from appropriate behavior outside the ring. A comment attributed to Tyson declaring that he had not "hurt" anyone, meaning Washington, suggested that evidence of his pugilistic skills was not visible.[26]

The petition drive led by black ministers in Indianapolis claiming that Tyson was victimized by the media and the jury shows the extent to which community leaders marginalized the sexual assault. Tyson supporters argued that the charge was sullying his image as a role model for youngsters. Apparently, the pro-Tyson forces did not consider the usefulness of the case in teaching impressionable children about the importance of not hurting anyone—physically or emotionally.[27]

Aside from violent crimes, nonviolent crimes take a great toll in the African American community. The mandatory minimum sentencing laws for the use of crack cocaine impose prison terms of as much as five years without possibility of parole for first-time offenders found guilty of possessing five grams of crack cocaine. Blacks are more likely to use crack cocaine than whites who seem to prefer powder cocaine. Possession of 500 grams of powder cocaine draws a five-year sentence. Differences in the amount of substances possessed mean crack cocaine users and dealers are destined to spend long periods of time in jail while possession of five grams of powder cocaine is a misdemeanor requiring no more than one year in jail.

The consequences of mandatory minimum sentencing is highly evident in the case of Kemba Smith, a middle-class teenager, who came of age in suburban Richmond, Virginia. During the nineteen-year-old's enrollment at Hampton University in the early 1990s, she met and fell in love with the Jamaican-born Peter Michael Hall, a drug dealer. Although Smith never used or sold drugs, she was an accessory and pled guilty to conspiracy, money laundering, and lying to federal agents about Hall's multimillion dollar business in crack cocaine stretching from New York to Virginia. As Smith, a first-time offender, tells her story, she was naive and afraid to disobey Hall, a man she describes as violently abusive. Smith's culpability drew a twenty-four-year sentence. How many young black boys and girls could identify with or be in similar situations as Kemba Smith? Eighty-eight percent of the persons arrested for crack cocaine possession are black.[28]

Smith might have languished in prison had her parents, Gus and Odessa Smith, not assumed a proactive and highly vocal role in fighting for her release through public lectures for high school and college students. Kemba Smith's story appeared in a 1996 *Emerge* and won additional supporters, including students in Dayton, Ohio's Colonel White School for the Arts. They formed a Kemba Smith Club based on their conviction that the mandatory minimum sentencing law was unfair. The NAACP participated in Smith's defense, and the case became a *cause celebre* because of the publicity and ostensible class and race biases in sentencing.[29]

In one of the final acts of his presidency, William Jefferson Clinton granted sixty-two pardons. Among the recipients were Kemba Smith and Dorothy Gains, another African American found guilty of her role in a drug ring. Laura Sager, director of Families Against Mandatory Minimum, said "President Clinton has shown mercy and integrity by releasing these individuals, who clearly aren't the drug kingpins Congress intended to target" when passing the mandatory minimum sentencing bill. Sager urged congress legislative to review and change the mandatory minimum sentencing laws.[30]

The tough anticrime legislation curtailed the number of violations and resulted in a greater disproportion of African Americans in the nation's prisons for drug offenses. Between 1985 and 1995, the American prison population of drug offenders increased from 38,900 to 224,900. Approximately 70 percent of the black males between sixteen and twenty-five years of age in Watts, California, were either incarcerated, on parole, or on probation in the 1990s. Many were substance abusers.[31]

Prison records often stand in the way of meaningful employment and the right to vote, even after convicted persons serve their sentences. Knowledge of this reality may dissuade some would-be-offenders. Certainly, the students at Colonel White School for the Arts learned more about the criminal justice system as a result of their interest in the Kemba Smith case.

Concomitant with the decline in violent crime rate is the decline in the birth rate among unwed teens. In fact, statistics show that the birth rate fell by 21 percent between 1991 and 1996. What accounts for this decline? Perhaps, the accessibility to more effective birth control is responsible as much as the fear of contracting sexually transmitted diseases. Community- and church-based organizations and programs along with the influence of mothers and fathers, who became parents while still children, also deserve credit.[32]

While the birth rate is down, a significant number of children are born to young single parents. Some of these children grow up in disadvantaged circumstances and depend upon public assistance. Seven percent of welfare recipients are teenaged mothers. The Welfare Reform Bill (1996) ended welfare as we knew it by redirecting guarantees of assistance from the federal government to state authorities. The new legislation requires recipients to support themselves after a specified term of public assistance. Passage of the Temporary Assistance for Needy Families prompted Mary Jo Bane, Assistant Secretary for Children and Families in the Department of Health and Human Services under President Clinton, to resign once he signed the bill. Bane was anxious about what would happen to poor children when states were no longer required to provide assistance and protection. According to Bane,

> Analyses produced by the Department of Health and Human Services and by the Urban Institute before the bill was enacted predicted that upward of a million children would be pushed into poverty as a result of the bill, and that some eight million families with children would lose income.

The findings are clear. Children, many of whom are black, will suffer if their parents do not conform in finding adequate gainful employment within the specified time limit.[33]

The state of affairs for black youth in America at the turn of the twenty-first century is mixed, like that for many of their other cohorts. How this will impact upon their places in American society in the next one, two, or three decades is unknown. This age group is often viewed with suspicion or disdain by their elders who see young people as irresponsible rebels disconnected from the real world because of their dress, attitudes, or music choices. Such perceptions lend themselves to stereotypical notions about all youngsters. As an acknowledgment of the disquiet adults hold for youth, one teenager spoke confidently in defense of her peers when she said, "It's important that my generation be able to show that we can take the place of the generation before us. Things aren't going to fall apart when we take over."[34]

NOTES

Introduction

1. Steven Mintz, "At the End of the Century of the Child," (Unpublished paper, presented at History of Childhood Conference, Benton Foundation, Washington, D.C., 2000, in possession of author).
2. See Alex Kotlowitz, *There Are No Children Here: The Story of Two Boys Growing Up in the Other America* (New York: Anchor Books, 1991); Patricia Riley, ed., *Growing Up Native American* (New York: Avon Books, 1993); Dorinda Makanaonalani Nicholson, *Pearl Harbor Child: A Child's View of Pearl Harbor—from Attack to Peace* (Honolulu: Arizona Memorial Museum Association, 1993); Zlata Filipović, *Zlata's Diary: A Child's Life in Sarajeo* (New York: Viking, 1994); Joyce A. Ladner, *Tomorrow's Tomorrow* (Lincoln: University of Nebraska, 1995); Rebecca Carroll, *Sugar in the Raw: Voices of Young Black Girls in America* (New York: Three Rivers Press, 1997); Sonsyrea Tate, *Little X: Growing Up in the Nation of Islam* (San Francisco: Harper San Francisco, 1997); Michael L. Cooper, *Indian School: Teaching the White Man's Way* (Wilmington: Clarion Books, 1999); Jordana Y. Shakoor, *Civil Rights Childhood* (Jackson: University Press of Mississippi, 1999); Frances Esquibel Tywoniak, *Migrant Daughter: Coming of Age As a Mexican American* (Berkeley: University of California Press, 2000); Laurel Holliday, ed., *Dreaming in Color, Living in Black and White: Our Own Stories of Growing Up Black in America* (New York: Pocket Books, 2000); Cathy Luchetti, *Children of the West: Family Life on the Frontier* (New York: W. W. Norton & Co., 2001); Harriet Hyman Alsonso, *Growing Up Abolitionist: The Story of the Garrison Children* (Amherst: University of Massachusetts Press, 2002); Sandra Day O'Connor and H. Alan Day, *Lazy B: Growing Up on a Cattle Ranch in the Southwest* (New York: Random House, 2002).
3. See Frederick Douglass, *Narrative of the Life of Frederick Douglass: An American Slave, Written by Himself* (Boston: Anti-Slavery Office, 1845); Frederick Douglass, *Life and Times of Frederick Douglass: Written by Himself* (New York: Collier Books, 1962); Frederick Douglass, *My Bondage and My Freedom* (New York: Dover Publications, Inc., 1969); Harriet Jacobs, *Incidents in the Life of a Slave Girl: Written by Herself*, edited by Jean Fagan Yellin (Cambridge: Harvard University Press, 1987); Booker T. Washington, *Up from Slavery, An Autobiography* (New York: Bantam, 1967); Ann Moody, *Coming of Age in Mississippi* (New York: Laurel Book, 1968).
4. See Robert E. Desroches, Jr., " 'Not Fade Away': The Narrative of Venture Smith, an African American in the Early Republic," *Journal of American History* 84 (June 1997), 42–44.
5. See Eugene D. Genovese, "The Treatment of Slaves in Different Countries: Problems in the Applications of the Comparative Method," in Eugene D. Genovese, ed., *In Red and Black: Marxian Explorations in Southern and Afro-American History* (New York: Pantheon Books, 1971), 158–172.

6. The scholarship on the work of black children focuses almost entirely on the chores of enslaved boys and girls. An exception is Vincent DiGirolamo, "The Negro Newsboy: Black Child in a White Myth," *Columbia Journal of American Studies* 4 (2000): 63–92.

Chapter One   Africa's Progeny Cast upon American Shores

1. Sarah Margru to George Whipple, September 18, 1847, American Missionary Association Archives, Tulane University, New Orleans Louisiana (hereafter cited as AMA); John W. Barber, *A History of the Amistad Captives: Being a Circumstantial Account of the Capture of the Spanish Schooner Amistad, by the Africans on Board; Their Voyage, and Capture Near Long Island, New York; With Biographical Sketches of each of the Surviving Africans. Also, An Account of The Trials Had on their Case, Before the District and Circuit Courts of the United States, For the District of Connecticut* (New Haven: E. L. & J. W. Barber, 1840), 3–5.
2. Olaudah Equiano, *The Interesting Narrative of the Life of Olaudah Equiano: Written by Himself,* edited by Robert J. Allison (Boston: Bedford Books of St. Martin's Press, 1995), 47, 51. See Vincent Carretta, "Olaudah Equiano or Gustavus Vassa? New Light on an Eighteenth-Century Question of Identity," *Slavery and Abolition* (hereafter cited as *S&A*) 20 (December 1999): 96–103.
3. Equiano, *The Interesting Narrative,* 34. See Daniel L. Schafer, "Shades of Freedom: Anna Kingsley in Senegal, Florida and Haiti," in Jane G. Landers, ed., *Against the Odds: Free Blacks in the Slave Societies of the Americas* (London: Frank Cass, 1996), 130–135; Daniel L. Schafer, *Anna Madgigine Jai Kingsley: African Princess, Florida Slave, Plantation Owner* (Gainesville: University Press of Florida, 2003), 4–8. See also Shelia Lambert, ed., *House of Commons Sessional Papers of the Eighteenth Century,* vol. 68, *George III, Minutes of Evidence on the Slave Trade 1788–1789* (Wilmington: Scholarly Resources, 1975), 73–76 for testimony regarding how persons became enslaved in Africa.
4. David Eltis, "The Volume, Age/Sex Ratios, and African Impact of the Slave Trade: Some Refinements of Paul Lovejoy's Review of the Literature," *Journal of African History* 31 (1990), 489. See Erik J. W. Hofstee, "The Great Divide: Aspects of the Social History of the Middle Passage in the Trans-Atlantic Slave Trade," (Michigan State University, Ph. D. diss., 2001), especially chapter two, "Children and Infants," 64–105.
5. See Augustino, " 'It Was the Same as Pigs in a Sty': A Young African's Account of Life on a Slave Ship (1849)," in Robert Edgar Conrad, ed., *Children of God's Fire: A Documentary History of Black Slavery in Brazil* (University Park: Pennsylvania State University Press, 1984), 37–38; Belinda (Belinda Royall), "Petition of an African Slave to the Legislature of Massachusetts (1782)," in Vincent Carretta, ed., *Unchained Voices: An Anthology of Black Authors in the English-Speaking World of the Eighteenth Century* (Lexington: University of Kentucky Press, 1996), 142–144; Boyrereau Brinch, *The Blind African Slave, or Memoirs of Boyrereau Brinch, Nicknamed Jeffrey Brace. Containing an Account of the Kingdom of Bow-Woo, in the Interior of Africa; with the Climate and Natural Productions, Laws, and Customs Peculiar to That Place. With an Account of His Captivity, Sufferings, Sales, Travels, Emancipation, Conversion to the Christian Religion, Knowledge of the Scriptures, & c. Interspersed with Stricture on Slavery, Speculative Observations on the Qualities of Human Nature, with Quotations from Scripture,* Electronic edition available at <http://docsouth.unc./neh/brinch/brinch.html>; Ottobah Cugoano, "Thoughts and Sentiments on the Evil and Wicked Traffic of the Slavery and Commerce of the Human Species," in Francis D. Adams and Barry Sanders, eds., *Three Black Writers in Eighteenth Century England* (Belmont, CA: Wadsworth Publishing Company, Inc., 1971); Philip D. Curtin, ed., *Africa Remembered: Narratives by West Africans from the Era of the Slave Trade* (Madison: University of Wisconsin, 1967); James Albert Ukawsaw Gronniosaw, "A Narrative of the Most Remarkable Particulars in the Life of James Albert Ukawsaw Gronniosaw, an African Prince, as Related by Himself." Electronic version available at <http://docsouth.unc.edu/neh/gronniosaw/ gronnios.html>; Florence Hall, "Memoir of

Florence Hall" (unpublished ca. 1820) Powel Family Papers, Historical Society of Pennsylvania, Philadelphia, Pennsylvania; Jerome S. Handler, "Survivors of the Middle Passage: Life Histories of Enslaved Africans in British America," *S&A* 23 (April 2002): 23–56; Jerome Handler, "Life Histories of Enslaved Africans in Barbados," *S&A* 19 (April 1998): 129–141; Vernon H. Nelson, ed., "John Archibald Monteith: Native Helper and Assistant in the Jamaica Mission at New Carmel," *Transaction Moravian Historical Society* 21 Part I (1966): 29–51; Venture Smith, *A Narrative of the Life and Adventures of Venture A Native of Africa, but a Resident Above Sixty Years in the United States of America*. Related by Himself in Arna Bontemps, ed., *Five Black Lives: The Autobiographies of Venture Smith, James Mars, William Grimes, The Rev. G. W. Offley, James L. Smith* (Middletown: Wesleyan University Press, 1971), 1–35. See also David Eltis, Stephen D. Behrendt, David Richardson, and Herbert S. Klein, eds., Trans-Atlantic Slave Trade: A Database on CD-ROM (Cambridge: Cambridge University Press, 1999).

6. "Memoirs of Florence Hall," Powel Collection, HSP; Ottobah Cugoano, "Narrative of the Enslavement of Ottobah Cugoano, a Native of Africa; Published by Himself, in the Year 1787," 120; Brinch, "Memoirs," 14, 68–71. Electronic edition available at "Documenting the American South, University of North Carolina at Chapel Hill Libraries," <http://docsouth.unc.edu/new/cugoano/cugoano.html>. Not all children lived under ideal conditions until kidnapped and transported to the Americas. Many children were already enslaved in Africa as a result of warfare that had little or nothing to do with the trans-Atlantic slave trade. See Hofstee, "The Great Divide," 67.

7. Smith, "A Narrative of the Life and Adventures of Venture," 8; Robert E. Desrochers, Jr., " 'Not Fade Away': The Narrative of Venture Smith, and African in the Early Republic," *Journal of American History* (hereafter cited as *JAH*) 84 (June 1997), 40.

8. Smith, "A Narrative of the Life and Adventures of Venture," 9.

9. Equiano, *The Interesting Narrative*, 39–40.

10. Ibid., 47–48.

11. Ibid., 48, 51.

12. Ibid., 48–50.

13. Ibid., 50.

14. Ibid., 51.

15. Ibid., 51.

16. Carretta, "Olaudah Equiano or Gustavus Vassa?" 96, 98–99, 102. See Handler, "Survivors of the Middle Passage," 23–56; Curtin, *Africa Remembered*; William L. Andrews, *To Tell a Free Story: The First Century of Afro-American Autobiography, 1760–1865* (Urbana: University of Illinois, 1988), 56–60.

17. Gronniosaw, "A Narrative," 6; Cugoano, "Narrative of the Enslavement of Ottobah Cugoano, a Native of Africa," 120; Augustino, "It Was the Same as Pigs in a Sty'," 38.

18. See Gronniosaw, "A Narrative," 7; Robert Edgar Conrad, ed., *Children of God's Fire: A Documentary History of Black Slavery in Brazil* (University Park: Pennsylvania State University Press, 1984), 38.

19. Paul E. Lovejoy, "The Impact of the Atlantic Slave Trade on Africa: A Review of the Literature," *Journal of African History* 30 (1989), 374. See "New Perspectives on the Transatlantic Slave Trade," *William and Mary Quarterly* (hereafter cited as *W&MQ*), special issue 58 (January 2001); Philip A. Curtin, *The Atlantic Slave Trade: A Census* (Madison: University of Wisconsin Press, 1969).

20. Hofstee, "The Great Divide," 66, 68; Colin Palmer, *Human Cargoes: The British Slave Trade to Spanish America, 1700–1739* (Urbana: University of Illinois Press, 1981), 121; Elizabeth Donnan, *Documents Illustrative of the History of the Slave Trade to America*, 4 vols. (Washington: Carnegie Institute of Washington, 1930), II: 220; Donnan, *Documents*, III: 138, 457.

21. Eltis, "The Volume, Age/Sex Ratios, and African Impact of the Slave Trade," 489; David Eltis, "Fluctuations in the Age and Sex Ratios of Slaves in the Nineteenth-Century

Transatlantic Slave Traffic," *Slavery and Abolition* 7 (1986), 258; Donnan, *Documents*, II: 289; Hofstee, "The Great Divide," 66, 73, 77.

22. Donnan, *Documents*, III: 584; Colin Palmer, *Human Cargoes: The British Slave Trade to Spanish America, 1700–1739* (Urbana: University of Illinois Press, 1981); Palmer, *Human Cargoes*, 121–122; Hofstee, "The Great Divide," 72, 78; Eltis et al. Trans-Atlantic Slave Trade CD-ROM, #18076.

23. R. Lynn Matson, "Phillis Wheatley—Soul Sister," *Phylon* 33 (Fall 1972), 228; Phillip M. Richards, "Phillis Wheatley and Literary Americanization," *American Quarterly* 44 (June 1992), 166–167, 177.

24. Gronniosaw, "A Narrative," 6; Robert Edgar Conrad, ed., *Children of God's Fire: A Documentary History of Black Slavery in Brazil* (University Park: Pennsylvania State University Press, 1984), 38; Sarah Margru [Kinson] to Mr. Whipple, [Sept] 18th 1847, May 2, 1847, AMA; John W. Barber, *A History of the Amistad Captives: Being a Circumstantial Account of the Capture of the Spanish Schooner Amistad, by the Africans on Board; Their Voyage, and Capture Near Long Island, New York; With Biographical Sketches of each of the Surviving Africans. Also, An Account of The Trials Had on their Case, Before the District and Circuit Courts of the United States, For the District of Connecticut* (New Haven: E. L. & J. W. Barber, 1840), 14–15.

25. Walter Rodney, "West Africa and the Atlantic Slave-Trade," Historical Association of Tanzania, Paper No. 2 (Nairobi: East Africa Publishing House, 1967), 7; John Thornton, *Africa and Africans in the Making of the Atlantic World, 1400–1680,* second edition (Cambridge: Cambridge University Press, 1998), 43. See Randy J. Sparks, "Two Princes of Calabar: An Atlantic Odyssey from Slavery to Freedom," *W&MQ* 59 (July 2002), 562–563.

26. Donnan, *Documents*, I: 282–283; Thornton, *Africa and Africans*, 52–53; Gronniosaw, "A Narrative," 9; Donald Wax, "A Philadelphia Surgeon on a Slaving Voyage to Africa, 1749–1751," *Pennsylvania Magazine of History and Biography* 94 (1968), 483. See George Metcalf, "A Microcosm of Why Africans Sold Slaves: Akan Consumption Patterns in the 1770s," *JAH* 28 (1987): 377–394; Robin Law, "Dahomey and the Slave Trade: Reflections on the Historiography of the Rise of Dahomey," *JAH* 27 (1986), 243–247, for discussions focusing upon motives for engaging in the Atlantic slave trade.

27. *Snow Greyhound* Log and Account book, New Port, Rhode Island Historical Society, New Port Rhode Island; Donnan, *Documents*, I: 283; Smith, "The Narrative of the Life and Adventures of Venture," 9–10; Gronniosaw, "The Narrative," 9. See Joseph C. Miller, *Way of Death: Merchant Capitalism and the Angolan Slave Trade, 1730–1830* (Madison: University of Wisconsin Press, 1988), 68–70.

28. Rodney, "*West Africa*," 6.

29. Michael L. Conniff and Thomas J. Davis, *Africans in the Americas: A History of the Black Diaspora* (New York: St. Martin's Press, 1994), 41–44; Rodney, "*West Africa*," 10–11; Thornton, *Africa and Africans*, 98–102.

30. Hall, "Memoirs of Florence Hall," HSP.

31. Donnan, *Documents*, I: 284.

32. George Francis Dow, *Slave Ships and Slaving* (Westport: Negro Universities Press, 1970), 172–173.

33. Ibid., 173.

34. Lovejoy, "The Impact of the Atlantic Slave Trade," 386–390; Eltis, "The Volume, Age/Sex Ratios, and African Impact of the Slave Trade," 485–492. See Thornton, *Africa and Africans*, 72–74.

35. John Thornton, "Sexual Demography: The Impact of the Slave Trade on Family Structure," in Darlene Clark Hine, Wilma King, and Linda Reed, eds., "*We Specialize in the Wholly Impossible*": *A Reader in Black Women's History* (Brooklyn: Carlson Publishing, Inc., 1995), 58–59; G. Ugo Nwokeji, "African Conceptions of Gender and the Slave Traffic," *W&MQ* 58 (January 2001): 47–67.

36. Thornton, "Sexual Demography," 59.

37. Donnan, *Documents*, I: 441.

38. Ibid., I: 442; I: 293.

39. Ibid., I: 459; Augustino, "It Was the Same as Pigs in a Sty," 39.

40. Ibid., I: 459; Conrad, *Children of God's Fire*, 33, 38; Equiano, *The Interesting Narrative*, 56. See Rawley, *The Transatlantic Slave Trade*, 283–306; Daniel P. Mannix and Malcolm Cowley, *Black Cargoes: A History of the Atlantic Slave Trade, 1518–1865* (New York: Viking Press, 1962), 104–130.

41. Wax, "A Philadelphia Surgeon," 468.

42. Equiano, *The Interesting Narrative*, 56; Augustino, "It Was the Same as Pigs in a Sty," 39. See Rawley, *The Transatlantic Slave Trade*, 283–306; Daniel P. Mannix and Malcolm Cowley, *Black Cargoes: A History of the Atlantic Slave Trade, 1518–1865* (New York: Viking Press, 1962), 104–130.

43. Augustino, "It Was the Same as Pigs in a Sty," 38, 39; Smith, "The Narrative of the Life and Adventures of Venture," 11.

44. Wax, "Philadelphia Surgeon," 486–487.

45. Brinch, "Memoirs," 103; James Pope-Hennessey, *Sins of the Fathers: A Study of the Atlantic Slave Traders, 1441–1807* (London: Weidenfeld and Nicolson, 1967), 99.

46. Quobna Ottobah Cugoano, "Thoughts and Sentiments on the Evil and Wicked Traffic of the Slavery and Commerce of the Human Species," in Vincent Carretta, ed., *Unchained Voices: Anthology of Black Authors in the English Speaking-World of the Eighteenth Century* (Lexington: University Press of Kentucky, 1996), 149; Bernard Martin and Mark Spurrell, eds., *The Journal of a Slave Trader (John Newton) 1750–1754* (London: The Epworth Press, 1962), 75, 105; Pope-Hennessy, *Sins of the Fathers*, 100; Dow, *Slave Ships & Slavers*, 174.

47. Pope-Hennessey, *Sins of the Fathers*, 100.

48. Ottobah Cugoano, "Narrative of the Enslavement of Ottobah Cugoano, a Native of Africa; Published by Himself, in the Year 1787," 120.

49. Dow, *Slave Ships & Slaving*, 173; Augustino, "It Was the Same as Pigs in a Sty," 39. See Hofstee, "The Great Divide," 100–102, for a discussion regarding children committing suicide in the Middle Passage.

50. David Richardson, "Shipboard Revolts, African Authority, and the Atlantic Slave Trade," *W&MQ* 58 (January 2001), 72.

51. Donnan, *Documents*, III: 45; Hofstee, "The Great Divide," 97. See Antonio T. Bly, "Crossing the Lake of Fire: Slave Resistance During the Middle Passage, 1720–1842," *Journal of Negro History* 83 (Summer 1998): 178–186; See Richardson, "Shipboard Revolts," 69–92.

52. Donnan, *Documents*, II: 334–335; Martin and Spurrell, *The Journal of a Slave Trader*, 103; Richardson, "Shipboard Revolts," 71.

53. Cugoano, "Narrative of the Enslavement of Ottobah Cugoano," 124; Pope-Hennessy, *Sins of the Fathers*; 100; Hofstee, "The Great Divide," 99.

54. Donnan, *Documents*, II: 266; John Atkins, *A Voyage to Guinea, Brazil, and The West Indies in His Majesty's Ships, The Swallow and Weymouth* (London: Frank Cass & Co. Ltd, 1970), 73.

55. Ibid., Atkins, *A Voyage*, 73.

56. Bly, "Crossing the Lake of Fire," 181–182.

57. Howard Jones, *Mutiny on the Amistad: The Saga of a Slave Revolt and Its Impact on American Abolition, Law, and Diplomacy* (New York: Oxford University Press, 1987), 3–26; Barber, *A History of the Amistad Captives*, 9–15.

58. Sarah Margru to George Whipple, September 18, 1847, AMA; Barber, *A History of the Amistad Captives*, 9–15. See Ellen Nickenzie Lawson, "Children of the Amistad," *Instructor* (February 1988): 44–48.

59. See J. C. Furnas, "Patrolling the Middle Passage," in Robert M. Spector, ed., *Readings in American History, 1607–1865* (New York: American Heritage Custom Publishing, 1993),

155–162; Robert E. Desrochers, Jr., "Slave-For-Sale Advertisements and Slavery in Massachusetts, 1704–1781," *W&MQ* 59 (July 2002): 623–664.

60. Solomon Northup, *Twelve Years a Slave: Narrative of Solomon Northup* in Gilbert Osofsky, ed., *Puttin' On Ole Massa: The Slave Narratives of Henry Bibb, William Wells Brown, and Solomon Northup* (New York: Harper Torchbooks, 1969), 338. See Wilma King, *Stolen Childhood: Youth in Bondage in Nineteenth-Century America* (Bloomington: Indiana University Press, 1995) for a discussion of enslaved children in the South.

61. Memoir of Florence Hall, Powel Collection, HSP.

Chapter Two   Minor Players in Bondage: Interactions between Enslaved and Slaveholding Children in the Old South

1. Manus Brown quoted in George P. Rawick, ed., *The American Slave: A Composite Autobiography* 6 Mississippi Narr. (Westport: Greenwood Press, 1972), 1: 270. See discussions of interactions between enslaved and slaveowning children in the antebellum South in Wilma King, *Stolen Childhood: Slave Youth in Nineteenth-Century America* (Bloomington: Indiana University Press, 1995), especially Chapter 3.

2. Launcelot Minor Blackford Diary, June 21, 1848, Southern Historical Collection, University of North Carolina, Chapel Hill, North Carolina (hereafter cited as SHC).

3. Thomas Jefferson, *Notes on the State of Virginia*, edited by William Peden (New York: W. W. Norton & Company, 1982), 162. See Daniel L. Schafer, *Anna Madgigine Jai Kingsley: African Princess, Florida Slave, Plantation Slaveowner* (Gainesville: University of Florida, 2003); John D. Russell, "Colored Freemen as Slave Owners in Virginia," *Journal of Negro History* (hereafter cited as *JNH*): 233–242; Philip J. Schwarz, "Emancipators, Protectors, and Anomalies: Free Black Slaveowners in Virginia," *Virginia Magazine of History and Biography* 95 (July 1987), 319, 322–323.

4. Kimberly S. Hanger, " 'The Fortunes of Women in America': Spanish New Orleans's Free Women of African Descent and Their Relations with Slave Women," in Patricia Morton, ed., *Discovering the Women in Slavery: Emancipating Perspectives on the American Past* (Athens: University of Georgia Press, 1996), 153–173; Paul Lachance, "The Limits of Privilege: Where Free Persons of Color Stood in the Hierarchy of Wealth in Antebellum New Orleans," in Jane G. Landers, ed., *Against the Odds: Free Blacks in the Slave Societies of the Americas* (London: Frank Cass, 1996), 65–84.

5. Carter G. Woodson, *Free Negro Owners of Slaves in the United States in 1830 Together with Absentee Ownership of Slaves in the United States in 1830* (New York: Negro Universities Press, 1968), v; Loren Schweninger, *James T. Rapier and Reconstruction* (Chicago: University of Chicago Press, 1978), 16; Loren Schweninger, "Property Owning Free African American Women in the South, 1800–1870," in Darlene Clark Hine, Wilma King, and Linda Reed, eds., *"We Specialize in the Wholly Impossible": A Reader in Black Women's History* (Brooklyn: Carlson Publishing, Inc., 1995), 259, 264; Schwarz, "Emancipators, Protectors, and Anomalies," 321–322; Larry Koger, *Black Slaveowners: Free Black Slave Masters in South Carolina, 1790–1860* (Columbia: University of South Carolina Press, 1995), 45, 57, 59–60; Mary Beth Corrigan, " 'It's a Family Affair': Buying Freedom in the District of Columbia, 1850–1860," in Larry E. Hudson, Jr., ed., *Working Toward Freedom: Slave Society and Domestic Economy in the American South* (Rochester: University of Rochester Press, 1994), 179.

6. Carter G. Woodson, "Free Negro Owners of Slaves in the United States in 1830," *JNH* 9 (January 1924): 6–35; Loren Schweninger, "John Carruthers Stanly and the Anomaly of Black Slaveholding," *North Carolina Historical Review* 67 (April 1990), 169, 171, 177–179; Gary B. Mills, *The Forgotten People: Cane River's Creoles of Color* (Baton Rouge: Louisiana State University, 1977), 117–118, 208–209. See Koger, *Black Slaveowner*, 80–101; R. Halliburton, Jr., "Free Black Owners of Slaves: A Reappraisal of the Woodson Thesis," *South Carolina Historical Magazine* 76 (July 1976): 129–142; John H. Russell, "Colored Freemen as Slave Owners in Virginia," *JNH* 1 (June 1916): 233–242. See also

T. H. Breen and Stephen Innes, *"Myne Owne Ground": Race and Freedom on Virginia's Eastern Shore, 1640–1676* (New York: Oxford University Press, 1980); Arthur Zilversmit, *The First Emancipation: The Abolition of Slavery in the North* (Chicago: University of Chicago Press, 1967).

7. Betsy Sompayrac, "Last Will and Testament," January 15, 1845, Office of the Parish Clerk, Natchitoches, Louisiana (hereafter cited as PCNLA). See Kimberly S. Hanger, "Patronage, Property and Persistence: The Emergence of a Free Black Elite in Spanish New Orleans," in Jane G. Landers, ed., *Against the Odds: Free Blacks in the Slave Societies of the Americas* (London: Frank Cass, 1996), 51–52.

8. The selection of godparents and sponsors varied by color and status. For example, in 1854 the North Carolina slaveowner Mary Ruffin Smith stood as sponsor at the baptism of the enslaved girl Lucy Battle Smith, a relative of Cornelia Smith whom Mary Ruffin Smith owned. The Reverend Henry T. Lee, served as rector of Chapel of the Cross, Chapel Hill, North Carolina, from 1856 to 1858. He baptized Ann Elisa, Henry, Patsy Alice, and Rufus, the enslaved children of Lissy and Sam on Easter Sunday, March 23, 1856. Their sponsors—white women—Mrs. William Horn Battle and her invalid daughter, Susan Catherine, also sponsored eight other black children baptized on the same day. Furthermore, Reverend Lee baptized George, a black youngster owned by the Chaves family. The records indicate that an enslaved woman was his sponsor. See Mary Arthur Stoudemire, "Black Parishioners of the Chapel of the Cross, 1844–1866," *North Carolina Genealogical Society Journal* 9 (May 1983), 78–84.

9. Sompayrac, "Last Will and Testament," PCNLA. See Michael P. Johnson and James L. Roark, " 'A Middle Ground': Free Mulattoes and the Friendly Moralist Society of Antebellum Charleston," *Southern Studies* 21 (Fall 1982), 253.

10. "Succession of Betsy Sompayrac, Petition," April 8, 1847, PCNLA. See Koger, *Black Slaveowners*, 83–85, 89, 93–95, for a comparison of wills bequeathing enslaved children to heirs. See also Wilma King, "The Mistress and her Maids: White and Black Women in a Louisiana Household, 1858–1868," in Patricia Morton, ed., *Discovering the Women in Slavery: Emancipating Perspectives on the American Past* (Athens: University of Georgia Press, 1996), 82–106; Drew Gilpin Faust, " 'Trying to Do a Man's Business': Slavery, Violence and Gender in the American Civil War," *Gender and History* 4 (Summer 1992): 197–214; LeeAnn Whites, *The Civil War as a Crisis in Gender, Augusta, Georgia, 1860–1890* (Athens: University of Georgia Press, 1995); LeeAnn Whites, "The Civil War as a Crisis in Gender," in Catherine Clinton and Nina Silber, ed., *Divided Houses: Gender and the Civil War* (New York: Oxford University Press, 1992), 3–21, for discussions of the challenges women faced when interacting with and managing slaves.

11. Anna Matilda King (hereafter cited as AMK) to Honble Thos. Butler King, December 27, 1844, Thomas Butler King Papers, SHC; AMK to Henry Lord King, September 28, 1948, March 10, 1857, SHC.

12. Frances Anne Kemble, *Journal of a Residence on a Georgian Plantation in 1838–1839*, edited by John A. Scott (Athens: University of Georgia Press, 1984), 93.

13. M. Cain to Minerva, April 14, 1833, Tod Robinson Caldwell Papers, SHC.

14. Eugene D. Genovese, *Roll, Jordan, Roll: The World the Slaves Made* (New York: Vintage Books, 1976), 518; Jo Anne Sellers Huber, "Southern Women and the Institution of Slavery" (M. A. thesis, Lamar University, 1980), 41; Sudie Duncan Sides, "Southern Women and Slavery," part I, *History Today* 20 (January 1970), 55; Kemble, *Journal of a Residence on a Georgian Plantation in 1838–1839*, 93; Blackford Diary, June 21, 1848, SHC.

15. Dick Journal, February 1808, Manuscripts Department, University of Virginia, Charlottesville, Virginia (hereafter cited as UVA).

16. Ibid.

17. Rawick, *The American Slave* 5 Texas Narr., 7–8, 242; Norman R. Yetman, ed., *Life Under the "Peculiar Institution": Selections from the Slave Narrative Collection* (New York: Holt, Rinehart and Winston, 1970), 327.

18. Theodore Rosengarten, *Tombee: Portrait of a Cotton Planter* (New York: Morrow, 1986), 172; Genovese, *Roll, Jordan, Roll*, 515.

19. Edwin Adams Davis and William Ransom Hogan, *The Barber of Natchez* (Baton Rouge: Louisiana State University Press, 1998), 54, 57.

20. Rawick, *The American Slave* 5 Texas Narr., 4, 156.

21. See Ira Berlin, "The Structure of the Free Negro Caste in the Antebellum United States," *Journal of Social History* 9 (Spring 1976), 298, 308–309; Michael P. Johnson and James L. Roark, "Strategies of Survival: Free Negro Families and the Problem of Slavery," in Carol Bleser, ed., *In Joy and In Sorrow: Women, Family, and Marriage in the Victorian South, 1830–1900* (New York: Oxford University Press, 1991), 88–102, 288–293. See also Whittington B. Johnson, *Black Savannah, 1788–1864* (Fayetteville: University of Arkansas Press, 1996), 1–2, 4; Tommy L. Bogger, *Free Blacks in Norfolk, Virginia, 1796–1860: The Darker Side of Freedom* (Charlottesville: University of Virginia Press, 1997), 103–104; Bernard E. Powers, Jr., *Black Charlestonians: A Social History, 1822–1885* (Fayetteville: University of Arkansas Press, 1994), 57–58, 61, 72.

22. Hogan and Davis, *The Barber of Natchez*, 56–57; William Ransom Hogan and Edwin Adams Davis, eds., *William Johnson's Natchez: The Antebellum Diary of a Free Negro* (Baton Rouge: Louisiana University Press, 1993), 764. See Virginia Meacham Gould, ed., *Chained to the Rock of Adversity: To Be Free, Black, & Female in the Old South* (Athens University of Georgia, 1998), 69–83.

23. Rawick, *The American Slave* 6 Mississippi Narr., Supplement 1:270 (emphasis added); Bernard Mergen, *Play and Playthings: A Reference Guide* (Westport: Greenwood Press, 1982), 42; David Thomas Bailey, "A Divided Prism: Two Sources of Black Testimony on Slavery," *Journal of Southern History* 46 (August 1980): 381–401.

24. Rawick, *The American Slave* 6 Mississippi Narr., 1:270 (emphasis added). See John W. Blassingame, "Using the Testimony of Ex-Slaves: Approaches and Problems," *Journal of Southern History* 41 (November 1975): 473–492.

25. Blackford Diary, February 3, 1849, SHC.

26. J. G. Clinkscales, *On the Old Plantation: Reminiscences of His Childhood* (New York: Negro Universities Press, 1969), 55–56. Sarah Alston, the widow of a great planter in antebellum North Carolina encouraged her grandson to do the same when she described a new two-seat child-sized carriage. When telling about his new toy, she wrote, "I reckon it will take all your little waiting men to pull it." She then offered an alternative, "unless you *hitch* the *old grey*." Alston planted the idea, and the child could decide between using his "little waiting men" or a draft animal. See Jane Turner Censer, *North Carolina Planters and Their Children, 1800–1860* (Baton Rouge: Louisiana State University Press, 1984), 147.

27. Rawick, *The American Slave* 2 South Carolina Narr., 1: 82.

28. Genovese, *Roll, Jordan, Roll*, 515.

29. See Albert J. Raboteau, *Slave Religion: The "Invisible Institution" in the Antebellum South* (New York: Oxford University Press, 1978), for a discussion of "hush harbors." See Schweninger, *James T. Rapier*, 16, 18.

30. Charles L. Perdue, Jr., Thomas E. Barden, and Robert K. Phillips, eds., *Weevils in the Wheat: Interviews with Virginia Ex-Slaves* (Bloomington: Indiana University Press, 1980), 109; Suzanne Lebsock, *The Free Women of Petersburg: Status and Culture in a Southern Town, 1784–1860* (New York: W. W. Norton & Company, 1984), 11; David K. Wiggins, "The Play of Slave Children in the Plantation Communities of the Old South, 1820–1960," *Journal of Sport History* 7 (Summer 1980), 31. Catherine Broun Diary, December 25, 1864, John Peter Broun Papers, SHC.

31. Dickson J. Preston, *Young Frederick Douglass: The Maryland Years* (Baltimore: John Hopkins University Press, 1980), 92; Perdue et al., *Weevils in the Wheat*, 84.

32. Herbert, "Reminiscences," SHC, 19. Although black and white children played together on occasions, their paths often diverged when white children entered school and their

enslaved counterparts entered the workplace. See "The White Boys Outgrow Charles," in Willie Lee Rose, ed., *A Documentary History of Slavery in North America* (New York: Oxford University Press, 1976), 406–411.

33. Frederick Douglass, *Life and Times of Frederick Douglass: Written by Himself, His Early Life as a Slave, His Escape from Bondage, and his Complete History* (New York: Collier Books, 1962), 71; Rawick, *The American Slave* 3 Texas Narr., Supplement 2: 667; Rawick, *The American Slave* 5 Texas Narr., 3: 242.

34. Rawick, *The American Slave* 15 North Carolina Narr., 2: 321.

35. See Andrew Fede, "Legitimized Violent Slave Abuse in the American South, 1619–1865: A Case Study of Law and Social Change in Six Southern States," *The American Journal of Legal History* 29 (April 1985): 93–150; Kermit L. Hall, William M. Wieck, and Paul Finkelman, eds., *American Legal History: Cases and Materials* (New York: Oxford University Press, 1991), 195–196.

36. See Catherine M. Hanchett, " 'What Sort of People & Families . . .': The Edmondson Sisters," *Afro-Americans in New York Life and History* 6 (July 1982), 25–26.

37. Yetman, *Life under the "Peculiar Institution,"* 137; Janet Cornelius, "We Slipped and Learned to Read: Slave Accounts of the Literacy Process, 1830–1865" *Phylon* 44 (September 1983), 176; J. G. Clinkscales, *On the Old Plantation: Reminiscences of His Childhood* (New York: Negro Universities Press, 1969), 44–46.

38. Susie King Taylor, *Reminiscences of My Life in Camp* (New York: Arno Press and the New York Times, 1968), 6.

39. Schweninger, *James T. Rapier*, 16, 18.

40. Rawick, *The American Slave* 6 Mississippi Narr., Supplement 1: 270; Rawick, *The American Slave* 3 Texas Narr., 3: 2, Supplement 2, 667; Michael P. Johnson and James L. Roark, *Black Masters: A Free Family of Color in the Old South* (New York: W. W. Norton & Company, 1984), 87.

41. Lunsford Lane, *The Narrative of Lunsford Lane* quoted in Steven Mintz, ed., *African American Voices: The Life Cycle of Slavery* (St. James: Brandywine Press, 1993), 93.

42. Jacqueline Jones, *Labor of Love, Labor of Sorrow: Black Women, Work and the Family, From Slavery to the Present* (New York: Vintage Books, 1985), 24.

43. Tryphena Blanche Holder Fox (hereafter cited as TBHF) to Anna Rose Holder (hereafter cited as ARH), September 5, 1858, November 15, 1858, January 1, 1860, Mississippi Department of Archives and History (hereafter cited as MDAH); Censer, *North Carolina Planters and Their Children*, 147; Maxine Lorraine Clark, "Race Concepts and Self-Esteem in Black Children" (Ph. D. diss., University of Illinois, 1979), 17–22.

44. Wilma King, ed., *A Northern Woman in the Plantation South: Letters of Tryphena Blanche Holder Fox, 1856–1876* (Columbia: University of South Carolina Press, 1997), 87.

45. TBHF to George Holder, May 20, 1861, MDAH, emphasis added; Genovese, *Roll, Jordan, Roll*, 515.

46. Rawick, *The American Slave,* Alabama Narr., l, Supplement 1, 1: 456.

47. Harriet Jacobs, *Incidents in the Life of a Slave Girl: Written by Herself,* edited by Jean Fagan Yellin (Cambridge: Harvard University Press, 1987), 18. See Douglass, *Life and Times*, 142; James Mellon, ed., *Bullwhip Days: The Slave Remember* (New York: Weidenfeld & Nicholson, 1988).

48. Jacobs, *Incidents in the Life of a Slave Girl*, 18, 20; John S. Jacobs, "A True Tale of Slavery," *The Leisure Hour: A Family Journal of Instruction and Recreation* 476 (February 7, 1861), 86.

49. Jacobs, *Incidents in the Life of a Slave Girl*, 5.

50. James W. C. Pennington, *The Fugitive Blacksmith; or, Events in the History of James W. C. Pennington, Pastor of a Presbyterian Church, New York, Formerly a Slave in the State of Maryland, United States* (Westport: Negro Universities Press, 1971), 2–3; Mintz, *African American Voices*, 91.

51. Jacobs, *Incidents in the Life of a Slave Girl*, 187.

52. L. Minor Blackford, *Mine Eyes Have Seen The Glory: The Story of A Virginia Lady Mary Berkeley Minor Blackford, 1802–1896 Who taught her sons to hate Slavery and to love the Union* (Cambridge: Harvard University Press, 1954), 29–31.

53. William Taylor Barry Letterbook (#2569), April 11, 1828, August 7, 1829, August 16, 1832, UVA.

54. Rawick, *The American Slave* 5 Texas Narr., 3: 236–237.

55. Johnson and Roark, *Black Masters*, 136–137, Schweninger, "John Carruthers Stanly," 177–181. Although there are many similarities in the behavior of these slaveholding freedmen, Stanly was more "charitable" than Ellison in emancipating and allowing selected slaves to purchase their freedom. He also accumulated good will in the community by posting bonds assuring good behavior and acted as guardian for several ex-slaves. See Schweninger, "John Carruthers Stanly," 171.

56. Daniel F. Littlefield, Jr., ed., *The Life of Okah Tubbee* (Lincoln: University of Nebraska Press, 1988), viii–ix, 132–133, fn. 17, 18. There are similarities between McCary's will and the February 28, 1817, will of William Hepburn, a prosperous Alexander, Virginia, merchant which contains similar conditions involving the five-year-old slave-born mulatto Moses Hepburn and two siblings, children of Ester. Hepburn had once owned the children and their mother before selling them to Hannah Jackson, Ester's sister. Following Ester's death in 1816 or 1817, Hepburn agreed to support the orphaned children. The Hepburn will also makes provisions for Moses' education and express the benefactor's "desire that Jerry shall serve his brother Moses, until 21 years, then he is to be free." It appears that Moses is William Hepburn's son but Jerry, who was not among the slaves sold by Hepburn to Jackson, is not. See Sara Revis, "Historical Case Studies of Alexandria's Archaeological Sites: Hannah Jackson, An African American Woman and Freedom," (Alexandria: Office of Historic Alexandria, 1985), 1–2, 5, 6.

57. Littlefield, *The Life of Okah Tubbee*, xiv. See Schweninger, "John Carruthers Stanly," 184, 186; Dickson D. Bruce, Jr., *Archibald Grimke: Portrait of a Independent* (Baton Rouge: Louisiana State University Press, 1993), 1–17, for insight into the relationships between slave-born and white siblings. See also Adrienne D. Davis, "The Private Law of Race and Sex: An Antebellum Perspective," *Stanford Law Review* 51 (January 1999): 223–284.

58. Littlefield, *The Life of Okah Tubbee*, xii–xiv.

59. See Kent Anderson Leslie, *Woman of Color, Daughter of Privilege: Amanda America Dickson* (Athens: University of Georgia Press, 1995), 1, 3, 8, 37, 136; Melton A. McLaurin, *Celia: A Slave* (Athens: University of Georgia Press, 1991), 20–30, 116–121; Thelma Jennings, " 'Us Colored Women Had To Go Through a Plenty': Sexual Exploitation of African-American Slave Women," *Journal of Women's History* 1 (Winter 1990): 45–74; Bertram Wyatt-Brown, *Southern Honor: Ethics & Behavior in the Old South* (New York: Oxford University Press, 1982), 296; Catherine Clinton, *The Plantation Mistress: Woman's World in the Old South* (New York: Pantheon, 1982), 87–88.

60. See Herbert G. Gutman, *The Black Family in Slavery and Freedom, 1750–1925* (New York: Vintage Books, 1977), 83; Rawick, *The American Slave* 2 South Carolina Narr., 2: 310.

61. See Gray B. Mills, *The Forgotten People: Cane River Creoles of Color* (Baton Rouge, Louisiana State University Press, 1977); Johnson and Roark, *Black Masters*.

Chapter Three   Within the Professional Household: Slave Children in the Antebellum South

An earlier version of this chapter appeared in *The Historian* 59 (Spring 1997): 523–540.

1. Frederick Douglass, *My Bondage and My Freedom* (New York: Dover Publications, Inc., 1969), 161.

2. Tryphena Blanche Holder Fox (hereafter cited as TBHF) to Anna Rose Holder (hereafter cited as ARH), October 14, 1860, Mississippi Department of Archives and History, Jackson,

Mississippi (hereafter cited as MDAH) emphasis in the original; Harriet Jacobs, *Incidents in the Life of a Slave Girl* (New York: Oxford University Press, 1987), 19; Willie Lee Rose, *Slavery and Freedom* expanded edition, edited by William W. Freehling (New York: Oxford University Press, 1982), 39. See Steven Mintz, ed., *African American Voices: The Life Cycle of Slavery* (St. James, NY: Brandywine Press, 1993); See Wilma King, *Stolen Childhood: Youth in Bondage in Nineteenth-Century America* (Bloomington: Indiana University Press, 1995).

3. See Eugene D. Genovese, "The Treatment of Slaves in Different Countries: Problems in the Applications of the Comparative Method," in Eugene D. Genovese, *In Red and Black: Marxian Explorations in Southern and Afro-American History* (New York: Pantheon Books, 1971), 158–172.

4. See Wilma King, ed., *A Northern Woman in the Plantation South: Letters of Tryphena Blanche Holder Fox, 1856–1876* (Columbia: University of South Carolina Press, 1993), 87, 89, 90, 95, 120, 126, 128, 157.

5. See Harriet Jacobs, *Incidents in the Life of a Slave Girl: Written by Herself*, edited by Jean Fagan Yellin (Cambridge: Harvard University Press, 1987); John S. Jacobs, "True Tale of Slavery," *The Leisure Hour: A Family Journal of Instruction and Recreation* (February 7, 1861), 86; Jean Fagan Yellin, *Harriet Jacobs: A Life* (New York: Basic Civitas Books, 2004).

6. See Pauli Murray, *Proud Shoes: The Story of an American Family* (New York: Harper & Row, 1984); Catherine Clinton, "Caught in the Web of the Big House: Women and Slavery," in Walter Fraser, ed., *The Web of Southern Social Relations: Women, Family, and Education* (Athens: University of Georgia Press, 1985), 19–34.

7. See Leland Winfield Meyer, *The Life and Times of Colonel Richard M. Johnson of Kentucky* (New York: Columbia University Press, 1932), 290–324.

8. See Archibald Grimké Papers, Founder's Library, Howard University, Washington, D.C.; Dickson D. Bruce, Jr., *Archibald Grimke: Portrait of a Black Independent* (Baton Rouge: Louisiana State University Press, 1993).

9. See George P. Rawick, ed., *The American Slave: A Composite Autobiography*, 19 vols. (Westport: Greenwood Press, 1972); George P. Rawick, ed., *The American Slave: A Composite Autobiography*, Supplement, Series 1, 12 vols. (Westport: Greenwood Press, 1978); George P. Rawick, ed., *The American Slave: A Composite Autobiography*, Supplement, Series 2, 10 vols. (Westport: Greenwood Press, 1979).

10. TBHF to ARH, November 15, 1857, November 27, 1857, December 27, 1857, MDAH.

11. Deborah Gray White, *Ar'n't I a Woman? Female Slaves in the Plantation South* (New York: W. W. Norton & Company), 69; Jacqueline Jones, *Labor of Love, Labor of Sorrow: Black Women, Work and the Family, From Slavery to the Present* (New York: Vintage Books, 1986), 18. See Robert Moore Riddick, Inventory and Appraisement, 1819, Prentis Family Papers, Earl Gregg Swem Library, the college of William and Mary, Williamsburg, Virginia; Rose, *A Documentary History*, 338–344; "Hand bill," Negro Collection, Slavery Division, William R. Perkins Library, Duke University, Durham, North Carolina (hereafter cited as Duke University).

12. Frederick Douglass, *My Bondage and My Freedom* (New York: Dover Publications, Inc., 1969), 93; Norman R. Yetman, ed., *Life Under the "Peculiar Institution": Selections from the Slave Narrative Collection* (New York: Holt, Rinehart and Winston, Inc., 1970), 40; Jacob Stroyer, *My Life in the South* (Salem: Salem Observer, 1889), 20.

13. Yetman, *Life Under the "Peculiar Institution,"* 40; Stroyer, *My Life in the South*, 20; Douglass, *My Bondage and My Freedom*, 93.

14. TBHF to ARH, June 13, 1859, MDAH.

15. TBHF to ARH, November 15, 1858, and June 13, 1859, MDAH. See Nell Irvin Painter, "Soul Murder and Slavery: Towards a Fully Loaded Cost Accounting," in Nell Irvin Painter, *Southern History Across the Color Line* (Chapel Hill: University of North Carolina Press, 2002), 15–39.

16. The first of the children, a boy was born February 28, 1860. A second son was born in March 1861, and the birth date of a third child, Maria, is unknown. ARH to TBHF, January 1, 1860, March 17, 1860, March 29, 1861, December 27, 1861, MDAH;

Rawick, *The American Slave*, 4, Georgia Narr., Part 2: 372; Jacobs, *Incidents in the Life of a Slave Girl*, 27, 28.

17. Jacobs, *Incidents in the Life of a Slave Girl*, 7–9, 15, 213.
18. Ibid., 20, 27.
19. Ibid., 10–12.
20. Ibid., 5–6, 223.
21. Jacobs, "The Tale of Slavery," 86; Jacobs, *Incidents in the Life of a Slave Girl*, 5, 9.
22. Ibid.
23. Jacobs, *Incidents in the Life of a Slave Girl*, 19, 27, 54, 55. For further discussions about the sexual abuse of enslaved women in the nineteenth century, see Catherine Clinton, "Caught in the Web of the Big House: Women and Slavery," in Walter Fraser, Jr., ed., *The Web of Southern Social Relations: Women, Family, and Education* (Athens: University of Georgia Press, 1985), 19–34; Melton A. McLaurin, *Celia, A Slave* (Athens: University of Georgia Press, 1991); Eugene D. Genovese, *Roll, Jordan, Roll: The World Slaves Made* (New York: Vintage, 1976); Thelma Jennings, " 'Us Colored Women Had To Go Through a Plenty': Sexual Exploitation of African-American Slave Women," *Journal of Women's History* 1 (Winter 1990): 45–74.
24. Jacobs, *Incidents in the Life of a Slave Girl*, 59, 61, 77, 81, 114, 142, 166, 227.
25. Murray, *Proud Shoes*, 42–47.
26. Ibid., 159.
27. Ibid., 48, 53; Mary Arthur Stoudemire, "Black Parishioners of the Chapel of the Cross, 1844–1866," *North Carolina Genealogical Society Journal* 9 (May 1983) 83–84; Clinton, "Caught in the Web," 21.
28. Murray, *Proud Shoes*, 44, 49–50, 162. The Smith sisters lived as virtually free persons without the benefit of emancipation. Others, including Amanda America Dickson, lived under similar circumstances. See Kent Anderson Leslie, "Amanda America Dickson: An Elite Mulatto Lady in Nineteenth-Century Georgia," in Virginia Bernhard, Betty Brandon, Elizabeth Fox-Genovese, and Theda Perdue, eds., *Southern Women: Histories and Identities* (Columbia: University of Missouri, 1992), 71–86.
29. Meyer, *The Life and Times of Colonel Richard M. Johnson*, 317–119.
30. Ibid., 317, 320–321.
31. Ibid., 318, 319.
32. Ibid., 317, 321, 322.
33. Ibid., 317, 321; Ian F. Haney Lopez, "The Social Construction of Race: Some Observations on Illusion, Fabrication, and Choice," *Harvard Civil Rights–Civil Liberties Law Review* 29 (Winter 1994): 1–62.
34. Theodore Hershberg and Henry William, "Mulattoes and Blacks: Intra-Group Color Differences and Social Stratification in Nineteenth-Century Philadelphia," in Theodore Hershberg, ed., *Philadelphia: Work, Space, Family, and Group Experience in the Nineteenth Century* (New York: Oxford University Press, 1981), 397; Charles H. Wesley, *Negro Labor in the United States* (New York: Vanguard Press, 1927), 40; Kwando Mbiassi Kinshasa, "Free Blacks' Quest for National Identity: Debates in the African American Press on Assimilation and Emigration" (Ph.D. diss., New York University, 1983), 94.
35. Meyer, *The Life and Time of Colonel Richard M. Johnson*, 322.
36. Dickson D. Bruce, Jr., *Archibald Grimke: Portrait of a Black Independent* (Baton Rouge: Louisiana State University Press, 1993), 1–5; Distinguished Biographers, eds., *The National Cyclopedia of American Biography* 17 (New York: James T. White, 1927), 55.
37. Bruce, *Archibald Grimke*, 6–7.
38. Ibid., 12–13.
39. Ibid., 14–15, 16, 67–74, 257.
40. Ibid., 23, 64, 68.
41. Myer, *Life and Times*, 319.

42. C. Vann Woodward, ed., *Mary Chesnut's Civil War* (New Haven: Yale University Press, 1981), 29.
43. Murray, *Proud Shoes*, 35, 44, 49.
44. Meyers, *Life and Times*, 318; Bruce, Archibald Grimké, 12–13.
45. Murray, *Proud Shoes*, 40, 47, 48.
46. Douglass, *My Bondage and My Freedom*, 161.
47. Bruce, *Archibald Grimke*, 10.
48. Jacobs, *Incidents in the Life of a Slave Girl*, 9.
49. Ibid., 10. Emphasis in the original.
50. Ibid., 5, 91. See Michael P. Johnson, "Runaway Slaves and the Slave Communities in South Carolina, 1799 to 1830" *William and Mary Quarterly* 38 (July 1981): 418–441; Judith Kelleher Schafer, "New Orleans Slavery in 1850 as Seen in Advertisements," *Journal of Southern History* 47 (February 1981): 33–56.
51. Jacobs, *Incidents in the Life of a Slave Girl*, 91, 101, 105–109, 154–155.

Chapter Four No Bondage for Me: Free Boys and Girls Within a Slave Society

1. Brenda Stevenson, ed., *The Journals of Charlotte Forten Grimké* (New York: Oxford University Press, 1988), 139–140.
2. See *Historical Statistics of the United States: From Colonial Times to 1970* 2 vols. (Washington: Government Printing Office, 1975), 18.
3. Marilyn Richardson, ed., *Maria W. Stewart, America's First Black Woman Political Writer: Essays and Speeches* (Bloomington: Indiana University Press, 1987), 45; Jermain Wesley Loguen, *Rev. J. W. Loguen, a Slave and as a Freeman: A Narrative of Real Life* (Syracuse: J. G. K. Truair & Co., 1859), 249. See *Douglass' Monthly*, August 1859, 125.
4. Julie Winch, " 'You Have Talents—Only Cultivate Them': Philadelphia's Black Female Literary Societies and the Abolitionist Crusade," in Jean Fagan Yellin and John C. Van Horne, eds., *The Abolitionist Sisterhood: Women's Political Culture in Antebellum America* (Ithaca: Cornell University Press, 1994), 103. See Linda Perkins, "Black Women and Racial 'Uplift' Prior to Emancipation," in Filomina Chioma Steady, ed., *The Black Woman Cross-Culturally* (Rochester, VT: Schenkman Books, Inc., 1985), 317–334; James Oliver Horton, "Generations of Protest: Black Families and Social Reform in Ante-Bellum Boston," *New England Quarterly* 49 (June 1976): 242–256.
5. *Population of the United States in 1860: Compiled from Original Returns of the Eighth Census by Joseph C. G. Kennedy* (Washington: Government Printing Office, 1864), 2.
6. Silvio A. Bedini, *The Life of Benjamin Banneker* (New York: Charles Scribner's Sons, 1972), 10–23.
7. Gary B. Nash, *Forging Freedom: The Formation of Philadelphia's Black Community, 1720–1840* (Cambridge: Harvard University Press, 1988), 61–63.
8. Nell Irvin Painter, *Sojourner Truth: A Life, A Symbol* (New York: W. W. Norton, 1996), 23; Robert William Fogel and Stanley L. Engerman, "Philanthropy at Bargain Prices: Notes on the Economics of Gradual Emancipation," *Journal of Legal Studies* 3 (June 1974), 381; Ira Berlin, *Many Thousands Gone: The First Two Centuries of Slavery in North America* (Cambridge: Belknap Press of Harvard University Press, 1998), 228, 234; Gary B. Nash, *Race and Revolution* (Madison: Madison House, 1990), 34; Gary B. Nash, *Red, White & Black: The Peoples of Early North America*, fourth edition (Upper Saddle River: Prentice Hall, 2000), 279–280; Joanne Pope Melish, *Disowning Slavery: Gradual Emancipation and 'Race' in New England, 1780–1860* (Ithaca: Cornell University Press, 1998).
9. William W. Freehling, "The Founding Fathers, Conditional Antislavery, and the Nonradicalism of the American Revolution," in Robert James Maddox, ed., *Annual*

Editions, American History: Pre-Colonial Through Reconstruction, fifteenth edition (Sluice Dock: Duskin/McGraw-Hill, 1999), 82. See Roger G. Kennedy, *Mr. Jefferson's Lost Cause: Land Farmers, Slavery, and the Louisiana Purchase* (New York: Oxford University Press, 2003); Constitution of the United States, Article IV, Section 2.

10. Bedini, *The Life of Benjamin Banneker*, 13–19, 23; Ian F. Haney Lopez, "The Social Construction of Race: Some Observations on Illusion, Fabrication, and Choice," *Harvard Civil Rights–Civil Liberties Law Review* 29 (Winter 1991), 1–5; Mary Beth Corrigan, " 'It's a Family Affair': Buying Freedom In the District of Columbia 1850–1860," in Larry E. Hudson, Jr., ed., *Working Toward Freedom: Slave Society and Domestic Economy in the American South* (Rochester: University of Rochester Press, 1994), 175–178.

11. Report on the condition of the people of color in the state of Ohio; proceedings of the Ohio Anti-Slavery Convention, held at Putnam (April 1835), 23. See "Negro Children Speak, 1834," in Herbert Aptheker, ed., *A Documentary History of The Negro People in the United States* (Secaucus: The Citadel Press, 1969), 158. Thanks to Nikki Taylor for this citation.

12. John Hope Franklin and Loren Schweninger, *Runaway Slaves: Rebels on the Plantation* (New York: Oxford University Press, 1999), 210–213.

13. Edmund S. Morgan, *American Slavery—American Freedom: The Ordeal of Colonial Virginia* (New York: W. W. Norton & Company, 1975), 333.

14. Elizabeth Keckley, *Behind the Scenes or Thirty Years a Slave, and Four Years in the White House* (New York: Oxford University Press, 1988), 47. See Michael P. Johnson and James L. Roark, *Black Masters: A Free Family of Color in the Old South* (New York: W. W. Norton & Company, 1984), 53–55.

15. Pauli Murray, *Proud Shoes: The Story of an American Family* (New York: Harper & Row, 1987), 49, 162.

16. Kent Anderson Leslie, *Woman of Color, Daughter of Privilege: Amanda America Dickson, 1849–1893* (Athens: University of Georgia Press, 1995), 36, 38, 47–49.

17. Leslie, *Woman of Color*, 1, 3, 36, 38, 45–49, 65.

18. Loren Schweninger, "A Slave Family in the Ante Bellum South," *Journal of Negro History* 60 (January 1975), 31–32, 34; Loren Schweninger, *James T. Rapier and Reconstruction* (Chicago: University of Chicago Press, 1978), 1.

19. Schweninger, "A Slave Family," 32, 34.

20. Ibid., 35.

21. Murray, *Proud Shoes*, 49. See Leland Winfield Meyer, *The Life and Times of Colonel Richard M. Johnson of Kentucky* (New York: Columbia University Press, 1932), 290–324; Michael P. Johnson and James L. Roark. *Black Masters: A Free Family of Color in the Old South* (New York: W. W. Norton & Company, 1984), 101–106, 242–243, 325; Gary B. Mills, *The Forgotten People: Cane River's Creoles of Color* (Baton Rouge: Louisiana State University, 1977).

22 Persons without legal proof of freedom relied on the testimony of white acquaintances who assured civil authorities that they were free, of good character, and would not be an economic liability to the community.

23. John J. Ormond, Arthur P. Bagby, George Goldthwaite, eds., *The Code of Alabama* (Montgomery: Brittan and De Wold, 1852), 241–245; Johnson and Roark, *Black Masters*, 42–43, 164; John Hope Franklin, *From Slavery to Freedom: A History of Negro Americans*, sixth edition (New York: Alfred A. Knopf, 1988), 142.

24. Johnson and Roark, *Black Masters*, 162–163. See George Firzhugh, "Slavery Justified," in *Sociology for the South, or the Failure of Free Society* (New York: Burt Franklin, 1965), 226–306.

25. *Arkansas State Gazette and Democrat*, July 31, 1858, 3: 2.

26. Billy D. Higgins, "The Origins and Fate of the Marion County Free Black Community," *Arkansas Historical Quarterly* 54 (Winter 1995), 439–440. See "*Arthur v. Chavis*, 6 Randolph 142, February 1828 [143]," in Helen T. Catterall, ed., *Judicial Cases Concerning American Slavery and the Negro*, volume I (Washington: Carnegie Institute of Washington, 1926), 151.

27. Stevenson, *The Journals*, 140.
28. Maritcha Lyons, "Memories of Yesterday All of Which I Saw and Part of Which I Was: An Autobiography" (Unpublished manuscript, Williamson Collection, Reel 1, Schomburg Research Center, New York, New York), 23; Dorothy Sterling, ed., *We Are Your Sisters: Black Women in the Nineteenth Century* (New York: W. W. Norton & Company, 1984, 1984), 188–189.
29. John Mercer Langston, *From the Virginia Plantation to the National Capitol or The First and Only Negro Representative from the Old Dominion* (Hartford: American Publishing Company, 1894), 42–43; Sterling, *We Are Your Sisters*, 138.
30. Janice Sumler-Lewis, "The Fortens of Philadelphia: An Afro-American Family and Nineteenth-Century Reform" (Washington, D.C.: Georgetown University, Ph.D. diss., 1978), 95.
31. Leonard W. Levy and Harlan B. Philips, "The Roberts Case: Source of the 'Separate by Equal' Doctrine," *American Historical Reiew* 56 (April 1951), 514. See Stephen Kendrick and Paul Kendrick, *Sarah's Long Walk: The Free Blacks of Boston and How Their Struggle for Equality Changed America* (Boston: Beacon Press, 2004).
32. Kendrick and Kendrick, *Sarah's Long Walk*, 176–177.
33. Ibid., 257.
34. Sterling, *We Are Your Sisters*, 187–188. Emphasis in the original.
35. Gerda Lerner, *Black Women in White America: A Documentary History* (New York: Vintage Books, 1973), 85–86.
36. Carter G. Woodson, ed., *The Mind of the Negro as Reflected in Letters Written during the Crisis, 1800–1860* (New York: Russell & Russell, 1969), 541.
37. Sterling, *We Are Your Sisters*, 187–188; Sumler-Lewis, "The Fortens," 39, 94.
38. Langston, *From the Virginia Plantation to the National Capitol*, 20. See John B. Reid, " 'A Career to Build, a People to Serve, a Purpose to Accomplish': Race, Class, Gender, and Detroit's First Black Women Teacher, 1865–1916," in Darlene Clark Hine, Wilma King, and Linda Reed, eds., *"We Specialize in the Wholly Impossible": A Reader in Black Women's History* (Brooklyn: Carlson Publishing, 1995), 303–320; Ruffin-Helsip Papers, Amistad Research Center, Tulane University, New Orleans, Louisiana; Ellen N. Lawson and Marlene Merrill, "Antebellum Black Coeds at Oberlin College," *Oberlin Alumni Magazine* (January/February 1980), 18–21; James Oliver Horton, "Black Education at Oberlin College: A Controversial Commitment," *Journal of Negro Education* 54 (1985): 477–499.
39. Albert S. Broussard, *African–American Odyssey: The Stewarts, 1853–1963* (Lawrence: University of Kansas Press, 1998), 16, 18.
40. Francis J. Grimké Papers, Moorland-Spingarn Collection, Howard University, Washington, D.C.; Dickson D. Bruce, Jr., *Archibald Grimke: Portrait of a Black Independent* (Baton Rouge: Louisiana State University Press, 1993), 8.
41. See Mary Niall Mitchell, " 'A Good and Delicious Country': Free Children of Color and How They Learned to Imagine the Atlantic World in Nineteenth-Century Louisiana," *History of Education Quarterly* 43 (Spring 2000): 123–144; Molly Mitchell, " 'After the War I Am Going to Put Myself a Sailor': Geography, Writing, and Race in Letters of Free Children in Civil War New Orleans," in James Marten, ed., *Children and War: A Historical Anthology* (New York: New York University Press, 2002), 26–37.
42. Mitchell, " 'After the War,' " 27–29; Mitchell " 'A Good and Delicious Country,' " 126–127.
43. Mitchell, " 'A Good and Delicious Country,' " 132–133.
44. John Hope Franklin and Alfred A. Moss, Jr., *From Slavery to Freedom: A History of Negro Americans* eighth edition (New York: McGraw Hill, 2000), 181.
45. Ibid.; Sterling, *We Are Your Sisters*, 129, 204; Darlene Clark Hine, William C. Hine, and Stanley Harrold, *The African-American Odyssey* (Upper Saddle River: Prentice Hall, 2000), 155.

46. Ellen N. Lawson and Marlene Merrill, "The Antebellum 'Talented Thousandth': Black College Students at Oberlin Before the Civil War," *Journal of Negro Education* 52 (1983), 143.

47. See William Cheek and Aimee Lee Check, *John Mercer Langston and the Fight for Black Freedom, 1829–65* (Urbana: University of Illinois Press, 1989), 302–306.

48. See Kirsten P. Buick, "The Ideal Works of Edmonia Lewis: Invoking and Inverting Autobiography," in Marianne Doezema and Elizabeth Milroy, eds., *Reading American Art* (New Haven: Yale University Press, 1998), 190–207; Elizabeth Martin and Vivian Meyer, *Female Gazes: Seventy-Five Women Artists* (Toronto: Second Story Press, 1997), 46.

49. Lawson, "The Antebellum 'Talented Thousandth,' " 147.

50. See Kathleen M. Brown, *Good Wives, Nasty Wenches, and Anxious Patriarchs: Gender, Race, and Power in Colonial Virginia* (Chapel Hill: University of North Carolina Press, 1996), 212–113, 231–236; Barbara L. Bellows, "My Children, Gentlemen, Are My Own: Poor Women, the Urban Elite, and the Bonds of Obligation in Antebellum Charleston," in Walter Fraser, Jr., *The Web of Southern Social Relations: Women Family, and Education* (Athens: University of Georgia Press, 1985), 52–71.

51. Joseph D. Ketner, *The Emergence of the African-American Artist: Robert S. Duncanson, 1821–1872* (Columbia: University of Missouri Press, 1993), 12–14.

52. HLC Diary, January 8, 1932, April 1, 1932, April 3, 1932; John Hope Franklin and Alfred A. Moss, Jr., *From Slavery to Freedom: A History of African Americans* eighth edition (New York: McGraw Hill, 2000), 371; Gail Buckley, *American Patriots: The Story of Blacks in the Military From the Revolution to Desert Storm* (New York: Random House, 2001), 193.

53. Ibid., 15–16.

54. Nancy Prince, *A Black Woman's Odyssey Through Russia and Jamaica: The Narrative of Nancy Prince* (New York: Markus Wiener Publishing, 1990), 6–7.

55. See Harriet E. Wilson, *Our Nig: or, Sketches from the Life of a Free Black in a Two-Story White House, North. Showing that Slavery's Shadows Fall Even There* (New York: Vintage Books, 1983).

56. Eliza Potter, *A Hairdresser's Experience in the High Life*, Henry Lewis Gates, Jr., ed. (New York: Oxford University Press, 1991), xlvi.

57. Langston, *From the Virginia Plantation*, 56.

58. Aptheker, "Negro Children Speak," 158.

59. Sumler-Lewis, "The Fortens," 39.

60. Ibid., 59.

61. Sterling, *We Are Your Sisters*, 222.

62. See Dickson D. Bruce, Jr. *Archibald Grimke: Portrait of a Independent* (Baton Rouge: Louisiana State University Press, 1993), 14–16.

63. Lucy A. Delaney, "From the Darkness Cometh the Light or Struggles for Freedom," in Henry Louis Gates, Jr., ed., *Six Women's Slave Narratives* (New York: Oxford University Press, 1988), 15–16.

64. Roger Bruns, ed., *Am I Not a Man and a Brother: The Antislavery Crusade of Revolutionary America, 1688–1788* (New York: Chelsea House Publishing, 1977), 306.

Chapter Five "Dis Was atter Freedom Come": Freed Girls and Boys Remember the Emancipation

1. Soloman Caldwell quoted in George P. Rawick, ed., *The American Slave: A Composite Autobiography* 2 South Carolina Narr. (Westport: Greenwood Press, 1972), 1: 172.

2. John Hope Franklin and Loren Schweninger, *Runaway Slaves: Rebels on the Plantation* (New York: Oxford University Press, 1999), 282; Ulrich B. Phillips, *American Negro Slavery: A Survey of the Supply, Employment and Control of Negro Labor As Determined by the Plantation Regime* (Baton Rouge: Louisiana State University Press, 1966), 293–296,

306–308, 328–329. See Eugene D. Genovese, *Roll, Jordan, Roll: The World the Slaves Made* (New York: Vintage Books, 1976), 648–657.

3. Ira Berlin, Barbara J. Fields, Steven F. Miller, Joseph P. Reidy, and Leslie S. Rowland, *Slaves No More: Three Essays on Emancipation and the Civil War* (Cambridge: Cambridge University Press, 1992), ix; Herbert G. Gutman, *The Black Family in Slavery and Freedom, 1750–1925* (New York: Vintage Books, 1977), 402; Joseph T. Glatthaar, *Forged in Battle: The Civil War Alliance of Black Soldiers and White Officers* (New York: Free Press, 1990), 4–5; James M. McPherson, *Ordeal by Fire: The Civil War and Reconstruction* (New York: Alfred A. Knopf, 1982), 158, 253–4, 267, 297.

4. See John W. Blassingame, "Using the Testimony of Ex-Slaves: Approaches and Problems," *Journal of Southern History* (hereafter cited as *JSH*) 41 (November 1875): 473–492; David Thomas Bailey, "A Divided Prism: Two Sources of Black Testimony on Slavery," *JSH* 46 (August 1980): 381–404; Paul D. Escott, *Slavery Remembered: A Record of Twentieth-Century Slave Narratives* (Chapel Hill: University of North Carolina, 1979), 3–17.

5. See Henry Steele Commager, ed., *Documents of American History*, sixth edition (New York: Appleton-Century-Crofts, Inc., 1958), I: 420–421, #222.

6. Ira Berlin, Thavolia Glymph, Steven F. Miller, Joseph P. Reidy, Leslie S. Rowland, and Julie Saville, eds., "Military Governor in the Department of the South to the Quartermaster General," *Freedom: A Documentary History of Emancipation 1861–1867*, Series I, volume III, *The Wartime Genesis of Free Labor: The Lower South* (New York: Cambridge University Press, 1990), 272; R. Saxton, "Proclamation by Gen Saxton: A Happy New Year's Greeting to the Colored People in the Department of the South," *Liberator* (January 3, 1863), 3.

7. Commager, *Documents of American History*, I: 421, #222.

8. Eighth Census of the United States, 1860; Eric Foner, *Reconstruction: America's Unfinished Revolution, 1863–1877* (New York: Harper & Row, Publishers, 1988), 1.

9. Charles L. Perdue, Jr., Thomas E. Barden, and Robert K. Phillips, eds., *Weevils in the Wheat: Interviews with Virginia Ex-Slaves* (Bloomington: Indiana University Press, 1980), 212; Dorothy Sterling, ed., *We Are Your Sisters: Black Women in the Nineteenth Century* (New York: W. W. Norton & Company, 1984), 243.

10. Norman R. Yetman, *Life Under the "Peculiar Institution": Selections from the Slave Narrative Collection* (New York: Holt, Rinehart and Winston Inc., 1970), 24. See Susie King Taylor, *Reminiscences of My Life in Camp With the 33d United States Colored Troops Late 1st S. C. Volunteers* (Boston: published by author, 1902), 18; Foner, *Reconstruction*, 1–2.

11. Brenda Stevenson, ed., *The Journals of Charlotte Forten Grimké* (New York: Oxford University Press, 1988), xxxvi, 37; Brenda Stevenson, "Charlotte Forten (1837–1914)," in G. J. Barker-Benfield and Catherine Clinton, eds., *Portraits of American Women: From Settlement to the Present* (New York: St. Martin's Press, 1991), 289; Foner, *Reconstruction*, 1–2.

12. Stevenson, *The Journals*, 37, 428; Janice Sumler Lewis, "The Fortens of Philadelphia: An Afro-American Family and Nineteenth-Century Reform" (Georgetown University: Ph.D. diss., 1978), 142. See Willie Lee Rose, *Rehearsal for Reconstruction: The Port Royal Experiment* (Indianapolis: Bobbs-Merrill Company, 1964).

13. Stevenson, *The Journals*, 428–429.

14. Taylor, *Reminiscences of My Life in Camp*, 18.

15. Rawick, *The American Slave*, 2 South Carolina Narr., 2: 124.

16. Ibid., 2 South Carolina Narr., 2: 216–217.

17. Booker T. Washington, *Up From Slavery* (New York: Airmont, 1967), 26.

18. Rawick, *The American Slave*, 2 South Carolina Narr., 2: 217.

19. Foner, *Reconstruction*, 82–83.

20. Yetman, *Life Under the "Peculiar Institution,"* 20–21.

21. Ibid., 21.

22. See Patricia Cline Cohen, "Women at Large: Travel in Antebellum America," *History Today* (December 1994): 44–50. See also, Cheryl Fish, "Voices of Restless (Dis)continuity: The Significance of Travel for Free Black Women in the Antebellum Americas," *Women Studies* 26 (1997): 475–495.

23. Yetman, *Life Under the "Peculiar Institution,"* 21. See Eliza Potter, *A Hairdresser's Experience in the High Life*, Henry Lewis Gates, Jr. ed. (New York: Oxford University Press, 1991), 30, 38, for references to traveling alone. See also Wilma King, "Eliza Johnson Potter: Traveler, Entrepreneur, and Social Critic," in Kriste Lendenmeyer, ed., *The Human Tradition Ordinary Women, Extraordinary Lives: Women in American History* (Wilmington: Scholarly Resources, Inc., 2000), 91–104.

24. Yetman, *Life Under the "Peculiar Institution,"* 21.

25. Ira Berlin, Josephy P. Reidy, and Leslie S. Rowland, eds., *Freedom's Soldiers: The Black Military Experience in the Civil War* (Cambridge: Cambridge University Press, 1998), 131. A search of Spottswood Rice's service and pension records failed to identify "Spott and Noah." It is possible that they were Rice's sons but used a different surname from that of their father when enlisting. See Spottswood Rice, Invalid #487999, Certificate #529570, Pension #880044 and #659773, National Archives, Washington, D.C. (hereafter cited as NA). Other references to Spott and Noah fighting in the Civil War come from their sister, Mary Bell. See Yetman, *Life Under the "Peculiar Institution,"* 23, 25.

26. Berlin, Reidy and Rowland, *Freedom's Soldiers*, 133.

27. See Kate Drumgoold, "A Slave Girl's Story: Being an Autobiography of Kate Drumgoold," in Henry Louis Gates, Jr., ed., *The Schomburg Library of Nineteenth-Century Black Women Writers: Six Women's Slave Narratives* (New York: Oxford University Press, 1988), 8; Annie L. Burton, *Memories of Childhood's Slavery Days* (Boston: Ross, 1909), 11–12; Dorothy Sterling, ed., *The Trouble They Seen: Black People Tell the Story of Reconstruction* (Garden City: Doubleday, 1978), 68. An abundance of data regarding women seeking the release of their children from former owners and apprenticeships may be found in the Freedmen's Bureau papers, RG 105, BRFAL, NA. Bureau of Refugees, Freedmen, and Abandoned Lands (hereafter cited as BRFAL), National Archives, Washington, D.C. (hereafter cited as NA).

28. F. W. Diggs, took exception to Spottswood Rice's letters and wrote to General William S. Rosecrans saying he did not believe Rice should be allowed to remain in the state. "To be thus insulted by such a black scoundrel," Diggs explained, "is more than I can stand." See Berlin, Reidy and Rowland, *Freedom: A Documentary History*, 689–691.

29. Yetman, *Life Under the "Peculiar Institution,"* 25. See Jim Cullen, " 'I's a Man Now': Gender and African American Men," in Catherine Clinton and Nina Silber, ed., *Divided Houses: Gender and the Civil War* (New York: Oxford University Press, 1992), 77–91.

30. Commager, *Documents of American History*, II: 1–2, #245; Foner, *Reconstruction*, 68–69.

31. Rawick, *The American Slave*, 14 North Carolina Narr., 1: 249. See Wilma King, *Stolen Childhood: Slave Youth in Nineteenth-Century America* (Bloomington: Indiana University Press, 1995), 145–146.

32. Gutman, *The Black Family in Slavery and Freedom*, 402–412; Rebecca J. Scott, "The Battle over the Child: Child Apprenticeship and the Freedmen's Bureau in North Carolina," in N. Ray Hiner and Joseph M. Hawes, ed., *Growing Up in America: Children in Historical Perspective* (Urbana: University of Illinois Press, 1985), 194; Barbara Jeanne Fields, *Slavery and Freedom on the Middle Ground: Maryland During the Nineteenth Century* (New Haven: Yale University Press, 1985), 139–142; Leslie A. Schwalm, *A Hard Fight for We: Women's Transition from Slavery to Freedom in South Carolina* (Urbana: University of Illinois Press, 1997), 250–251; Karin L. Zipf, "Reconstructing 'Free Woman': African-American Women, Apprenticeship, and Custody Rights during Reconstruction," *Journal of Women's History* 12 (Spring 2000): 9. See "Indentures of Apprenticeship between Daniel E. Jones, and Epec, Nancy & Richard Jones, January 16, 1866, District of Arkadelphia, Box I, Arkansas, RG 105, BRFAL.

33. Black Codes recognized limited rights of freed persons but made it nearly impossible for them to exercise the rights. See the "Mississippi Apprentice Law," in Commager, *Documents of American History*, I: 2–5, #246; I: 5–7, #247. See W. E. B. Du Bois, *Black Reconstruction in America, 1860–1880* (Cleveland: Meridian Books, 1965) for discussions of Black Codes by states.

34. Schwalm, *A Hard Fight For We*, 250–251.

35. See "Records of Indentures, Reports of Indentures Made and Cancelled, North Carolina, 1868," Box 29, RG 105, BRFAL, NA; "Indentures for Orphaned Children, Louisiana," vol. 144, 1865–1867, RG 105 (e1377), BRFAL, NA; "Indentures of Apprenticeship," 1865–1866, Microfilm M843, Roll 35, RG 105, BRFAL, NA; King, *Stolen Childhood*, 152; Scott, "Battle over the Child," 197. See also Barbara L. Bellows, " 'My Children, Gentlemen, Are My Own': Poor Women, the Urban Elite, and the Bonds of Obligation in Antebellum Charleston," in Walter Fraser, Jr., ed., *The Web of Southern Social Relations: Women, Family, and Education* (Athens: University of Georgia, 1985), 52–71.

36. Indentures for Orphaned Children, Louisiana, vol. 144, RG 105, BRFAL, NA. See "Records of Indentures, Reports of Indentures Made and Cancelled, North Carolina, 1868," Box 28, RG 105, BRFAL, NA; District of Arkaldelphia, Box 1, RG 105, BRFAL, NA.

37. See "Records of Indentures, Reports of Indentures Made and Cancelled, North Carolina, 1868," Box 29, RG 105, BRFAL, NA; "Indentures for Orphaned Children, Louisiana," vol. 144, 1865–1867, R. G. 105 (e1377), BRFAL, NA. See also "Indentures," December 15, 1867, Cass County, vol. 3, Reel C15183, Missouri State Archives, Jefferson City, Missouri (hereafter cited as MSA); "Indentures," October 10, 1867, October 28, 1867, December 31, 1867, December 17, 1868, August 2, 1870, December 8, 1870, June 25, 1886 Saline County, vol. 4, Reel C11414, MSA, for comparative purposes.

38. "Indentures," December 15, 1867, Cass County, vol. 3, Reel C15183; "Indentures," October 10, 1867, October 28, 1867, December 31, 1867, December 17, 1868, August 2, 1870, December 8, 1870, June 25, 1886 Saline County, vol. 4, Reel C11414, MSA.

39. See "Records of Indentures, Reports of Indentures Made and Cancelled, North Carolina, 1868," Box 29, RG 105, BRFAL, NA.

40. Ibid.

41. King, *Stolen Childhood*, 152–154; Schwalm, *A Hard Fight for We*, 250; Leon F. Litwack, *Been in the Storm so Long: The Aftermath of Slavery* (New York: Vintage Books, 1980), 237–238.

42. King, *Stolen Childhood*, 152; Scott, "Battle over the Child," 198–207; Ira Berlin, Steven F. Miller, and Leslie Rowland, "Afro-American Families in the Transition from Slavery to Freedom," *Radical History Review* 42 (1988), 102. See Arkansas Register of Complaints, March 1866, vol. 89, BRFAL, NA; Virginia Register of Complaints, March 15, 1867, Series 3839, vol. 143, BRFAL, NA; Kentucky Register of Complaints, May 4, 1866, December 31, 1866, Series 1216–1219, vol. 152, BRFAL, NA; South Carolina Register of Complaints, July 30, 1866, August 21, 1866, Series 3308–3309, vol. 254, BRFAL, NA; Fields, *Slavery and Freedom on the Middle Ground*, 139–140. See also Kentucky Register of Complaints, August 1, 1866, Series 1216–1219, vol. 152; Arkansas Register of Complaints, March 1866, vol. 89, 26; Virginia Register of Complaints, March 15, 1867, Series 3839, vol. 143; Kentucky Register of Complaints, May 4, 1866, December 31, 1866, Series 1216–1219, vol. 152; South Carolina Register of Complaints, July 30, 1866, August 21, 1866, Series 3308–3309, vol. 254, BRFAL, NA.

43. Arkansas Register of Complaints, March 1867, vol. 89, BRFAL, NA.

44. Arkansas Register of Complaints, March–April, 1867, vol. 89, BRFAL, NA.

45. South Carolina Register of Complaints, July 4, 1866, Series 3308–3309, vol. 254, BRFAL, NA.

46. See Daniel F. Littlefield, Jr., ed., *The Life of Okah Tubbee* (Lincoln: University of Nebraska Press, 1988).

47. See Zipf, "Reconstructing 'Free Woman,' " 19–22; Laura Edwards, *Gendered Strife and Confusion: The Political Culture of Reconstruction* (Urbana: University of Illinois Press, 1997), 42–45.

48. Zipf, "Reconstructing 'Free Women,' " 20.
49. Ibid., 21.
50. Scott, "Battle over the Child," 205–206; Zipf, "Reconstructing 'Free Woman,' " 17–23; Edwards, *Gendered Strife and Confusion*, 43–44. The binding out of orphaned and poor children continued. See "Indentures," January 8, 1870, August 2, 1870, Saline County, vol. 4, Reel C11141, MSA.
51. "Indenture," July 22, 1865, Benjamin Cudworth Yancy Papers, Southern Historical Collection, University of North Carolina, Chapel Hill, North Carolina. See Jacqueline Jones, *Labor of Love, Labor of Sorrow: Black Women, Work and the Family, From Slavery to the Present* (New York: Vintage Books, 1986), 60–61; Foner, *Reconstruction*, 103–104. See also Ronald L. F. Davis, *Good and Faithful Labor: From Slavery to Sharecropping in the Natchez District, 1860–1890* (Westport: Greenwood Press, 1982), 3–23, for a discussion regarding the emergence of sharecropping.
52. "Contract of January 29, 1866," Alonzo T. Mial Papers, North Carolina Department of Archives and History, Raleigh, North Carolina (hereafter cited as NCDAH); Alonzo T. Mial to Ruffin Horton, December 6, 1859, Mial Papers, NCDAH.
53. "Contract of January 29, 1866," Mial Papers, NCDA.
54. Ibid.
55. Ibid.
56. L. Maria Child, *The Freedmen's Book* (Boston: Fields, Osgood, 1869), 267. See Reidy, "Master and Slave, Planters and Freedmen," 220–221; Thelma Jennings, " 'Us Colored Women Had to go Through a Plenty': Sexual Exploitation of African-American Slave Women," *Journal of Women's History* 1 (Winter 1990), 60–63.
57. Leon F. Litwack, *Been in the Storm so Long: The Aftermath of Slavery* (New York: Vintage Books, 1980), 245; Berlin, et al., *Freedom: A Documentary History*, 69; Schwalm, *A Hard Fight for We*, 194–199, 204–211, 214–217; Brown, "To Catch the Vision of Freedom," 71.
58. See Paul A. Cimbala, *Under the Guardianship of the Nation: The Freedmen's Bureau and Reconstruction in Georgia, 1865–1870* (Athens: University of Georgia Press, 1997), 111–112.
59. Marilyn Richardson, ed., *Maria W. Stewart, America's First Black Woman Political Writer: Essays and Speeches* (Bloomington: Indiana University Press, 1987), 36; W. E. Burghardt Du Bois, *Black Reconstruction in America: An Essay Toward a History of the Past Which Black Folk Played in the Attempt to Reconstruct Democracy in America, 1860–1880* (Cleveland/New York: Meridian, World, 1965), 638.
60. Robert C. Morris, ed., *Freedmen's Schools and Textbooks: Semi-Annual Report on Schools for Freedmen*, vol. 1 (New York: AMS Press, Inc., 1980), 5–6; Bell Irvin Wiley, *Southern Negroes, 1861–1865* (New Haven: Yale University Press, 1965), 267–268.
61. Wiley, *Southern Negroes*, 267–268.
62. Morris, *Freedmen's School an Textbooks*, 7.
63. Washington, *Up From Slavery*, 30–31. See James D. Anderson, *The Education of Blacks in the South, 1860–1935* (Chapel Hill: University of North Carolina Press, 1988), 5–78.
64. Wiley, *Southern Negroes*, 271; Alvord, "Inspector's Report," January 1, 1866, in Morris, *The Freedmen's Schools and Textbooks*, 2, 3, 7, 12. The Freedmen's Bureau's educational arm covered the District of Columbia along with the eleven former-Confederate and four border states in addition to West Virginia and Kansas. The General Superintendent headed the Educational Division which also had local agents, superintendents, and inspectors.
65. Morris, *The Freedmen's Schools and Textbooks*, i, vi, viii–ix.
66. Washington, *Up From Slavery*, 30–31.
67. Morris, "Inspector's Report," January 1, 1866, in Morris, *The Freedmen's Schools and Textbooks*, 3, 4, 7, 8.
68. See Alvord's reports for discussions about the incorporation of needlework classes for women.
69. Morris, *The Freedmen's Schools and Textbooks*, 75–76.
70. Washington, *Up From Slavery*, 31.

71. Edgar A. Toppin, *A Biographical History of Blacks in America Since 1528* (New York: David McKay, 1971), 121–122.

72. Rawick, *The American Slave*, 2 South Carolina Narr., 1: 90.

73. See Elsa Barkley Brown, "Negotiating and Transforming the Public Sphere: African American Political Life in the Transition from Slavery to Freedom," *Public Culture* 7 (Fall 1994): 107–146.

74. See Catherine Clinton, "Reconstructing Freedwomen," in Nina Silber, ed., *Divided Houses: Gender and the Civil War* (New York: Oxford University Press, 1992); Report of the Joint Select Committee to Inquire into the Affairs of the Late Insurrectionary States. Made to the two Houses of Congress February 19, 1872, 13 vols. (Washington: Government Printing Office, 1872); Beverly Greene Bond, " 'Till Fair Aurora Rise': African-American Women in Memphis, Tennessee, 1840–1915" (Ph.D. diss., University of Memphis, 1996), 69–103; James Gilbert Ryan, "The Memphis Riots of 1866: Terror in a Black Community During Reconstruction," *JNH* 62 (July 1977): 243–257; Hannah Rosen, " 'Not That Sort of Women': Race, Gender, and Sexual violence during the Memphis Riot of 1866," in Martha Hodes, ed., *Sex, Love, Race: Crossing Boundaries in North American History* (New York: New York University Press, 1999), 267–293; Martha Hodes, "The Sexualization of Reconstruction Politics: White Women and Black Men in the South After the Civil War," *Journal of the History of Sexuality* 3 (1993): 402–417.

75. Rawick, *The American Slave*, 5 Texas Narr., 3: 152–153; Rawick, *The American Slave*, 2 South Carolina Narr., 1: 12. Emphasis added.

Chapter Six   Black and Red Education at Hampton Institute: A Case Study of the Shawnee Indians, 1900–1925

An earlier version of this chapter appeared in the *Journal of Negro Education* 57 (Fall 1988): 524–535.

1. See David Wallace Adams, "Schooling the Hopi: Federal Indian Policy Writ Small, 1887–1917" in Leonard Dinnerstein and Kenneth T. Jackson, eds., *American Vistas, 1877 to the Present* (New York: Oxford University Press, 1995), 27–44; Margaret Connell Szasz, "Federal Boarding Schools and the Indian Child: 1920–1960," in N. Ray Hiner and Joseph M. Hawes, eds., *Growing Up in American in Historical Perspective: Children* (Urbana: University of Illinois Press, 1985), 209–218; Robert A. Trennert, "Educating Indian Girls at Nonreservation Boarding Schools, 1878–1920," in Ellen Carol DuBois and Vicki L. Ruiz, eds., *Unequal Sisters: A Multicultural Reader in U. S. Women's History* (New York: Routledge, 1990), 224–237; Donal F. Lindsey, *Indians at Hampton Institute, 1877–1923* (Urbana: University of Illinois Press, 1995). See also Julie Davis, "American Indian Boarding School Experiences: Recent Studies from Native Perspectives," *Organization of American Historians Magazine of History* 15 (Winter 2001): 20–22.

2. Adams, "Schooling the Hopi," 34; Trennert, "Educating Indian Girls," 226.

3. Elaine Goodale Eastman, *Pratt: The Red Man's Moses* (Norman: University of Oklahoma Press, 1935), 59, 63; Lindsey, *Indians at Hampton Institute*, 28–31; William H. Robinson, "Indian Education at Hampton Institute," in Keith Schall, ed., *Stony the Road: Chapters in the History of Hampton Institute* (Charlottesville: University of Virginia Press, 1977), 1–6; Trennert, "Educating Indian Girls," 225.

4. Samuel Chapman Armstrong to Emma Armstrong, June 5, 1872, Williamsiana Collection, Williams College, Williams, Massachusetts; Robert F. Engs, "Red, Black, White: A Study in Intellectual Inequality," in J. Morgan Kousser and James M. McPherson, eds., *Region, Race, and Reconstruction: Essays in Honor of C. Van Woodward* (New York: Oxford University Press, 1982), 244.

5. Lindsey, *Indians at Hampton Institute*, 19.
6. Caroline W. Andrus (cited hereafter as CWA) to Sara House, November 7, 1910, CWA Letterbook, Hampton University Archives, Hampton, Virginia (cited hereafter as HUA); Hollis B. Frissell (cited hereafter as HBF) [form letter] to potential employers of Native American students, July 3, 1900, HUA; Lindsey, *Indians at Hampton Institute*, 34, 36–38; Robinson, "Indian Education," 15–16; Trennert, "Educating Indian Girls," 226–227.
7. "Hampton Normal and Agricultural Institute," Bulletin no. 27 (Washington, D.C.: Government Publication Office, 1923); Robinson, "Indian Education," 7.
8. Francis Greenwood Peabody, *Education for Life: The Story of Hampton Institute* (New York: Doubleday, 1918), 148–150; Trennert, "Educating Indian Girls," 226; Engs, "Red, Black and White," 245; Robinson, "Indian Education," 23; William G. McLoughlin, "Red Indians, Black Slavery, and White Racism: America's Slaveholding Indians," *American Quarterly* 25 (October 1974): 375.
9. Peabody, *Education for Life*, 149–150; Engs, "Red, Black and White," 245. Many Native American students could not speak English in the first years of the program; therefore, the school arranged special language classes. Hampton Institute gradually abandoned the classes as it raised entrance and academic standards. See *The Annual Report of the Principal to the Hampton Institute Board of Trustees* (cited hereafter as *AR*) (Hampton: Hampton Institute Press, 1903), 38, HUA.
10. Typewritten note attributed to William Scoville, Eva Shawnee File, HUA. All information regarding the Shawnees comes from the official student records. See Kathryn E. Holland Braund, "The Creek Indians, Blacks, and Slavery," *Journal of Southern History* 57 (November 1991): 601–636; Daniel F. and Mary Ann Littlefield, "The Beams Family: Free Blacks in Indian Territory," *Journal of Negro History* 41 (January 1976): 16–35. See also B. Ann Rodgers and Linda Schott, " 'My Mother was a Mover': African American Seminole Women in Bracettville, Texas, 1914–1964," in Elizabeth Jameson and Susan Armitage, eds., *Writing the Range: Race, Class, and Culture in the Women's West* (Norman: University of Oklahoma Press, 1997), 585–599; John Hope Franklin and John Whittington Franklin, eds., *My Life and An Era: The Autobiography of Buck Colbert Franklin* (Baton Rouge: Louisiana State University Press, 1997), 1–5, 18–19, 255–256.
11. Wilma King Hunter, "Coming of Age: Hollis B. Frissell and the Emergence of Hampton Institute, 1893–1917" (Indiana University, Ph.D. diss., 1982), 14–18, 24–26; Lindsey, *Indians at Hampton Institute*, 1–2.
12. Braund, "The Creek Indians, Blacks, and Slaves," 615; Ian F. Haney Lopez, "The Social Construction of Race: Some Observations in Illusion, Fabrication, and Choice," *Harvard Civil Rights-Civil Liberties Law Review* 29 (Winter 1994): 3–62. See Richard Delgado and Jean Stefanic, eds., *Critical Race Theory: The Cutting Edge* (Philadelphia: Temple University Press, 1995), especially 48–55. See also Littlefield and Littlefield, "The Beams Family," 19, for reference to the 1839 Cherokee constitution wherein the descendants of Cherokee women and black men were privileged with Cherokee citizenship. However, the children of Cherokee men and black women were denied citizenship.
13. King Hunter, "Coming of Age," 111; Lindsey, *Indians at Hampton Institute*, 204.
14. George P. Phenix to CWA, November 11, 1912; Helen Townsend (hereafter cited as HT) to CWA, November 14, 1912; Leta Meyers to CWA, September 4, 1912; George P. Phenix to Garry Meyers, November 14, 1912, Leta Meyers File, HUA; Lindsey, *Indians at Hampton Institute*, 204.
15. Leta Meyers to CWA, September 4, 1912; George P. Phenix to Garry Meyers, November 14, 1912, Leta Meyers File, HUA.
16. See notations, November 7, 1906, Lydia Shawnee File, HUA. Lindsey, *Indians at Hampton Institute*, 205–220.
17. Mary E. Williams to HBF, August 14, 1899, June 7, 1900, HUA.
18. See notations, November 7, 1906, Lydia Shawnee File, HUA.

19. Helen W. Ludlow, *Ten Years' Work Among the Indians at Hampton, Virginia, 1878–1888* (Hampton: Hampton Institute Press, 1888), 4; Engs, "Red, Black and White," 249; Eastman, *Pratt*, 65.
20. Robinson, "Indian Education," 24.
21. Engs, "Red, Black and White," 242.
22. Hampton Institute Faculty Minutes, February 2–9, 1910, HUA.
23. Martha Waldron to HBF, April 7, 1908, HUA.
24. Margaret Muir, "Indian Education at Hampton Institute and Federal Policy" (Brown University: M.A. thesis, 1970), 81; Ludlow, *Ten Years' Work*, 13.
25. See Muir, "Indian Education," 79; *1912 AR*, 19, HUA.
26. *The Southern Workman* 13 (September 1884), 95.
27. Muir, "Indian Education," 82.
28. Eva Shawnee to scholarship donor, February 4, 1901, Eva Shawnee File, HUA; Rebecca Shawnee to scholarship donor, January 3, 1905, Rebecca Shawnee File, HUA.
29. David Shawnee to scholarship donor, March 3, 1920, David Shawnee File, HUA; Julia Shawnee Application, June 6, 1908, Julia Shawnee File, HUA.
30. Eva Shawnee to Elizabeth Hyde, June 30, 1909, Eva Shawnee File.
31. David Shawnee to scholarship donor, March 3, 1920, David Shawnee File, HUA.
32. See copies of special occasion programs, newspaper clippings, *Talks and Thoughts*, and Christian Endeavor Society correspondence between 1900 and 1912, HUA.
33. See Lydia Shawnee's outing records 1903, 1904, and 1905; Elinor R. Hodges to Indian Office, August 31, 1903; C. A. Manchester to Indian Office, undated handwritten letter, emphasis in the original; Mrs. George Clark to Indian Office, September 9, 1905, Lydia Shawnee File, HUA.
34. Mrs. R. F. Troy to HT, September 11, 1911, Emaline Shawnee File, HUA.
35. Mrs. R. F. Troy to HT, September 18, 1911, Emaline Shawnee File, HUA.
36. Undated, unsigned, handwritten memorandum, Emaline Shawnee File, HUA.
37. See rules governing the outing, Indian Department File, HUA.
38. *1898 AR*, 14–15, HUA.
39. Frank Thackery to Lafayette Shawnee, January 2, 1911, February 20, 1911, Lafayette Shawnee File, HUA; Frank Thackery to HBF, February 6, 1911, Lafayette Shawnee File, HUA; L. J. Burt and R. Shaha to HBF, May 14, 1911, Lafayette Shawnee File, HUA.
40. HBF to Thomas Sloan, June 29, 1911, HUA; Lafayette Shawnee to William Scoville, June 23, 1911, Lafayette Shawnee File, HUA.
41. Lydia Shawnee to CWA, August 23, 1912, Lydia Shawnee File, HUA; Emaline Shawnee to CWA, August 23, 1912, Lydia Shawnee File, HUA.
42. Emaline Shawnee to HT, July 13, 1912; Emaline Shawnee File, HUA; Lafayette Shawnee to CWA, September 27, 1912, Lafayette Shawnee File, HUA, Lydia Shawnee to CWA, August 23, 1912, Lydia Shawnee File, HUA.
43. Lindsey, *Indians at Hampton Institute*, 252.
44. U.S. Congress, House, 62nd. Congress, 2nd Session, April 8, 1912, *Congressional Record* 48: 4457; Joseph W. Tingey, "Indians and Blacks Together: An Experiment in Biracial Education at Hampton Institute, 1878–1923" (Teacher's College, Columbia University: Ed. D. diss., 1978), 323.
45. J. D. Eggleston to John H. Stephens, February 9, 1912 C. B. Miller to Clarence H. Kelsey, February 30, 1912, Indian Appropriation File, HUA. Booker T. Washington forwarded copies of this correspondence to Frissell.
46. *Congressional Record*, 48: 4455; Tingey, "Indians and Blacks Together," 321–322.
47. *Congressional Record*, 48: 4456, 48: 4459; Tingey, "Indians and Blacks Together," 322–324.
48. Hampton Institute Faculty Minutes, February 2, 1912, May 11, 1912, HUA. See student petition *The Southern Workman* 41 (May 1912), 166–167; "Editorial," *The Southern Workman* 4 (October 1912), 545–546.

49. Hampton Institute Faculty Minutes, May 11, 1912, HUA; CWA to Mrs. J. S. Howe, March 12, 1914, CWA letter book, HUA. See Lafayette Shawnee to HBF, September 2, 1915; Lafayette Shawnee to CWA, October 6, 1915, Lafayette Shawnee File, HUA.

50. CWA to HBF, undated, CWA Letterbook, HUA. Emphasis added.

51. See Lafayette Shawnee to Hampton Institute, 1912–1930, Lafayette Shawnee File, HUA.

52. Lafayette Shawnee to Arthur Howe, June 15, 1931; August 19, 1935; August 28, 1935; October 15, 1935; Lafayette Shawnee to K. B. Read, November 9, 1939, Lafayette Shawnee File, HUA.

53. Rebecca Shawnee to Christian Endeavor Society, December 27, 1932; December 22, 1933; January 9, 1938; Rebecca Shawnee File, HUA.

54. Adams, "Schooling the Hopi," 40.

55. Trennert, "Educating Indian Girls," 233.

Chapter Seven   What a "Life" This Is: An African American Girl Comes of Age during the Great Depression in Urban America

1. The Hattie Lee Cochran 1931 and 1932 Diaries (cited hereafter as HLC Diary) along with a "1925 Ready Reference Diary," and a 1929 autograph book are in the possession of her son, Alvin Russel Hunter (1938–), retired Major, U. S. Air Force, Columbia, Missouri.   There is no positive identification of the 1925 diary's owner, but its contents focusing on church meetings, housekeeping, and marketing suggest that they belonged to Mary Banks Cochran, Hattie's mother. The 1929 autograph book belonged to the adolescent girl and contains witty sayings, signatures, and photographs of her friends.

2. "Adolescence" is defined as a special time in the lives of children after the onset of puberty but before they assume full adult responsibilities, including gainful employment outside the home.

3. The Western Reserve Historical Society, Cleveland, Ohio, houses the interviews, "Preserving Our African-American Heritage," collected by the Sadie J. Anderson Missionary Society of St. James African Methodist Episcopal Church, Cleveland, Ohio, with support from the Ohio Humanities Council (hereafter cited as Interview, WRHS).

4. See Gail Lumet Buckley, *The Hornes: An American Family* (New York: Signet, 1988); Pearl Bailey, *The Raw Pearl* (New York: Pocket Book, 1971); Robert O'Meally, *Lady Day: The Many Faces of Billie Holiday* (New York: Arcade Publishing, 1991). See also Carole Ione, *Pride of Family: Four Generations of American Women of Color* (New York: Avon Books, 1993).

5. Pearl Bailey, *The Raw Pearl*, 11–16.

6. Gail Lumet Buckley, *The Hornes: An American Family* (New York: Signet Book, 1986), 84, 129–131.

7. "In Memoriam: Margaret Walker Alexander (1915–1998), December 4, 1998," Central United Methodist Church, Jackson, Mississippi (Obituary in possession of the author).

8. According to the 1992 Cochran Family Reunion Souvenir booklet, Perry and Mary were the parents of twelve children. Two of the children died before the family moved to Cleveland in 1915.

9. See U.S. Population Census for Laudedale County, Mississippi and Cayhouga County, Ohio for 1910, 1920, 1930.

10. See Emmett J. Scott, *Negro Migration During the War* (New York: Oxford University Press, 1920). A large body of literature exists on the Great Migration, see Joe William Trotter, Jr., ed., *The Black Migration in Historical Perspective: New Demensions of Race, Class and Gender* (Bloomington: Indiana University Press, 1991); Carol Marks,

Farewell—We are Good and Gone: The Great Black Migration (Bloomington: Indiana University Press, 1989); Malaika Adero, ed., *Up South: Stories, Studies, and Letters of this Century's African-American Migrations* (New York: New Press, 1993); Kenneth L. Kusmer, *A Ghetto Takes Shape: Black Cleveland, 1870–1930* (Urbana: University of Illinois Press, 1976). See also Nicholas Lemann, *The Promised Land: The Great Black Migration and How it Changed America* (New York: Vintage Press, 1991); Ted Ownby, *American Dreams in Mississippi: Consumers, Poverty, & Culture, 1830–1998* (Chapel Hill: University of North Carolina Press, 1999).

11. See James D. Anderson, *The Education of Blacks in the South, 1860–1935* (Chapel Hill: University of North Carolina, 1988); The Thirteenth Census of the United States, 1910, Lauderdale County, Mississippi (55, 21), microfilm, National Archives, Washington, D.C; Interview by Wilma King with Mildred Cochran Talbot, the daughter of Arenzia and Fannie Cochran, December 30, 1998. Where Cochran worked prior to his employment at Kelly, a company established in 1928, is unknown. See *The Cleveland City Directory* (Cleveland: The Cleveland Directory Co., 1930), 955.

12. Kenneth L. Kusmer, *A ghetto takes shape: Black Cleveland, 1870–1930* (Urbana: University of Illinois Press, 1976), 61–65; Grace Palladino, *Teenagers: An American History* (New York: Basic Books, 1996), 12–14; Wilma King Hunter, "Coming of Age: Hollis B. Frissell and the Emergence of Hampton Institute, 1893–1917" (Unpublished Ph.D. diss., Indiana University, 1982), 268–317; Theodore Kornweibel, Jr., "An Economic Profile of Black Life in the Twenties," in Theodore Kornweibel, Jr., ed., *In Search of the Promised Land: Essays in Black Urban History* (Port Washington: Kennikat Press, 1981), 140–147.

13. "Bicentennial Souvenir Journal, Central High School, 1846–1952," Western Reserve Historical Society, Cleveland, Ohio.

14. Benjamin O. Davis, Jr., *Benjamin O. Davis, Jr., American: An Autobiography* (Washington, D.C.: Smithsonian Institution Press, 1991), 15; Roy Roseboro, Interview, WRHR.

15. See Francis Ellen Watkins, "The Two Offers," in Judith A. Hammer and Martin J. Hammer, eds., *Centers of the Self: Short Stories by Black American Women From the Nineteenth Century to the Present* (New York: Hill and Wang, 1994), 21–30. See also Frances Smith Foster, ed., *Minnie's Sacrifice, Reaping and Sowing, Trial and Triumph: Three Rediscovered Novels by Frances E. W. Harper* (Boston: Beacon Press, 1994); Ian F. Haney Lopez, "The Social Construction of Race: Some Observations on Illusion, Fabrication, and Choice," *Harvard Civil Rights–Civil Liberties Law Review* 29 (Winter 1994): 1–62.

16. The data came from the diary which contains many scattered references to classes and teachers.

17. HLC Diary, October 15, 1931; Hattie L. Cochran, "Autograph Book."

18. HLC Diary, September 14, 1931; October 1, 1931.

19. Davis, *Benjamin O. Davis, Jr., American,* 15; Interview, WRHS; HLC Diary, March 4, 1931; "Obituaries," *Cleveland Plain Dealer*, March 5, 1931.

20. HLC Diary, January 15, March 27, 1931.

21. HLC Diary, January, 1931; Carl Wittke, *The First Fifty Years: The Cleveland Museum of Art 1916–1966* (Cleveland: Press of Western Reserve University, 1966), 85–87.

22. "Stage Is Set for View of Geulph Treasure Tonight," *Cleveland Plain Dealer*, January 11, 1931.

23. See *Thirteenth Census of the U.S.,* "Table 53—Families Having Radio Sets, by Color and Nativity of Head for Cities of 100,000 or More," 449.

24. "Stage Is Set," *Cleveland Plain Dealer*, January 11, 1931.

25. HLC Diary, January 12, 1931.

26. HLC Diary, January 19, 1931; Wittke, *The First Fifty Years* reports that the museum acquired nine objects while the *Cleveland Plain Dealer* (January 10, 1931) reports that the museum director purchased six objects.
27. See 1931 *City Directory, Cleveland, Ohio*, Western Reserve Historical Society, Cleveland, Ohio.
28. HLC Diary, January 2, and July 18, 1931.
29. Palladino, *Teenagers*, xiv.
30. HLC Diary, July 16, November 16, 1931; Palladino, *Teenagers*, 8–9.
31. HLC Diary, May 30, 1931. It appears that the Cochrans, or at least Tom, either owned a car or had access to one. Even if the family owned a car, Hattie's fascination was with roadsters, "big Packards," and other "machines" driven by young males she knew. While at Central High School, Benjamin O. Davis, Jr. owned a car in partnership with a friend. The boys paid $25.00 for the automobile and shared the cost equally. Davis, *Benjamin O. Davis, Jr., American*, 15.
32. HLC Diary, August 16–18, 1931.
33. Ibid., August 21, 1931.
34. Ibid., January 7, 1931.
35. See Corinna Jenkins Tucker, Bonnie L. Barber, and Jacquelynne S. Eccles, "Advice About Life Plans and Personal Problems in Late Adolescent Sibling Relationships," *Journal of Youth and Adolescence* 26 (February 1997), 63–76.
36. HLC Diary, October 2, 1931.
37. See Glen Elder, *Children of the Depression: Social Changes in the Life Experience* (Chicago: University of Chicago Press, 1974). See also Brenda Stevenson, ed., *The Journal of Charlotte Forten Grimké* (New York: Oxford University Press, 1988) for a comparison of the two diaries. The nineteenth-century Forten Grimké journals are the only published sources of an African American girl's daily experiences in the nineteenth century.
38. See Cheryl J. Sanders, *Saints in Exile: The Holiness-Pentecostal Experience in African American Religion and Culture* (New York: Oxford University Press, 1996).
39. See Sonia Usmiani and Judith Daniluk, "Mothers and Their Adolescent Daughters: Relationships between Self-Esteem, Gender Role Identity, and Body Image," *Journal of Youth and Adolescence* 26 (February 1997): 45–62.
40. References to the barbeque stand:

Monday, May 18, 1931,	stayed until nearly 11:00	Wednesday May 20
Pop stand—		
Monday June 1		
Tuesday June 2, 1931 test in cooking	stayed until 12:00	
Wednesday June 3, 1931 test in history	stayed until 10:00	
Friday June 5,	stayed until 10:00	
Thursday June 11	stayed a few minutes	
Saturday June 13	stayed from late afternoon until 11:00	
Tuesday June 16	stayed a little while	
Thursday June 18	went in the afternoon	
Friday June 19	stayed a few minutes	

The references ended but resumed after nearly three months.

Thursday September 10, 1931	
Friday September 11	stayed for a while
Saturday September 12	stayed for a while
Monday September 14	went by
Tuesday September 15	stayed for a while

Wednesday September 16	stayed for a while
Thursday September 17	stayed until 11:00
Saturday September 19	stayed until about 11:15
Monday September 21	stayed until 8 o'clock
Wednesday September 23	stayed a while

See HLC Diary for the above dates.

41. See note above.
42. See map in the "I Could Stop on a Dime and Get Ten Cents Change," program brochure, The Cleveland Play House, 8500 Euclid Avenue, Cleveland, Ohio 44106-0189.
43. Cochran had tests in cooking June 2, and history June 3 and June 4, 1931. School closed June 10 and resumed September 8, 1931. See Fairbanks, *Days of Rondo*, 72; and Palladino, *Teenagers*, 32 for references to *True Confessions*.
44. See *Cleveland Plain Dealer*, January through March, 1931.
45. See HLC Diary, September 25, 1931, and afterward; Palladino, *Teenagers*, xxi.
46. HLC Diary, September 28, 1931; October 3, 1931; October 6, 1931, October 7, 1931.
47. See Studs Terkel, *Hard Times: An Oral History of the Great Depression* (New York: Pantheon Books, 1970).
48. There is only one reference to Hattie Cochran working outside the home. See November 1, 1931 entry when she wrote: "Ollie Mae & I [went] out to the Weyers house this eve.— Serving a dinner party."
49. See HLC 1929 autograph book.
50. HLC Diary, April 14, 1931. See Hattie L. Cochran's 1929 autograph book also contained photographs of friends mentioned in the 1931 diary.
51. HLC Diary, April 14, 1931.
52. HLC Diary, January 8, 1932, April 1, 1932, April 3, 1932; John Hope Franklin and Alfred A. Moss, Jr., *From Slavery to Freedom: A History of African Americans* eighth edition (New York: McGraw Hill, 2000), 371.
53. HLC Diary, June 8, 1932.
54. HLC Diary, June 18, 1932; June 19, 1932; June 25, 1932; June 27–29, 1932.
55. HLC Diary, June 21, 1932, July 13, 1932, July 27, 1932.
56. When Cochran met the Hunters is not clear, but her May 2, 1932, entry says: "Hunter girls from Meadville were up by the house. Went with Rufus down on 46th & Woodland to Convention didn't get back til late." The following day, she wrote: "Very Beautiful day. Rufus came by the School [during] lunch period & Hattie, Louise & I went riding down By the Lake Erie."
57. HLC Diary, August 15, 1932; August 18–19, 1932.
58. HLC Diary, August 20, 1932.

Chapter Eight   The Long Way from the Gold Dust Twins to the Williams Sisters: Images of African American Children in Selected Nineteenth- and Twentieth-Century Print Media

1. Walter White to Editor, September 22, 1954, Segregation and Discrimination, Complaints and Responses, 1940–1955, Microfilm Part 15, Series B, Administrative Files, Papers of the National Association for the Advancement of Colored People (hereafter cited as NAACP Papers) (Frederick, MD: University Publications of America, 1982). For a general discussion of the treatment of blacks in advertisements see Marilyn Kern-Foxworth, *Aunt Jemima, Uncle Ben, and Rastus: Blacks in Advertising, Yesterday, Today, and Tomorrow* (Westport, CN: Praeger, 1994).
2. White to Editor, September 22, 1954, NAACP Papers. That watermelon serves as a stereotypical derision of African is evident. Egyptians cultivated fruit well before the

trans-Atlantic trade began, and its African origin, like that of enslaved blacks served as the basis for myths embracing the notion that all blacks love the melon and have gargantuan appetites for the fruit. See Manthia Diawara, "The Blackface Stereotype." <http://www.blackculturalstudies.org/m_diawara/blackface.html>.

3. White to Editor, September 22, 1954, NAACP Papers.

4. See Leonard C. Archer, *Black Images in the American Theatre: NAACP Protest Campaigns—Stage, Screen, Radio & Television* (Brooklyn: Pageant-Poseidon, Ltd., 1973); Nickieann Fleener-Marzec, "D. W. Griffith's *The Birth of a Nation*: Controversy, Suppression, and the First Amendment as It Applies to Filmic Expression, 1915–1973," (Ph.D. diss., University of Wisconsin-Madison, 1977); Thomas Cripps, *Slow Fade to Black: The Negro in American Film, 1900–1942* (New York: Oxford University Press, 1977), 41–49; Thomas Cripps, "The Reaction of the Negro to the Motion Picture 'Birth of a Nation,'" *The Historian* 26 (May 1963): 244–262.

5. The focus is on images of black children in selected print media. Most images in white controlled productions are negative; however, not all white artists and illustrators produced stereotypical characters. See Carolyn Dean, "Boys and Girls and 'Boys': Popular Depictions of African-American Children and Childlike Adults in the United States, 1850–1930," *Journal of American Culture* 23 (Fall 2000): 17–35; J. L. Mashburn, *Black Postcard Price Guide*, second edition (Enka, NC: Colonial House, 1999). See also David R. Roediger, *The Wages of Whiteness: Race and the Making of the American Working Class* (London: Verso, 1993), 115–131; Eric Lott, *Love & Theft: Blackface Minstrelsy and the American Working Class* (New York: Oxford University Press, 1995). Identification numbers, dates of publication, and names of production companies are provided when available.

6. See "Alligator Bait," Stereotypes, Photographs and Prints Division, Schomburg Center for Research in Black Culture, New York Public Library, New York, New York; Postcard Collection, Special Collections, Main Library, Michigan State University, East Lansing, Michigan (hereafter cited as Postcards, MSU); Kern-Foxworth, *Aunt Jemima*, 31; Dean, "Boys and Girls and 'Boys,'" 33, fn 8.

7. Frederick Douglass, "The Negro as Man," [n.d.] Frederick Douglass Papers, Library of Congress, Washington, D.C. Thanks to Donna M. Wells for bringing this citation to my attention. See Donna M. Wells, "Frederick Douglass and the Power of the Photograph: Annotated Bibliography" (unpublished paper in possession of the author), 6; Hugh Honour, *The Image of the Black in Western Art: From the American Revolution to World War I, Black Models and White Myths*, vol. IV (Cambridge: Harvard University Press, 1989). See also Harriet Beecher Stowe, *Uncle Tom's Cabin or, Life among the Lowly* (New York: Penguin Books, 1986), especially Chapter XIV, "Evangeline," and Chapter XX, "Topsy"; Dean, "Boys and Girls and 'Boys,'" 20.

8. See "Greetings from Dixieland," #D-5129 (1937) Curt Teich & Co., Chicago, Illinois, in possession of author. Thanks to Ralph and Carol Gephart for the souvenir postcard folder from their private collection.

9. Ibid., in possession of author.

10. Clarence Brooks & Co. Fine Coach Varnishes, Postcards, MSU for all references to the varnish ads. Currier & Ives produced more than one hundred prints in the comic "Darktown Series" with predominately black characters. Images of blacks in the series are negative uniformly. "The Colored Beauty" is a rare exception. See *Currier & Ives: A Catalogue Raisonné: A Catalogue of the Lithographs of Nathaniel Currier, James Merritt Ives and Charles Currier, including Ephemera Associated with the Firm, 1834–1907* [introduction by Bernard F. Reilly, Jr.,], vol. 1 (Detroit: Gale Research Company, 1984); Bryan F. Le Beau, "Fresh Eyes," *Smithsonian* 32 (December 2001): 78–83; Bryan F. Le Beau, *Currier & Ives: America Imagined* (Washington: Smithsonian Institution Press, 2001), 216–244.

11. Undated, copyrighted trade card (Boston), Postcards, MSU. See Grace Elizabeth Hale, *Making Whiteness: The Culture of Segregation in the South, 1890–1940* (New York: Pantheon Books, 1998), 155.

12. Undated trade card, Postcards, MSU.

13. Undated trade cards, Postcards, MSU.

14. "Who Are We?" Afro-Americana, Warshaw Collection of Business Americana-Soap, Archives Center, National Museum of American History, Smithsonian Institution, Washington, D.C. (hereafter cited as NMAH). See Dean, "Boys and Girls and 'Boys,'" 22.

15. "Who Are We?" Warshaw Collection, NMAH; Kern-Foxworth, *Aunt Jemima*, 48; Hale, *Making Whiteness*, 163.

16. "Who Are We?" Warshaw Collection, NMAH; Hale, *Making Whiteness*, 163.

17. Warshaw Collection, NMAH; Hale, *Making Whiteness*, 166; Kern-Foxworth, *Aunt Jemima*, 47.

18. Warshaw Collection, NMAH.

19. Warshaw Collection, NMAH; Jan Nederveen Pieterse, *White on Black: Images of Africa and Blacks in Western Popular Culture* (New Haven: Yale University Press, 1992), 195.

20. Pearline Soap trade card, Postcards, MSU; Hale, *Making Whiteness*, 162; Kern-Foxworth, *Aunt Jemima*, 31–33. Advertisements for both Pear and Pearline soap are available.

21. Elliot Paint & Varnish Company Trade Card (1935) and Norfolk Paint and Varnish Company Trade Card #7A-H359, Curt Teich Postcard Archives, Lake County Museum, Wauconda, Illinois (hereafter cited as CTA).

22. See Le Beau, *Currier & Ives*, 242, for a discussion regarding the two-part Currier and Ives prints, "Cause and Effect (1887)." One panel, "A Timely Warning," shows an older black man cautioning a child not to bathe for it will ruin his color. The second panel, "A Natural Result," suggests that the child did not heed the advice. As a result, the inside of his hands is white. The man exclaims, "Dar, I tole you so! Now yous done gone spile a little nigger."

23. Pieterse, *White on Black*, 199. Dean, "Boys and Girls and 'Boys,'" 26. Fruit as a sex symbolic may be linked to the interpretation of the Biblical "origin sin." See Genesis 2: 15–17; 3: 1–7.

For a general overview of sexuality among children born in the nineteenth century, based in part on Works Progress Administration narratives on the 1930s, see Anthony S. Parent, Jr. and Susan Brown Wallace, "Childhood and Sexual Identity under Slavery," *Journal of the History of Sexuality* 3 (1993): 363–401.

The Teich Company did not print comparable illustrations of white children on its cards; however, #C-691 comments about the sexuality of adults. The card's focus is on a young scantily clad white woman sitting adjacent to a wooden box marked "XX Brand" which serves as a bed for her two small children. An older woman wearing mixed-matched clothes with a corncob pipe in her hand asks, "Did that travelin' salesman say he'd write to yuh Sadie?" Sadie avoids the question and says, "He shore wuz han'some, maw—" The older bearded man smoking a corncob pipe in the background, presumably Sadie's father, holds a shotgun as if waiting patiently for the handsome salesman's return and to attend his own "shotgun wedding."

The reference is to "Sadie Hawkins," a cartoon character in the "Li'l Abner" comic strip by Al Capp in the 1930s. According to the script, Sadie's father, Hekzebiah, was weary of waiting for his homely daughter to marry. Therefore, as mayor of Dog Patch, U.S.A., he created an occasion for her and other single women to "chase" the town's eligible bachelors with the intent of marrying. Obviously, the woman on the Teich postcard "caught" herself a man but failed to marry him.

The popularity of Capp's comic event generated annual "Sadie Hawkins" days among high school and college students across the country.

See "Sadie Hawkins Day," <http://www.lil-abner.com/sadiehawk.html>; "Sadie Hawkins Day," <http://www.uchaswv.edu/library/sadie.html>.

24. Postcard #2CH291 (1952), CTA. See Evelyn Brooks Higginbotham, "African-American Women's History and the Metalanguage of Race," in Darlene Clark Hine, Wilma King, and Linda Reed, eds., *"We Specialize in the Wholly Impossible": A Reader in Black Women's History* (Brooklyn: Carlson Publishing, 1995), 11–13; Deborah Gray White, *Ar'n't I A Woman? Female Slaves in the Plantation South* (New York: W. W. Norton & Company, 1985), 28–34; Winthrop D. Jordan, *White Over Black: American Attitudes Toward the Negro, 1550–1812* (New York: W. W. Norton & Company, 1977), 136–178.

25. Postcard #2BH591 (1942), CTA. See Jordan, *White over Black,* 158–159; Dean, "Boys and Girls and 'Boys,' " 30.

26. Postcard #7AH2680 (1937), CTA. See Postcard #7AH2675 (1937), CTA of a boy and girl with the caption: "Some folks to be happy / Gotta have a heap o'money / But ah has music in my soul / And de love of mah sweet honey"; Postcard #7AH2674 (1937), CTA of a boy and girl with the caption: "When de golden moon comes creepin' up / Across de fah horizon / Dah's a suttin sweet hone chile / Ah's espeshul got mah eyes on"; Postcard #OBH1404 (n.d.), CTA of a boy and girl with the caption: "Check to Cheek / And heart to heart / You'r really missing / The Grandest part." See also White, *Ar'n't I A Woman?,* 27–46.

27. Honour, *The Image of the Black in Western Art,* 52–54; Londa Schiebinger, *Nature's Body: Gender in the Making of Modern Science* (Boston: Beacon Press, 1993), 160–172; Pieterse, *White on Black,* 181. See Sander L. Gilman, "Black Bodies, White Bodies: Toward an Iconography of Female Sexuality in Late Nineteenth-Century Art, Medicine, and Literature," in Henry Louis Gates, Jr., ed., *"Race," Writing, and Difference* (Chicago: University of Chicago Press, 1985), 223–261.

28. Postcard #2CH414 (1952), CTA.

29. Postcard #6BH1009, CTA. At the turn of the twentieth century, an advertisement for Wool Toilet and Bath Soap features two young white girls. One wearing only a shirt as she stands before a wash basin but appears less interested in bathing than in blowing bubbles. According to the ad, "Blowing Wool Soap bubbles is great fun, but it is greater fun to know that by using Wool soap . . . it means a savings in household expenses." For six soap wrappers, children could receive a "double-bubble soap pipe" and make bubbles within bubbles to entertain themselves. There is no sexual innuendo or mixed company involved in this child's play. In fact, the innocuous activity makes the white child's semi-nudity seem misplaced. The same kind of innocence did not surround black children in advertisements or postcards. See Wool soap advertisement, *Harper's Weekly* (September 30, 1899).

30. Nell Irvin Painter, "Sojourner Truth in Life and Memory: Writing the Biography of an American Exotic," *Gender & History* (Spring 1990), 9; Hazel V. Carby, *Reconstructing Womanhood: The Emergence of the Afro-American Woman Novelist* (New York: Oxford University Press, 1987), 33. See Patricia Morton, *Disfigured Images: The Historical Assault on African American Women* (Westport: Greenwood Press, 1991), chapter 2.

31. Jordan, *White Over Black,* 136–137; White, *Ar'n't I a Woman?,* 31–32.

32. Jordan, *White Over Black,* 150.

33. Postcard #7AH2676 (1937), CTA.

34. Postcard #6BH1160 (1946), Postcard #6B1158, n.d., Postcard #OB1407, 1940, CTA. A search of the Teich Collection for trade and postcards featuring white children in advertisements reveals respectful treatment of white subjects. Photographs and illustrations of white children appear in advertisements by shoe companies, including Poll-Parot (#6BH581), Weather-Bird (#9BH67), Dr. Posner (#6BH807), Child Life (#6BH817), and Walk-Rite (#ZBH759), CTA.

35. Postcard #OBH1730 (1940), CTA; Postcard #OB-H1150 (1940), CTA.

36. E[ulah]. B. to Anna Carlisle, March 6, 1909, May 19, 1909, Carbon Photo Series, #525 and #531, in possession of author. Many of the postcards used herein were found in

archival collections of libraries or museums. The greater majority did include handwritten messages. By contrast, a few cards secured from individual collectors who had purchased them at trade shows, flea markets, or antique malls, contained postmarked messages. This is true of the cards sent by Eula.

On the reverse side of a card showing an alligator eating a black child, the following note appears:

> They tell me that these alligators really do eat colored babies if they can reach them. These [alligators] are only in the St Johns River. Not here in Orlando. This is a town of about 8 square blocks in size. Nice people. Full of tourist at this time of the year.

This card is unusual because of the connection between the card and note on the reverse. Ironically, the author did not mail the card but used the message space as a diary or journal entry.

See Post Card Collection (Black Archives, Florida A. & M. University, Tallahassie, Florida, hereafter cited as Postcards, FAMU).

37. Wendy Morris, "The Researcher's Guide to Ethnic Imagery in the Rustcraft Greeting Card Collection of Occasional Cards, 1927–1959," Unpublished Finding Aid (December 1993) NAMH, 23. See Hallmark Greeting Cards "To Cheer You" and "De sun do shine," (#157951) NAACP Papers.

38. Kenneth B. Clark, *Prejudice and Your Child* (Middletown: Wesleyan University Press, 1988), ix–x, 18–19, 22–23; Richard Kluger, *Simple Justice: The History of Brown v. Board of Education and Black America's Struggle for Equality* (New York: Vintage Books, 1977), 315–345, 555–557.

39. Kluger, *Simple Justice*, 556.

40. Morris, "The Researcher's Guide," figure 5, 6, 7, 8, 9; Pieterse, *White on Black*, 166–167. See William S. Baring-Gould and Ceil Baring-Gould, *The Annotated Mother Goose: Nursery Rhymes Old and New, Arranged and Explained* (New York: Bramhall House, 1962), 304 for a comparable rhyme, "Ten Little Injuns." The "Injuns" are as prone to mishaps as the "Little Niggers." Similarly, the last of the boys marry and "disappear." See also "Ten Little Pickaninnies," *Beaham's Faultless Starch Library* (Kansas City: Faultless Starch Company, n. d.), Postcards, FAMU.

41. Cynthia Sobsey to Children's Activities, January 14, 1954, NAACP Papers; Cynthia Sobsey to [Walter] White, January 14, 1954, NAACP Papers; Mildred H. Lanser to National Association for the Advancement of Colored People, December 1, 1953, NAACP Papers. See Alligator and child postcard (#218 94260) Ashville Postcard, Ashville, North Carolina, Postcard, FAMU. See also, undated, unmailed, Phonostint Card, Detroit Publishing Company, in Postcards, FAMU with the handwritten comment: "They tell me that these alligators really do eat colored babies if they can reach them. These are only in the St Johns River. Not here in Orlando" on a postcard featuring an alligator devouring a black infant suggests the existence of supportive folklore.

42. Adrienne Ashby to Gentlemen, March 2, 1954, NAACP Papers.

43. See Irving Sternberg to Sidney L. Jackson, April 6, 1954, NAACP Papers; Henry L. Moon (hereafter cited as HLM) to Irving Sternberg, April 13, 1954, NAACP Papers; M. H. Lanser to NAACP, December 1, 1953, NAACP Papers; HLM to M. H. Lanser, December 11, 1953, NAACP Papers; Sarah C. Randolph to Gentlemen, January 6, 1954, NAACP Papers. See also Springs Cotton Mills, Burgess flashlight batteries, Mamby doll toaster cover, and "Sambo" chocolate covered ice milk advertisements, NAACP Papers.

44. Herbert L. Wright (hereafter cited as HLW) to Dear Sirs [Contemporary Arts, Inc.] November 27, 1953, NAACP Papers.

45. Alan Fox to HLW, November 30, 1953, NAACP Papers.

46. HLW to Fox, December 3, 1953, NAACP Papers.

47. See ad enclosed in Hollywood Shoe Polish, Inc. and NAACP correspondence, NAACP Papers.

48. HLM to Irving Sternberg, April 13, 1954, NAACP Papers.
49. White to Editor, September 22, 1954, NAACP Papers; Helen De Motte to Walter White, September 24, 1954, NAACP Papers.
50. HLM to Gentlemen, January 11, 1954, NAACP Papers.
51. Hallmark Cards, NAACP Papers; Robinson Family Scrapbook, NMAH. Cards in the Robinson Family Scrapbook are pasted directly on pages; therefore, company trademark or identification number are not available.
52. John A. Boppart to HLM, January 20, 1954, NAACP Papers.
53. Memorandum to the Files from Henry Lee Moon, February 10, 1954, NAACP Papers.
54. Mark L. Finch to Henry Lee Moon, February 11, 1954, NAACP Papers.
55. Louis Marcus to Hallmark, August 12, 1955, NAACP Papers.
56. Maxine Lorraine Clark, "Race Concepts and Self-Esteem in Black Children" (Ph.D. diss., University of Illinois-Urbana, 1979) argues that recent studies measuring color preference among black children yield mixed results with the children selecting black dolls on some occasions but choosing white puppets over brown ones on other occasions.
57. See Morris, "The Researcher's Guide to Ethnic Imagery," NAHM.
58. Mashburn, *Black Postcard Price Guide*, 183; "Obsolete Labels from the Archives of Louisiana Trade Labels, Inc.," published and distributed by G2 Ltd, P. O. Box 56277, New Orleans, Louisiana. See Kenneth W. Goings, *Mammy and Uncle Mose: Black Collectibles and American Stereotyping* (Bloomington: Indiana University Press, 1994).
59. "Got Milk?" Venus and Serena Williams, celebrity moustache advertisement, courtesy National Fluid Milk Processor Promotion Board, Bozell Worldwide, Inc., Advertising, New York, NY (hereafter cited as "Got Milk?"), in possession of author; M. M. Manring, *Slave in a Box: The Strange Career of Aunt Jemima* (Charlottesville: University of Virginia Press, 1998), 116.
60. "Got Milk?"; Stephen Wilson, "Williams sisters double up for title," *USA Today* (July 11, 2000), 13C. See Michael McCarthy, "Lanktree weighs in on Williams' endorsements," *USA Today* (March 22, 2001) <http://www.marcommpartners.com/williams.html> for a discussion of the Williams sisters agreeing to a Doublemint endorsement with Wm. Rigley Jr. Company. As winners of "doubles," the tennis plays "fit nicely with the Doublemint's longtime 'doubles' ad theme." See also Michael McCarthy, "Advertisers shift focus to female athletes," *USA Today* December 12, 2000.

Chapter Nine   African American Youth Face Violence and Fear of Violence in Nineteenth- and Twentieth-Century America

1. Stewart E. Tolnay and E. M. Beck, *A Festival of Violence: An Analysis of Southern Lynchings, 1882–1930* (Urbana: University of Illinois Press, 1992), ix; Vincent Vinikas, "Specters in the Past: The Saint Charles, Arkansas, Lynching of 1904 and the Limits of Historical Inquiry," *Journal of Southern History* (hereafter cited as *JSH*) 65 (August 1999), 541.
2. See Christopher Waldrep, "War of Words: The Controversy over the Definition of Lynching, 1899–1940," *JSH* 66 (February 2000): 75–100; Vinikas, "Specters in the Past," 543–544; Joel Williamson, *The Crucible of Race: Black-White Relations in the American South Since Emancipation* (New York: Oxford University Press, 1984), 183–189.
3. See Jacqueline Jones Royster, ed., *Southern Horrors and Other Writings: The Anti-Lynching Campaign of Ida B. Wells* (Boston: Bedford Books, 1997); Neil R. McMillen, *Dark Journey: Black Mississippians in the Age of Jim Crow* (Urbana: University of Illinois Press, 1989); Martha Hodes, *White Women, Black Men: Illicit Sex in the Nineteenth-Century South* (New Haven: Yale University Press, 1997), 176–177; Edward D. Ayers, *Vengeance and Justice: Crime and Punishment in the 19th Century American South* (New York: Oxford University Press, 1984), 243–244; Leon Litwack, *Trouble in Mind: Black Southerners in the Age of Jim Crow* (New York: Alfred A. Knopf, 1998), 306–309;

Lisa Lindquist Dorr, "Black-on-White Rape and Retribution in Twentieth-Century Virginia: 'Men, Even Negroes, Must Have Some Protection,' " *JSH* 66 (November 2000): 711–748. See Historical American Lynch Data Collection Project accessible at <www.uncwil.edu/earscil/projectHAH.htm>.

4. Ann Moody, *Coming of Age in Mississippi* (New York: Laurel Book, 1968), 125–126; Vinikas, "Specters in the Past," 546.

5. *Nashville Republican*, August 12, 1828; W. Fitzhugh Brundage, *Lynching in the New South: Georgia and Virginia* (Urbana: University of Illinois Press, 1993), 5–6; *Nashville Republican*, August 12, 1828. See Iver Bernstein, *The New York City Draft Riots: Their Significance for American Society and Politics in the Age of the Civil War* (New York: Oxford University Press, 1990), 27–30; for a discussion of mobs lynching free black men during the 1863 draft riots in New York City.

6. *Nashville Republican*, August 12, 1828; Marquis James, *Andrew Jackson: Portrait of a President* (New York: The Universal Library, Grosset & Dunlap, 1937), 29, 31.

7. *Nashville Republican*, August 12, 1828.

8. Ibid.

9. Ibid.

10. Ibid.

11. Ibid. Emphases added; Andrew Jackson to The Coroner of Davidson County [William] Faulker, August 28, 1827, Thi-Murdock, Collection, Overton Papers; Andrew Jackson to William Berkeley Lewis, Septer 1rst. 1827.

    Copies of correspondence from Andrew Jackson were available to the author by Harold D. Moser, editor-director, The Papers of Andrew Jackson, Hopkins Library, University of Tennessee, Knoxville, Tennessee, and by the public programs administrator, The Hermitage, Nashville, Tennessee.

12. Frederick Douglass, *Life and Times of Frederick Douglass: Written by Himself* (New York: Collier Books, 1962), 66–67.

13. Ibid.

14. See Andrew Fede, "Legitimized Violent Slave Abuse in the American South, 1619–1865: A Case Study of Law and Social Change in Six Southern States," *American Journal of Legal History* 29 (April 1985): 93–150; Laurence J. Kotlikoff, "The Structure of Slave Prices in New Orleans, 1804–1862,") *Economic Inquiry* 17 (October 1979): 496–518.

15. Harriet Jacobs, *Incidents in the Life of a Slave Girl Written by Herself*, ed., Jean Fagan Yellin, (New York: Oxford University Press, 1987), 27.

    See Thelma Jennings, " 'Us Colored Women Had to go Through a Plenty': Sexual Exploitation of African-American Slave Women," *Journal of Women's History* 1 (Winter 1990), 60–63; Jacqueline Jones, "Race, Sex, and Self-Evident Truths: The Status of Slave Women During the Era of the American Revolution," in Catherine Clinton, ed., *Half Sisters of History: Southern Women and the American Past* (Durham: Duke University Press, 1994), 23–24; Helen Tunnicliff Catterall ed., *Judicial Cases Concerning American Slavery and the Negro* (Washington: Carnegie Institute, 1929, reprinted by University Microfilms, Ann Arbor, 1969), 2: 513, 2: 520, 3: 363.

    See also "An Act to punish negroes and mulattoes for rape committed on Indians," Mississippi, 1858, *State Slavery Statutes* [microfilm] (Frederick, MD: UPA Academic Editions, 1989), 180, wherein the legislature approved "any number of lashes on the bare back, not exceeding one hundred, on each day, for five successive days, or suffer death as the jury may determine."

    The act further stipulated that if a free black or mulatto raped, or attempted to rape any white woman or had carnal knowledge of any white female under fourteen years of age, the punishment was death. There was no mention of punishment for the rape of a black female.

    On December 18, 1859, the Mississippi legislature made "the rape by a negro or mulatto on a female negro or mulatto, under twelve years of age" punishable with lashes

not to exceed one hundred per day for five successive days, "or suffer death as the jury may determine." The statute makes no distinction between enslaved and free black children.
Mississippi, 1860, *State Slavery Statutes*, 102.

16. Eugene D. Genovese, *Roll, Jordan, Roll: The World the Slaves Made* (New York: Vintage Books, 1976), 423.

17. Solomon Northup, "Twelve Years a Slave: Narrative of Solomon Northup," in Gilbert Osofsky, ed., *Puttin' On Ole Massa: The Slave Narratives of Henry Bibb, William Wells Brown, and Solomon Northup* (New York: Harper Torchbooks, 1969), 267–268. See Willie Lee Rose, ed., *A Documentary History of Slavery in North America* (New York: Oxford University Press, 1976), 423–427, for a discussion regarding unions between women of color and white men.

18. Catherine M. Hanchett, " 'What Sort of People and Families . . .': The Edmondson Sisters," *Afro-Americans in New York Life and History* 6 (July 1982), 21–37; Northup, "Twelve Years a Slave," 267–268; Genovese, *Roll, Jordan, Roll*, 417.

19. Hanchett, "What Sort of People," 22–27.

20. Susan Brownmiller, *Against Our Will: Men, Women, and Rape* (New York: Simon and Schuster, 1975), 153–154; Deborah Gray White, *Ar'n't I a Woman?*, 152–153; Pauli Murray, *Proud Shoes: The Story of an American Family* (New York: Harper & Row, 1984), 41–44; Catherine Clinton, "Caught in the Web of the Big House: Women and Slavery," in Walter Fraser, Jr., ed., *The Web of Southern Social Relations: Women, Family, and Education* (Athens: University of Georgia Press, 1985), 20–21.

21. See Melton A. McLaurin, *Celia, a Slave* (Athens: University of Georgia Press, 1991).

22. McLaurin, *Celia*, 107.

23. See Peter W. Bardaglio, "Rape and the Law in the Old South: 'Calculated to excite indignation in every heart,' " *JSH* 60 (November 1994): 749–772 for a discussion of race, rape, and southern laws.

24. Jacobs, *Incidents in the Life of a Slave Girl*, 19. See White, *Ar'n't I a Woman?* 27–46.

25. Jacobs, *Incidents in the Life of a Slave Girl*, 51.

26. George P. Rawick, ed., *The American Slave: A Composite Autobiography* Texas Narr., 10 Supplement 2 (Westport: Greenwood Press, 1979), 9: 4121–4123.

27. Ibid., 9: 4118–4120.

28. Rawick, *The American Slave* 17 Florida Narr., 128.
    See Genovese, *Roll, Jordan, Roll*, 505; Winthrop D. Jordan, *White Over Black: American Attitudes toward the Negro, 1550–1812* (New York: W. W. Norton & Company, 1977), 159.

29. Rawick, *The American Slave* 17 Florida Narr., 128. Emphasis added; Frederick Douglass, *My Bondage and My Freedom* (New York: Dover, 1969), 161.

30. Rawick, *The American Slave* 10 Texas Narr., 9: 4122–4123.

31. Ibid., 9: 4120–4121, 9: 4123.

32. See Darlene Clark Hine, "Rape and the Inner Lives of Black Women: Thoughts on the Culture of Dissemblance," in Darlene Clark Hine, ed., *Hine Sight: Black Women and The Re-Construction of American History* (Brooklyn: Carlson Publishing, Inc., 1994), 37–38; George A. Awad, "Father-Son Incest: A Case Report" *Journal of Nervous and Mental Disorders* 162 (February 1976), 135–139.

33. Norrece T. Jones, Jr., "Rape in Black and White: Sexual Violence in the Testimony of Enslaved and Free Americans" (Unpublished paper delivered at the Porter L. Fortune, Jr., History Symposium, October 30, 2000, University of Mississippi, Oxford, Mississippi, in possession of author), 19, 29; Nell Irvin Painter, "Race, Class, and Gender in the Slave South," in Leonard Dinnerstein and Keneth T. Jackson, eds., *America Vistas*, seventh edition (New York: Oxford University Press, 1995), 274; Orlando Patterson, *Rituals of Blood: Consequences of Slavery in Two American Centuries* (Washington, D.C.: Basic Civitis, 1998), 289; Wainwright Churchill, *Homosexual Behavior Among Males: A Cross-Cultural and Cross-Species Investigations* (New York: Hawthorn Books, Inc., 1967), 103–104.

See Richard R. Troiden, *Gay and Lesbian Identity: A Sociological Analysis* (Dix Hills, NY: General Hall, Inc., 1988), 17–18.

34. Jacobs, *Incidents in the Life of a Slave Girl*, 192. Unlike Jacobs, Sam and Louisa Everett offered more explicit comments about an owner's sexual interests. Aside from Jim McClain forcing slaves to copulate while he watched, the Everetts agreed that:

> He enjoyed these orgies very much and often entertained his friends in this manner; quite often he and his guests would engage in these debaucheries, choosing for themselves the prettiest of the young women. Sometimes they forced the unhappy husbands and lovers of their victims to look on.

Rawick, *The American Slave* 17 Florida Narr., 127.

35. Churchill, *Homosexual Behavior Among Males*, 85. See Jeffrey Weeks, "The Social Construction of Sexuality," in Kathy Peiss, ed., *Major Problems in the History of American Sexuality: Documents and Essays* (Boston: Houghton Mifflin Company, 2002), 2–10.

36. See George Chauncey, *Gay New York: Gender, Urban Culture, and the Makings of the Gay Male World, 1890–1940* (New York: Basic Books, 1994); Troiden, *Gay and Lesbian Identity*, 18–19; Tim Edwards, *Erotics & Politics: Gay Male Sexuality, Masculinity and Feminism* (London: Routledge, 1994), 14–15.

37. Hine, "Rape and the Inner Lives of Black Women," 37. There is no body of literature covering this topic for the slave era. More recent findings may be useful but there is a danger in reading current scholarship backward in time. See Andrea G. Hunter and James Earl Davis, "Constructing Gender: An Exploration of Afro-American Men's Conceptualization of Manhood," *Gender & Society* 6 (September 1992) 464–479; John D. Wrathall, "Reading the Silences Around Sexuality," in Peiss, *Major Problems in the History of American Sexuality*, 16–25. See also Churchill, *Homosexual Behavior Among Males*, 79–81, which reports that "homoerotophobic cultures are definitely in the minority."

38. L. Maria Child, *The Freedmen's Book* (Boston: Fields, Osgood, 1869), 267.

39. Catherine Clinton, "Reconstructing Freedwomen," in Catherine Clinton and Nina Silber, eds., *Divided Houses: Gender and the Civil War* (New York: Oxford University Press, 1992), 316, 318 Vinikas, "Specters in the Past," 556–557; Joel Williamson, "Wounds Not Scars: Lynching, the National Conscience, and the American Historian," *Journal of American History* (hereafter cited as *JAH*) (March 1997), 1236–1237.

40. Brownmiller, *Against Our Will*, 32, 37–38; Victor B. Howard, "The Civil War in Kentucky: The Slave Claims His Freedom," *Journal of Negro History* (hereafter cited as *JNH*) 67 (Fall 1982): 245–256.

41. Rawick, *The American Slave*, South Carolina Narr., 2.1: 46. See *Report of the Joint Select Committee to Inquire into the Conditions of Affairs in the Late Insurrectionary States. Made to the two Houses of Congress February 19, 1872* vols. 1–13 (Washington: D.C. Government Printing Office, 1872).

42. Rawick, *The American Slave* South Carolina Narr., 2.1: 46.

43. "Memphis Riots and Massacre," House Report No. 101, 30th Congress, 1st Session (1866), 13–14. Emphasis in the original. See Beverly Greene Bond, " 'Till Fair Aurora Rise': African-American Women in Memphis, Tennessee, 1840–1915" (Ph.D. diss., University of Memphis, 1996), 69–103; James Gilbert Ryan, "The Memphis Riots of 1866: Terror in a Black Community During Reconstruction," *JNH* 62 (July 1977): 243–257; Hannah Rosen, " 'Not That Sort of Women': Race, Gender, and Sexual violence during the Memphis Riot of 1866," in Martha Hodes, ed., *Sex, Love, Race: Crossing Boundaries in North American History* (New York: New York University Press, 1999), 267–293.

44. Victoria E. Bynum, *Unruly Women: The Politics of Social & Sexual Control in the Old South* (Chapel Hill: University of North Carolina Press, 1992), 88–89; Bertram Wyatt-Brown,

Southern Honor: Ethics & Behavior in the Old South, 315. See Martha Hodes, *White Women, Black Men: Illicit Sex in the Nineteenth-Century South* (New Haven: Yale University Press, 1997).

45. Martha Hodes, "The Sexualization of Reconstruction Politics: White Women and Black Men in the South After the Civil War," *Journal of the History of Sexuality* 3 (1993), 402–403; Hodes, *White Women, Black Men*, 11–14, 211–212; Diane Miller Sommerville, "The Rape Myth in the Old South Reconsidered," *JSH* 61 (August 1995): 481–518; Diane Miller Sommerville, "Rape, Race, and Castration in Slave Law in the Colonial and Early South," in Catherine Clinton and Michele Gillespie, eds., *The Devil's Lane: Sex and Race in the Early South* (New York: Oxford University Press, 1997), 75–76.

46. See W. E. B. Du Bois, *Black Reconstruction in America: An Essay Toward a History of the Past Which Black Folk Played in the Attempt to Reconstruct Democracy in America, 1860–1880* (New York: Meridian Books The World Publishing Company, 1965); Steven Hahn, "Hunting, Fishing, and Foraging: Common Rights and Class Relations in the Postbellum South," *Radical History Review* 26 (1982): 37–64. See also Karin L. Zipf, " 'The WHITES shall rule the land or die': Gender, Race, and Class in North Carolina Reconstruction Politics," *JSH* 65 (August 1999): 499–534.

47. Williamson, "Wounds not Scars," 1237.

48. See Royster, *Southern Horrors*, 28; Crystal Nichole Feimster, " 'Ladies and Lynching': The Gendered Discourse of Mob Violence in the New South, 1880–1930" (Ph.D. diss., Princeton University, 2000), 246–247, 258, for references about the lynching of black teenagers.

   The exact number of lynch victims is not known due to differences in defining what constituted a summary execution and underreporting the homicides.

   The preponderance of lynch victims were men; however, women and children under eighteen years of age were also killed by mobs. Historic American Lynch Project based upon the statistics kept by Tuskegee Institute lists victims by name, date, color, sex, and offense. The database contains statistics about the lynching of several families including the October 3, 1908, Fulton County, Kentucky, deaths of David Walker, accused of cursing a white woman, along with his wife, daughter, and son. Four other children of unknown sexes, including an infant, also died along with their parents.

   HAL database in possession of author.

49. Williamson, "Wounds not Scars," 1229, 1235, 1238, 1242–1244, 1246; David Levering Lewis, "Referees' Report," *JAH* 83 (March 1997), 1263; Robin D. G. Kelley, "Referees' Report," *JAH* 83 (March 1997), 1260. See Vinikas, "Specters in the Past," 536, 539–540. See also Rayford W. Logan, *The Betrayal of the Negro from Rutherford B. Hayes to Woodrow Wilson* (New York: Collier Books, 1965).

50. Vinikas, "Specters in the Past," 541. See Sandra Gunning, *Race, Rape, and Lynching: The Red Record of American Literature, 1890–1912* (New York: Oxford University Press, 1996); Harper Lee, *To Kill a Mockingbird* (New York: Warner Books, 1982); Gloria T. Hull, *Color, Sex, & Poetry: Three Women Writers of the Harlem Renaissance* (Bloomington: Indiana University Press, 1987); 128, 131–132, 171–172; Robyn Wiegman, *American Anatomies: Theorizing Race and Gender* (Durham: Duke University Press, 1995), 81–113; Robyn Wiegman, "The Anatomy of Lynching," *Journal of the History of Sexuality* 2 (1993): 445–467; Richard Wright, "Big Boy Leaves Home," in Richard Barksdale and Keneth Kinnamon, eds., *Black Writers of America: A Comprehensive Anthology* (New York: McMillian Company, 1972), 548–564; Hazel V. Carby, " 'On the Threshold of Woman's Era': Lynching, Empire, and Sexuality in Black Feminist Theory," in Henry Louis Gates, Jr., ed., *"Race," Writing, and Difference* (Chicago: University of Chicago Press, 1985), 301–316, for representative literary publications or discussions about lynching.

51. Sterling A. Brown, "Ole Lem," in *The Collected Poems of Sterling A Brown* (Evanston: Northwestern University Press, 1980), 180–181; James M. SoRelle, "The 'Waco Horror': The Lynching of Jesse Washington," *Southwestern Historical Quarterly* 86 (April 1986), 526–528; Hodes, *White Women, Black Men*, 176–177; McMillen, *Dark Journey*, 233–235; Litwack, *Trouble in Mind*, 280–281, 288.

   See W. Fitzhugh Brundage, *Lynching in the New South: Georgia and Virginia, 1880–1930* (Urbana: University of Illinois Press, 1993); James Allen and John Littlefields, *Without Sanctuary: Lynching Photography in America* (Santa Fe: Twin Palms Publishers, 2000); Gail Williams O'Brien, *The Color of the Law: Race, Violence, and Justice in the Post-World War II South* (Chapel Hill: University of North Carolina Press, 1999).

   Thanks to John Hope Franklin for bringing *The Color of the Law* to my attention.
52. Claude McKay, "The Lynching," in Richard Barksdale and Keneth Kinnamon, eds., *Black Writers of America: A Comprehensive Anthology* (New York: Macmillan Company, 1972), 494; Litwack, *Trouble in Mind*, 288. See *Without Sanctuary*, especially 26, 38, 51, 54–55, 56–57, 79 for the unmistakably calm resolve of white women and young white children photographed at lynch sites.
53. SoRelle, "The 'Waco Horror,' " 528.
54. Robert O'Meally, *Lady Day: The Many Faces of Billie Holiday* (New York: Arcade Publishing, 1991), 133–140.
55. Rackham Holt, *Mary McLeod Bethune: A Biography* (Garden City: Doubleday, 1964), 17–18; Joyce A. Hanson, *Mary McLeod Bethune & Black Women's Political Activism* (Columbia: University of North Carolina Press, 2003), 15.
56. Brundage, *Lynching in the New South*, 1–2; Deborah Gray White, *Too Heavy a Load: Black in Defense of Themselves, 1894–1994* (New York: W. W. Norton & Company, 1999), 24–25.
57. Clarence Norris and Sybil D. Washington, *The Last of the Scottsboro Boys: An Autobiography* (New York: G. P. Putnam's Sons, 1979), 229. See Dan T. Carter, *Scottsboro: A Tragedy of the American South*, revised edition (Baton Rouge: University of Louisiana Press, 1979); James A. Miller, Susan D. Pennybacker, and Eve Rosenhaft, "Mother Ada Wright and the International Campaign to Free the Scottsboro Boys, 1931–1934," *American Historical Review* 106 (April 2001): 387–430; Felecia G. Jones Ross, "Mobilizing the Masses: *The Cleveland Call and Post* and the Scottsboro Incident," *JNH* 84 (Winter 1999): 48–60.
58. Norris and Washington, *The Last of the Scottsboro Boys*, 9, 21–22.
59. See Timothy B. Tyson, "Robert F. Williams, 'Black Power', and the Roots of the African American Freedom Struggle," *JAH* 85 (September 1998), 551–556; Timothy B. Tyson, *Radio Free Dixie: Robert F. Williams & the Roots of Black Power* (Chapel Hill: University of North Carolina Press, 1999), 90–136.
60. See Tyson, "Robert F. Williams," 551–556; Tyson, *Radio Free Dixie*, 90–136.
61. Tyson, *Radio Free Dixie*, 101–136.
62. O'Brien, *The Color of the Law*, 79.
63. Ibid., 78–79.
64. Ibid.
65. Ibid., 79–81.
66. McKay, "The Lynching," 494; James L. Garrett Interview, January 10, 1934, Robert Minor Papers, Rare Book and Manuscript Library, Columbia University, New York, New York (hereafter cited as Minor Papers); O'Brien, *The Color of the Law*, 81–82; Moody, *Coming of Age in Mississippi*, 126.

   Castration, like lynching, was not the ordinary punishment for black men accused of rape or attempted rape of white women prior to emancipation. Its widespread use in conjunction with rape allegations and lynching is a post-emancipation phenomenon associated with the restoration of white masculine power and sexual anxiety of the time.

   See Sommerville, "Rape, Race, and Castration," 76–82.

67. Garrett Interview, 3, 4.
68. Ibid., 4.
69. Dr. A. E. Barnett, "Data Regarding the Lynching of Cordie Cheek," 8, Robert Minor Papers.
70. John Hope Franklin, "John Hope Franklin: A Life of Learning," in *Race and History: Selected Essays, 1938–1988* (Baton Rouge: Louisiana State University, 1989), 281. John Hope Franklin to Wilma King, November 28, 2001, telephone conversation.
71. J. R. Hill to Wilma King, telephone conversation October 20, 2000. See "Summary of Events Relating to Lynching of Cordie Cheek," and Thomas E. Jones, "The Cordie Cheek Lynching," Minor Papers.
72. Rosen, " 'Not That Sort of Women,' " 283. Hull, *Color, Sex, and Poetry*, 131. The widespread violent brutality associated with the rape of black women by whites during the Reconstruction era subsided, but the sexual abuse by white men did not disappear entirely.
73. Tyson, "Robert F. Williams," 540–541.
74. Ibid., 540; Tyson, *Radio Free Dixie*, 1, 48.
75. Norris and Washington, *The Last of the Scottsboro Boys*, 51. The court dropped charges against Roy Wright, Eugene Williams, Olen Montgomery, and Willie Roberson. They were released from prison July 24, 1937. The remaining Scottsboro Boys received paroles between November 17, 1943 and February 17, 1947. Parole violations and other causes resulted in several of them returning to prison. Haywood Patterson escaped July 17, 1948. Andy Wright, the last of the men to leave the prison, was released June 9, 1950. See Norris and Washington, *The Last of the Scottsboro Boys*, 249–255.
76. Ibid., 227–228.
77. Ibid., 13.

Chapter Ten   Emmett Till Generation: African American Schoolchildren and the Modern Civil Rights Movement in the South, 1954–1964

1. Victor B. Howard, "The Civil War in Kentucky: The Slave Claims his Freedom" *Journal of Negro History* 67 (Fall 1982), 247–248. See Martin Luther King, Jr., "I Have a Dream," in Richard Barksdale and Keneth Kinnamon, eds., *Black Writers of America: A Comprehensive Anthology* (New York: Macmillan Company, 1972), 871–883.
2. Steven Kasher, *The Civil Rights Movement: A Photographic History, 1954–68* (New York: Abbeville Press, 1996), 97. King was referring to Isaiah 11:6, *Holy Bible*.
3. Jack Mendelsohn, *The Martyrs: Sixteen Who Gave Their Lives for Racial Justice* (New York: Harper & Row, Publishers, 1966), 88, 96.
4. Booker T. Washington, *Up from Slavery, An Autobiography* (New York: Airmont Publishing Company, Inc., 1967), 18.
5. See James D. Anderson, *The Education of Blacks in the South, 1860–1935* (Chapel Hill: University of North Carolina Press, 1988); Robert C. Morris, *Reading, 'Riting, and Reconstruction: The Education of Freedmen in the South, 1861–1870* (Chicago: University of Chicago Press, 1981).
6. See Wilma King, " 'Inherently Unequal': The Access and Right to a Basic Education in the United States," <http://www.connectforkids.org/benton_topics1544/benton_topics_show.htm?doc_id=21149, 1-7>; Vicki L. Ruiz, "South by Southwest: Mexican Americans and Segregated Schooling, 1900–1950), *OAH Magazine of History* 15 (Winter 2001): 23–27.
7. Robert Weisbrot, *Freedom Bound: A History of America's Civil Rights Movement* (New York: Plume, 1991), 8.
8. See Richard Kluger, *Simple Justice: The History of Brown v. Board of Education and Black America's Struggle for Equality* (New York: Vintage Books, 1975), and especially 705 for the quote.

9. See descriptions of and commentary about Elizabeth Eckford's encounter with the Arkansas National Guards at Central High School in Melba Pattillo Beals, *Warriors Don't Cry: Searing Memoir of the Battle to Integrate Little Rock's Central High School* (New York: Washington Square Press, 1995), 49–50, 83.

    See description of Ruby Bridges walking with federal marshals in Ruby Bridges, *Through My Eyes* (New York: Scholastic, 1999), 24 quoted from John Steinbeck, *Travels with Charley: In Search of America* (New York: Bantham Books, 1963).

10. Wilma King in telephone conversation with spokesperson for the Norman Rockwell Family Trust Museum, October 2000.

    Of the many paintings by Normal Rockwell only a limited number contain persons of color or deal with issues reflecting the racial climate in the United States, such as "The Golden Rule," "New Neighbors," and "The Problem We all Live With." Nevertheless, Ruby Bridges identifies with Rockwell's "The Problem We all Live With" and includes it in her *Through My Eyes*. She asserts that Rockwell received his inspiration for the painting from John Steinbeck's *Travels with Charley*. During a southern trip with his dog, Steinbeck did stop at Frantz School where he saw Ruby Bridges being escorted into the building by federal marshals and included a description in *Travels*.

    The Rockwell spokesperson maintained that the artist worked from photographs. If this is the case, it is very likely that he saw photographs of the child with federal escorts, especially those attributed to AP World Wide wire service, in his local papers.

11. Beals, *Warriors Don't Cry*, 308; Dorothy Sterling (with Donald Gross), *Tender Warriors* (New York: Hill and Wang, 1958), 25; Audrey Edwards and Fr. Craig K. Polite, *Children of the Dream: The Psychology of Black Success* (New York: Doubleday, 1992), 60.

    This is not to suggest that parents or others concerned citizens were unmindful of the potential danger. They simply did not know it would escalate to the extent that it did. In Little Rock, the governor's actions seemed to have exacerbated the situation which degenerated to the degree that the President called in the 101st Airborne Division.

12. Sterling, *Tender Warriors*, 26.

13. A larger number of black students were selected to attend Central High School, but only nine entered.

    See Alexander Leidholdt, *Standing Before the Shouting Mob: Lenoir Chambers and Virginia's Massive Resistance to Public School Integration* (Tuscaloosa: University of Alabama Press, 1997), 87 for a discussion of Norfolk, Virginia's criteria for evaluating students for enrollment at previously all-white schools.

    The standards purported to take the would-be transfer students' health, academic background, physical and moral fitness, mental ability, social adaptability, and cultural backgrounds into account, as well as the health, safety, and cultural backgrounds of the pupils already enrolled in the requested school.

14. Gloster B. Current, "Crisis in Little Rock," *The Crisis* (November 1957), 526; "Troop Use an Error, Gov. Faubus Asserts: Urges Calm and Order," *Washington Post* (September 27, 1957), 1A, 4A; "Ike Blames Gov. Faubus For Crisis," *Washington Post* (September 29, 1957), A; Beals, *Warriors Don't Cry*, xxi.

15. Beals, *Warriors Don't Cry*, 110–113, 147–148, 152–154, 163–165, 259.

16. Kasher, *The Civil Rights Movement*, 56.

17. Alexander Leidholdt, *Standing Before the Shouting Mob: Lenoir Chambers and Virginia's Massive Resistance to Public-School Integration* (Tuscaloosa: University of Alabama Press, 1997), 96.

    See Beals, *Warriors Don't Cry*, 222, 233; Grace Palladino, *Teenagers: An American History* (New York: BasicBooks, 1996), 180.

18. Margaret Anderson, "Clinton, Tenn.: Children in a Crucible," *New York Times Magazine* (November 2, 1958), 12.

19. Anderson, "Clinton, Tenn.," 12. According to the news article, the following day Anderson used the incident to teach her students about American citizenship and

constitutional law. Some students received the lesson in the spirit of its intent while others labeled her as a "Nigger Lover."

20. Beth Roy, *Bitters in the Honey: Tales of Hope and Disappointment across Divides of Race and Time* (Fayetteville: University of Arkansas Press, 1999), 176, 178–179 (emphasis added); Beth Roy, "Goody Two-Shoes and the Hell-Raisers: *Women's Activism, Women's Reputations in Little Rock*," in Kathleen Blee, ed., *No Middle Ground: Women and Radical Protest* (New York: New York University Press, 1999), 96.

21. Roy, "Goody Two-Shoes and the Hell Raisers," 101.

22. Kasher, *The Civil Rights Movement*, 54.

23. See Beals' *Warriors Don't Cry* for a full discussion of her relationship with a white insider, who maintained a *link* or association with segregationists while helping her avoid potentially disastrous situations.

24. Elizabeth Huckaby, *Crisis at Central High: Little Rock, 1957–58* (Baton Rouge: Louisiana State University Press, 1980), 152.

25. Kasher, *The Civil Rights Movement*, 56; Beals, *Warriors Don't Cry*, 218–220, 243; Roy, "Goody Two-Shoes and the Hell-Raisers," 100.

26. See Roy, *Bitters in the Honey*, 271–300.

27. See Kasher, *The Civil Rights Movement*, 51; Will Count, *A Life Is More Than a Moment: The Desegregation of Little Rock's Central High* (Bloomington: Indiana University Press, 1999), 40. See also Roy, "Goody Two-Shoes and the Hell-Raisers," 102–110.

28. Henry Hampton and Steve Fayer with Sarah Flynn, eds., *Voices of Freedom: An Oral History of the Civil Rights Movement from the 1950s through the 1980s* (New York: Bantam Books, 1990), 51.

29. Bridges, *Through My Eyes*, 31. While Ruby Bridges attended William Frantz, three other African American children integrated McDonogh No. 19, an elementary school in New Orleans with a normal enrollment of 467 children. As of November 17, 1960, only four children remained at McDonogh No. 19. Afterward, white children did not attend but entered hastily established private schools or enrolled in schools in other parishes. Federal marshals escorted the African American children to and from McDonogh No. 19 as they did in the case of Ruby Bridges.

30. Bridges, *Through My Eyes*, 20. Two of the black children at McDonogh also associated the crowd with Mardi Gras, which raised questions about the true intensity of the crowds or mobs. Alan Wieder suggests that the vitriolic reactions from the mob at Frantz Elementary School were not directed at Ruby Bridges but at the few white parents, eight families, who kept their children enrolled there. See Alan Wieder, "From Crowds to Mobs: School Desegregation in New Orleans, A Case Study of Collective Behavior," *Equality & Excellence* 24 (Fall 1988), 4, 5.

31. Bridges, *Through My Eyes*, 23.

32. Ibid., 40.

33. Ibid., 50.

34. See Robert Coles, *The Story of Ruby Bridges* (New York: Scholastic Inc., 1995).

35. Beals, *Warriors Don't Cry*, 217, 249, 257, 260, 263.

36. H. R. 2560 Little Rock Nine Medals and Coin Act Sec. 101. The Congress hereby finds the following

(1) Jean Brown Trickey, Carlotta Walls LaNier, Melba Pattillo Beals, Terrence Roberts, Gloria Ray Karlmark, Thelma Mothershed Wair, Ernest Green, Elizabeth Eckford, and Jefferson Thomas, hereafter in this section referred to as the "Little Rock Nine," voluntarily subjected themselves to the bitter stinging pains of racial bigotry.

(2) The Little Rock Nine are civil rights pioneers whose selfless acts considerably advanced the civil rights debate in this country.

(3) The Little Rick Nine risked their lives to integrate Central High School in Little Rock, Arkansas, and subsequently the Nation.

(4) The Little Rock Nine sacrificed their innocence to protect the American principle that we are all "one nation, under God, indivisible."

(5) The Little Rock Nine have indelibly left their mark on the history of this Nation.

(6) The Little Rock Nine have continued to work toward equality for all Americans.

37. Beals, *Warriors Don't Cry*, 170, 182, 186, 217. See collection of press comments and excerpts about the "Little Rock Nine" in *The Crisis* (November 1957), 536–542.

38. Clenora Hudson-Weems, *Emmett Till: The Sacrificial Lamb of the Civil Rights Movement* (Troy, MI: Bedford Publishers, 1994), 311–313. See Jacqueline Goldsby, "The High and Low Tech of It: The Meaning of Lynching and the Death of Emmett Till," *Yale Journal of Criticism* 9 (1996): 245–282.

39. See Goldsby, "The High and Low Tech of It," 249, 253–254.

40. Hudson-Weems, *Emmett Till*, 306, 313. See Goldsby, "The High and Low Tech of It," for a discussion of the widespread media coverage and its impact upon the American public. See also "700 Are Jailed in Negro Protest at Birmingham: Students Play Hooky to March," *The Atlanta Constitution* (May 3, 1963), 1.

41. "700 Are Jailed," 1; Sally Belfrage, *Freedom Summer* (New York: Viking Press, 1965), 50. See Ellen Levine, *Freedom's Children: Young Civil Rights Activists Tell Their Own Stories* (Thorndike, Maine: Thorndike Press, 1993), 134–157, for first hand accounts of participation in the Children's Crusade.

42. John Dittmer, *Local People: The Struggle for Civil Rights in Mississippi* (Urbana: University of Illinois Press, 1994), 85.

43. Ben H. Bagdikian, "Negro Youth's New March on Dixie," *The Saturday Evening Post* 235 (September 8, 1962), 16, 17.

44. Bagdikian, "Negro Youth's New March on Dixie," 16, 18; Palladino, *Teenagers,* 177; Sally Belfrage, *Freedom Summer* (New York: Viking Press, 1965), 68–69.

45. Dittmer, *Local People*, 110–115.

46. Kasher, *The Civil Rights Movement*, 93; Glenn T. Eskew, *But for Birmingham: The Local and National Movement in the Civil Rights Struggle* (Chapel Hill: University of North Carolina Press, 1999), 261; David Halberstam, *The Children* (New York: Random House, 1998), 259–262.

47. Halberstam, *The Children*, 438–439; Levine, *Freedom's Children*, 146–147.

48. Don McKee, "Dogs and Hoses Used to Stall Negro Trek at Birmingham," *The Atlanta Constitution* (May 4, 1963), 1, 11; Kasher, *The Civil Rights Movement*, 95; Eskew, *But for Birmingham*, 268.

49. Eskew, *But for Birmingham*, 299.

50. Bill Shipp, "Shots Kill 2 Youths Afterward," *The Atlanta Constitution* (September 16, 1963), 1, 6; Bill Shipp, "Thirteen Fires and Shooting Shake Birmingham as Negroes Appeal for GIs, King asks President To Step In," *The Atlanta Constitution* (September 17, 1963), 1, 11; Claude Sitton, "Guard Summoned: Wallace Acts on City Pea for Help as 20 Are Injured," *New York Times* (September 16, 1963), 26; Mendelsohn, *The Martyrs,* 95–96; Robin D. G. Kelley, *Race Rebels: Culture, Politics, and the Black Working Class* (New York: Free Press, 1994), 91; Eskew, *But for Birmingham*, 321. See Spike Lee, "4 Little Girls," HBO (1998).

In 1977, fourteen years after the bombing, a jury convicted Robert Edward Chambliss for his role in the bombing. A Neshoba County, Mississippi jury found the eighty-year-old Edgar Ray Killen guilty of manslaughter in the deaths of three civil rights activists, James Chaney, Andrew Goodman, and Michael Schwerner. On June 23, 2005, Killen received a sixty-year sentence for his role in the murders.

51. Donna Leinwand and Deborah Sharp, "Bombing is a wound that has never closed," *USA Today* (May 18, 2000), 3A.

52. Mendelsohn, *The Martyrs*, 100–101.

53. John Lewis with Michael D'Orso, *Walking with the Wind: A Memoir of the Movement* (San Diego: Harvest Book, 1998), 237.

54. Howard, "The Civil War in Kentucky," 248; Belfrage, *Freedom Summer*, 50.

Afterword   African American Children in Contemporary Society

1. Ellis Cose, "The Good News about Black America (and Why Many Blacks aren't Celebrating)," *Newsweek* (June 7, 1999), 30.
2. Cose, "The Good News," 36–37.
3. A. Reynaldo Contreras and Jessica E. Stephens, "FORTY YEARS AFTER BROWN: The Impact of Immigration Policy on Desegregation," *Education and Urban Society* 29 (February 1997), 183–184. <http://www.law.harvard.edu/groups/ . . . /publications/ resegretation99.html>; Gary Orfield and John T. Yun, "Resegregation in American Schools" (Cambridge: Harvard University Civil Rights Project, 1999) <http:// www.law.harvard.edu/groups/ . . . /publications/ resegregation99.html>.

   See Derrick Bell, *Racism and American Law* third edition (Aspen: Aspen Publishers, Inc., 1992), 618–621.
4. Robin D. G. Kelley and Earl Lewis, *To Make Our World Anew* (New York: Oxford University Press, 2000), ix; Robin D. G. Kelley and Earl Lewis, eds., *The Young Oxford History of African Americans* (New York: Oxford University Press, 1995); Darlene Clark Hine and Clayborne Carson, eds., *Milestones in Black American History* (New York: Chelsea House Publishers, 1995).
5. Samuel Eliot Morison and Henry Steele Commager, *The Growth of the American Republic* (New York: Oxford University Press, 1950), 537.

   See John Hope Franklin and Alfred Moss, Jr., *From Slavery to Freedom* (New York: McGraw Hill, 2000); Darlene Clark Hine, William C. Hine, and Stanley Harrold, *The African-American Odyssey* (Upper Saddle River: Prentice Hall, 2003); James Oliver Horton and Lois E. Horton, *Hard Road to Freedom* (Rutgers: Rutgers University Press, 2001); Colin A. Palmer, *Passageways* (New York: Harcourt Brace, 1998); Joe William Trotter, Jr., *The African American Experience* (New York: Houghton Mifflin, 2001); Rodney D. Coates, *Annual Editions: African American History* (Sluice Dock: Dushkin/ McGraw Hill, 2000); Leonard Dinnerstein and Kenneth T. Jackson, eds., *America Vistas* (New York: Oxford University Press, 1995); Robert James Maddox, ed., *Annual Editions: American History* (Sluice Dock: Dushkin/McGraw Hill, 2000); and William R. Scott and William G. Shade, eds., *Upon These Shores* (New York: Routledge, 2000); Thomas C. Holt and Elsa Barkley Brown, eds., *Major Problems in African-American History: From Slavery to Freedom, 1619–1877*, volume I (Boston: Houghton Mifflin, 2000).

   See also Alan Brinkley, *The Unfinished Nation* (New York: McGraw Hill, 2000); John A. Garraty and Mark C. Carnes, *The American Nation* (New York: Longman, 2000); James A. Henretta, David Brody, and Lynn Dumenil, *America* (Boston: Bedford/ St. Martin, 1999); Mary Beth Norton et al., *A People and a Nation* (New York: Houghton Mifflin, 1998); and Michael P. Johnson, James Roark et al., *The American Promise* (Boston: Bedford Books, 1998).
6. See George M. Fredrickson, "The Skeleton in the Closet," *New York Review of Books* (November 2, 2000), 61–65.

   See also Steven Mintz, *Huck's Raft: A History of American Childhood* (Cambridge: Belknap Press, 2004), 94–117; Marie Jenkins Schwartz, *Born in Bondage: Growing Up Enslaved in the Antebellum South* (Cambridge: Harvard University Press, 2000); Wilma King, *Children of the Emancipation* (Minneapolis: CAROLHODA BOOKS, 2000); Wilma King, *Toward the Promised Land: From Uncle Tom's Cabin to the Onset of the Civil War, 1851–1861* (New York: Chelsea House Publishers, 1995); Kate Connell, *Tales From the Underground Railroad* (Austin: Steck-Vaughn, 1993); Gwen Everett, *John Brown: One Man Against Slavery* (New York: Rizzoli, 1993); Virginia Hamilton, *Many Thousand Gone: African Americans from Slavery to Freedom* (New York: Random House, 1993); Joyce Hansen, *The Captive* (New York: Scholastic, Inc., 1994); Richard and Judy Alan, eds., *African American Folktales for Young Readers* (Little Rock: August House Publishers, Inc., 1993).

7. See Harvard Sitkoff, "Segregation, Desegregation, Resegregation: African American Education, A Guide to the Literature," *OAH Magazine of History* 15 (Winter 2001): 6–13.

8. Rev. E. Martin Lewis to Walter White, December 20, 1945, Segregation and Discrimination, Complaints and Responses, 1940–1955, Microfilm Part 15, Series B, Administrative Files, Papers of the National Association for the Advancement of Colored People (Frederick, MD: University Publications of America, 1982).

9. See Helen Bannerman, *The Story of Little Black Sambo* (Bedford: Applewood Books, Reprint of the 1921 edition); Barbara Bader, "Sambo, Babaji, and Sam," *The Horn Book Magazine* (September–October 1996): 536–547; Michelle H. Martin, " 'Hey, Who's the Kid with the Green Umbrella?' Re-evaluating the Black-a-Moor and Little Black Sambo," *The Lion and The Unicorn* 22 (1998), 151.

10. Phyllis J. Yuill, *Little Black Sambo: A Closer Look* (New York: Council on Interracial Books for Children, 1976), 9, 13. See John W. Blassingame, *The Slave Community: Plantation Life in the Antebellum South*, revised edition (New York: Oxford University Press, 1979), for a discussion of slave personalities including Sambo, 203–205, 224–230, 233–238.

    See also Nancy Arnez and Henry Hankerson, "Reinforcing Cultural Excellence through Literature for Children and Youth," *Negro History Bulletin* 49 (January–December 1986): 21–25.

11. Yuill, *Little Black Sambo: A Closer Look*, 15, 19.

12. Martin, "Hey, Who's the Kid with the Green Umbrella?" 154, 155, 156. See Bill Yoffee, *Black Sambo's Saga: The Story of Little Black Sambo, Revisited at Age 98* (Kinsington, MD: privately published, 1997).

13. Yuill, *Little Black Sambo: A Closer Look*, 28, 30. *Little Black Sambo* is often available in special collections of libraries today rather than on open shelves. The J. B. Lippincott Company produces "the only authorized American editions" of the book.

14. See Julius Lester, *Sam and the Tigers* (New York: Dial Books, 1996); Bader, "Sambo, Babaji, and Sam," 545–547.

15. Ibid.

16. See Connie Porter, *Meet Addy: An American Girl* (Middleton, Wisconsin: Pleasant Company, 1993); "Breaking the Barbie Mold, a Doll Company Finds Success: Rejecting Barbie, Doll Maker Gains," *New York Times* (September 1, 1993). Each of the fictional characters in the American Girl Series is the subject of multiple volumes about American life and adventures in her own time. See Gordon Patterson, "Color Matters: The Creation of the Sara Lee Doll," *Florida Historical Quarterly*, (Winter 1995): 147–165, for the discussion regarding the creation of a black doll in the 1940s.

17. Fredrickson, "The Skeleton in the Closet," 63; Wayne Dawkins, "Children's Books Link Past to Today," *Courier-Post* (NJ) (October 18, 1993); James Tobin; James Tobin, "Slave Doll: History lesson, or is it an insult to blacks?" *The Detroit News* (September 5, 1993), 1 A, 13A.

    Writing about slavery in children's book is not a new area of interest. See Steven C. Tracy, ed., *The Collected Works of Langston Hughes: Works for Children and Young Adults: Biographies* (Columbia: University of Missouri Press, 2001).

18. Elizabeth Lenhard, "Playing with the Past," Living, *The Atlanta Journal/The Atlanta Constitution* (September 24, 1993), G1, G4; "Young Slave's Journey to Freedom Is Focus of Latest American Girls Series," *The Council Chronicle* (September 1993), 6–7; Susan B. Griffith, "Addy is more than a doll," *Call & Post (Cleveland, Ohio)* September 23, 1993; Marsha Mitchell, "The Pleasant Company Has a Living Doll on Its Hands," *Los Angeles Sentinel* (September 30, 1993).

19. Lisa C. Jones, "Toys that Teach: Black–oriented playthings inspire, educate, and entertain," *Ebony* (November 1993), 56–66. See Carolivia Herron, *Nappy Hair* (New York: Alfred A. Knopf, 1997). See also "NAPPY HAIR! Oh, my! Almost as Silly as 'Nigardly'!

<http://www. adversity. net/special/nappy_hair.htm>; Martin Mbugua, "Book-Flap Teach Regrousps: Queens school opens doors," *New York Daily News Online* (December 8, 1998).

20. Donna Leinwand and Deborah Sharp, "Ex-Klansmen in their 60s are accused in fatal church bombing," and "Bombing is a wound that has never closed," *USA Today* (May 18, 2000), 1A, 3A. See <http://www.4littlegirls.com/renospch.htm>.

21. See "Belated bombing arrests help U.S. confront ugly past," *USA Today* (May 19, 2000), 14A; <http://www.cnn.com/2005/LAW/06/21/mississippi.killings>.

22. See Jesse Kornbluth, "The Woman who Beat the Klan," *New York Times Magazine* (November 1, 1987), 26–39. <http://www.courttv.com/archive/trials/brewer/092399_pm_sentence_ctv.html>; <http://www.infoplease.com/ipa/A078179.html>.

23. "Justice officials meet with Mississippi family," (AP) *Columbia* (Missouri) *Daily Tribune* (July 13, 2000), 5A.

24. See "Special Report," U.S. Department of Justice, Office of Justice Programs, Bureau of Justice Statistics, Washington, D.C. <http://www.ojp.usdoj.gov/bjs/pub/ascii/apvsvc.txt>; Darlene Clark Hine, "Stop the Global Holocaust," in *Hine Sight: Black Women and the Re-Construction of American History* (Brooklyn: Carlson Publishing, Inc., 1994), 249–250; Cose, "The Good News about Black America," 30.

   See also Carl S. Taylor, *Girls, Gangs, Women, and Drugs* (East Lansing: Michigan State University Press, 1993), a sociological study of black girls, women, and crime in Detroit.

25. Sari Horwitz and Michael E. Ruane, *Sniper: Inside the Hunt for the Killers Who Terrorized the Nation* (New York: Random House, 2003), 55, 236. See Angie Cannon, *23 Days of Terror: The Compelling True Story of the Hunt and Capture of the Beltway Snipers* (New York: Pocket Books, 2003); Charles A. Moose and Charles Fleming, *Three Weeks in October: The Manhunt for the Serial Sniper* (New York: Dutton, 2003).

26. See "Special Report," U.S. Department of Justice, Office of Justice Programs, Bureau of Justice Statistics, Washington, D.C. <http://www.ojp.usdoj.gov/bjs/pub/ascii/apvsvc.txt>; Michael Awkward, " 'You're Turning Me On': The Boxer, the Beauty Queen, and the Rituals of Gender," in Devon W. Carbado, ed., *Black Men on Race, Gender, and Sexuality: A Critical Reader* (New York: New York University Press, 1999), 128–146; Kevin Brown, "The Social Construction of a Rape Victim: Stories of African American Males about the Rape of Desiree Washington," in Carbado, *Black Men on Race, Gender, and Sexuality*, 147–158; John M. Sloop, ". . . Mike Tyson and the Perils of Discursive Constraints: Boxing, Race, and the Assumption of Guilt," in Aaron Baker and Todd Boyd, eds., *Out of Bounds* (Bloomington: Indiana University Press, 1997), 102–122.

   See also, Robin D. G. Kelley, *Hammer and Hoe: Alabama Communists During the Great Depression* (Chapel Hill: University of North Carolina Press, 1990), 84–85.

27. A jury found Tyson guilty of the rape of Desiree Washington, and the court sentenced him to six years in the Indiana Youth Center, Plainfield, Indiana. He served three of the six year sentence and was released on parole March 25, 1995.

28. Libby Copeland, "Kemba Smith's Hard Time," *Washington Post* (February 13, 2000); Reginald Stewart, "Kemba's Nightmare," *Emerge* (May 1996), 28–48; Reginald Stuart, "Justice Denied: Kemba's Nightmare Continues as Movement to Reverse Mandatory Minimum Grows," *Emerge* (May 1998): 41–48.

29. Stuart, "Justice Denied," 48.

30. "Clinton grants 62 convicts clemency," *USA Today* (December 26, 2000), 3A.

31. Cose, "The Good News," 39. See "Justice Voice Commentary" <http://www.geocities.com/CapitolHill/Lobby/8899/ jv.html>.

32. Audrey Edwards, "Bubble Gum and Birth Control: A Girl's World," *Essence* (September 1998), 92, 94. See Dorothy Roberts, *Killing the Black Body: Race, Reproduction and the*

Meaning of Liberty (New York: Vintage Books, 1999), 104–149, for a discussion about Norplant, a controversial contraceptive.

33. Mary Jo Bane, "Welfare as We Might Know It," *The American Prospect* 30 (January–February 1997): 47–53; Roberts, *Killing the Black Body*, 113, 208–209; Barbara Ransby, "US: the Black Poor and the Politics of Expendability," *Race & Class* 38 (1996), 2–3.

34. Edwards, "Bubble Gum and Birth Control," *Essence*, 164.

INDEX